RELIGION
IN AMERICA

THE DAEDALUS LIBRARY

Each of these volumes is available as a Beacon Paperback.

RELIGION IN AMERICA

EDITED BY WILLIAM G. MC LOUGHLIN
AND ROBERT N. BELLAH

BEACON PRESS   BOSTON

Copyright © 1966, 1968 by the
American Academy of Arts and Sciences

First published as a Beacon Paperback in 1968
by arrangement with Houghton Mifflin Company

Beacon Press books are published under the auspices of
the Unitarian Universalist Association

The Introduction by William G. McLoughlin, "Religion and the Churches
in Contemporary America" by Bryan Wilson, "America's Institutions of
Faith" by Edwin S. Gaustad, "Churches and Families" by Donald Meyer,
"American Religion and the Cure of Souls" by William A. Clebsch,
"Alternatives Within Contemporary American Judaism" by Joseph L.
Blau, and "Catholicism in America" by Sister Marie Augusta Neal are
published here for the first time. The other essays in the book
appeared originally, some of them in slightly different form, in the
Winter 1967 issue of *Daedalus*, the Journal of the American Academy
of Arts and Sciences.

Printed in the United States of America
International Standard Book Number: 0–8070–1153–3

9 8 7 6 5 4 3

ACKNOWLEDGMENTS

THE EDITORS wish to express their appreciation to the authors of the essays in this volume and also to the following people who participated in the conferences held at the House of the American Academy of Arts and Sciences, and without whose counsel and co-operation this volume could not have been produced: Father Joseph Fichter, Mr. George T. Harris, Professors Frank Manuel, Henry Murray, Talcott Parsons, David Riesman, Krister Stendahl, and Paul van Buren; also, Father Robert Drinan, Mr. Henry Ansgar Kelly, and Professors C. Conrad Cherry, Jeffrey K. Hadden, Philip B. Kurland, Charles S. Liebman, and David Little. Thanks are also due to M. Alain Clement of *Le Monde* and Mr. John Cogley of *The New York Times* who attended the Academy conference. Mr. Jones B. Shannon, who was Executive Director of the Church Society for College Work, shared a continued interest in this study. A particular debt is owed Mr. Donald Cutler who from the beginning offered valuable suggestions and criticism, and helped guide the work to its completion.

Support for this study came to the American Academy through the Church Society for College Work. A number of friends of the Reverend W. Brooke Stabler, a founder and former officer of the Church Society, provided funds, intending that the work be a memorial tribute to Mr. Stabler. A second gift was made available through the General Division of Women's Work of the Episcopal Church. The Church Society for College Work is to be thanked for its initiative in suggesting the study and for its help.

CONTENTS

Contents

III. Pluralism and Its Problems

IV. Predictions and Reorientations

WILLIAM G. MC LOUGHLIN

Introduction: *How Is America Religious?*

WHEN, in the spring of 1950, *The Partisan Review* conducted a symposium on "Religion and the Intellectuals," there was considerable difference of opinion not only as to whether the United States was going through a new religious revival, but also as to whether it would be a good thing if it were. John Dewey, Sidney Hook, Irving Howe, and a group of contributors who (like the editors of *The Partisan Review*) considered themselves "naturalists," "positivists," or "secular radicals," described the new interest in religion and the supernatural as escapism, defeatism, or "a failure of nerve"—a turn to otherworldliness out of despair of reforming this world. In their view, the incipient religious revival reflected a gloomy loss of confidence in science, in social reform, and in rationalism and a return to the Puritan belief in original sin and the evangelical search for "a power beyond ourselves." On the whole, these intellectuals deplored the revival as a reactionary rejection of the New Deal's pragmatic liberalism.

Subsequent events in the Eisenhower years seemed in some ways to confirm this. The revival began in an aura of "piety on the Potomac," of presidential prayer breakfasts, Billy Graham's "engineering of mass consent," Norman Vincent Peale's "Let the churches stand up for capitalism," Msgr. Fulton J. Sheen's equation of Christianity with Americanism, Rabbi Liebman's *Peace of Mind* poultice, and the various neo-evangelical anti-Communist crusades feeding upon the paranoia of McCarthyism, Korea, and the Cold War. No doubt this was what Irving Howe had in mind when he spoke of "the religious turn" in 1950 as "part of a historical moment of sickness." As another of these secular radicals put it, what was needed was more "determination and courage" to meet the challenges and anxieties of the postwar years on a rational basis and not a prayerful turning to God to solve our problems. In short, the intellectuals of 1950 defined "religion" in pejorative terms—in terms of the militant agnosticism of the 1920's and 1930's. Religion for them signified either "pie-in-the-sky" fundamentalism, the hypocritical religiosity of the bourgeoisie, or the reactionary Anglo-Catholicism of aesthetes like T. S. Eliot and Allen Tate. It was significant that the editors of *The Partisan Review* turned for "intellectual comment" almost wholly to literary artists and not to teachers of theology.

This current symposium, sponsored by *Dædalus* eighteen years later, indicates that the doubters of 1950 essentially misunderstood the real nature of America's new wave of revivalism; it was nothing short of a Great Awakening. The postwar "turn to religion," which almost all of the contributors in this volume accept both as fact and as a positive good, went much deeper and wider than prayer breakfasts, mass evangelistic campaigns, and anti-Communist crusades. It constituted a general re-orientation of the whole social and intellectual climate of Western society, just as America's previous Great Awakenings had done. In the history books of the future, this revival will be associated with the rise of existential philosophy, neo-orthodox theology, the election of the first Roman Catholic President, the *aggiornamento* of Vatican II, the peace movement and the civil rights movement, the revival of pacifism, the war on poverty, and the quest for a new politics. In 1950, few could have foreseen this. Martin Luther King, Jr., was still in seminary; Adlai Stevenson and the Kennedy family were just entering national politics; Benjamin Spock was still a kindly, unruffled pediatrician; Reinhold Niebuhr's books were just becoming required reading in Ivy League colleges; and the new generation of hard-headed, realistic reformers in theology and politics was known only among the avant-garde intellectuals of the yet unborn "New Frontier."

This Great Awakening is by no means over yet, as the vigorous debate in this symposium demonstrates. Great Awakenings usually take a generation to mature. This volume is not a postmortem on a dead movement, but part of the intellectual revolution in search of consensus, the product of an Awakening still at high tide. It is a document of its times. While the Awakening has proceeded far enough to receive general commendation here as a healthy search for new ways to meet new problems, there is no agreement yet upon ways, means, or goals. As the titles of many and the contents of all these essays reveal, this symposium is primarily a search for definitions framed in terms of questions. Where question marks do not appear in the titles or opening sentences, the word *quest, search,* or *crisis* expresses a lack of clear formulation. Obviously many kinds of social and intellectual revolution are currently under way in American life—in theology and ecclesiology, in ethics and education, in politics and social work. The writers in this symposium emphasize on almost every page the idea of "turning point," of changes, challenges, new directions, new opportunities, new dangers and re-orientations. The mood, though occasionally pessimistic, is generally one of hope, excitement, and exhilaration. Even those Jewish and Roman Catholic contributors who acknowledge the danger for their faith (especially among the young), in the rapid pace of secularization in this generation and in the breakdown of old guidelines, prefer to emphasize the openness and creativity of religion today in a pluralistic society. The so-called "immigrant faiths" (Catholic, Jewish, Lutheran, Eastern Orthodox) have emerged from the discrimination, self-consciousness, and introversion of the first and second generation. Today the Jew considers the competition among the Orthodox, Hassidim, Reconstructionists, Reform, and Conservatives within his faith not as a threat or scandal to solidarity, but as complementary variations upon a theme. The Roman Catholic intellectuals see the de-ethnicization and de-Romanization of their church in the United States not as assimilation to Americanism, but as the ability of their members to rise above Old World provincialisms and rivalries. Perhaps the salient feature of this Great Awakening is the fact that for the first time Roman Catholics and Jews are sharing equally with Protestants in all its manifestations.

There are some important and probably unfortunate omissions from this symposium, although it was never intended to be encyclopedic. Efforts to obtain an article on the Negro and religion in America proved unavailing. Nor are there any articles devoted specifically to major issues like religion and education, religion and the younger generation, ethnic and regional aspects of American religion, religion and science, ecumenism, or changing religious attitudes toward sex, censorship, birth control, drugs, and divorce. To include all of these would lead to continual overlapping. Most of these topics are dealt with in some way in the articles which are included.

The choice of topics was not random but representative, as with the choice of contributors. Naturalists and secular radicals are perhaps underrepresented and so are the conservative or new evangelicals. Though the contributors are professionally concerned with religion in one way or another, they are not all ministers, nor are they all committed adherents to some religious faith. But they are generally sympathetic toward religion. This is perhaps an indication that in this Awakening the radical secularists of 1950 were the Old Lights, those out of step with their times or the mood of their generation. The historian is tempted to draw the following parallels between the participants in this Awakening and those of previous Awakenings in terms of the radical secularists of *The Partisan Review* debate and the contributors to this volume: The *Dædalus* contributors obviously belong with the pietistic Calvinists of the First Great Awakening, the Evangelicals of the Second Great Awakening, the Social Gospelers and higher critics of the Third Great Awakening, while the *Partisan Review* contributors can be compared to the rationalists and Unitarians, to the deists, and to the agnostic Darwinians and pragmatists. In this sense, the current or Fourth Great Awakening is simply another round in the perennial dialogue between what Reinhold Niebuhr called "the pious and the secular" in America.

While the editors tried to assemble a representative group of New Lights to comment upon the current religious situation, they did not assign them more than general topics within their respective areas of professional competence. In a series of preliminary discussions, however, some of the more general issues of religion in our times were articulated by eminent scholars not represented in this volume. It seems worthwhile in this introduction to touch upon some of the central themes or problems which run throughout these papers creating unsought-for patterns both for the present and the past.

Reading the volume as a whole, I find four themes arranged in two contrasting or paradoxical pairs which provide the overarching pattern for this symposium. It may well be that they have been the fundamental paradoxes of American religious history from the beginning.

The first and often-noted paradox is that while the United States has a reputation for being the most materialistic nation in the world, it is also acknowledged to be (and usually thinks of itself as being) one of the most religious nations. The second and equally well-known paradox is that while American religious leaders are now, as always, deeply involved in social and reform movements, these same leaders constantly express the fear that they, their churches, and their doctrines are somehow inconsequential or irrelevant to the religious needs of their constituents.

Stated another way, the four themes which provide the warp and woof of these articles are that while the current religious revival indicates the continued vitality of religion in the United States, the nation is becoming an increasingly secular society; while the clergy of America are pre-eminently activists who bring their religious principles into the realm of the everyday lives of their people, the churches seem increasingly irrelevant to the needs of the times and the clergy seem to have lost the greater part of their function to doctors, psychiatrists, and social workers. All of the writers in this volume are fully aware that in the First and Second Great Awakenings the ministry and churches were so concerned with saving souls that they tended to forget the social implications of religion, while in the Third Great Awakening (and the twentieth century as a whole) the ministry and churches became so involved in political activities that they tended to neglect the spiritual and personal aspects of religion. But how is this dichotomy to be bridged? Jews and Roman Catholics (who played less significant parts in previous Awakenings) recognize that their history in the United States has been similarly distorted—helping the immigrant to keep his faith and yet insistent upon giving primary attention to the bricks and mortar of institutional growth. Now that the immigrants' grandchildren are accepted within the culture, what role is left for the priest and rabbi, the cathedral and synagogue?

The basic question for this symposium might have been phrased in terms of these complementary paradoxes: Given the increasing secularization of American society in this generation, should the churches work harder to bring the Kingdom of God upon earth by demonstrating the relevance of religion in the *social* aspects of people's lives, or should the clergy address themselves to the *individual* himself, seeking to give his personal life some transcendent identity, meaning, and dignity in relation to God. It is the age-old problem of the vertical and horizontal meanings of religion. It received dramatic expression at one of the preliminary conferences for this symposium in the following exchange between Father Joseph Fichter of Harvard, Professor Paul van Buren of Temple, and Professor Talcott Parsons of Harvard:

Fichter: This is a tremendously important theme partly, I feel, because our definitions are too sharp. I don't think the distinction between the secular and the religious exists in the way we often express it. Often the secular and the religious are together in the same person and groups. Secularism often means to me a correct and rational use of our created faculties—man using his abilities in very practical ways that do not necessarily deny a supernatural or spiritual or religious aspect. If we could get at secularism from this point of view with broader definitions than we have tended toward, we will make some progress.

Van Buren: The unhelpfulness of the polls on American religion is related to their intention to answer only the question *whether* America is religious, as though one knew what "being religious" meant. The more interesting question is *how* America is religious, some description of the variety of forms which religiosity takes . . . .

Parsons: I certainly agree that "the secular and the religious" ought to be a major theme [of this symposium]. The [preliminary] papers have already sketched a number of aspects of it. I don't know whether it is more among intellectuals than others that the prejudice still lingers, as Father Fichter noted, that when one is acting in a secular context, . . . religion ceases altogether to be relevant to action. Of course, what we think of as the secular sphere of human activity has enormously expanded with the development of modern society. The basic economic, political, and a very large part of the educational and other functional areas have been secularized in this sense: If you go back to the Middle Ages, the scope of the church was very much broader than it is today. But this differentiation has nothing to do with the strength or weakness of religious orientation as a fundamental underlying factor in human motivation.

There is throughout this symposium a fluctuation in contexts which the reader would do well to keep in mind. The two obvious contexts, as noted already, are the contemporary situation and the historical one: that is, the conflict between the absolutes of transcendent religion and the relative values of culture which has been a perennial one for Judeo-Christians and which in the mid-twentieth century has become peculiarly acute. Some essays talk about the contemporary problem in terms of the broader historical context of religion and culture; others talk about it specifically in the context of the present moment. But, in addition, the contributors are continually forced to notice another context—that religion in America plays and has always played a different role and with a different quality than religion in Europe.

Religion in Europe has always been closely allied with the state; the rise of democracy and individualism there has meant the rise of anti-clericalism and atheism among a large segment of the population, and especially among the intellectuals. In Europe, for example, the notion that God is dead or that the churches are operating in a post-Christian civilization has been significant and accepted at least since the days of Marx, if not since the French Revolution. To Americans both in and outside the churches, these views still seem strange, shocking, and newsworthy. Professor Krister Stendahl of Harvard Divinity School expressed the important contextual difference between the religious situation in Europe and America in another portion of the preliminary discussions in preparation for this anthology:

When one reads these papers, even the papers critical of religion and pointing out the failures of the past two thousand years, one is struck, if one reads as a European, by the fact that everything here has been written in a religious framework. The sociologists are pointing out to the "death-of-God" theologians that God is not so dead as the theologians think. What impresses one is the general cultural phenomenon of the relative absence of vocal atheism or agnosticism in a negative key in America. A few months ago I sat down with the Swedish Consul General in New York to help decide which Americans the Royal Swedish Commission on the separation of church and state should meet when the august body came to this country. They had intended to meet roughly as many atheists as churchmen because that is how, in Sweden, they saw the issue. There were some difficulties in arranging such an agenda, difficulties not attributable, I guess, to my moving in too pious circles. There is a very drastic cultural difference here. In Europe, if you get tired of church, you would never organize an Ethical Culture Society to meet at 11:00 on Sunday morning in order to have something a little like going to church but unlike it too. Even the atheists in America speak in a religious key. There is more to this phenomenon than saying that Marxism is another kind of eschatology.

Professor Stendahl could find plenty of agnosticism or behavioristic atheism among the faculties of many departments of sociology, psychology, political science, and philosophy in America, but he is certainly correct about the general respect for religion in the nation as a whole. The burgeoning of Unitarian and Universalist churches around college campuses across the nation indicates that intellectuals who leave the more orthodox denominations still like to have some Sunday-morning ritual and some non-professional, value-oriented organization to belong to. Religion is a serious matter in America from politicians to pentecostals and from Babbitts to beatniks. American political and diplomatic history cannot be written without a consideration of this quality in our national character, and much of our literary criticism finds this the key to our poetry and novels. Even in the 1930's, which was a period of low ebb in American religious vitality by churchly standards, the proletarian writing was more pietistic than Marxist. "The 1930's were an Age of Faith," wrote Malcolm Cowley in *The New York Times* a few years ago, and "their faith was apocalyptic and millennial."

The continual denunciation of American materialism, hucksterism, and lusting for "the Almighty Dollar" by our social commentators is, like our muckraking tradition and political reform movements, a testimony to our commitment to religion. And even our dreams of success, our continual evaluation of the pursuit of happiness in terms of higher standards of living and the mass distribution of "creature comforts" can be described better as a variant upon the search for a new Eden or the coming of the Kingdom of God on earth as we think it is in heaven. So that even economic historians conclude that American exploiters, entrepreneurs, political manipulators, empire-builders, and sharp-traders have acted out of a total commitment which precludes any satisfactory resolution to their endeavors. The industrial statesman (or robber baron) and the dedicated reformer (or do-gooder) are both working for the same millennial state of peace, plenty, and "happiness" for all. There are as few cynics as there are atheists in America, and our pragmatists simply claim to practice a more common-sense approach to meliorism.

William Barrett, one of the secular radicals of *The Partisan Review* symposium, expressed the attitude of most Americans who call themselves agnostics in giving his reasons for doubting the validity of the turn to religion in 1950: "Religion is total or it is nothing, and I will begin to believe that a new leaven is working when I see the Catholic faithful walking barefooted through the streets of our cities on Good Friday, or climbing the steps of St. Patrick's Cathedral on their knees." In short, the thesis of the atheist or agnostic in America is not that there is no God, but that those who claim to be committed to him are not demonstrating the total commitment he deserves. American secularists are more correctly defined as overly pious rather than anti-religious or anti-clerical. And when the overly pious find hypocrisy in the traditional churches, they develop a totalistic religion of their own choosing—Marxism for the friend of the masses, pentecostalism for the Biblical literalist, Zen Buddhism for the avant-garde, ritual or mysticism for the highbrow, third-party politics for the activist, affluent hedonism or professional absorption for the middle class. As Barrett put it, "Like a good many other people in the modern world, I have my own private religion."

The reader of this symposium might well keep in mind a question central to all of these papers, but directly faced by almost none of them: Why have Americans defined religion or being religious in terms which only an Old Testament prophet or medieval saint could measure up to? Why have pragmatic secularists like William James chosen to hold up St. Teresa or St. John of the Cross as models of religious commitment? Why did Henry Adams, an alienated intellectual of the Gilded Age, look back longingly to the faith which worshiped the Virgin Mary and built Chartres Cathedral? Why did that professional atheist, Mark Twain, idolize St. Joan (contrast the skeptical European portrait of "Saint" Joan written at almost the same time by George Bernard Shaw)?

What emerges from this symposium, and perhaps what is emerging from this Fourth Great Awakening, is an effort of Americans to break out of this religious totalism and to construct a new definition of what it means to be religious. Our efforts at "ecumenism" are one way to break down total commitment to a particular variety of faith and doctrine. Our acceptance of "pluralism" is a way of granting equal validity to other faiths and doctrines. Our definition of a religious person as one who demonstrates "ultimate concerns" is a way around the rigid distinction between the saved and the damned. To preach against "absolutizing the relative" is an effort to dissociate American manifest destiny from God's will and to see American democracy as merely our way of finding "proximate solutions to insoluble problems."

If, in search for a more mature understanding of faith, advanced religious leaders not only accept but lead in this breakdown of institutional rigidity, pietistic totalism, and popular stereotypes about religion, many churchmen and churchgoers deplore their action as a sign of weakness in the church. New spiritual sophistication has caused considerable shock and confusion and helps to account for the paroxysms of chauvinism which have gripped so many Americans since World War II. They long for the simpler religious definitions of former days. And if the church has no standards, then the state must set them.

Will Herberg saw the Awakening in 1955 as the merging of all faiths into the "culture religion" of "the American way of life." The Jew coming out of his ghetto, the Catholic out of his hyphenated nationalism, the Protestant out of his denominationalism all seemed to agree that "faith in faith" was the highest form of religious pluralism. Herberg saw the revival as essentially a deterioration of all ultimate religious values. "To be a Protestant, a Catholic, or a Jew," he wrote, "has become simply another way of being an American." For Herberg, the turn toward religion was a sign of the triumph of secularism.

Few of the writers in this symposium appear to agree with him. Although some of the essays wrestle seriously with the possibility that we have entered a post-Judeo-Christian era in Western civilization (including the United States), I do not sense in them either the militant agnosticism of *The Partisan Review* intellectuals or the jeremiad of Will Herberg. I sense, rather, the mood of "New Lights" in all American Awakenings—the conviction that God has yet further light to reveal to his followers in this world and yet new ways of expressing himself. There is more than faith in faith underlying this revival and more than Kierkegaardian despair in the theology of crisis which undergirds this generation's search for values. Underneath the querulous searching of these and other intellectuals stirs a faith more nearly like that of Job facing the whirlwind, anxious but ready to believe—the faith of the apostle saying, "Lord, I believe, help thou my unbelief."

The major difficulty for the reader throughout this symposium will undoubtedly lie in the failure of the participants to agree upon any common definition of terms. A barrier of language, expression, terminology, and activity exists here as in all periods of social and intellectual re-orientation. Do the writers mean by "religion" the belief in God, the affirmation of a creed, membership in a church or synagogue, affiliation with a faith or denomination, ethical commitment, humanitarian idealism, experiential conversion? Do they mean by non-religion or secularism a lack of any or all of these? Is it possible to be religious in some ways and not in others? Is a secularist someone pre-occupied with material well-being, with professional concerns, with family, with self-expression? Is he one who seeks escape through drugs, alcohol, sex, the alienated cultism of beatniks, hipsters, Hell's Angels, or jet-set bohemians? Or does he, like the Black Muslims, Jehovah's Witnesses, or Zen Buddhists, create a new and more meaningful religion for himself outside the Judeo-Christian tradition?

Similarly, the contributors approach the "relevance" or "functionalism" of religion in many different ways. Sometimes they are concerned with the relevance of the individual church or synagogue to the lives of the members of the congregation; other times with the meaning of "the church" as an institution or as God's chosen, with the function of the minister as a man of God, with the relevance of dogma and doctrine, ritual and liturgy, prayer and worship.

These essays operate on many different levels and in many dimensions. It may be either the failing or the vitality of this symposium that it imposes no order upon the participants and arrives at no conclusions. The writers do not even agree on the points at which the religious dimension is most truly expressing itself in our society today. Does the most vital religion now lie in the churches or in the reform movements, in the synagogues or on the college campuses, in the suburbs or in the slums? Are the best expressions of religious thought and feeling today found among the college students, the adolescents, the artists, the architects, the poets, the playwrights, the novelists, or the political and social agitators? While the participants in this volume may often be talking past one another, there seems to me to be sufficient understanding and mutual interchange to call this a dialogue. If it is a dialogue without consensus, it is perhaps better for that.

The contributors all seem to agree on one point—that religion is still worth talking about because it is playing a significant part in the social reform causes of the times: civil rights, peace, academic freedom, civil liberties, poverty, social justice in general. Here there is real commitment to ultimate concerns. Not since the days of the Social Gospel Movement have so many ministers entered into the efforts to change society and joined the organizations, marches, rallies, pickets, and petitioners for the protests and the oppressed. Not since then have the social-action committees of religious denominations and interdenominational agencies issued so many formal pronouncements on behalf of such activities. And most important, and novel, never before have the Roman Catholics and Jews been so conspicuously united with the Protestants in these endeavors. The most dramatic picture of the Americanization of the immigrant faiths in this generation was not the election of John F. Kennedy, the participation of a Roman Catholic archbishop in his inaugural, or the high mass at his funeral, but rather the news photographs of priests, nuns, and rabbis marching in civil rights rallies and being stoned and spat upon by their own parishioners for doing it.

It is worth quoting here another bit of dialogue from a preliminary conference for this volume which reflects the manner in which the revivalistic fervor of American religion and Protestant activism have provided the tone for this new social gospel mood:

T. George Harris (senior editor of *Look* and a Southern Baptist): What is happening, I think, is that we have got a gap, a substantial gap, between what people are doing and the concepts by which they are representing their actions. The rate of change in American life is so great that I find it impossible to live even in New York and think that the language means anything. In some sense, the young people at Berkeley who are using a religious jargon are trying to find a notion of beatification. There's a parish in Oakland where they are writing their own liturgies. They are deeply involved in civil rights action in an aesthetic or irrational way; civil rights is not a legal problem for them, but involves instead a projection of the self into the lives of other human beings in a way that can only be described as ecstatic. The people from the Bible Belt who previously represented the ecstatic in American religion—at whose revivals the Devil was so visibly present that he led to sluggings in the back row—have become rationalists, and talking with them is rather like a Harvard dialogue. The cutting edge of change is among the people for whom religion means an effort to break out of the pigeonholes of what has become essentially a rococo culture. The ethnic basis of religion has shifted. The real crisis for the human is finding identity. What is essential can only be described as a search for personal style.

Daniel Callahan (editor of *Commonweal*, Catholic layman): Paradoxically, those in religious groups who are most active in social protests are those who are most disturbed about traditional Christianity. Among Roman Catholics a decade ago, those concerned about social questions tended to act fairly moderately. They knew what theological grounds they stood on when they acted: papal encyclicals in the case of Catholics. They were applying solid principles "in the world" as many of them would say. Now, curiously, the intensity of social commitment is stronger, but there is a parallel loss of the theological roots. The most disturbed Christians are active in civil rights. That their motivation does get vague is often a matter of personal style, not of Christological principles . . . .

Harris: Neither was Christ based on such principles.

Callahan: Pardon?

Harris: Neither was Christ. What we are constantly running up against is a continued attempt to impose a medieval metaphysic on a religious figure. But what is happening among these young people is a more vivid identification with a Christian figure, and in such a personal sense that it cannot be expressed in logical categories. The Committee for the South was able to break the ground in civil rights early because they had the encyclicals. Now one sees more of a direct and curious escape from an empty life. It is irrational, but to indict an action because it does not fit into the tidy categories of rationality seems to me to move the discussion into "the religious category."

Callahan: It is not clear to me what one means here by "irrational." Is identification with Christ somehow seeing Christ as a social prophet with a personality which seems especially relevant to the world we live in? Perhaps this could be called irrational in the sense that if one says, "Who was Christ or who is he today?" no answer is forthcoming. The point is that he provides some kind of model, but there are no theological rationales for the model other than his aura of attractiveness.

Harvey Cox (professor at Harvard Divinity School, Congregationalist): This is really the discussion of a Southern Baptist and a Roman Catholic in its modern terms. On the one side, the intense feeling which sometimes has not only no great intellectual rationale, but even an anti-systematic bias: When you are saved, you are done with all this cold abstraction. And then one moves on to gradual rationalization of the process. I am not saying this to degrade. What we are seeing now is the new expression of what has traditionally happened to revivalism in America. It is certainly not separable from the whole tradition of American Protestant revivals.

Talcott Parsons (professor of sociology, Harvard): And bringing non-Protestants into the revival tradition.

Callahan: Yes. Among Roman Catholics, one can find something of an uneasiness toward or distaste for technical theological argument as putting one on the wrong track right away. In the past, I would have taken this as a purely Protestant kind of thought.

In short, the revivalistic tradition which in the past has permeated American social reform and social protest activity among Protestants, now includes the Roman Catholic and the Jew. This Awakening, like those of the past, has social, cultural, and political overtones which go far beyond the traditional definitions of the terms religion and religious. The search for a new vocabulary, for ultimate values, for transcendent meaning and self-identity has entered all realms of life. The sacred and the secular merge into each other; something profound in our culture is being transformed. New ways of thinking, believing, and acting are producing a proliferation of value-oriented expressions and actions which still lack a common definition.

It is clear from these papers that there are many aspects of contemporary life with which the churches as institutional purveyors of truth seem unable to cope. The Harvard psychologist Henry Murray, speaking from outside the churches, gave this problem forceful articulation in a preliminary discussion, and it deserves mention here because the question of reaching the younger generation is so basic to all of the discussion in these pages. Murray put it this way:

My interest is the "fitness of Christianity" (I am not speaking only of North America because it would apply to Christianity everywhere, and I am not including Judaism because I have not enough experiential knowledge). I mean fitness in its Darwinian sense, "to survive," and in its Hendersonian sense of the fitness of the environment to serve man's needs. I begin with the assumption that religion is for man rather than man for religion.

I would start by defining what seems to me a desperate situation. We have a great affluent society, and lots of encouraging things are happening. Just underneath, however, it seems reminiscent of 1912 when everyone thought the world was beautiful and two wars were on the horizon. On the international level, the problems of war and population control and, on the national level, the juvenile revolution are of enormous proportions. I recall Boris Sidis, after he had made his reputation as an intellectual at Harvard at age twelve, coming to ask me for a job, any job, at the age of twenty-eight. And he said—this was after the First World War—"there is going to be one more war, a war between generations, all the children against all the parents with armaments." Almost ever since I have seen this conflict increasing. Have you read *Up the Down Staircase?* I would like to take vandalism, a symbol of that whole problem, as being meaningless destruction but yet having a special meaning for these kids. They call it raising hell, and I think literally it is that kind of thing. In the private domain, finally, all those sensitive, somewhat neurotic, alienated people speak of the absurdity [of life], of a meaninglessness. None of these things was mentioned this morning as dilemmas involving religion.

My next point would be that we do not have a religion to deal with these problems. A standard might be the Christianity of the thirteenth century, permeating everything and in a superordinate position with respect to any question raised at the time. Why does Christianity as it now stands not serve man? . . . Christianity does not cover enough. It does not say enough to different kinds of people . . . . None of us mentioned the deplorable deficiency of Christianity in presenting a model for sex and dyadic love. We are paying the penalty for this, and it is absolutely crucial.

(It is interesting that Murray, like Barrett and Henry Adams, seeks a parallel with some totalism of religious culture.) Whether or not the Judeo-Christian tradition does lack the means to cope with the demands and questions of the new generation, this effort to maintain some nexus between the old and the new lies at the heart of this symposium and the intellectual-religious ferment of our times. The participants in this symposium are not, on the whole, so pessimistic as Murray about the potential of Christianity to adjust itself to meet this need. But neither are they sanguine enough to think the adjustment a simple one. For many, perhaps for the best, in the younger generation (and particularly for the younger Negroes in America) this is a real question.

Murray, of course, was not saying that Christianity was relevant to no one anymore. Nor in raising the issues of relevance are the participants in this symposium stating their doubts about relevance in all areas. No one doubts that as centers of middle-class, suburban socialization, and do-goodism, the churches and synagogues are relevant and necessary—they usually provide the first group that mobile Americans join when they enter a new neighborhood; they certainly provide the basis for marriages and friendships, for discussions and charitable activities, for at least a minimal level of worship and self-transcendence in weekly worship. In the context of suburbia, where religion thrives statistically and financially, the priests, ministers, and rabbis do have a function even if it is only for baptisms, circumcisions, confirmations, bar mitzvahs, marriages, funerals, and church suppers. Admittedly it is a minimal function, and to the devout it seems hypocritical, if not narrowly conformist. But it provides at least a possible bridge from the religious to the secular. Though he lacks the stature of his Puritan or nineteenth-century counterpart, the man of God in America is still more than a ceremonial figure. The clergy have not been so much in the news, so well known, so quoted, and so lionized or criticized for half a century.

As a document of this Fourth Great Awakening, this symposium well may become a benchmark for future historians. It marks a level of dialogue and analysis which seems to indicate that the meaning of this revival is about to become clear. For one thing, it demonstrates that religion is neither dead nor irrelevant in America, but that it has reached a new plane of sophistication. If it has lost some optimism, it has also lost some naïveté. Probably, too, it will mean that Americans at last recognize the dangers of treating religion as an ideology whose totality can and should be imposed upon the culture by the majority. Perhaps it means that secularists are now a majority and that henceforth believers in religion will have to maintain their influence and prestige by the intrinsic virtues of their faith and action rather than by the extrinsic weight of their institutions and power.

Perhaps what this symposium says in the end is that America is really coming of age as a culture. It has lost its innocence with its acceptance of power and responsibility. It has now to exchange the zealous millennial faith of the young convert for the stoical, questioning faith of the battle-weary and worldly-wise. If this means a less buoyant America, it will also mean a more resilient one. On the eve of its third century as a nation, the United States may no longer see the glory of the coming of the Lord but rather, as Reinhold Niebuhr said, that history is "essentially unpredictable."

GENERAL EVALUATIONS

ROBERT N. BELLAH

Civil Religion in America

WHILE SOME have argued that Christianity is the national faith, and others that church and synagogue celebrate only the generalized religion of "the American Way of Life," few have realized that there actually exists alongside of and rather clearly differentiated from the churches an elaborate and well-institutionalized civil religion in America. This article argues not only that there is such a thing, but also that this religion—or perhaps better, this religious dimension—has its own seriousness and integrity and requires the same care in understanding that any other religion does.[1]

The Kennedy Inaugural

Kennedy's inaugural address of 20 January 1961 serves as an example and a clue with which to introduce this complex subject. That address began:

We observe today not a victory of party but a celebration of freedom—symbolizing an end as well as a beginning—signifying renewal as well as change. For I have sworn before you and Almighty God the same solemn oath our forebears prescribed nearly a century and three quarters ago.

The world is very different now. For man holds in his mortal hands the power to abolish all forms of human poverty and to abolish all forms of human life. And yet the same revolutionary beliefs for which our forebears fought are still at issue around the globe—the belief that the rights of man come not from the generosity of the state but from the hand of God.

And it concluded:

Finally, whether you are citizens of America or of the world, ask of us the same high standards of strength and sacrifice that we shall ask of you. With a good conscience our only sure reward, with history the final judge of our deeds, let us go forth to lead the land we love, asking His blessing and His help, but knowing that here on earth God's work must truly be our own.

These are the three places in this brief address in which Kennedy mentioned the name of God. If we could understand why he mentioned God, the way in which he did it, and what he meant to say in those three references, we would understand much about American civil religion. But this is not a simple or obvious task, and American students of religion would probably differ widely in their interpretation of these passages.

Let us consider first the placing of the three references. They occur in the two opening paragraphs and in the closing paragraph, thus providing a sort of frame for the more concrete remarks that form the middle part of the speech. Looking beyond this particular speech, we would find that similar references to God are almost invariably to be found in the pronouncements of American presidents on solemn occasions, though usually not in the working messages that the president sends to Congress on various concrete issues. How, then, are we to interpret this placing of references to God?

It might be argued that the passages quoted reveal the essentially irrelevant role of religion in the very secular society that is America. The placing of the references in this speech as well as in public life generally indicates that religion has "only a ceremonial significance"; it gets only a sentimental nod which serves largely to placate the more unenlightened members of the community, before a discussion of the really serious business with which religion has nothing whatever to do. A cynical observer might even say that an American president has to mention God or risk losing votes. A semblance of piety is merely one of the unwritten qualifications for the office, a bit more traditional than but not essentially different from the present-day requirement of a pleasing television personality.

But we know enough about the function of ceremonial and ritual in various societies to make us suspicious of dismissing something as unimportant because it is "only a ritual." What people say on solemn occasions need not be taken at face value, but it is often indicative of deep-seated values and commitments that are not made explicit in the course of everyday life. Following this line of argument, it is worth considering whether the very special placing of the references to God in Kennedy's address may not reveal something rather important and serious about religion in American life.

It might be countered that the very way in which Kennedy made his references reveals the essentially vestigial place of religion today. He did not refer to any religion in particular. He did not refer to Jesus Christ, or to Moses, or to the Christian church; certainly he did not refer to the Catholic Church. In fact, his only reference was to the concept of God, a word which almost all Americans can accept but which means so many different things to so many different people that it is almost an empty sign. Is this not just another indication that in America religion is considered vaguely to be a good thing, but that people care so little about it that it has lost any content whatever? Isn't Eisenhower reported to have said, "Our government makes no sense unless it is founded in a deeply felt religious faith—and I don't care what it is,"[2] and isn't that a complete negation of any real religion?

These questions are worth pursuing because they raise the issue of how civil religion relates to the political society, on the one hand, and to private religious organization, on the other. President Kennedy was a Christian, more specifically a Catholic Christian. Thus, his general references to God do not mean that he lacked a specific religious commitment. But why, then, did he not include some remark to the effect that Christ is the Lord of the world or some indication of respect for the Catholic Church? He did not because these are matters of his own private religious belief and of his relation to his own particular church; they are not matters relevant in any direct way to the conduct of his public office. Others with different religious views and commitments to different churches or denominations are equally qualified participants in the political process. The principle of separation of church and state guarantees the freedom of religious belief and association, but at the same time clearly segregates the religious sphere, which is considered to be essentially private, from the political one.

Considering the separation of church and state, how is a president justified in using the word *God* at all? The answer is that the separation of church and state has not denied the political realm a religious dimension. Although matters of personal religious belief, worship, and association are considered to be strictly private affairs, there are, at the same time, certain common elements of religious orientation that the great majority of Americans share. These have played a crucial role in the development of American institutions and still provide a religious dimension for the whole fabric of

American life, including the political sphere. This public religious dimension is expressed in a set of beliefs, symbols, and rituals that I am calling the American civil religion. The inauguration of a president is an important ceremonial event in this religion. It reaffirms, among other things, the religious legitimation of the highest political authority.

Let us look more closely at what Kennedy actually said. First he said, "I have sworn before you and Almighty God the same solemn oath our forebears prescribed nearly a century and three quarters ago." The oath is the oath of office, including the acceptance of the obligation to uphold the Constitution. He swears it before the people (you) and God. Beyond the Constitution, then, the president's obligation extends not only to the people but to God. In American political theory, sovereignty rests, of course, with the people, but implicitly, and often explicitly, the ultimate sovereignty has been attributed to God. This is the meaning of the motto, "In God we trust," as well as the inclusion of the phrase "under God" in the pledge to the flag. What difference does it make that sovereignty belongs to God? Though the will of the people as expressed in majority vote is carefully institutionalized as the operative source of political authority, it is deprived of an ultimate significance. The will of the people is not itself the criterion of right and wrong. There is a higher criterion in terms of which this will can be judged; it is possible that the people may be wrong. The president's obligation extends to the higher criterion.

When Kennedy says that "the rights of man come not from the generosity of the state but from the hand of God," he is stressing this point again. It does not matter whether the state is the expression of the will of an autocratic monarch or of the "people"; the rights of man are more basic than any political structure and provide a point of revolutionary leverage from which any state structure may be radically altered. That is the basis for his reassertion of the revolutionary significance of America.

But the religious dimension in political life as recognized by Kennedy not only provides a grounding for the rights of man which makes any form of political absolutism illegitimate, it also provides a transcendent goal for the political process. This is implied in his final words that "here on earth God's work must truly be our own." What he means here is, I think, more clearly spelled out in a previous paragraph, the wording of which, incidentally, has a distinctly Biblical ring:

Now the trumpet summons us again—not as a call to bear arms, though arms we need—not as a call to battle, though embattled we are—but a call to bear the burden of a long twilight struggle, year in and year out, "rejoicing in hope, patient in tribulation"—a struggle against the common enemies of man: tyranny, poverty, disease and war itself.

The whole address can be understood as only the most recent statement of a theme that lies very deep in the American tradition, namely the obligation, both collective and individual, to carry out God's will on earth. This was the motivating spirit of those who founded America, and it has been present in every generation since. Just below the surface throughout Kennedy's inaugural address, it becomes explicit in the closing statement that God's work must be our own. That this very activist and non-contemplative conception of the fundamental religious obligation, which has been historically associated with the Protestant position, should be enunciated so clearly in the first major statement of the first Catholic president seems to underline how deeply established it is in the American outlook. Let us now consider the form and history of the civil religious tradition in which Kennedy was speaking.

The Idea of a Civil Religion

The phrase *civil religion* is, of course, Rousseau's. In Chapter 8, Book 4, of *The Social Contract,* he outlines the simple dogmas of the civil religion: the existence of God, the life to come, the reward of virtue and the punishment of vice, and the exclusion of religious intolerance. All other religious opinions are outside the cognizance of the state and may be freely held by citizens. While the phrase *civil religion* was not used, to the best of my knowledge, by the founding fathers, and I am certainly not arguing for the particular influence of Rousseau, it is clear that similar ideas, as part of the cultural climate of the late-eighteenth century, were to be found among the Americans. For example, Franklin writes in his autobiography,

I never was without some religious principles. I never doubted, for instance, the existence of the Deity; that he made the world and govern'd it by his Providence; that the most acceptable service of God was the doing of good to men; that our souls are immortal; and that all crime will be punished, and virtue rewarded either here or hereafter. These I esteemed the essentials of every religion; and, being to be found in all the religions we had in our country, I respected them all, tho' with different degrees of respect, as I found them more or less mix'd with other

7

articles, which, without any tendency to inspire, promote or confirm morality, serv'd principally to divide us, and make us unfriendly to one another.

It is easy to dispose of this sort of position as essentially utilitarian in relation to religion. In Washington's Farewell Address (though the words may be Hamilton's) the utilitarian aspect is quite explicit:

Of all the dispositions and habits which lead to political prosperity, Religion and Morality are indispensable supports. In vain would that man claim the tribute of Patriotism, who should labour to subvert these great Pillars of human happiness, these firmest props of the duties of men and citizens. The mere politician, equally with the pious man ought to respect and cherish them. A volume could not trace all their connections with private and public felicity. Let it simply be asked where is the security for property, for reputation, for life, if the sense of religious obligation *desert* the oaths, which are the instruments of investigation in Courts of Justice? And let us with caution indulge the supposition, that morality can be maintained without religion. Whatever may be conceded to the influence of refined education on minds of peculiar structure, reason and experience both forbid us to expect that National morality can prevail in exclusion of religious principle.

But there is every reason to believe that religion, particularly the idea of God, played a constitutive role in the thought of the early American statesmen.

Kennedy's inaugural pointed to the religious aspect of the Declaration of Independence, and it might be well to look at that document a bit more closely. There are four references to God. The first speaks of the "Laws of Nature and of Nature's God" which entitle any people to be independent. The second is the famous statement that all men "are endowed by their Creator with certain inalienable Rights." Here Jefferson is locating the fundamental legitimacy of the new nation in a conception of "higher law" that is itself based on both classical natural law and Biblical religion. The third is an appeal to "the Supreme Judge of the world for the rectitude of our intentions," and the last indicates "a firm reliance on the protection of divine Providence." In these last two references, a Biblical God of history who stands in judgment over the world is indicated.

The intimate relation of these religious notions with the self-conception of the new republic is indicated by the frequency of their appearance in early official documents. For example, we find in Washington's first inaugural address of 30 April 1789:

It would be peculiarly improper to omit in this first official act my fervent supplications to that Almighty Being who rules over the universe, who presides in the councils of nations, and whose providential aids can supply every defect, that His benediction may consecrate to the liberties and happiness of the people of the United States a Government instituted by themselves for these essential purposes, and may enable every instrument employed in its administration to execute with success the functions allotted to his charge.

No people can be bound to acknowledge and adore the Invisible Hand which conducts the affairs of man more than those of the United States. Every step by which we have advanced to the character of an independent nation seems to have been distinguished by some token of providential agency. . . .

The propitious smiles of Heaven can never be expected on a nation that disregards the eternal rules of order and right which Heaven itself has ordained. . . . The preservation of the sacred fire of liberty and the destiny of the republican model of government are justly considered, perhaps, as *deeply,* as *finally,* staked on the experiment intrusted to the hands of the American people.

Nor did these religious sentiments remain merely the personal expression of the president. At the request of both Houses of Congress, Washington proclaimed on October 3 of that same first year as president that November 26 should be "a day of public thanksgiving and prayer," the first Thanksgiving Day under the Constitution.

The words and acts of the founding fathers, especially the first few presidents, shaped the form and tone of the civil religion as it has been maintained ever since. Though much is selectively derived from Christianity, this religion is clearly not itself Christianity. For one thing, neither Washington nor Adams nor Jefferson mentions Christ in his inaugural address; nor do any of the subsequent presidents, although not one of them fails to mention God.[3] The God of the civil religion is not only rather "unitarian," he is also on the austere side, much more related to order, law, and right than to salvation and love. Even though he is somewhat deist in cast, he is by no means simply a watchmaker God. He is actively interested and involved in history, with a special concern for America. Here the analogy has much less to do with natural law than with ancient Israel; the equation of America with Israel in the idea of the "American Israel" is not infrequent.[4] What was implicit in the words of Washington already quoted becomes explicit in Jefferson's second inaugural when he said: "I shall need, too, the favor of that Being in whose hands we are, who led our fathers, as Israel of old, from their native land and planted them in a country flowing with all the necessaries and comforts of life." Europe is Egypt; America, the promised land. God has led his people to establish a new sort of social order that shall be a light unto all the nations.[5]

This theme, too, has been a continuous one in the civil religion. We have already alluded to it in the case of the Kennedy inaugural. We find it again in President Johnson's inaugural address:

They came here—the exile and the stranger, brave but frightened—to find a place where a man could be his own man. They made a covenant with this land. Conceived in justice, written in liberty, bound in union, it was meant one day to inspire the hopes of all mankind; and it binds us still. If we keep its terms, we shall flourish.

What we have, then, from the earliest years of the republic is a collection of beliefs, symbols, and rituals with respect to sacred things and institutionalized in a collectivity. This religion—there seems no other word for it—while not antithetical to and indeed sharing much in common with Christianity, was neither sectarian nor in any specific sense Christian. At a time when the society was overwhelmingly Christian, it seems unlikely that this lack of Christian reference was meant to spare the feelings of the tiny non-Christian minority. Rather, the civil religion expressed what those who set the precedents felt was appropriate under the circumstances. It reflected their private as well as public views. Nor was the civil religion simply "religion in general." While generality was undoubtedly seen as a virtue by some, as in the quotation from Franklin above, the civil religion was specific enough when it came to the topic of America. Precisely because of this specificity, the civil religion was saved from empty formalism and served as a genuine vehicle of national religious self-understanding.

But the civil religion was not, in the minds of Franklin, Washington, Jefferson, or other leaders, with the exception of a few radicals like Tom Paine, ever felt to be a substitute for Christianity. There was an implicit but quite clear division of function between the civil religion and Christianity. Under the doctrine of religious liberty, an exceptionally wide sphere of personal piety and voluntary social action was left to the churches. But the churches were neither to control the state nor to be controlled by it. The national magistrate, whatever his private religious views, operates under the rubrics of the civil religion as long as he is in his official capacity, as we have already seen in the case of Kennedy. This accommodation was undoubtedly the product of a particular historical moment and of a cultural background dominated by Protestantism of several varieties and by the Enlightenment, but it has survived despite subsequent changes in the cultural and religious climate.

Civil War and Civil Religion

Until the Civil War, the American civil religion focused above all on the event of the Revolution, which was seen as the final act of the Exodus from the old lands across the waters. The Declaration of Independence and the Constitution were the sacred scriptures and Washington the divinely appointed Moses who led his people out of the hands of tyranny. The Civil War, which Sidney Mead calls "the center of American history,"[6] was the second great event that involved the national self-understanding so deeply as to require expression in the civil religion. In 1835, Tocqueville wrote that the American republic had never really been tried, that victory in the Revolutionary War was more the result of British pre-occupation elsewhere and the presence of a powerful ally than of any great military success of the Americans. But in 1861 the time of testing had indeed come. Not only did the Civil War have the tragic intensity of fratricidal strife, but it was one of the bloodiest wars of the nineteenth century; the loss of life was far greater than any previously suffered by Americans.

The Civil War raised the deepest questions of national meaning. The man who not only formulated but in his own person embodied its meaning for Americans was Abraham Lincoln. For him the issue was not in the first instance slavery but "whether that nation, or any nation so conceived, and so dedicated, can long endure." He had said in Independence Hall in Philadelphia on 22 February 1861:

All the political sentiments I entertain have been drawn, so far as I have been able to draw them, from the sentiments which originated in and were given to the world from this Hall. I have never had a feeling, politically, that did not spring from the sentiments embodied in the Declaration of Independence.[7]

The phrases of Jefferson constantly echo in Lincoln's speeches. His task was, first of all, to save the Union—not for America alone but for the meaning of America to the whole world so unforgettably etched in the last phrase of the Gettysburg Address.

But inevitably the issue of slavery as the deeper cause of the conflict had to be faced. In the second inaugural, Lincoln related slavery and the war in an ultimate perspective:

If we shall suppose that American slavery is one of those offenses which, in the providence of God, must needs come, but which, having continued through His appointed time, He now wills to remove, and that He gives to both North and South this terrible war as the woe due to those by whom the offense came, shall we discern therein any departure from those divine attributes which the believers in a living God always ascribe to Him? Fondly do we hope, fervently do we pray, that this mighty scourge of war may speedily pass away. Yet, if God wills that it continue until all the wealth piled by the bondsman's two hundred and fifty years of unrequited toil shall be sunk, and until every drop of blood drawn with the lash shall be paid by another drawn with the sword, as was said three thousand years ago, so still it must be said "the judgements of the Lord are true and righteous altogether."

But he closes on a note if not of redemption then of reconciliation— With malice toward none, with charity for all. . . ."

With the Civil War, a new theme of death, sacrifice, and rebirth enters the civil religion. It is symbolized in the life and death of Lincoln. Nowhere is it stated more vividly than in the Gettysburg Address, itself part of the Lincolnian "New Testament" among the civil scriptures. Robert Lowell has recently pointed out the "insistent use of birth images" in this speech explicitly devoted to "these honored dead": "brought forth," "conceived," "created," "a new birth of freedom." He goes on to say:

The Gettysburg Address is a symbolic and sacramental act. Its verbal quality is resonance combined with a logical, matter of fact, prosaic brevity. . . . In his words, Lincoln symbolically died, just as the Union soldiers really died—and as he himself was soon really to die. By his words, he gave the field of battle a symbolic significance that it had lacked. For us and our country, he left Jefferson's ideals of freedom and equality joined to the Christian sacrificial act of death and rebirth. I believe this is a meaning that goes beyond sect or religion and beyond peace and war, and is now part of our lives as a challenge, obstacle and hope.[8]

Lowell is certainly right in pointing out the Christian quality of the symbolism here, but he is also right in quickly disavowing any sectarian implication. The earlier symbolism of the civil religion had been Hebraic without being in any specific sense Jewish. The Gettysburg symbolism (". . . those who here gave their lives, that that nation might live") is Christian without having anything to do with the Christian church.

The symbolic equation of Lincoln with Jesus was made relatively early. Herndon, who had been Lincoln's law partner, wrote:

For fifty years God rolled Abraham Lincoln through his fiery furnace. He did it to try Abraham and to purify him for his purposes. This made Mr. Lincoln humble, tender, forbearing, sympathetic to suffering, kind, sensitive, tolerant; broadening, deepening and widening his whole nature; making him the noblest and loveliest character since Jesus Christ. . . . I believe that Lincoln was God's chosen one.[9]

With the Christian archetype in the background, Lincoln, "our martyred president," was linked to the war dead, those who "gave the last full measure of devotion." The theme of sacrifice was indelibly written into the civil religion.

The new symbolism soon found both physical and ritualistic expression. The great number of the war dead required the establishment of a number of national cemeteries. Of these, the Gettysburg National Cemetery, which Lincoln's famous address served to dedicate, has been overshadowed only by the Arlington National Cemetery. Begun somewhat vindictively on the Lee estate across the river from Washington, partly with the end that the Lee family could never reclaim it,[10] it has subsequently become the most hallowed monument of the civil religion. Not only was a section set aside for the Confederate dead, but it has received the dead of each succeeding American war. It is the site of the one important new symbol to come out of World War I, the Tomb of the Unknown Soldier; more recently it has become the site of the tomb of another martyred president and its symbolic eternal flame.

Memorial Day, which grew out of the Civil War, gave ritual expression to the themes we have been discussing. As Lloyd Warner has so brilliantly analyzed it, the Memorial Day observance, especially in the towns and smaller cities of America, is a major event for the whole community involving a rededication to the martyred dead, to the spirit of sacrifice, and to the American vision.[11] Just as Thanksgiving Day, which incidentally was securely institutionalized as an annual national holiday only under the presidency of Lincoln, serves to integrate the family into the civil religion, so Memorial Day has acted to integrate the local community into the national cult. Together with the less overtly religious Fourth of July and the more minor celebrations of Veterans Day and the birthdays of Washington and Lincoln, these two holidays provide an annual ritual calendar for the civil religion. The public-school system serves as a particularly important context for the cultic celebration of the civil rituals.

The Civil Religion Today

In reifying and giving a name to something that, though pervasive enough when you look at it, has gone on only semiconsciously, there is risk of severely distorting the data. But the reification and the naming have already begun. The religious critics of "religion in general," or of the "religion of the 'American Way of Life,'" or of "American Shinto" have really been talking about the civil religion. As usual in religious polemic, they take as criteria the best in their own religious tradition and as typical the worst in the tradition of the civil religion. Against these critics, I would argue that the civil religion at its best is a genuine apprehension of universal and transcendent religious reality as seen in or, one could almost say, as revealed through the experience of the American people. Like all religions, it has suffered various deformations and demonic distortions. At its best, it has neither been so general that it has lacked incisive relevance to the American scene nor so particular that it has placed American society above universal human values. I am not at all convinced that the leaders of the churches have consistently represented a higher level of religious insight than the spokesmen of the civil religion. Reinhold Niebuhr has this to say of Lincoln, who never joined a church and who certainly represents civil religion at its best:

An analysis of the religion of Abraham Lincoln in the context of the traditional religion of his time and place and of its polemical use on the slavery issue, which corrupted religious life in the days before and during the Civil War, must lead to the conclusion that Lincoln's religious convictions were superior in depth and purity to those, not only of the political leaders of his day, but of the religious leaders of the era.[12]

Perhaps the real animus of the religious critics has been not so much against the civil religion in itself but against its pervasive and dominating influence within the sphere of church religion. As S. M. Lipset has recently shown, American religion at least since the early-nineteenth century has been predominantly activist, moralistic, and social rather than contemplative, theological, or innerly spiritual.[13] Tocqueville spoke of American church religion as "a political institution which powerfully contributes to the maintenance of a democratic republic among the Americans"[14] by supplying a strong moral consensus amidst continuous political change. Henry Bargy in 1902 spoke of American church religion as "la poésie du civisme."[15]

It is certainly true that the relation between religion and politics in America has been singularly smooth. This is in large part due to the dominant tradition. As Tocqueville wrote:

The greatest part of British America was peopled by men who, after having shaken off the authority of the Pope, acknowledged no other religious supremacy: they brought with them into the New World a form of Christianity which I cannot better describe than by styling it a democratic and republican religion.[16]

The churches opposed neither the Revolution nor the establishment of democratic institutions. Even when some of them opposed the full institutionalization of religious liberty, they accepted the final outcome with good grace and without nostalgia for an *ancien régime*. The American civil religion was never anticlerical or militantly secular. On the contrary, it borrowed selectively from the religious tradition in such a way that the average American saw no conflict between the two. In this way, the civil religion was able to build up without any bitter struggle with the church powerful symbols of national solidarity and to mobilize deep levels of personal motivation for the attainment of national goals.

Such an achievement is by no means to be taken for granted. It would seem that the problem of a civil religion is quite general in modern societies and that the way it is solved or not solved will have repercussions in many spheres. One needs only to think of France to see how differently things can go. The French Revolution was anticlerical to the core and attempted to set up an anti-Christian civil religion. Throughout modern French history, the chasm between traditional Catholic symbols and the symbolism of 1789 has been immense.

American civil religion is still very much alive. Just three years ago we participated in a vivid re-enactment of the sacrifice theme in connection with the funeral of our assassinated president. The American Israel theme is clearly behind both Kennedy's New Frontier and Johnson's Great Society. Let me give just one recent illustration of how the civil religion serves to mobilize support for the attainment of national goals. On 15 March 1965 President Johnson went before Congress to ask for a strong voting-rights bill. Early in the speech he said:

Rarely are we met with the challenge, not to our growth or abundance, or our welfare or our security—but rather to the values and the purposes and the meaning of our beloved nation.

15

The issue of equal rights for American Negroes is such an issue. And should we defeat every enemy, and should we double our wealth and conquer the stars and still be unequal to this issue, then we will have failed as a people and as a nation.

For with a country as with a person, "What is a man profited, if he shall gain the whole world, and lose his own soul?"

And in conclusion he said:

Above the pyramid on the great seal of the United States it says in Latin, "God has favored our undertaking."

God will not favor everything that we do. It is rather our duty to divine his will. I cannot help but believe that He truly understands and that He really favors the undertaking that we begin here tonight.[17]

The civil religion has not always been invoked in favor of worthy causes. On the domestic scene, an American-Legion type of ideology that fuses God, country, and flag has been used to attack nonconformist and liberal ideas and groups of all kinds. Still, it has been difficult to use the words of Jefferson and Lincoln to support special interests and undermine personal freedom. The defenders of slavery before the Civil War came to reject the thinking of the Declaration of Independence. Some of the most consistent of them turned against not only Jeffersonian democracy but Reformation religion; they dreamed of a South dominated by medieval chivalry and divine-right monarchy.[18] For all the overt religiosity of the radical right today, their relation to the civil religious consensus is tenuous, as when the John Birch Society attacks the central American symbol of Democracy itself.

With respect to America's role in the world, the dangers of distortion are greater and the built-in safeguards of the tradition weaker. The theme of the American Israel was used, almost from the beginning, as a justification for the shameful treatment of the Indians so characteristic of our history. It can be overtly or implicitly linked to the idea of manifest destiny which has been used to legitimate several adventures in imperialism since the early-nineteenth century. Never has the danger been greater than today. The issue is not so much one of imperial expansion, of which we are accused, as of the tendency to assimilate all governments or parties in the world which support our immediate policies or call upon our help by invoking the notion of free institutions and democratic values. Those nations that are for the moment "on our side" become "the free world." A repressive and unstable military dictatorship in South Viet-Nam becomes "the free people of South Viet-Nam and their government." It is then part of the role of America as the New Jerusalem and "the last best hope of earth" to defend such governments with treasure and eventually with blood. When our soldiers are actually dying, it becomes possible to consecrate the struggle further by invoking the great theme of sacrifice. For the majority of the American people who are unable to judge whether the people in South Viet-Nam (or wherever) are "free like us," such arguments are convincing. Fortunately President Johnson has been less ready to assert that "God has favored our undertaking" in the case of Viet-Nam than with respect to civil rights. But others are not so hesitant. The civil religion has exercised long-term pressure for the humane solution of our greatest domestic problem, the treatment of the Negro American. It remains to be seen how relevant it can become for our role in the world at large, and whether we can effectually stand for "the revolutionary beliefs for which our forebears fought," in John F. Kennedy's words.

The civil religion is obviously involved in the most pressing moral and political issues of the day. But it is also caught in another kind of crisis, theoretical and theological, of which it is at the moment largely unaware. "God" has clearly been a central symbol in the civil religion from the beginning and remains so today. This symbol is just as central to the civil religion as it is to Judaism or Christianity. In the late-eighteenth century this posed no problem; even Tom Paine, contrary to his detractors, was not an atheist. From left to right and regardless of church or sect, all could accept the idea of God. But today, as even *Time* has recognized, the meaning of the word *God* is by no means so clear or so obvious. There is no formal creed in the civil religion. We have had a Catholic president; it is conceivable that we could have a Jewish one. But could we have an agnostic president? Could a man with conscientious scruples about using the word *God* the way Kennedy and Johnson have used it be elected chief magistrate of our country? If the whole God symbolism requires reformulation, there will be obvious consequences for the civil religion, consequences perhaps of liberal alienation and of fundamentalist ossification that have not so far been prominent in this realm. The civil religion has been a point of articulation between the profoundest commitments of the Western religious and philosophical tradition and the common beliefs of ordi-

17

nary Americans. It is not too soon to consider how the deepening theological crisis may affect the future of this articulation.

The Third Time of Trial

In conclusion it may be worthwhile to relate the civil religion to the most serious situation that we as Americans now face, what I call the third time of trial. The first time of trial had to do with the question of independence, whether we should or could run our own affairs in our own way. The second time of trial was over the issue of slavery, which in turn was only the most salient aspect of the more general problem of the full institutionalization of democracy within our country. This second problem we are still far from solving though we have some notable successes to our credit. But we have been overtaken by a third great problem which has led to a third great crisis, in the midst of which we stand. This is the problem of responsible action in a revolutionary world, a world seeking to attain many of the things, material and spiritual, that we have already attained. Americans have, from the beginning, been aware of the responsibility and the significance our republican experiment has for the whole world. The first internal political polarization in the new nation had to do with our attitude toward the French Revolution. But we were small and weak then, and "foreign entanglements" seemed to threaten our very survival. During the last century, our relevance for the world was not forgotten, but our role was seen as purely exemplary. Our democratic republic rebuked tyranny by merely existing. Just after World War I we were on the brink of taking a different role in the world, but once again we turned our back.

Since World War II the old pattern has become impossible. Every president since Roosevelt has been groping toward a new pattern of action in the world, one that would be consonant with our power and our responsibilities. For Truman and for the period dominated by John Foster Dulles that pattern was seen to be the great Manichaean confrontation of East and West, the confrontation of democracy and "the false philosophy of Communism" that provided the structure of Truman's inaugural address. But with the last years of Eisenhower and with the successive two presidents, the pattern began to shift. The great problems came to be seen as caused not solely by the evil intent of any one group of men, but as stemming from much more complex and multiple sources. For Kennedy, it was not so much a struggle against particular men as against "the common enemies of man: tyranny, poverty, disease and war itself."

But in the midst of this trend toward a less primitive conception of ourselves and our world, we have somehow, without anyone really intending it, stumbled into a military confrontation where we have come to feel that our honor is at stake. We have in a moment of uncertainty been tempted to rely on our overwhelming physical power rather than on our intelligence, and we have, in part, succumbed to this temptation. Bewildered and unnerved when our terrible power fails to bring immediate success, we are at the edge of a chasm the depth of which no man knows.

I cannot help but think of Robinson Jeffers, whose poetry seems more apt now than when it was written, when he said:

> Unhappy country, what wings you have! . . .
> Weep (it is frequent in human affairs), weep for
>   the terrible magnificence of the means,
> The ridiculous incompetence of the reasons, the
>   bloody and shabby
> Pathos of the result.

But as so often before in similar times, we have a man of prophetic stature, without the bitterness or misanthropy of Jeffers, who, as Lincoln before him, calls this nation to its judgment:

When a nation is very powerful but lacking in self-confidence, it is likely to behave in a manner that is dangerous both to itself and to others.

Gradually but unmistakably, America is succumbing to that arrogance of power which has afflicted, weakened and in some cases destroyed great nations in the past.

If the war goes on and expands, if that fatal process continues to accelerate until America becomes what it is not now and never has been, a seeker after unlimited power and empire, then Vietnam will have had a mighty and tragic fallout indeed.

I do not believe that will happen. I am very apprehensive but I still remain hopeful, and even confident, that America, with its humane and democratic traditions, will find the wisdom to match its power.[19]

Without an awareness that our nation stands under higher judgment, the tradition of the civil religion would be dangerous indeed. Fortunately, the prophetic voices have never been lacking. Our present situation brings to mind the Mexican-American war that Lincoln, among so many others, opposed. The spirit of civil disobedience that is alive today in the civil rights movement and the opposition to the Viet-Nam war was already clearly outlined by Henry David Thoreau when he wrote, "If the law is of such a nature that it requires you to be an agent of injustice to another, then I say, break the law." Thoreau's words, "I would remind my countrymen that they are men first, and Americans at a late and convenient hour,"[20] provide an essential standard for any adequate thought and action in our third time of trial. As Americans, we have been well favored in the world, but it is as men that we will be judged.

Out of the first and second times of trial have come, as we have seen, the major symbols of the American civil religion. There seems little doubt that a successful negotiation of this third time of trial—the attainment of some kind of viable and coherent world order—would precipitate a major new set of symbolic forms. So far the flickering flame of the United Nations burns too low to be the focus of a cult, but the emergence of a genuine trans-national sovereignty would certainly change this. It would necessitate the incorporation of vital international symbolism into our civil religion, or, perhaps a better way of putting it, it would result in American civil religion becoming simply one part of a new civil religion of the world. It is useless to speculate on the form such a civil religion might take, though it obviously would draw on religious traditions beyond the sphere of Biblical religion alone. Fortunately, since the American civil religion is not the worship of the American nation but an understanding of the American experience in the light of ultimate and universal reality, the reorganization entailed by such a new situation need not disrupt the American civil religion's continuity. A world civil religion could be accepted as a fulfillment and not a denial of American civil religion. Indeed, such an outcome has been the eschatological hope of American civil religion from the beginning. To deny such an outcome would be to deny the meaning of America itself.

Behind the civil religion at every point lie Biblical archetypes: Exodus, Chosen People, Promised Land, New Jerusalem, Sacrificial Death and Rebirth. But it is also genuinely American and genuinely new. It has its own prophets and its own martyrs, its own sacred events and sacred places, its own solemn rituals and symbols. It is concerned that America be a society as perfectly in accord with the will of God as men can make it, and a light to all the nations.

It has often been used and is being used today as a cloak for

petty interests and ugly passions. It is in need—as is any living faith
—of continual reformation, of being measured by universal standards. But it is not evident that it is incapable of growth and new insight.

It does not make any decision for us. It does not remove us from
moral ambiguity, from being, in Lincoln's fine phrase, an "almost
chosen people." But it is a heritage of moral and religious experience from which we still have much to learn as we formulate the
decisions that lie ahead.

REFERENCES

1. Why something so obvious should have escaped serious analytical attention
   is in itself an interesting problem. Part of the reason is probably the controversial nature of the subject. From the earliest years of the nineteenth
   century, conservative religious and political groups have argued that
   Christianity is, in fact, the national religion. Some of them have from time
   to time and as recently as the 1950's proposed constitutional amendments
   that would explicitly recognize the sovereignty of Christ. In defending the
   doctrine of separation of church and state, opponents of such groups have
   denied that the national polity has, intrinsically, anything to do with
   religion at all. The moderates on this issue have insisted that the American
   state has taken a permissive and indeed supportive attitude toward
   religious groups (tax exemption, et cetera), thus favoring religion but still
   missing the positive institutionalization with which I am concerned. But
   part of the reason this issue has been left in obscurity is certainly due to
   the peculiarly Western concept of "religion" as denoting a single type of
   collectivity of which an individual can be a member of one and only one
   at a time. The Durkheimian notion that every group has a religious dimension, which would be seen as obvious in southern or eastern Asia, is
   foreign to us. This obscures the recognition of such dimensions in our
   society.

2. Quoted in Will Herberg, *Protestant-Catholic-Jew* (New York, 1955), p. 97.

3. God is mentioned or referred to in all inaugural addresses but Washington's
   second, which is a very brief (two paragraphs) and perfunctory acknowl-
   edgment. It is not without interest that the actual word *God* does not
   appear until Monroe's second inaugural, 5 March 1821. In his first inaugural,
   Washington refers to God as "that Almighty Being who rules the universe,"
   "Great Author of every public and private good," "Invisible Hand," and
   "benign Parent of the Human Race." John Adams refers to God as "Providence," "Being who is supreme over all," "Patron of Order," "Fountain of
   Justice," and "Protector in all ages of the world of virtuous liberty." Jefferson speaks of "that Infinite Power which rules the destinies of the universe,"
   and "that Being in whose hands we are." Madison speaks of "that Almighty

Being whose power regulates the destiny of nations," and "Heaven." Monroe uses "Providence" and "the Almighty" in his first inaugural and finally "Almighty God" in his second. See, *Inaugural Addresses of the Presidents of the United States from George Washington 1789 to Harry S. Truman 1949*, 82d Congress, 2d Session, House Document No. 540, 1952.

4. For example, Abiel Abbot, pastor of the First Church in Haverhill, Massachusetts, delivered a Thanksgiving sermon in 1799, *Traits of Resemblance in the People of the United States of America to Ancient Israel*, in which he said, "It has been often remarked that the people of the United States come nearer to a parallel with Ancient Israel, than any other nation upon the globe. Hence OUR AMERICAN ISRAEL is a term frequently used; and common consent allows it apt and proper." Cited in Hans Kohn, *The Idea of Nationalism* (New York, 1961), p. 665.

5. That the Mosaic analogy was present in the minds of leaders at the very moment of the birth of the republic is indicated in the designs proposed by Franklin and Jefferson for a seal of the United States of America. Together with Adams, they formed a committee of three delegated by the Continental Congress on July 4, 1776, to draw up the new device. "Franklin proposed as the device Moses lifting up his wand and dividing the Red Sea while Pharaoh was overwhelmed by its waters, with the motto 'Rebellion to tyrants is obedience to God.' Jefferson proposed the children of Israel in the wilderness 'led by a cloud by day and a pillar of fire at night.'" Anson Phelps Stokes, *Church and State in the United States*, Vol. 1 (New York, 1950), pp. 467-68.

6. Sidney Mead, *The Lively Experiment* (New York, 1963), p. 12.

7. Quoted by Arthur Lehman Goodhart in Allan Nevins (ed.), *Lincoln and the Gettysburg Address* (Urbana, Ill., 1964), p. 39.

8. *Ibid.*, "On the Gettysburg Address," pp. 88-89.

9. Quoted in Sherwood Eddy, *The Kingdom of God and the American Dream* (New York, 1941), p. 162.

10. Karl Decker and Angus McSween, *Historic Arlington* (Washington, D. C., 1892), pp. 60-67.

11. How extensive the activity associated with Memorial Day can be is indicated by Warner: "The sacred symbolic behavior of Memorial Day, in which scores of the town's organizations are involved, is ordinarily divided into four periods. During the year separate rituals are held by many of the associations for their dead, and many of these activities are connected with later Memorial Day events. In the second phase, preparations are made during the last three or four weeks for the ceremony itself, and some of the associations perform public rituals. The third phase consists of scores of rituals held in all the cemeteries, churches, and halls of the associations. These rituals consist of speeches and highly ritualized behavior. They last for two days and are climaxed by the fourth and last phase, in which all the separate celebrants gather in the center of the business district on the

afternoon of Memorial Day. The separate organizations, with their members in uniform or with fitting insignia, march through the town, visit the shrines and monuments of the hero dead, and, finally, enter the cemetery. Here dozens of ceremonies are held, most of them highly symbolic and formalized." During these various ceremonies Lincoln is continually referred to and the Gettysburg Address recited many times. W. Lloyd Warner, *American Life* (Chicago, 1962), pp. 8-9.

12. Reinhold Niebuhr, "The Religion of Abraham Lincoln," in Nevins (ed.), *op. cit.*, p. 72. William J. Wolfe of the Episcopal Theological School in Cambridge, Massachusetts, has written: "Lincoln is one of the greatest theologians of America—not in the technical meaning of producing a system of doctrine, certainly not as the defender of some one denomination, but in the sense of seeing the hand of God intimately in the affairs of nations. Just so the prophets of Israel criticized the events of their day from the perspective of the God who is concerned for history and who reveals His will within it. Lincoln now stands among God's latter-day prophets." *The Religion of Abraham Lincoln* (New York, 1963), p. 24.

13. Seymour Martin Lipset, "Religion and American Values," Chapter 4, *The First New Nation* (New York, 1964).

14. Alexis de Tocqueville, *Democracy in America*, Vol. 1 (New York, 1954), p. 310.

15. Henry Bargy, *La Religion dans la Société aux États-Unis* (Paris, 1902), p. 31.

16. Tocqueville, *op. cit.*, p. 311. Later he says, "In the United States even the religion of most of the citizens is republican, since it submits the truths of the other world to private judgment, as in politics the care of their temporal interests is abandoned to the good sense of the people. Thus every man is allowed freely to take that road which he thinks will lead him to heaven, just as the law permits every citizen to have the right of choosing his own government" (p. 436).

17. U. S., *Congressional Record*, House, 15 March 1965, pp. 4924, 4926.

18. See Louis Hartz, "The Feudal Dream of the South," Part 4, *The Liberal Tradition in America* (New York, 1955).

19. Speech of Senator J. William Fulbright of 28 April 1966, as reported in *The New York Times*, 29 April 1966.

20. Quoted in Yehoshua Arieli, *Individualism and Nationalism in American Ideology* (Cambridge, Mass., 1964), p. 274.

FRANKLIN H. LITTELL

The Churches and the Body Politic

Two REPRESENTATIVE judgments on American religion, by wise and able men, may serve to introduce a consideration of the widespread confusion as to its true nature, condition, and influence. Summarizing his view of the American churches, gained during his first visit to the new world, Dietrich Bonhoeffer wrote:

God has granted American Christianity no Reformation. . . . Anything of the churches of the Reformation which has come to America either stands in conscious seclusion and detachment from the general life of the church or has fallen victim to Protestantism without Reformation. . . . The decisive task for today is the dialogue between Protestantism without Reformation and the churches of the Reformation.[1]

A few months ago Eugene Carson Blake, former Stated Clerk of the United Presbyterian Church, told a ministerial gathering in Chicago that the influence of religion in America had reached its lowest ebb in seventy-five years. For this reason, he favored a national union of Methodist, United Church, Presbyterian, and Episcopal forces,[2] apparently to reverse a flagging public effectiveness.

Both Bonhoeffer and Blake illustrate the confusion in assessing American church life and its public impact. Bonhoeffer was writing, to be sure, before the tragic shape of the church struggle in Germany led him virtually to abandon hope in institutional forms of Christianity. He was yet to write about "the secular" and "a world come of age" in the way that would later set off an avalanche of writing about "worldly Christianity" among the younger theologians of Europe and America. He was also writing before the renascence of theological and historical concern among American Lutherans and Mennonites, as well as among German Evangelicals and German Reformed in America, introduced a new and more consciously confessional force into the main stream of religious life. But significantly, what he then observed of religion in America failed to convince him of the value of religious liberty and voluntaryism and the viability of the American experiment. When, in debates in the Finkenwalde Seminar and in synods of the Confessing Church, the abandonment of the establishment and espousal of the Free-Church style were advocated, Bonhoeffer remained unconvinced. To the last, he perceived no effective organized alternative to the pattern of church-state relations known as "Christendom."

Blake, to be sure, has been one of the most articulate and influential churchmen in American public life. His role in achieving greater justice for Negro citizens has been especially noteworthy. He was also joint sponsor of the most promising organized effort toward inter-church union launched in recent years. Shortly after his pessimistic expression as to the effectiveness of contemporary religion, his election to a post of great eminence in the ecumenical movement was announced. He succeeds W. A. Visser 't Hooft as Secretary-General of the World Council of Churches—a post through which, after years of international experience as Secretary of the World's Student Christian Federation, his predecessor wielded enormous influence in inter-church and public affairs.

Bonhoeffer, whose inadequate understanding of the nature of the church was the most tragic element in his eventual martyrdom, looked back to the sixteenth century. Blake is apparently among the many who look back to an early period of American religious history—perhaps to the founding fathers of the American republic, or to the abolitionist crusade, or to the churches' role in the nation's manifest destiny during the latter part of the nineteenth century. Both, however, missed the point completely. The self-consciousness of American Christianity will not be served by referring to past ages at all. Religion in America, for a variety of reasons, has been future-oriented.

The key question is whether we must look backward to attain a genuine self-consciousness in American religion, or whether the clue to understanding the present is to be derived from the view of the future. For many of the forefathers, at least, the planting of America represented a major break from past history and a radical advance into a new age. God had hidden America until such a time as the Reformation could guarantee that the religion planted on these shores would be pure and evangelical. Certain writers linked three great events by which God's Providence prepared the coming of the New Age: (1) the invention of printing, whereby the Bible was made available to all; (2) the Reformation, whereby cult and confession were purified; (3) the discovery of America. Even such relatively sober men as Cotton Mather and Jonathan Edwards linked the discovery of America with the coming triumph of the eternal gospel.

In a later time, faith in America was linked to the unique experiment in religious liberty and voluntaryism. The great church historian Philip Schaff, although educated in the traditions of Christendom, became a vigorous champion of the separation of church and state and a sensitive interpreter of the peculiar significance of the American experiment. On one occasion he wrote:

The Reformation of the sixteenth century is by no means the last word which God has spoken to His people. He has other and greater Pentecosts in store. By His providence all nationalities and creeds are brought together in this land of freedom, of which the Reformers could not dream. Here is the material, the possibility and opportunity for a settlement of the controversies of Christendom.[3]

With Schaff, a new element has entered the picture. In the American experiment, religious liberty has been joined with an ecumenical motif. The coercive system of the Old World, with confessional conformity enforced by the state, was destructive of both liberty and open discussion. In America, the practice of liberty is conducive to cooperation. Moreover, the revelation of divine truth has not been completed in some truth once delivered to the saints: God has yet more truth to break forth from his Word in Israel.

To put the question in the language of the Pilgrim John Robinson, as in the preceding sentence, draws us closer to a very important watershed in the historical consciousness of the religious groups in America. By no means all of them regard the sixteenth century or the fourth century, let alone the nineteenth century of the great statistical successes, as normative. To some, the whole concept of "Christendom" has been repelling. The goal for the future, a goal uniquely fitted to the possibilities of America, is the restitution of high religion as it flourished in the primitive church before the time of the great Christian emperors, when the "fall of the church" brought to the Christian religion outward prosperity but inward impoverishment.

The End of the Constantinian Era

The establishment of Christianity, at the end of the apostolic age, not only changed the nature and style of that religion. It also introduced the persecution of heretics and the harassment of the Jews. A Jewish scholar has recently dealt very vigorously with the whole system of established religion and state-church cooperation maintained by the church since that time.

The Christian era did not start with the birth of Jesus. It dates from the first half of the fourth century, commencing when Constantine the Great established Christianity as the state religion of the Roman Empire. The characteristic mark of the era was militancy.[4]

In the opinion of the author, Rabbi Eliezer Berkovits, the intolerance natural to established Christianity reached its final fruition in the murderous policies of the Third Reich. And the present turn toward tolerance and ecumenism results, in his judgment, from the church's loss of status and power in the world rather than from increase in wisdom and virtue. For the Jew, he feels, there is little point to Christian-Jewish dialogue—at least until enough time has passed for the Nazi's "final solution to the Jewish question," Christendom's last spasm, to be expiated. Granted that Dr. Berkovits has failed to distinguish sufficiently between "Christendom" and "Christianity," his periodization of the church history fits very neatly that of a number of Christian movements which have contributed substantially to the American experiment.

A number of Christian leaders and movements, very influential in launching America's radical experiment in religious liberty and voluntaryism, have also condemned the coercive policies of Christendom. They have spoken of the union of church and state following Constantine as a descent from and a betrayal of the faith. Maintaining as normative the early church, they have longed for the restitution of the church at Jerusalem. They have despised the bishops who at Constantine's behest "went over to the world." The radical Reformation achieved in the New World an influence never acquired in Europe.[5] These groups of the "Left Wing of the Reformation" played a mighty part in the achievement of religious liberty and the establishment of the principle of voluntary support and membership. To do so they had to defy the state-church system that obtained in the eleven colonies besides Rhode Island and Pennsylvania, to win the understanding and support of some representatives of the more traditional churches that still favored the pattern and style of established religion, and to prove that religious groups could take a responsible role in the public forum without falling back into the old ways of establishmentarian politics.

To a certain extent, these targets have been scored. Yet the full implications of a constitutional affirmation of the voluntary principle, of the separation of the two covenants, religious and political, have yet to be drawn. Will the churches devote the same energy to the positive obligations of freedom once the negative dimension of religious liberty has been lined out, with a bar against political interference in religious matters? Will they slip back into some form of social establishment once legal establishment has been eliminated? Will a new form of "Christendom" take the place of that which obtained for so long at law? The litmus test of whether a final shift to a new base has occurred is the relationship to the Jews. During the second period of American church history, after disestablishment had been largely achieved, the political problem was to make religious liberty viable. Today, with the last remnants of the Protestant public liturgy being removed, we are entering the age of pluralism and the dialogue.

When voluntary membership and support were proving themselves, when missions and ecumenical cooperation were giving a richer texture to a religious life based on voluntaryism, much of the mythology of Christendom was perpetuated. Many churchmen and theologians continued to think of the American scene as an extension of European Christendom. The missionary movement itself, even though the leaders of the home boards acted on the assumption that America was missionary territory, contributed to the confusion until recently. In a classic work, *The Church and Missions*, Robert E. Speer presented without flinching two conflicting views of the religious situation. He stated the case for "Christian America":

In Great Britain and the United States the State is Christian in theory and principle.

Christ is and has a right to be acknowledged as the head of the State, and all acts of the State ought to be in conformity with the law of Christianity.[6]

Later in his discussion, however, he concluded that the alliance of church and state has become detrimental to the cause of religion. "Most powerful of all things in discrediting Christianity and weakening the force of the missionary's presentation has been the example of the nominally Christian nations," he wrote. He then quoted a Hindu statesman who, reaching the same conclusion as Gandhi and Nehru, had said after observing the conduct of the "Christian" West during World War I:

The European War, and no less the European Peace, have discredited the Christianity of the Churches. The Christian missionary has no chance of getting a hearing now, unless he distinguishes between Christ and Christianity and between Christianity and western civilization.[7]

After the widespread apostasy revealed by the "Christian" nations in Nazism and Fascism, the necessity of distinguishing between "Christendom" and "Christianity" became imperative. The former mission fields began to prefer the term *younger churches* and hastened to cut the ties of control to agencies in London, Paris, and New York. The stress on "indigenization" of the churches of Africa, Asia, and the islands, along with the upsurge of a host of native cults, documents the churches' rejection of an earlier identification with the European states and America. The crisis posed by the rise of anti-Christian systems and ideologies in the heart of Christendom, accompanied by large-scale abandonment of any pretense to Christian standards, has brought the younger theologians of European and American Catholicism and Protestantism to write of "the post-Christian era." Whether Christians in America will continue to think of themselves as citizens of a Christian nation or whether they will accept the reality of their existence as a minority in a Gentile world is of fatal consequence not only for their stance in the Age of Dialogue with representatives of other high religions; it also determines their conduct in the political forum.

Many Protestants still cling to the mythology of the earlier age even though the effort to maintain national Prohibition and to use the law to forbid the teaching of evolution in the public schools of many states discredited the state-church style among a majority of Americans. Beyond this, the question basic to the self-understanding of American Catholics and American Jews is whether America is an extension of European Christendom or an area in which something fundamentally new and different in the history of religions is being attempted.

Unfortunately, many Jewish writers still assume that "Christendom" remains intact, if shaken. They fail to distinguish between "Christian society" and "Gentile society." Since *Gentile* means, etymologically, "non-Jewish," the continuing commitment of these writers to ethnicity is all too evident. Furthermore, there is nothing in the valuable "American Schema," the Declaration on Religious Freedom of Vatican II, to clarify this issue. Religious liberty, there defined in the natural-law terms made familiar by the great encyclicals *Mater et Magistra* (15 May 1961) and *Pacem in Terris* (11

April 1963), could still become merely the toleration of the dignity and integrity of dissenting individuals and groups within a state governed by sacral assumptions. What is needed, and is lacking, is a series of cross references from religious liberty to the ecclesiological documents ("Lumen Gentium," Dogmatic Constitution on the Church; and "Gaudium et Spes," Pastoral Constitution on the Church in the Modern World).[8] The American experiment in religious liberty and voluntaryism involves a new kind of church, with matters appropriate to religious discipline discussed in a different context and in part in a different language from matters appropriate to political decision.

The separation of the religious and political covenants has resulted in greater toleration of dissent, "heresy," and atheism in American society. Since the church has the right as a voluntary association to fix its own terms of reference, this separation does not, however, necessarily involve a great toleration of such activities within the religious communities. But a healthy functioning of such religious societies within the body politic does involve a positive note. It is not enough for religious bodies to exact freedom from political interference, important as this is. They have, beyond the negative phase of religious liberty, a positive obligation to communicate to their neighbors what they consider important to the general welfare. The positive phase of religious liberty is expressed in service to the neighbor, in the practice of dialogue, in loyal support and defense of "secular" government. Non-sacral government is as important to religious liberty as free churches.

Clarification of the prevailing confusion of "Christendom" and "Christianity" is even more imperative for the American Jewish communities than it is for Protestants or Catholics. American Catholics might, as leaders like Cardinal Spellman and Archbishop Sheen appeared to intend during the public controversy over the "Prayer Amendments," graft themselves onto the earlier Protestant tradition which held that Christianity is part of the common law of the land. For American Jews, however, it is of utmost importance to know whether they are a hard-shelled minority in a Christian nation or a complex of minorities of legal and social status equal to that of other religious minorities (including various Protestant and Catholic ones) in a Gentile civilization ruled by a secular government. American Jews, distinctly children of the Enlightenment who are indebted to the process of secularization that brought them in European nations a modicum of peace and security, have often failed to perceive that the American experiment stands for neither establishment nor secularism. American Protestants and Catholics, overcome by the vertigo of freedom, often revert to an earlier style of hegemony, while American Jews are tempted to cultivate the mind-set of the ghetto that Christendom produced and enforced.

In Europe the situation is becoming increasingly clear despite the attempt of various "Christian" parties and governments in the West to maintain the traditional façade. As one theologian, a leader in the church struggles with Nazism and Communism, has put it:

By alert spirits, the situation of Christianity in Europe is characterized by the fact that the end of the Constantinian period is at hand. The Barmen Theses, in which by the proclamation of the sole Lordship of Jesus Christ all hyphenated Christianity is rejected, remain significant as the charter of liberty for the Biblical proclamation, out of a Babylonian capitivity.

The Constantinian alliance marked the interruption of the common way of the church of Jesus Christ, which according to the view of the New Testament is to be a way of suffering in contradiction and contrast to the world. With the end of illusions about the Constantinian period, and in return to the witness of the Early Church, we no longer have the right to demand privileges from the state and a monopoly of support of the gospel.[9]

His argument has special poignancy since he is a Christian leader in the D. D. R. (Communist East Germany), and has lived and worked for more than thirty years under totalitarian ideological establishments.

In America the break from the traditions and practice of "Christendom" occurred at the beginning of the nation's existence, with the Great Bill of Religious Freedom in Virginia (1784-86) and the First Amendment to the Federal Constitution (1791). And in spite of the pleas of the totalitarians, America has not become "post-Christian" enough to retrogress to Fascist or Marxist sacralism. Religious liberty and secular government still bracket our greatest possibilities, although the courts have had to carry a larger share of the burden of defending the American experiment than would be necessary in an area where the churches were alert to the true nature of their freedom.

It is a mistake to suppose that the American experiment in religious liberty and secular government derived from practical necessity or from pragmatic response to the problems of religious diversity. As the debates in the state conventions that ratified the

Federal Constitution make clear, the new and radical approach to the relations of church and state derived from a view of church and a view of government quite different from that which had obtained for centuries in Christendom. The Rhode Island resolution, adopted at the point when both that state and North Carolina refused to ratify until basic liberties were guaranteed, bears quotation.

That religion, or the duty which we owe to the Creator, and the manner of discharging it, can be directed only by reason and conviction, and not by force and violence; and therefore all men have a natural, equal and unalienable right to the exercise of religion according to the dictates of conscience; and that no particular religious sect or society ought to be favored or established, by law, in preference to others.[10]

As believing men, which most of them were, and as champions of the full, free, and informed discussion that is the lifeblood of liberty, they left open the possibility that diverse creeds might be able to prove their case and win their way to general voluntary support. Other advocates of liberty in other regions shared what was asserted in Rhode Island. This assertion was liberating to both church and state. High religion can only be, and of right ought to be, voluntary and uncoerced. This freed the church to be what the radical Reformation called "a True Church," a community of faithful people in no sense beholden to or intimidated by outside force in matters of faith. And, of barely secondary importance, it freed the state to be what government is intended to be: a human invention, limited in ultimate claims, modest in use of power, established to achieve specific ends—in a word, theologically speaking, a "creature."

Against the background of this historical development, the twin perils of dogmatic secularism and "Christian America" stand clearly defined. The ideology of secularism, always to be distinguished carefully from the historical process of secularization, is chiefly important for its influence among the intellectuals. Only occasionally has it distorted the American experiment in religious liberty, although a few published opinions in the U. S. Supreme Court report give concrete reality to the threat. Far more general is the casual acceptance of the premises of social establishment of religion, of the claims of culture-religion. Here even some outstanding church leaders have preferred to defend the mythology of "Christian America" rather than to accept the perils of religious liberty, voluntaryism, and pluralism. The public statements of such men of distinction as Henry P. Van Dusen and Reinhold Niebuhr criticizing the Supreme Court's decisions in the prayer cases attest to this. Most pertinent, however, is the way in which spokesmen for the radical right, such as Robert Welch, Carl McIntire, and George Wallace, have attempted to make defense of "Christian America" (the earlier tradition of white, Anglo-Saxon, Protestant America) a major bulwark of reactionary politics.

Quite plainly there are many who have not yet accepted the unique character of the American experiment in religious liberty and voluntaryism. The significance of the collapse of European Christendom and of the post-Christian nature of virulent anti-Semitism and ideological politics has escaped them. For those who love liberty and are prepared to live with the problems and challenges of the dialogue, the lesson is equally plain: Secular government is the partner of religious freedom.

The end of the Constantinian era has brought quite different problems to Europe and America. Europe is certainly "post-Christendom" and probably "post-Christian" as well. America is "post-Christendom," but the churches still have a chance to prove their case for Christianity on its merits. The failure to distinguish between the two situations is, more than anything else, responsible for perpetuating the confusion of language evident in theological circles. On the one hand are traditional theologians who still draw their supplies through a long tunnel that reaches back four hundred years to the great Reformers of the sixteenth century, and who still discuss the relations of church and state in the language of Luther and Calvin, Canisius and Cassander, in a situation that would have horrified all four. On the other hand are the theologians of the "Death of God" who assume the continued existence of Christendom and attack it in ecstatic utterance. In reference to the nineteenth-century culture-religion, their words have the impact if not the form of prophecy. For those who have accepted the reality of pluralism, liberty, and the dialogue, however, their message is as out of date—if not as dull—as the Syllabus of Errors or the platform of Abraham Kuyper's Anti-Revolutionary Christian Party.

In Europe, the end of the Constantinian era came after the churches had exhausted their credit, after they had lost both proletariat and intellectuals, after they had given birth to violent anti-Christian ideologies. In America, the Constantinian pattern and style were proclaimed at an end by Christians who had caught a new vision of the nature of high religion and just government. Separation of church and state has in Europe been the product of ideology, with a new sacralism frequently replacing the old. Separation in America has been largely nonideological; it has brought inestimable gains to both church and state.

Cooperative Separatism

There is no need at this point to discuss the process by which constitutional provisions once applicable only in restraint of the Congress have more recently been, by extension of the "due-process" clause of the Fourteenth Amendment, directed toward state and municipal instruments of government as well. Suffice it to say that the free exercise of religion and the prohibition of any establishment of religion are now securely established against misguided action by any political or quasi-political agency at any level. The transition to religious liberty and voluntaryism, with all its ramifications, has been slow and sometimes painful. In recent years, with the process nearing completion, the courts have had to carry a heavier load than is healthy in an area of popular sovereignty. In the polarization of public opinion that feeds the extremists, the courts have all too often had to defend the particulars of secular government—thereby being cast in the role of "secularists" undermining "Christian America." Advocates of high religion should have challenged a debased public liturgy (including the exploitation of a shapeless and formless religion in the public schools) long before the matter was brought to court at all. In sum, religious liberty is not something that was achieved once and for all. On the contrary, a standard was raised at the time of the beginning of the American republic toward which we have gradually been progressing. And in no area is there more confusion still to be found than in interpreting and implementing the proper role of the churches in influencing public opinion and political action.

If America were still an extension of "Christendom," religious groups could choose between the state-church style of establishments and the a-political style of conventicles. In some circles, it is still insisted that America is a Christian nation and that certain laws and public decrees should reflect that type of religious commitment. Against this image, vehement secularists claim that a high wall of separation between church and state requires that organized religion avoid participation in the political forum. Both positions, establishmentarian and secularist, ideologically buttressed and articulated though they be, ignore the actual historical record and compound confusion as to how free churches may and should function in a society with a secular government and a high degree of popular sovereignty. Americans have yet to work out most of the guidelines for churches in this new and indeed unique experiment in liberty. Neither the defenders of "Christian America" nor the ideological secularists are much help. Both were formed in the European situation and presuppose the kind of religion and anti-religion that Christendom produces.

During the first period of American church history, the colonial era, the dominant churches functioned in the same way as the established churches of the Old World. During the second period of American church history—when new methods of mass evangelism won the people back to the churches on a voluntary basis and made religious liberty a viable proposition—two conflicting motifs were evident. On one side, lectures, public sermons, writings, and proc-lamations of political bodies kept alive the image of America as a Christian nation. On the other, those who actually developed the new methods, carried on the home missions work, and reclaimed the population to voluntary membership treated North America as missionary territory in the same sense as Africa or Asia. As Timothy L. Smith has shown, most of the great social crusades of the first half of the nineteenth century were products of the missionary societies and the great revivals.[11] They reflected the determination to prove the case for religion by persuasion, to "Christianize" an otherwise pagan people. Yet at the same time, although church-membership rolls represented less than 20 per cent of the popula-tion during the Civil War, Abraham Lincoln assumed a non-sec-tarian Christianity to be the faith of the nation, and Jefferson Davis explicity declared it to be the faith of the peoples of the Confed-erate states. Not until the modern period, when Catholics and Jews and others have come into full and unabashed participation in the public life of the nation, as symbolized by the 1960 election, has the old Protestant culture-religion been frontally challenged.

In the third period of American church history, the Age of Dialogue, the Protestant churches that once dominated the scene are no longer unchallenged from within the evangelical ranks either. During the first period, Congregationalism and Anglicanism were dominant. During the second period, Baptists, Methodists, and Disciples or Christians achieved major statistical growth and influence. In the contemporary scene, "late-bloomers" like the Luth-erans—once confined to linguistic ghettos—are exercising a major liturgical and theological influence in Protestant ecumenical circles. For one thing, the tradition of the magisterial Reformation has grown strong, to balance the heritage of the radical Reformation. For another, the bridge to understanding of and cooperation with Catholics has been considerably strengthened. Finally, the defense and interpretation of religious liberty has now produced noteworthy statements from Vatican II, from the Presbyterians, and from the Lutherans. The case for religious liberty is no longer a virtual monopoly of those radical Protestant groups that in Europe and in colonial America once found themselves cast outside the political main stream.

In spite of the twin myths of "Christian America" and radical separation, and the effort to apply either ideology at law in the contemporary scene, religious liberty and its implications are more the occasion of constructive thought than ever before in America. A recent report of the Lutheran Church of America came close to the genius of the American solution to church-state relations: "We shall defend both the institutional separation and the functional interaction of church and state in the United States and Canada."[12] This is the solution that Paul G. Kauper of the University of Michigan Law School has called "cooperative separatism."[13] It better describes the uniqueness of the American experiment than would either a modified theory of Christendom or a dogmatic secularism. With free churches and a secular government, the churches still have a positive responsibility to participate vigorously in forming public opinion and shaping political consensus. Their style is quite different, however, from that of the conspiracies and cabals by which religious and ideological blocs corrupt politics in more primitive societies.

Part of the conceptual confusion in defining the public and political function of the American churches arises because there is no word to comprehend all of the various forms of religious association that may combine to make their weight felt on a given issue.[14] In this essay, *church* and *churches* have been used in a generic sense, with intention to comprehend synagogues, communions, confessions, sects, and the like, unless a distinction is clearly indicated. But what does it mean to speak of a "United Buddhist Church" in South Viet-Nam? It was simple enough to distinguish *church* from *sect* in Christendom, since *church* was whatever the law approved and *sect* was everything else neither Jewish nor Moslem.[15] The typology of *church* and *sect* developed by Ernst Troeltsch,[16] and popularized in this country by H. Richard Niebuhr,[17] is also more confusing than clarifying. As a matter of record, Troeltsch himself declared it inapplicable to the modern period and especially to England and America.

However we define the various religious bodies, and for internal purposes almost every group requires some normative term, it is becoming increasingly clear that in America religious bodies neither flee the world like traditional sects nor dominate it like established churches. The teachings of Luther, Calvin, Butzer, and Hooker on church and state, along with the Canons and Decrees of the Council of Trent, have almost as little relevance to our situation as the political views of Hochmann von Hochenau and the Hermit of the Wissahickon. We still have a few religious fossils of sectarian movements, of which Cassius Clay has been the most vocal recent representative, who refuse to vote, hold office, or serve in civic capacity. We have even more councils of bishops, synods, and assemblies that, when they pass resolutions, sometimes sound as though they were members of the old House of Lords or princes of the realm. When they do speak, their words sound "moralistic"—that is, presumptive of a status, authority, and constituency that no longer obtains.

American religious liberty, voluntaryism, and pluralism have created a new situation for both church and state. Politically, Americans are exploring the meaning of secular government while, religiously, they are discovering the potential of free churches. The church must first look to the integrity of its own constituency and discipline to ensure that whatever is recommended to fellow-citizens may reflect consistency of thought and principled action. Because the government is "secularized," it must function according to the language and concerns of the "secular city"[18] rather than in pursuit of specific religious objectives. The religious and political covenants have been separated. The effect of this separation on the churches' style of politics is monumental.

The Age of the Laity

In the old style of relating religion to the public life, both government and church were led by ruling classes. For centuries of Christendom, a "good" layman was defined in terms of silence, docility, and obedience. A loyal subject had similar qualities. But with the appearance of "citizens" (rather than subjects) and the rise of popular participation in government, there has developed within the churches a growing emphasis upon "the ministry of the laity," "the apostolate of the laity." Established churches of the old type are inevitably hierarchical, just as a class of ruling nobility was necessary to the function of politics before the emergence of self-government.

The Age of Dialogue is also the Age of the Laity. The role of all people can no longer be designated by a ruling element alone—whether within the church or within the civil society. To function, popular sovereignty requires a full measure of civic initiative on the part of the citizenry. This in itself dictates that the churches, along with other voluntary associations, shall participate fully in the formation of public opinion and the determination of public policy. Beyond that, the roles of both clergy and people (*laos*, from which *laity*) have substantially changed in a period of history where attention is given to the dignity of every human person and where appeal is made to the consciences of men of good will everywhere. The dialogue reaches far beyond the circles of the specially trained and commissioned. The initiative of men of conscience, especially in areas where popular sovereignty functions substantially, is essential to both healthy religion and sound politics.

In Christendom, the churches' style of leadership was structured and hierarchical. In the "sects," it was patriarchal and familial. In the American experiment, lay initiative and civic initiative are inter-related and reinforce each other. The laity, living and working in the world, carry a far larger share of the responsibility for discussing and determining political action (or inaction) than ever before.

A New Style of Politics

During the century and a half of mass evangelism, church membership was brought from about 7 per cent to about 70 per cent of the population, with well over 90 per cent claiming church affiliation in population surveys. While the Protestants of the most successful revivalist churches developed the characteristically American Protestant forms of recruitment, the Roman Catholics developed the equally unique parochial school system from first grade through graduate school. The Jews, coming later although in large numbers, have developed an elaborate network of cultural and charitable enterprises to hold their own. As we enter the third period of American church history, the Age of Dialogue, all three great faith groups are enjoying an unparalleled prosperity and strength as a result of the religious liberty and voluntaryism that almost all of them once feared.

Never before in human history has the attempt been made to hold a society together and move it forward under great strain and stress without a common public liturgy, without a creed established by law. When William Penn and Roger Williams proposed the experiment, in colonial times, the wise and experienced scorned the thought. When the Great Bill of Religious Freedom was brought forward later in Virginia, patriots like George Washington and Patrick Henry opposed it. Today, as religious liberty and the separation of the two covenants are being achieved, the inter-religious dialogue has a heavy weight placed upon it. In areas of dialogue where an establishment has learned to practice tolerance and to respect dissent, traditional patterns still supply a frame of order. In America, both religious and civic order greatly depend upon the consensus of all concerned. The inter-relation of religious and political forces enters territory never before explored.

As an example of the type of initiative appropriate to our situation, we may take the National Conference on Religion and Race, held in Chicago in January of 1963. At this Conference, which centered upon an issue of deep religious concern and civic moment, leaders of the three great traditions (organized in seventy-seven different official sponsoring groups) officially cooperated for the first time in history.[19] The Conference launched an avalanche of regional, state, and local conferences. It took, thereby, a substantial part in winning support for the passage of the Civil Rights Act of 1964. In the future, successful religious initiative in the political arena will most probably be based upon this alliance of Catholic, Protestant, and Jewish forces, rallying about them other civic groups and societies of men of good will.

The American churches are not, by and large, pietist conventicles content to avoid politics and public controversy. The effort of the dogmatic secularists and the radical right to push them back into the corner of individual and familial devotion will not succeed. Nor are they established churches, although they will continue to act as such for a time in smaller towns and isolated areas (for example, Utah—where the Mormon ethos still perpetuates in many respects the old New England folklore and folk-style of politics and economics).

If a new style of politics appropriate to free churches and secular government is to emerge, two things are needed of the churches. The first requirement is attention to the internal integrity and discipline of the religious bodies. When they enter the political arena in various cooperative efforts, they must be able to speak and act with clarity and consistency. It may seem strange to attribute political significance to church discipline. But those who propose some new pattern of public order, some new piece of legislation, have the obligation to prepare a "model"—to demonstrate the meaning and workability of what is declared. The second requirement, in which all citizens and not just church members share responsibility, is the development of a language and political style appropriate to America's present role as a world city. To be experimented with at many levels is political action based on discussions and agreements within the primary religious communities, among the faith groups, and in concert on specific issues with all men of good will. The appeal for dialogue and cooperation among all "men of good will" made in *Pacem in Terris* (11 April 1963) and implicit in the Declaration on Religious Freedom of Vatican II will be more and more the broadened base upon which the churches' style of political action will be based. But thorough discipline and a solid consensus within the ranks of the churches' membership must back this appeal if credible action is to ensue.

To be de-mythologized are the twin myths of America as a Christian nation[20] and America as an area dominated by the ideology of secularism, under which religious and political concerns are separated by a high wall. Neither of these myths fits the realities of our history and our present possibilities. Both represent a retrogression to the unsatisfactory alternatives afforded men of sensitive conscience in an earlier period of religious and political history.

Churches that wish to be taken seriously in the public forum must recover discipline within their ranks. Each must speak and act within the frame of reference it has chosen. The present writer is a Methodist. Two things have weakened the credibility of Methodist initiative on political issues. First, the Methodists, along with those other denominations of British background most successful during the great revivals, virtually abandoned membership standards to achieve statistical success.[21] Second, they have tended to perpetuate the language and image of "Christian America." They frequently speak of themselves as a representative national church. Accepting the self-image of social establishment has proved almost as debilitating as accepting that of the legal establishment. Precisely at the time when cheap membership practices made it virtually impossible for church leaders to maintain traditional Wesleyan discipline against the use of alcohol, the church supported vigorously the politics of the Anti-Saloon League, the W.C.T.U., and state and national prohibition.

As Methodists learn to accept their role as one of several religious minorities in a secular society, both religious obligation and civic responsibility will be clarified. The churches in a society with a large measure of self-government must talk up the consensus and develop the models of human relations that may commend themselves to the society at large. These models are desperately needed. The process of "talking up" helps to form public opinion, to sustain the law once it has been enacted. The community with a right to be heard by fellow-citizens is one that has already discussed and adopted the style of life it is recommending to the commonwealth. Petitions for legislation against public racial segregation come ill from a segregated church. Defense of labor's right to organize reads strangely when published by a "scab" press.

When political action is taken or legislation proposed, it must be stated in language appropriate to a pluralistic and secular society. If distinctions are to be preserved between the two covenants, the form of words is important. Sabbath observance may be enjoined among believers and maintained within the church by the authority of Holy Writ. In the public forum, however, the case for Sabbath observance must be made on the basis of protecting individuals and society from excessive work hours and ensuring them a decent alternation of work and rest. Within the ranks, mutual aid may be grounded in the *Lex Christi*. In the society at large, the case for insuring the poor and helpless against the exigencies of indigency must be made by pointing out the nature of a just state. The religious initiative penetrates and informs the body politic, but in our situation the Church Meeting and the Town Meeting have been separated. They operate within different contexts and with different constituencies.

The language of the secular society is created in good part by the religious tradition—for example, "just state." And the value judgments upon which public policy is based are shaped more largely than sometimes realized by Judaeo-Christian norms. This framework within which the public policy is discussed, this oral tradition by

41

which the language is shaped, is created among free churches in a secular society not by fiat or legislation, but by the teaching and action that win voluntary acceptance. Analytical and critical analysis can be built into a generation by required schooling. Wisdom, the unconscious and subconscious responses that bind the generations together in a common idiom of thought and action, can only be instilled and altered by "the thoughts that wound from behind."

The kinds of political cooperation open to Jews, Catholics, Protestants, and all men of good will are many and various. In the genius of the American experiment, this varied cooperation will be pedestrian and problem-solving; ideological dogmatics will be eschewed. Fair-housing practices, equal-employment possibilities, "shared-time" programs between public and private schools, "cluster programs" in higher education, improved schooling and Head-Start programs, equal justice for all at law—these and many other areas are suitable for political initiative by religious groups. In each case, high religion and sound politics require the maintenance of a genuine dialectic. The integrity of the church must be carefully guarded from political manipulation, and the integrity of the created order must be respected. Neither government nor social welfare nor the secular city exists to be the object of religious imperialism.

America is called to become a world city, a meeting place of the peoples. Even the reform movements of Islam, Buddhism, and Hinduism, once ethnic religions, are sending missionaries to the great cities of North America.[22] The style of a universal spirit of dialogue is replacing the old order of coercion and arbitrament by the knife. The mind locked in a fortress, defending an ethnic complex called "Christendom," would resist such encounter by writ and by law. The mind that is fearless in faith and open to the dialogue will welcome it; it will accept the truth that a religion that cannot win its case and grow on its merits is unworthy of the future. The churches will continue to influence the form and direction of the world city, perhaps more than they did during the time when the pluralism of loyalties was hidden behind a façade of established orthodoxy. But they will earn the right to be heard by their evidence of internal integrity and inter-religious amity. They will no longer inherit the right to rule.

REFERENCES

1. Dietrich Bonhoeffer, *No Rusty Swords*, ed. Edwin H. Robertson (New York, 1965), pp. 117-18.

2. *Chicago Sun-Times,* November 5, 1965, p. 12.

3. David Schaff, *The Life of Philip Schaff* (New York, 1897), pp. 472-73.

4. Eliezer Berkovits, "Judaism in the Post-Christian Era," *Judaism,* Vol. 15, No. 1 (1966), p. 74.

5. Kenneth Scott Latourette, *A History of the Expansion of Christianity, III: Three Centuries of Advance* (New York, 1939), pp. 188-89.

6. Robert E. Speer, *The Church and Missions* (New York, 1926), pp. 121-22.

7. *Ibid.,* pp. 171-73.

8. Walter M. Abbott (ed.), *The Documents of Vatican II* (New York, 1966), pp. 672f, 9f, 183f.

9. Günter Jacob, "Der Raum für das Evangelium in Ost und West," *Bericht über die ausserordentliche Synode der evangelischen Kirche in Deutschland, 1956* (Hannover-Herrenhausen, 1956), pp. 17-29.

10. Jonathan Elliot, *The Debates on the Federal Constitution,* Vol. 1 (2d ed.; Philadelphia, 1881), pp. 334-35.

11. Timothy L. Smith, *Revivalism and Social Reform* (Nashville, 1956), *passim.*

12. *Church and State: A Lutheran Perspective* (New York, 1963), p. 36.

13. Paul G. Kauper, "Church and State: Cooperative Separatism," *Michigan Law Review,* Vol. 60 (reprint; 1961).

14. See the discussion in Joachim Wach, *Sociology of Religion* (Chicago, 1944), pp. 144-45.

15. See article by Kawerau on "Sektenwesen in Deutschland," *Realenzyklopädie für protestantische Theologie und Kirche,* Vol. 18 (3d ed.; 1906), pp. 155-56, defining *sect* on p. 154: "Gemeinschaften, welche unter Organisierung eines ihnen eigenen Lehramtes und Regimentes, oder doch unter Trennung von kirchlichen Regiment und Lehramt, sich in Bezug auf Lehre und Bekenntnis mit keiner der durch den westfälischen Frieden und nachher in Deutschland öffentlich anerkannten Kirchen in übereinstimmung befinden und sich vom Bekenntnis dieser Kirchen losgesagt haben."

16. Ernst Troeltsch, *The Social Teachings of the Christian Churches* (2 vols.; New York, 1931; German original: 1912). Definition of *church* is given in Vol. 1, p. 288; of *sect,* Vol. 1, p. 336.

17. H. Richard Niebuhr, *The Social Sources of Denominationalism* (New York, 1957; paper), pp. 19-20 for description of how a "sect" may become a "church."

18. The contrast of religious and political life in sacral society and under secularized government has been treated by Harvey Cox in *The Secular City* (New York, 1965); note especially Chapters 3 and 4.

19. See the Conference report: Mathew Ahmann (ed.), *Race: Challenge to Religion* (Chicago, 1963).

20. This is the burden of my tract for the times: *From State Church to Pluralism* (New York, 1962).

21. See my paper, "The Methodists," *What's Ahead for the Churches?*, eds. Kyle Haselden and Martin E. Marty (New York, 1964), pp. 74-93.

22. See Ernst Benz, *Kirchengeschichte in ökumenischer Sicht* (Leiden, 1961), Chapter 5; Kurt Hutten and Siegfried von Kortzfleisch (eds.), *Asien missioniert im Abendland* (Stuttgart, 1963), *passim*.

WILLIAM G. MC LOUGHLIN

Is There a Third Force in Christendom?

HISTORIANS, CHURCHMEN, sociologists, and journalists have recently become intrigued with the tremendous upsurge of activity among the fundamentalists, the small sects, the religious Conservatives, and the revival-oriented pietists. Several years ago, at the height of the great revival of the 1950's, the Reverend Henry P. Van Dusen of Union Theological Seminary wrote an article for *Life* in which he described this activity as "the third force in Christendom" competing with Catholicism and traditional Protestantism for the conversion of mankind to Christianity.[1] Van Dusen concentrated upon the rapidly expanding pentecostal, holiness, and Adventist groups that have attracted so much attention in recent years—the Churches of Christ, Assemblies of God, Church of God in Christ, Seventh Day Adventists, Church of the Nazarene, Jehovah's Witnesses. According to the *Life* article, these "third-force" or "fringe-sect" groups had a world membership of twenty million people, roughly one third of whom were members of sixty different denominations in the United States. The most significant aspect of these groups is that they have increased their membership by 500 to 700 per cent over the past twenty years, while the traditional Protestant denominations and the Roman Catholic have increased by only 75 to 90 per cent, barely keeping up with the growth in population.

The implications seemed obvious: The traditional denominations were losing their grasp upon the more ardent Christians of the world and might soon find themselves challenged by a religious movement similar to the Protestant revolt against the Church of Rome in the sixteenth century, the Puritan revolt of the seventeenth century, or the evangelical movement of the eighteenth century. Sociologists pointed to the archetypal patterns of sectarian revolt defined by Ernst Troeltsch in his *Social Teachings of the Christian Churches.* Roman Catholics seemed equally worried over their losses to these zealous sects, particularly in Latin-American countries and in the Philippines where social discontent breeds religious as well as political rebellion against the establishment.

Not only the numerical growth of this third force but also its emotional and missionary power were a source of concern. Third-force pietists seemed to represent the most zealous, dedicated, and enthusiastic members of Christendom. Their loss to traditional Christian denominations signified a serious decline in vitality; the lifeblood was draining out of the orthodox churches. Some of these fringe sects were so fanatical and so alienated that their energy was said to pose a serious threat to the stability of society as well as to the well-being of the religious establishment here and abroad. Visions of an Anabaptist uprising or a millennarian crusade were called to mind, especially in discussions of groups like Jehovah's Witnesses, the radical Negro sects, or the faith-healing cults.

And where fear was not expressed, envy or frustration often was. The leaders of the established denominations looked longingly upon the transforming power of faith at work in the personal lives and Christian activity of these third-force pietists—the self-sacrificing evangelism of Jehovah's Witnesses in Russia and Spain, the tithing and missionary activity of the Adventists, the creation of Christian schools, hospitals, and colleges by the fundamentalists. In order to make Christianity a living option in the secular world of the mid-twentieth century, in order to give the traditional denominations the dynamic vigor needed to face the tremendous challenges of contemporary society, the regular Christians, it was argued, should display the same ardor for their cause, the same enthusiastic fellowship, the same self-sacrificing dedication, the same commitment to their faith that the third-force believers displayed. Americans have always measured faith in terms of the activistic, enthusiastic self-commitment exemplified by the fringe sects. Not even the Liberal Protestants seemed to question these criteria. Despite the steadily increasing size of church enrollments, the apparently inexhaustible supplies of money available, and the obvious interest in religion evinced by the revivals of Billy Graham, the book sales of Norman Vincent Peale, and the television popularity of Fulton Sheen, most leaders of the major denominations acknowledged that secularism was invading rather than retreating from the churches. American churchmen, who measure national religious commitment by the same "total" standards they apply to individual commitment, considered it clear proof of the superficiality of the revival of the 1950's that less than 50 per cent of the church members attended services regularly. Compared to the revivalism of the fringe sects, that of Graham, Peale, and Sheen seemed itself secularized. Some religious leaders concluded that the world had entered "the post-Christian era"; others, more recently, have announced that "God is dead."

Americans have unquestionably been going through a major reorientation in religious outlook during the past twenty years. We are still too close to this shift to see it in historical perspective. But it seems apparent that the pietistic upthrust by fringe-sect dissenters and come-outers does not in itself constitute the creation of a significant new religious movement in Christendom. Rather, the fringe sects appear to be the usual and inevitable emotional and institutional effluvia of a major alteration within Christendom. They may be a comment upon the confused state of religion and world affairs in this generation, but they do not constitute a dynamic new force capable of replacing or seriously threatening the old order. All evidence indicates that the traditional denominations are still intact and that they are demonstrating once again the flexibility and inherent vitality that has enabled them to survive similar reorientations in the past. Even the Roman Catholic Church, probably the most conservative and ponderous institution in Christendom, has recently displayed its remarkable ability to reform, from within, both its institutions and its doctrine.

Upon examination it appears to be the fringe groups that refuse to face reality and try to deny or thwart change. And their appeal seems limited to those least willing or capable of contributing to a new religious or social order. While it is undoubtedly true that secularism is increasing in American denominations, this is an unavoidable consequence of the denominations' rapid expansion. No ecclesiastical system that includes, as American religion does, over two thirds of the population among its members can avoid taking on the cultural coloration of the secular environment. It is not difficult to show that large segments of the traditional denominations are only superficially "religious" in outlook or practice, as Americans would define the term *religious*. Yet, Will Herberg quite rightly points out, "To be a Protestant, a Catholic, or a Jew are today the alternative ways of being an American."[2] Significantly, American church membership and church participation are considered a fundamental part of being a good citizen. Americans have such high standards of "religiousness" that they are constantly berating themselves for failing to live up to them. What distinguishes American from European Christendom more than anything else is the pietistic quality of American culture. To say, as Herberg does, that the traditional denominations (including Catholicism and the Jewish faith) simply embody a "culture religion" is not necessarily to say that these denominations are secularist. It depends upon the standard of measurement. If the United States is a pietistic nation, as I think it to be, even its "establishment" can be religiously radical.[3] Many historians, foreign observers, and theologians have noted the messianic quality of the American character. In *The Kingdom of God in America*, H. Richard Niebuhr points out that Americans have always considered themselves to be God's Chosen People, a people with a divine mission in the universal destiny of man. To be an American is to belong to a pietistic sect—similar to the situation of being a Jew in the Old Testament era. Sometimes this mission expresses itself in terms of an example to the world— as in the case of the Bible Commonwealth of the Puritan city upon a hill or the new nation of 1776 dedicated to certain inalienable rights of man; sometimes it expresses itself in more aggressive forms as "manifest destiny" or "the white man's burden" to bring democracy and Christianity to the heathen or "the undeveloped"; sometimes it makes war to end colonialism (1898), to make the world safe for democracy (1917), or to prevent the immoral aggression of atheistic, totalitarian Communism (today); sometimes it dedicates its most idealistic young men to missionary endeavor and to Peace Corps evangelism; and sometimes it simply gives away its "filthy lucre" to help the poor, the weak, and the unfortunate, as in the Marshall Plan, Point Four, the Alliance for Progress, and foreign aid in general. Despite all the charges of self-interest, pragmatism, or hypocrisy that can be leveled at these actions, European observers have generally recognized that the United States is unique among nations because it professes to a conscience as well as to a mission.

But, as H. Richard Niebuhr has also demonstrated, the religious definition of the national mission and conscience has not always been the same. In the colonial period it was inspired by a predominantly Calvinistic consensus; in the revolutionary era by a deistic (but still essentially Christian) consensus; in the nineteenth century by an evangelical consensus; and in the first half of the twentieth century by a Social Gospel consensus. The recurrent periods of revivalism or "Great Awakenings" in American history have coincided with the shifts from one to another of these consensuses. The old Social Gospel consensus that informed the Progressive Era, World War I, the New Deal, and World War II has run its course. Since 1945, it has given way to a new and as yet ill-defined consensus ranging from Barthian neo-orthodoxy through Niebuhrian Christian realism to Coxian New Worldliness.

Each of the major religious reorientations in American history has produced fanatical fringe sects—antinomians, perfectionists, communitarians, Adventists, faith healers, and pentecostalists. Each of these "Great Awakenings" was marked by important reformers, at work within the traditional denominations, who espoused "New Light" or "New Side," "New Divinity" or "Progressive Orthodoxy," "Modernism" or "Neo-orthodoxy." In each case, after perhaps a generation of furious polemical warfare, institutional infighting, and bitter schisms or exscindings, the New Lights have emerged triumphant. They have produced a reformulation of the Old-Light orthodoxy into a new consensus that is able to maintain its claim of orthodoxy and, at the same, to adjust Christian doctrines and practices to the new needs of a changing social order. If there is any significant third force at work in American religion today, it is the force that is leading toward a new orientation in America's pietistic culture religion.[4]

Assuming, then, that we are in such an Awakening and that American religion today is divided between New Lights and Old Lights, what is the role being played by the "Conservative" religious groups? Is it simply to oppose change? Or can the Conservative perhaps be "the New Light" in an era of revolution against a decadent "Liberalism"? Certainly many Conservatives see themselves in this role, and apparently many leaders of the traditional denominations are fearful of the radicalism or "extremism" that threatens their well-established position.[5]

The problem of assessing the role of "Conservative" religious groups begins, as always, with definitions. Obviously it is impossible simply to employ denominational labels. Most of the major denominations contain such a broad spectrum of religious views among their members and ministers that, like the Democratic and Republican Parties, they fit into no neat definition. Hence historians and sociologists have had to derive other bases of measurement.

Over the years at least five basic ways of measuring "Conservatism" in religion have been employed.

The first is theological. Here the effort is to establish a continuum from the sophisticated, scholarly, "Liberal," or intellectualized method of dealing with religious dogma and doctrine to the unsophisticated, literalistic, or "fundamentalist" method. This spectrum is loosely used to differentiate the modernist from the fundamentalist in American theology. By this measurement, most Congregationalists or Northern Presbyterians fall at the Liberal end of the scale and most Southern Baptists or Jehovah's Witnesses at the Conservative. All sects that hold to millennialism, perfectionism, dispensationalism, Adventism, and so on are lumped among the Conservatives because of their unsophisticated reliance upon literalistic interpretations of Scriptural prophecies. But this theological continuum for measuring Conservatism very often runs into grave difficulties when it equates certain doctrines with a Conservative stance. Highly sophisticated theologians can be very dogmatic about the Trinity or the Virgin Birth, and very scholarly works have been written to defend the millennial, perfectionist, apocalyptical beliefs usually associated with anti-intellectual fundamentalists. Many Roman Catholics and high-church Episcopalians can be as dogmatic as any pentecostalist about the miraculous or "mysterious" in Christianity. Consider the interest of even sophisticated churchmen in faith healing and glossalalia (speaking in tongues). And where in this continuum does one place such groups as Christian Scientists, New Thought, Baha'ism, or Theosophy? The mystic can be found at both ends of the continuum, just as the Christian doctrine of perfectionism, or "growing in grace," in varying degrees of definition, can be found at all points along the line.

The second common way of measuring Conservatism, which also has its uses and its shortcomings, is on the basis of the psychological aspects of religious experience and worship. William James first popularized this approach, and a recent book by Charles Glock and Rodney Stark indicates that sociologists still find it meaningful.[6] This continuum begins with a religious experience or worship service in which the individual asserts only a bare intellectual assent to belief and experiences almost no emotional contact with the deity whom he worships. This is defined as the Liberal attitude, and it is characterized by, say, a Unitarian or an urban Congregationalist. At the other end of the continuum is the ecstatic, highly emotional worship of the pentecostal or holiness groups in which the individual experiences such a direct, personal encounter with the deity that he becomes possessed, loses himself, rolls on the floor in the power of the Holy Ghost who speaks through him. This form of measurement also has its difficulties with the mystic at either end; the Thoreauvian transcendentalist's experience with the Over-Soul in the woods is almost as clear a case of possession, though more intellectualized afterward, as that of the pentecostalist. It is also difficult to place on this continuum the more sedate, but perhaps equally ecstatic, encounter of liturgical worship services in which emotionalism is ritualized but nevertheless highly sensuous (the music, incense, robes, candles, stained glass, and images of Roman Catholic, Anglo-Catholic, or Eastern Orthodox churches).

The third common form of measurement is more sociological than psychological; the continuum moves from upper-class, in-group, establishment "church" allegiance to lower-class, out-group, "disinherited," or "alienated" sect allegiance. The criteria here are partly in terms of wealth, status, security, and partly in terms of psychological equivalents or symbols for status and wealth. Troeltsch's sect-church formulation of religious groups relies primarily upon this type of measurement. But Troeltsch's categories seem less helpful in America where it is difficult to distinguish sect, denomination, and church, and where the status of a denomination varies greatly in different regions. Most denominations have poor as well as rich members, and many sects contain wealthy laymen. Moreover, the Southern Baptists, Missouri Synod Lutherans, and Mormons, though sectarians, have a range in wealth and status that probably represents a fair cross section of the national stratification. It is commonly assumed that in-group denominations are more Liberal and out-group sects more Conservative because the out-group denominations or "hole-in-the-corner" sects are other-worldly: that is, they reject the standards of this world (from which they are excluded by wealth, race, education, or other social criteria) and concentrate upon the rewards of the next life of the millennium. But socioeconomic measurements of religion also cut both ways. The out-group may find in its religion a justification for changing the system that excludes it from full participation as equals; it may be a major force for reform rather than for Conservatism. The Anabaptists, Levelers, Diggers, Fifth Monarchy Men, Puritans, and Black Muslims are prime examples of this. Also, the question of Liberalism versus Conservatism becomes reversible depending upon whether one typifies "the disinherited" in terms of Wesley's Methodists or Cromwell's Puritans. Historians are still wrangling over whether the Massachusetts Bay Colony was a theocentric, totalitarian society, a Christian utopia, or a seed-bed of the American democratic system because it was all three.

A fourth and more limited kind of measurement, closely related to this question of Puritanism and revolution, is in terms of church polity and social philosophy. This is the "no bishop, no king" criterion. Here, the standard formulation of the continuum holds that hierarchical church systems which utilize bishops, arch-bishops, and a supreme head are also inclined to favor monarchy or autocracy in social affairs, while church systems which hold to the priesthood of all believers and a congregational, autonomous polity are apt to be democratic in their social philosophy. By this measurement, the Catholic Church exemplifies the Conservative; the Baptist, the Liberal; the presbyterian system of the Calvinist or Reformed churches is said to come in between and to favor a representative or republican form of government. The difficulties with this measurement are too apparent to need discussion: The Scottish Presbyterians were not republicans; the Massachusetts Puritans were congregational, but not democratic; and Catholicism manages to thrive under all forms of government.

The inadequacy of these four criteria either jointly or singly has led me to favor a fifth kind of measurement—in terms of the New Light versus the Old Light within a specific historical framework, such as America's four Great Awakenings. In this system, the continuum is included within the moving main stream of America's pietistic culture. Thus, it is possible to give the terms *Conservative* or *Liberal* significance within the context of a particular era. This historical-context system of measurement makes it easier to understand why some of today's Conservatives are both Old Lights, because they oppose the avant-garde of American theological and social reformulation, and New Lights because they have joined in the current Awakening as a revolt against the "Liberal Protestant" consensus of the past fifty years. By using this system, I think I can also indicate why the fringe groups, for all their pietistic radicalism and extremism, are essentially Conservative or, perhaps more accurately, apolitical within the culture.

If by a third force one means a force that is capable of significantly altering a culture or that is symptomatic of a significant new shift in the dynamics of a culture, then neither those who call themselves "the Conservatives" (or neo-evangelical or fundamentalists) in America, nor the sects, cults, and fringe groups are a third force. By this definition I think it could be said that the third force is no longer solidly Protestant, but a pluralistic combination of Catholics, Protestants, and Jews, all of whom are now part of the pietistic American culture system. In fact, a good case could be made for the claim that the main thrust of American pietism today (defined in this continuum) lies with the Liberal wing of the Catholic Church.[7] If the fringe groups are apolitical, the "Conservatives" are reactionary.

To understand what is commonly referred to as the third force in American Christendom today, it is necessary to begin by defining historically the various segments of today's Old-Light movement, which means those groups that are opposed to the current reorientation in religious thought and practice—the pentecostal, holiness, and Adventist groups, the fundamentalists or neo-evangelicals outside or within the traditional churches, most of the Negro churches and cults, most of the Lutherans, the Mormons, the Southern Baptists, not to mention the scores of tiny come-outer sects led by some charismatic leader (Father Divine or Daddy Grace) or united around a particular rite (snake-handling or foot-washing). Such a historical analysis must begin as far back as the 1860's, for most of the important Conservative groups in existence today had their rise in the last Great Awakening when the American Protestant consensus shifted from evangelical Protestantism to Social Gospel Protestantism. Evangelical Protestantism (the Protestantism of most Americans in the nineteenth century) rested upon a literalistic interpretation of the Bible with primary importance given to individual conversions in a crisis experience. The basic ethic of this form of Protestantism was in complete harmony with the individualistic, laissez-faire social outlook of the nineteenth century. It equated the old Puritan sense of mission with the missionary movement at home and abroad; through missionaries, revivals, and soul-winning preaching, God was gradually spreading the gospel and converting the world to the Christian (and also the Anglo-Saxon, democratic, capitalistic, and American) way of life. Essential to this was the Protestant ethic of hard work, thrift, piety, and sobriety. In the euphoric atmosphere of America's growing wealth, prestige, and power, the mood of evangelicalism was as optimistic as its morality was Victorian. Most of those who call themselves "Conservative" today look back to this old nineteenth-century evangelicalism as the standard of Christian orthodoxy from which the "Liberals," "modernists," or "Social Gospelers" have departed.

Evangelicalism, even at its height, however, never embraced the whole of American Protestantism. The Lutheran synods, particularly the more Conservative German Lutheran synods of Missouri, Wisconsin, and Buffalo were for the most part outside the main stream of American Protestantism. These German (as well as some Scandinavian) evangelicals were alienated partly by language barriers and national customs, and partly by American theology and church practices. In order to preserve their separateness from a culture into which they did not wish to be assimilated, they founded Lutheran parochial schools, seminaries, and magazines conducted in their own language. A similar alienation, both social and geographical, was forced upon the Mormons, a millennarian and perfectionist sect born in the pre-Civil War era and driven by mobs out of "respectable" Protestant society into exile in Utah. Also suffering a forced alienation from the main stream of American culture were the Negro churches and, to a lesser extent, the Southern Baptists, Methodists, and Presbyterians who had split from their northern brethren over abolitionism before the Civil War and who remained separated by the resentments arising from the war and its aftermath. Southern white evangelicals and Negro evangelicals shared essentially the same doctrines and ethical values as the northern evangelicals in this period. Revivalists like Dwight L. Moody and Samuel Porter Jones, one a Congregationalist, the other a Southern Methodist, were able to conduct city-wide crusades in the nation's largest cities during the latter part of the nineteenth century; they received wholehearted support from almost all denominations—including the Episcopal Church and the Congregational Church which then, as now, were generally within the Liberal wing of Protestantism. But southern white evangelicals, like Negro evangelicals, lacked the money and the incentive to produce a learned ministry. Thus, they failed to keep within the moving context of the theological, social, and intellectual trends of the times, and subsequently became doubly alienated.

In the generation following 1865, the American evangelical consensus underwent a series of crises that gradually produced a drastic reorientation in Protestantism: the conflict between religion and science highlighted by the Darwinian controversy; the conflict over the higher criticism of the Bible that undermined the literalistic infallibility of Scripture; the development of the social teaching of the gospel that sought to replace the rugged individualism of the Protestant ethic with a new social ethic now familiar as the Welfare State. By 1890 most of the educated clergy in the North had accepted evolution and "the New Theology"; by 1912 most of them had accepted at least the Progressive Era's concept of the positive state. The rank and file of American Protestants probably did not accept the new Social Gospel or Liberal Protestant consensus until after Clarence Darrow made a monkey out of Bryan in the Scopes trial. But by 1925 the new consensus was established, and the defenders of the old evangelicalism, now called fundamentalists, were in the minority.[8] Already socially, regionally, or (in the case of the Negro) racially alienated, they now became theologically alienated.

At the same time that this reorientation was getting under way in the 1870's, another group of dissenters broke with the evangelical consensus at a different level and for different reasons. These were the Adventists, holiness, and pentecostal groups which were in a sense left over from the pre-Civil War perfectionist era and which found the evangelical consensus increasingly cold, formal, and corrupt after 1860. These dissenters pulled away from the evangelical consensus at the bottom just as the radical Social Gospelers or Christian socialists pulled away at the top. Both groups found the evangelical consensus too culture-bound, too willing to compromise with the prevailing order, too much concerned with respectability, conformity, and the *status quo*. But while the Christian socialists put the American sense of mission into a dynamic thrust for social reform in order to create the Kingdom of God on earth through political and economic action, the pentecostalists, holiness sects, and Adventists put the sense of mission into a program of withdrawal from the corruptions of the traditional churches and into a millennial hope for the creation of the Kingdom of God on earth through the Second Coming of Christ. The traditional churches, themselves originally very sectarian in the early-nineteenth century, had by 1870 become stolid, middle-class, suburban-centered institutions that disliked the more fervent and apocalyptic aspects of Christianity. Their learned ministers and respectable congregations in their richly furnished brownstone churches wanted no emotionalism in church services, no holiness or perfectionist enthusiasm, no mention of hell-fire, Satan, or the Second Coming of Christ. They had made peace with this world. It was all they could do to put up with the greatly toned-down urban revivalism of Moody and Sankey. They were decidedly cool toward the prophetic conventions and Bible conferences that sought to retain the old sectarian doctrines and practices.

Premillennialism, the doctrine that the world is getting worse and worse and that only the Second Coming can set it right, became especially appealing to many rural-born and unsophisticated Americans who found it difficult to adjust to the changing thought patterns and living conditions brought by science, technology, urbanism, and industrialism. For those seeking other means of self-expression and fulfillment in a world they could not comprehend, there was a resurgence of other pietistic practices with deep roots in Christian tradition—the baptism of the Holy Ghost, talking in tongues, faith healing, sanctification, perfectionism. Discontented and increasingly alienated evangelicals found greater satisfaction for their spiritual and psychological needs in the new sects that emphasized one or another of these teachings than they had found in the routine services of their old denominations. The holiness sects provided escape from this sin-filled world by concentrating upon the perfect state of sinlessness granted true believers under "baptism of the Holy Ghost with fire"; they drew heavily from Methodist denominations where a long-established doctrine of perfectionism was falling into disuse. The pentecostals found escape in "the endue-ment of power" or "the bestowment of charismatic gifts" that the Holy Ghost gives to true believers enabling them to speak in tongues or practice faith healing; they drew heavily from the Baptist denominations where ecstatic revivalism had formerly been prominent. Both groups agreed with the Adventists that the world would soon come to a horrendous end and that they, being the only true saints, would be saved from the holocaust while the wicked, apostate, unconverted, imperfect worldings in the regular churches would be annihilated or sent to hell. The psychological frustrations and anxieties of these alienated groups are clearly evident in their transvaluations, but to them the special supernatural powers and favors they receive in their religious life are justified and provable by the revealed word of God and are made manifest by the direct, personal, miraculous actions of the Holy Ghost. All the fringe sects are pneumatocentric.

The Seventh Day Adventists, formed in 1860 through the prophetic visions of Ellen G. White out of the remnants of William Miller's millennial movement of the 1840's, are only one form of this withdrawal from the present world to await and prepare for the Second Coming. Jehovah's Witnesses, formed in 1872 by Charles T. Russell, altered the Adventist emphasis by insisting that Christ had returned in the spirit in 1874. They maintain that Christ ascended the throne of heaven in 1914 and turned Satan loose on earth preparatory to the Second Coming; most of them believe that by 1972 Christ will set up his Kingdom on earth. The Biblical exegesis behind the doctrines of the Adventists and other fringe sects is often highly complicated. The elaborate theological riddles of dispensationalism, pyramidism, chiliasm are accepted on faith from the leaders of these movements and memorized; they serve as mythical explanations of a spiritual world that the believer prefers to the confusion and despair of his existence in the real world. In the real world, the believer is rejected, despised, left out, powerless, and afraid. In his own world, he is accepted, annointed, the friend of Jesus and God, endowed with supernatural power, destined to inherit the world or to sit with Jehovah in heaven; those who now deride and persecute him will sooner or later receive the annihilation or punishment they deserve.

H. Richard Niebuhr, following Ernst Troeltsch, called these sects the churches of "the disinherited." Whether one calls them disinherited or alienated, they are essentially apolitical and withdrawn. They have washed their hands of this world except to proselytize for followers who will accept their exclusive version of truth—apart from which there can be no salvation. They are as opposed to ecumenism as a nationalist is to yielding sovereignty to a world government. But such groups pose no serious threat to the social order so long as they remain apolitical and small. If, indeed, there are six or ten million adherents to them in the United States (and the figures are subject to serious doubts and problems),[9] they are still a comparatively small and powerless segment of 121 million church members. Their rapid growth is large only in terms of percentage. Only by including their overseas membership (an even more debatable figure) do any of these sects reach significant proportions. Jehovah's Witnesses, for example, who claimed 1,040,836 members in 1965, noted that only 308,370 of these are located in the United States[10]; and three quarters of the Seventh Day Adventists, who claim a larger membership than Jehovah's Witnesses, are also overseas.[11] It is not surprising that these energetic and apocalyptic missionary sects should make large temporary gains in those parts of the world where colonialism is waning or social revolution is long overdue.[12] But only total social and political chaos in Christendom, or for that matter in any of the new nations, would ever make them a potential threat. They may be an annoyance and a scandal to the traditional churches in the United States, but they are not competitors. Few middle-class Americans need or want what the fringe sects have to offer.

A more serious problem is posed for the traditional denominations by those who call themselves "Conservatives," "evangelicals," or "fundamentalists." *Fundamentalism* was a term coined about 1910 in order to define those who opposed the modernist and Social Gospel movements within the established denominations. They were also called "essentialists" and "restorationists," though these terms have now died out. Several historical monographs have traced the ways in which these Conservative evangelicals, within each denomination, fought for control of the institutional bureaucracy—seeking first to impose creedal tests for orthodoxy, to unfrock any minister who refused to sign or conform to the creed, to purge faculty members from seminary, or denominational college posts who were deemed unorthodox by fundamentalist standards, to authorize no missionaries who would not conform to the creed, and to control even the denominational publishing houses and Sunday schools along fundamentalist lines.[13] These fights extended from 1910 to 1930 and produced serious problems in every major denomination in the North. They were especially bitter among the northern Baptists, Methodists, Presbyterians, and Disciples. Eventually, by the mid-1920's, the fundamentalists had become so narrowly dogmatic, so bitterly intransigent, that they lost the good will of the moderates who had formerly given them some sympathy.

Defeated and embittered after 1925, most of the fundamentalists withdrew from all association with "Liberals." Many fundamentalists left their denominations to join the fringe sects; fundamentalist congregations declared themselves independent from denominational ties, joined new denominations founded by fundamentalists, or remained, reluctantly and sulkily, within their old denominations. The southern denominations, where Liberalism had always been weak, were saved from these schisms; certain of them, like the Southern Baptists, advanced northward to absorb many of the disaffected northern fundamentalists. The most embittered fundamentalists vented their spleen by rallying in the 1930's around revivalistic demagogues like Gerald B. Winrod and Gerald L. K. Smith who linked the fundamentalist version of Christianity to 100-per cent Americanism and spouted protofascist doctrines in their diatribes against political as well as theological Liberalism.

But most fundamentalists in the 1930's voted for the New Deal and kept politics out of their religion. In those regions of the country where they remained numerous, the South and Midwest, they continued to practice "the old-time religion." In the South, they kept the public schools free from heresy by outlawing the teaching of evolution; in areas where they found themselves too few to do this, they tithed their incomes to establish Christian schools—really Protestant parochial schools—to preserve the faith of their children. To sustain their fundamentalist subcultures, they developed a host of religious and social institutions. They established their own summer Bible camps and "Christian" vacation resorts, their own Bible colleges and seminaries, their own publishing houses, newspapers, magazines, and their own radio stations, phonograph and motion-picture companies. They created and sustained numberless foreign-missionary agencies and home evangelistic associations to provide outlets for their activistic, pietistic yearning to save the world.[14] Having been shut out of the consensus-dominated religious and social institutions of America, they, like the Lutherans, Negroes, Jews, Catholics, and Mormons, created their own.[15] In order to coordinate some of the multifarious and overlapping associations and institutions and to combat what they considered the nefarious ecumenism of the National Council of Churches (dominated by the main-line Liberals), the fundamentalists decided in 1941 to form their own federation. The American Council of Christian Churches, led by Carl McIntire, claimed by 1965 to speak for fifteen denominations and more than a million and a half fundamentalists.[16] But the great bulk of the twenty million or more Americans who could be called fundamentalists or Conservatives distrusted ecumenism too much to join even this loose federation.[17]

Then came World War II and the breakdown of the Liberal consensus in its aftermath. Just as the evangelical consensus had broken up under the impact of a series of social and intellectual crises at the end of the nineteenth century, so the Liberal consensus found itself unable to withstand the impact of Hitlerism, World War II, the atomic bomb, the Cold War, the Korean War, and the rising tide of nationalism and anticolonialism that threw the world into turmoil. The basically optimistic rationale of Liberal theology proved unable to assimilate these catastrophes. New philosophical and theological rationales arose to challenge its premises.

The reaction against the optimistic faith of Social Gospel idealism had begun in Europe following World War I and reached the more avant-garde religious thinkers in America in the 1930's. The new theology in Europe stemmed from the work of Karl Barth and Emil Brunner and was variously called neo-orthodoxy, dialectical theology, the theology of paradox, crisis, or despair. In America where it was called Christian existentialism or Christian realism, its foremost exponents were, and are, Reinhold Niebuhr, John C. Bennett, Paul Tillich, Robert Calhoun, and William M. Horton.

This new theology sought to correct the overly optimistic, moralistic, idealistic faith of Liberalism by re-emphasizing the dual nature of man, the transcendental mystery of God, and the insoluable riddle of human destiny. Because it produced a new emphasis on the sinful, irrational nature of man, many considered it a swing to the right in theology. But, at the same time, it endorsed the liberal views of politics, and some of its advocates even supported Marxism for a time as a more hardheaded analysis of social reform than the Social Gospel. Dropping the modernists' amorphous theology of divine immanence—God seen as working out his redemption of man through historical progress—the new theology returned to a more direct reliance upon the supernatural aspects of theology, and many Liberals accused it of being as obscurantist as fundamentalism.

Out of this breakup of the Liberal Protestant consensus emerged the great revival of the 1950's. Both the fringe sects and the fundamentalists benefited from this religious reorientation, but it was the latter that posed the more serious threat to the traditional denominations. Any swing to the right in theology might well be taken as a return to the old-time religion by the average churchgoer, as the immense popularity of Billy Graham's interdenominational, city-wide revival crusades amply demonstrated. Many Liberal pastors refused to join in these crusades lest they lead to a rejuvenation of fundamentalism in their midst.[18] At the outset of his career in the 1940's, Graham's revivals were supported almost wholly by fundamentalist, evangelistic associations and youth groups. Only later was he able to win support from the main-line denominations by his obvious sincerity, his charismatic appeal, and his adroit salesmanship. In the confusion over religion that prevailed in the 1950's, his revivals were a convenient rallying point for men of all shades of opinion.

Graham himself came out of a background different from that of the hard-core fundamentalism of the 1920's and 1930's. As a graduate of Wheaton College in Illinois (one of the very few accredited fundamentalist colleges) who had majored in anthropology and earned a Bachelor of Science degree, Graham was an educated fundamentalist, a neo-fundamentalist. He represented a new level of sophistication in this sub-culture religion. Out of the long battle between Liberals and fundamentalists, there had emerged a group of fundamentalist "scholars" who had taken the trouble to read the arguments of the Liberals carefully and who were now ready to argue on their terms instead of in terms of nineteenth-century evangelicalism. The level of sophistication was not high, and few Liberal theologians took even the best neo-fundamentalist scholars seriously. But the disorganized state of the Liberal consensus after 1950 lent a certain attractiveness to the strong, fervent, unquestioning faith of the neo-fundamentalists,[19] and many American churchgoers were ready to give them a hearing.

The neo-fundamentalists bought their new prestige at a high price, however. They were forced to split with brethren who proved unwilling to abandon their literalistic Biblicism and their virulent hostility to Liberals even to the extent of engaging in dialogue with them, let alone in evangelistic cooperation. The more Graham hobnobbed with Liberals in his revivals, the more he was accused by ultraconservative fundamentalists of selling out their cause. Eventually they refused to maintain fellowship with him.[20] In opposition to these old-line fundamentalists and to the exclusiveness of the American Council of Christian Churches, the neo-fundamentalists formed their own federation in 1942 called the National Association of Evangelicals. The founders of the N.A.E. prefer not to call themselves fundamentalists or neo-fundamentalists, adopting instead the term "evangelicals" or "Conservatives." They, too, erected a whole network of religious associations and institutions to integrate their followers and to promote their evangelism.

In competition with the A.C.C.C., they collected thirty-four denominations, some of them pentecostals, holiness, and Adventist groups, with a total membership of 1,654,278 by 1965.[21] In addition, the N.A.E. claims "through its affiliated agencies" to "service a constituency of 10,000,000." Its ultimate aim is to win the allegiance of twenty-two million "unaligned" Protestants who are associated neither with the National Council of Churches nor with the American Council of Christian Churches. Most of these unaligned Protestants tend, like the Southern Baptists and Missouri Synod Lutherans, toward Conservatism.

In 1957 the magazine that speaks most effectively for these neo-fundamentalists or evangelicals, *Christianity Today,* employed the Opinion Research Corporation to conduct a poll of the Protestant clergy of the United States in order to determine how they were aligned. The survey reported that 12 per cent of the clergy considered themselves to be "neo-orthodox" followers of Barth and Brunner, 14 per cent called themselves "Conservative," and 29 per cent, "fundamentalist."[22] This poll apparently led some evangelicals to describe themselves as "a new 'third force' in American religious life," occupying "the great middle space between the fringe sects and the Liberal leadership in the older church bodies."[23] But the failure of the poll to clarify the definitions of *Liberal, Conservative,* and *fundamentalist* left considerable doubt as to just what most Protestant clergymen meant by giving themselves these labels.

Since the National Council of Churches still maintained the allegiance of thirty-one denominations with 41,341,466 members in 1965, even though the N.A.E. spokesmen continued to denounce it as dominated by "rationalistic modernism" or "Liberalism," it does not appear that the evangelical "third force" made much headway between 1957 and 1965. It seems more likely that a theological reorientation was going on within the traditional denominations in the N.C.C. without any schisms that would materially swell the ranks of the N.A.E. or the A.C.C.C. On the other hand, it is also clear that the Liberal Protestant consensus was divided into a radical neo-orthodox wing, a "New Light" or Liberal-realist wing, and a large group of old Liberals still in a state of confusion. It was these confused Liberals who were supporting Billy Graham in the 1950's and whom the new evangelicals hoped to win over.

But any such possibility was, and is, extremely unlikely: first, because the theological gap between the old Liberals and the new evangelicals is far too wide and deep to be bridged by the kind of "scholarly" neo-fundamentalism to which even the most enlightened evangelicals adhere; second, because Graham's apocalyptic revivalism has not succeeded, and will not, in converting the Liberals (with the possible exception of the more socially conservative of Norman Vincent Peale's followers); third, because the N.A.E.'s outlook on political and economic affairs is so deeply committed to nationalistic, laissez-faire ultraconservatism that it shocks even the most chastened Liberal Protestant. The new evangelicals, if one can judge from their social philosophy as expressed in *Christianity Today, United Evangelical Action, Christian Economics,* and in Billy Graham's books, sermons, and political comments, are lock, stock, and barrel with Senator Barry Goldwater. For them, applied Christianity is still basically evangelistic soul-winning; they equate Christianity with "the American way of life" as defined by the National Association of Manufacturers; they are hysterically anti-Communist in foreign policy and totally opposed to any extension of the Welfare State in domestic policy. And while they profess sympathy with the civil rights movement and oppose the die-hard segregationists, they still believe that the principle function of the Christian churches in social reform is "proclamation of the gospel" and not social action to "legislate" reform. They regularly denounce Martin Luther King and the leaders of C.O.R.E., S.N.C.C., and the N.A.A.C.P. as radical agitators who do more harm than good.[24] For the evangelicals, as for Billy Graham, the greatest problems facing America today are the Supreme Court's rulings on Bible reading and prayer in the public schools, the "spiraling divorce rate," "the poor showing of many soldiers in North Korean prison camps, the upsurge of juvenile delinquency, the increase of illegitimate births, and the spread of addiction to alcohol and dope."[25]

Probably the high-tide of this neo-evangelical "third force" was the selection of Barry Goldwater as the Republican candidate for the Presidency in 1964. The bitter disappointment of all evangelicals at his smashing defeat is graphically exemplified by an editorial comment in *Christianity Today:* "The outcome of the 1964 election apparently demonstrated that a generalized appeal for moral recovery elicits little response from the American people. Goldwater's plea for 'law and order' seemed only to produce its own kind of backlash: the antagonisms of liberal churchmen."[26] If the new evangelical movement is any threat whatsoever as a third force, it is merely because the Goldwater movement demonstrated that the United States now has a permanent, powerful, and respectable ultra-right wing in its political spectrum. The new evangelicals are the spiritual hard-core of the radical right.[27]

One other potential third force among religious Conservatives—the Negro denominations and sects—deserves mention. Without question, the Negro churchgoers in America are still overwhelmingly fundamentalist in outlook. Although the Negro revolution owes a great deal to the religious faith of the Negro churches and their leaders, especially in the South, the best evidence indicates that the younger generation of Negroes who are the real and future leaders of the civil rights movement are much less religious than their elders. The most vigorous spokesmen for Negro equality, although they grew up in the Negro fundamentalist churches, are now operating from an existential, pragmatic, or humanist faith that is secular if not anti-religious. The views of James Baldwin, James Farmer, Floyd McKissick, and Stokely Carmichael are more appealing to the Negro militants than those of Martin Luther King, Jr., Ralph Abernathy, Hosea Williams, Andrew Young, and Milton Galamison. C. Eric Lincoln, a sociologist who is close to the movement, maintains that Martin Luther King is "anathema" to the urban Negroes in the North. The militant civil rights workers now see the Conservative, fundamentalist churchgoers among the Negroes as a major drag upon, if not opponents of, "the movement." The members of "the black bourgeoisie," like those of the white, are essentially conservative socially and politically. They are afraid of vigorous action. They caution the young to go more slowly; they want to be accepted and respected by the whites rather than to antagonize them. Their conservative attitude toward civil rights activists offers prime evidence for the reactionary character of Conservative theology in its fundamentalist form. As a result, the Negro churchgoers are badly split over civil rights problems and seem unable to provide the necessary unity and guidance that the movement needs. Dr. Joseph H. Jackson, president of the National Baptist Convention, U.S.A., Inc., the largest Negro denomination in the United States with 5,500,000 members, so consistently pulled back from civil rights activities and deplored sit-ins and demonstrations on their behalf that Martin Luther King, Jr., felt obliged to lead a schism from this group in 1962. Only a minority followed him. Among these churchgoers in the South, among Negroes over thirty generally, King and his Southern Christian Leadership Conference may provide effective leadership. But the majority of American Negroes no longer live in the South, and the most active civil rights workers, North and South, are under thirty. The S.C.L.C. probably has more influence upon white churchgoers than upon churchgoers in the Negro denominations. If the Negro revolution is successful, it should mean the end of Negro denominations, for they are a mark not of Christianity's strength in America but of its failure. If the "movement" is successful, it will not be the result of the fundamentalist convictions of the Negroes. Insofar as religion is a factor in the civil rights movement, it supplies important sources of courage, stamina, faith, and hope. But the reform impulse, the initiative, the drive and thrust of this revolutionary movement are essentially secular and cultural. The Negro is fighting for his rights as a citizen and as a man, not as a Christian believer.[28]

When the historian comes to evaluate the meaning of the current Great Awakening or reorientation in American religion, he may well conclude that its most significant aspect is its pluralistic quality. For the first time in American history, Roman Catholics and Jews have taken a full share at every level of America's culture religion. The election of John F. Kennedy was only the most conspicuous sign of this. More important are the new ecumenical movement and the obvious respect Protestants, Jews, and Catholics have for one another as they engage in direct dialogue as equals. If being a Protestant, a Catholic, or a Jew is now accepted as just a different way of being a good American rather than as a problem in assimilation; if Protestants, Catholics, and Jews can now make jokes about one another and themselves without self-conscious embarrassment (just as Negro comedians are at last joking honestly about American racism); if surveys reveal that Roman Catholics and Jews now have as many friends outside their own faith as within it, then America has indeed become a pluralistic rather than a Protestant culture.[29]

It may even be that the most dynamic and healthy pietistic elements in the American culture religion today are now coming from Roman Catholicism. The Protestant churches seem to lack sufficient unity to act with their old confident vigor. They seem querulous and confused. While the voice of the National Council of Churches still speaks for reform and change, it has no way of implementing its policies. The Jews are still too small a group, though their activity and influence far exceeds their numerical strength. Catholicism, however, has both the unity, the flexibility, and the will to seek new and dynamic solutions for the major issues of the day, both at home and abroad. If the Catholic Church is not yet Liberal, it nevertheless possesses a sufficient quota of Liberalism to be in the main stream. It might not be too much to say that the recognition of Americans that this is a pluralistic and not an exclusively Protestant nation has come with the realization that the Catholic Church has at last become Americanized. Priests are publicly rebelling against their bishops, the laity is demanding a larger and more meaningful role; the hierarchy itself seems ready to move forward. Catholic priests and cardinals no longer fear to let their members go to hear Protestant revivalists; they no longer feel obliged to defend birth-control laws; they no longer seek strict censorship. Even the old frictions over parochial schools seem to be dissolving as the need for educational reform is recognized as a national rather than a local problem. At the same time, Catholics are acknowledging the virtues of the Protestant concept of liberty of conscience and the necessity for Christian social action, which they had previously deplored. As the Catholic cleric and layman move out into the cultural main stream, they bring with them a dynamic religious impulse and assurance very much like that which animated the Protestant reform impulse of the nineteenth century; they bring a belief that the Kingdom of God can be achieved on earth by human effort. To this extent the American Catholic has absorbed the spirit of the New Adam in the New World. And this is the measure of his de-Romanization.[30]

Ultimately, then, the third force in Christendom may not be any form of Protestant Conservatism or Negro or Catholic Liberalism, but the pietistic spirit of American culture itself—not only the American sense of mission which leads it into world leadership for the containment of Communist expansion in the name of democratic freedom for all men, and not only the sense of charity or stewardship which leads it into giving economic assistance in billions of dollars each year to help others to help themselves, but the sense of religious commitment and ideals that Americans inscribe to democracy and their way of life.[31]

While Americans are imbued with the faith that they have been given a set of universal and inalienable truths to guide them in the search for ultimate truth, they see their system as a means rather than as an end. Being pietists, Americans believe that God has yet "further light" to shed to them as well as to the rest of the world. This faith in the *search* for truth, this belief that happiness must constantly be pursued—though it cannot be caught short of the millennium—is still the dynamic religious force in America as a civilization.[32]

REFERENCES

1. Henry P. Van Dusen, "The Third Force's Lessons for Others," *Life* (June 9, 1958), pp. 122-23.

2. Will Herberg, *Protestant, Catholic, Jew* (New York, 1955), p. 274.

3. I use the term *pietism* here not in its usual narrow sense of puritanical, fanatical, fundamentalist religiosity, but in its broader configuration as defined by Ernst Troeltsch: individualistic, self-perfecting, anti-institutional; and I include also the quality that George Kennan has called "the moralistic-legalistic" approach of Americans toward foreign policy. For a more extensive discussion of this point, see W. G. McLoughlin, "Pietism and the American Character," *American Quarterly* (Summer, 1965), pp. 163-86.

4. The articles in this issue of *Dædalus* by Harvey Cox, Daniel Callahan, and Michael Novak all bear directly on this current Awakening or reorientation in American religion.

5. I recognize that the term *traditional denominations* like the term *establishment* is so imprecise in America as to beg the questions seeking definition here. I use it in this paper simply as shorthand for the older, larger, more prosperous denominations that constitute the core of the National Council of Churches. A more precise attempt to differentiate Liberal and Conservative religious outlooks follows *infra*.

6. See William James, *The Varieties of Religious Experience* (New York, 1903); and Charles Y. Glock and Rodney Stark, *Religion and Society in Tension* (Chicago, 1965).

7. This is explained more fully *infra*.

8. The word *fundamentalism* is badly in need of definition. In one sense, it may apply only to those who subscribe to a fixed set of doctrines, such as the famous Five Points of the Niagara Bible Conference of 1895. In another sense, it may mean simply those who rely on the Bible in its literalistic sense as the ultimate authority. Or, in the broadest sense, it may signify a whole set of cultural or tribalistic values associated with nineteenth-century rural, southern, Anglo-Saxon America. I use the term here and throughout in the historical context to designate those who, for both theological, ecclesiastical, and social reasons, were opposed to "modernism" or Liberal Protestantism.

9. The fringe sects are notoriously opposed to giving out their statistics partly because they have no accurate figures, partly because they fear persecution, and partly because of sheer cantankerousness toward investigators (for all of which they find suitable proof texts). One of the most active and fastest growing ultra-conservative evangelical groups in the United States is the Churches of Christ, which broke off from the Disciples in 1906. The 1936 religious census listed its membership as 309,551; the 1945 edition of the *Yearbook of American Churches* still listed its membership at that figure, but since then its membership has been listed in rounded figures to the nearest 50,000 or 100,000: in 1955 it was 1,500,000; in 1965, 2,250,000. It is difficult to put much stock in such gross estimates.

10. *Yearbook of American Churches,* ed. B. Y. Landis (New York, 1965), p. 55.

11. "The Third Force in Christendom," *Life* (July 9, 1958), p. 120, and William J. Whalen, *Armageddon* (New York, 1962). For the best general analyses of the theological views of the various fringe sects, see F. E. Mayer, *The Religious Bodies of America* (St. Louis, 1956), and Elmer T. Clark, *The Small Sects in America* (New York, 1937).

12. One of the significant statistical and programmatic differences between the Conservative and the Liberal churches today is that the former spend a far higher percentage of their money and manpower in missionary activities. To cite just one example, of the total of 28,486 American missionaries abroad in 1964, only 34.7 per cent came from the denominations associated with the National Council of Churches although these denominations constitute 61.7 per cent of the Protestant church members in the United States. See charts in *Christianity Today* (January 29, 1965), pp. 4, 8.

13. For histories of the fundamentalist movement, see S. G. Cole, *History of Fundamentalism* (New York, 1931); P. A. Carter, *The Decline and Revival of the Social Gospel* (Ithaca, 1956); and Norman F. Furniss, *The Fundamentalist Controversy* (New York, 1957).

14. The high priority given among fringe sects and fundamentalists to overseas missionary endeavor (at a time when the traditional denominations are drastically retrenching in such work) unquestionably results from their alienation from their own culture—a very different motivation from that of traditional missionary endeavor. Jehovah's Witnesses, for example, consider themselves people without a country and are thus able to dissociate their missionary work from American national policies and actions. The missionary work of the neo-fundamentalists or "evangelicals," however, is very closely geared to right-wing foreign-policy attitudes and thrives best in places like South Korea and Taiwan, which are dominated by the United States for military reasons.

15. Glock and Stark demonstrated the solidarity of these self-contained religious groups by measuring the friendship ties among them and finding that the members of Conservative religious groups (fringe sects, Southern Baptists, American Baptists) reported fewer friends outside their own congregation than did the members of main-line Liberal denominations (*op. cit.*, pp. 163-164). The same would undoubtedly hold for intermarriage and business relationships. It is notable that this solidarity was markedly higher among the fringe sects in the 1960's than among Roman Catholics—the significance of which is noted *infra*.

16. For a sympathetic account of the American Council of Christian Churches and a list of its member denominations, see *Christianity Today* (January 29, 1965), pp. 9-11; for an unsympathetic account, see Ralph L. Roy, *Apostles of Discord* (Boston, 1953). Its most important member group is the American Baptist Association (or Landmark Baptists) with a membership of 655,200 in 1965.

17. It is virtually impossible to draw any clear-cut line between fundamentalists and Conservatives. But, in general, those who would accept the

former designation are the more rigid, backward-looking, and narrow-minded literalists associated with the A.C.C.C. Those who prefer the designation "Conservatives" or "evangelicals" are those who look to the National Association of Evangelicals for leadership or who belong to the Lutheran denominations. See *infra.*

18. Graham became a revivalist through his connection with the Youth for Christ movement, a fundamentalist agency designed to combat juvenile delinquency by flamboyant rallies and community sings. Liberal ministers saw Youth for Christ as a threat to their own more sedate youth groups and were at first decidedly cool toward Graham on this account. See W. G. McLoughlin, *Billy Graham* (New York, 1960), pp. 35-43.

19. Among the theologians whom the neo-fundamentalists or evangelicals describe as "Conservative scholars" are E. J. Carnell, P. K. Jewett, Bernard Ramm, S. J. Mikolaski, R. V. G. Tasket, and Pierre Corthiel. See *Christianity Today* (January 1, 1965), p. 26.

20. One of the leading opponents of Billy Graham today is Bob Jones, Sr., the founder of Bob Jones College in Cleveland, Tennessee (since moved to Greenville, South Carolina), which Graham once attended. For his most recent attacks upon Graham see Larry L. King, "Bob Jones University," *Harper's* (June, 1966), pp. 51-58.

21. For a list of these member denominations and a sympathetic discussion of the N.A.E., see *Christianity Today* (January 29, 1965), pp. 3-5.

22. See *Christianity Today* (January 1, 1965), p. 26.

23. *Christianity Today* (October 9, 1964), pp. 5-6.

24. It is only fair to say, however, that in the traditional context of the Southern Baptist position, Billy Graham has made a useful contribution to desegregation by his refusal since 1954 to allow Jim Crow seating in any of his revival meetings and by his insistence that all choirs which sing for his revival meetings be integrated. See Samuel Southard, "Segregation and Southern Churches," *Journal of Religion and Health* (April, 1962), pp. 197-221. On the other hand, this contribution may be more than offset by Graham's insistence that demonstrations, sit-ins, and marches to initiate action for civil rights are un-Christian and undemocratic.

25. See *Christianity Today* (October 9, 1964), pp. 5-6.

26. *Christianity Today* (November 20, 1964), p. 44.

27. Professor Jeffrey K. Hadden of Purdue sent a questionnaire to 726 Baptist ministers in December, 1965, asking them to identify their theological position and state how they voted in the 1964 election. Sixty-nine per cent of the 49 who called themselves "fundamentalist" voted for Goldwater; 51 per cent of 383 who called themselves "Conservative" voted for Goldwater; 11 per cent of 128 who called themselves "neo-orthodox" voted for Goldwater; and 5 per cent of 140 who called themselves "liberal" voted for Goldwater.

28. The civil rights movement has recently been fractured by two new elements—the advocates of "Black Power" and the opponents of the war in Viet-Nam. Martin Luther King, Jr., by linking the settlement of the Negro's domestic problems to demands that the government reverse its policies in Southeast Asia and withdraw from Viet-Nam, may temporarily have avoided a split with the militant young secularists of S.N.C.C. who find the religious leaders of the civil rights movement generally too conservative. But at the same time King's apparent alliance with "Black Power" advocates like Carmichael and McKissick has lost him the support of many who thought his religious commitment to nonviolence would serve as a moderating force upon the secular radicals. It is becoming clear that despite King's efforts, Negroes in the civil rights movement are going to be split between the churchgoing, Bible-believing, middle-class, older generation and the non-religious, slum-dwelling, younger generation for whom nonviolence has always been a strategical tactic and not a religious commitment.

    For a good study of the role of religion in the civil rights movement, see Joseph R. Washington, Jr., *Black Religion* (Boston, 1964). Washington is convinced that King provides no inspiration for the younger Negroes in the movement. King, incidentally, is not a fundamentalist; as Washington points out, he is a Liberal Protestant. But on this issue he is able to appeal to Negroes more theologically Conservative than he. It would be worth some study to know whether the Negro fundamentalists in the South are, proportionately, more Conservative in theology and yet more radical about civil rights than those in the North. While the rise of the Black Muslim or Black Nationalist movement is indicative of the desperation and alienation of many Negroes in the North, its failure to attract more than 100,000 out of the nation's 20,000,000 Negroes is a measure of the Negro's commitment to the prevailing American value system.

29. Milton Himmelfarb may be right in his article in this issue that it is difficult for a non-practicing Jew to resist the cultural pull toward Christianity upon his children or grandchildren, but I suspect that this is more the weight of numbers and of cultural habit than of any significant religious or Christian quality in American life today. The culture is increasingly secular; a non-practicing Jew, like a non-practicing Protestant or Catholic, can make terms with it with comparative ease—and so can his children if they choose. But the pietistic quality of this culture is another matter; this it is almost impossible to escape.

30. See Edward Wakin and Joseph F. Scheuer, *The De-Romanization of the American Catholic Church* (New York, 1966). It should be added, however, that the Roman Catholic reform impulse will operate out of different premises and with a different mood from that of nineteenth-century evangelical reform. It is obvious, for example, that the nuns and priests who engage in civil rights activities bring to their activism for the Kingdom of God a point of view both as individuals and as part of their religious tradition which is quite different from that of the Protestant activist. "De-Romanization" is by no means the equivalent of "assimilation."

31. Robert Bellah's article on America's "civil religion" in this issue of *Dædalus* points out how the American pietistic tradition has been politicized without losing its essential transcendental quality.

32. Since this article first appeared in *Dædalus,* I have received several thoughtful letters which tax me with being too dogmatic in asserting the ultra-conservatism of all Evangelicals. The documentation presented in some of these letters, while not conclusive, has led me to modify my position—at least to the point of admitting that there undoubtedly are some signs of liberalism stirring among the Evangelicals which may eventually bring them into closer rapport with the main-line denominations.

Several correspondents noted that Senator Mark Hatfield, a liberal in Republican circles, is a conservative evangelical in theological circles, a member of the Conservative Baptist Association.

One letter pointed out that my own statistical evidence for the fact that all Evangelicals were supporters of Senator Goldwater does not bear me out. In note 27, Professor Hadden's survey indicates that 49 per cent of those ministers who considered themselves religious "conservatives" in 1964 voted for President Johnson. While this is a much smaller proportion than President Johnson received from the public at large, and while it may simply reflect the traditional Democratic allegiance of many southern Fundamentalists, it nevertheless does indicate that the equation between Evangelical conservatives and Goldwater-type political thinking is not so clear-cut as I have implied.

I am also indebted to a letter from Professor Alan Graebner of Concordia College for pointing out that the table on page 164 of the Glock and Stark book does not prove that the Missouri Synod Lutherans whom they questioned lacked friends outside their own congregations. Unfortunately, the sampling of this denomination used by Glock and Stark is very small and perhaps unrepresentative; they questioned Missouri Synod Lutherans living in northern California rather than in the more tightly-knit Lutheran communities of Missouri where this denomination is strongest. Nevertheless, my equation of religious conservatism and social conservatism may again be overdrawn. This group, too, may be coming out of its shell.

And finally, I should like to quote from a provocative letter written by Professor Richard L. Millett of Southern Illinois University which indicates there is a more widespread division of political and economic views among Evangelicals than my article implies:

Voting for Goldwater is not synonymous with "ultraconservatism." Most evangelicals whom I know who voted for Goldwater did so very reluctantly, seeing him only as the lesser of two evils. They simply felt that Johnson, even more than Goldwater, was morally unfit for the Presidency. (Their assessment of him has since been joined, if my reading of the *New Republic,* etc., does not deceive me, by a large segment of America's liberals.)

A further point of fact comes from the political stance of the evangelical periodicals. Those you mention are conservative indeed, but in at least one case (*Christian Economics*) your choice is hardly major or typical. Have you ever looked at the other side of the coin? Such magazines as *Eternity* (edited by the late Dr. Donald G. Barnhouse) or *His* (Inter-Varsity Christian Fellowship) take a quite different stance. For example see Barnhouse's article on "Communism and the National Council of Churches" in the September, 1960, issue of *Eternity*; or see the June, 1965, issue of *His* dealing with the original Berkeley disturbances. You might even go back to *Christianity Today* and read something other than Henry's editorials. Many articles and columns (notably those by John Warwick Montgomery of Trinity) have taken a rather Liberal position, and Henry prints them.

You might also note that when Carl F. H. Henry asked a carefully picked group of conservative businessmen to criticize the involvement of the church in social issues the response, judged by his own mail, was overwhelmingly negative.

On a related note you might examine many of the recent publications of William B. Eerdmans Publishing Company, the leading Evangelical press. These include a slashing attack on the John Birch Society, a strong rebuttal of those who seek a Biblical basis for segregation (James O. Buswell, Vol. 3, *Slavery, Segregation and Scripture*) and a defense of Social Action (*Inasmuch* by David Moberg). None of these fit your stereotype.

Your examples of evangelical "scholars" were also rather dated and inadequate. Carnell and Rahm certainly fit (and it might be noted that their writings, notably Carnell's *Case for Orthodox Christianity*, can hardly be labeled as politically conservative), but Bruce Metzger of Princeton, F. F. Bruce of Manchester, Culbert Rutenber of Andover-Newton (a socialist and pacifist to boot), G. C. Berkouwer of the Free University of Amsterdam, and Helmut Thielicke of Tübingen are certainly much more influential than any of the others you cited.

I would suggest that there is a broad division on political questions among evangelicals, with a decided tendency among younger adherents toward the left. Inter-Varsity Christian Fellowship perhaps best exemplifies this. Most of its staff . . . supported Johnson in 1964. They now have contacts with over one thousand faculty members in nonevangelical colleges, and from my experience at numerous faculty meetings, from East to West, they are predominantly young, rather liberal in social and political outlook, rather conservative in theology, but rebels in organization and concentrated among the sciences (although historians are well represented, including members on six of the "Big Ten" history faculties).

While Professor Millett's letter and evidence does not negate my general conclusions, it does indicate that more is stirring than I have indicated. As such his statement, a document in itself, deserves to be weighed into my assessment. But whether these younger, more liberal, and rebellious evangelicals can reform the Evangelical movement from within or whether they will eventually have to drift away from it, only time will tell.

BRYAN WILSON

Religion and the Churches in Contemporary America

I

AMERICAN CHRISTIANITY inherits its traditional elements—its teachings, its authority structure and organization, and its church practices and rituals—from Europe. Each of these has undergone modification, since traditional theology, church organization, and sacred rituals appear to be fundamentally irreconcilable with the values, life styles, and functional imperatives of advanced industrial society. Today, religion in America is characterized by its secularity,[1] its denominational pluralism,[2] the absence of substantial ideological distinctions among at least most of the Protestant denominations (despite some differences within them),[3] and its irrelevance to everyday life.[4] The most distinctive American contribution to Christianity has been the development of denominational pluralism, which is a qualitatively different phenomenon from the European dichotomy of church and sect, and an elaboration of the limited non-conformist denominationalism of eighteenth-century England.[5] Denominational pluralism has been a logical response to the secular style of the American Constitution, the diversity of faiths, and the formal equality established between them. In an increasingly secular world, denominational pluralism as an appropriate religious pattern of organization has been diffused to most other English-speaking countries. But in those societies, and particularly in England, the denominations are less diverse in origin, retain a higher and more distinctive ideological commitment, but fail, even collectively, to mobilize a very high proportion of the total population. Paradoxically, although the traditional elements of Christianity are accepted and denominational pluralism is frequently exposed to attack in America (as "the sin of disunity"), pluralism remains a

73

much more conspicuous feature, and shows more resilience, despite attack, than do the traditional elements which have experienced a process of erosion. And, withal, the churches maintain and increase their memberships and attendances. This transformation of Christianity and its worldly success are aspects of the paradox of the persistence of non-rational values in an increasingly rationalized world.

The irrelevance of traditional Christian teachings has been acknowledged by contemporary theologians, and its secularization has been promoted by the fashion for de-mythologizing, and the current postmortem examination of the death of God. The very thought patterns of theology appear to be at odds with those of modern society. As one English philosopher, who, after strenuous efforts to defend it, has now abandoned Christian belief, comments, "When theology is interpreted to make it relevant to the substantial secular life of the modern world, it always seems to lose any distinctive theological content and often, too, any logical consistency."[6] Traditional church organization has undergone steady modification, particularly in urban America, toward greater rationalization and extensive innovation, especially in ancillary agencies, and the evolution of central bureaucracy. The process has not been without its critics, nor have the traditional parish organization and the ecological organization of the church. Perhaps because they are most completely insulated from the impact of secular society, traditional and received ritual procedures have experienced the least disturbance, although Europeans have sometimes commented that dignity, solemnity, and gentility were lacking in American ritual performance. Ritual has, possibly, been protected from change as it has acquired enhanced importance as the unique specialist function of the ministry and as a persisting agency of reassurance for the laity, but some theologians would suggest that the maintenance of ritual, once its supportive dogma has been destroyed, must be problematical. As the primary activity of religion, ritual may, nonetheless, prove also to be its ultimate concern, even though, in a "privatized" society, it has little consequence for the community and little relevance for morality.

If these received aspects of Christianity are exposed to the corrosive influences of American life, denominational pluralism, considering the weakness of ideological distinction between many denominations, has been surprisingly resistant to attack. This relatively successful persistence is a subsidiary paradox for our attention.

American denominations came into being partly as consequences of the differences in ethnicity, community, and social status of their clientele. Their continuance as separate bodies has increasingly rested on their established organizational identity. It is not distinctive teachings and practice which sustains them, although these half-remembered traditions provide the rationalizations for it. The denominations have ceased to claim the unique possession of truth. But, as a system, pluralism espouses principles—of tolerance, competition, pragmatism, and freedom of choice—well attuned to the ethos of American society.[7] Denominational pluralism has facilitated the acceptance by religious bodies of rational organizational structures characteristic of other social institutions. Although this has been especially true of Protestantism, it has affected Catholicism, and has been increasingly true of Judaism.[8] It is these background values and the defense mechanisms that organizations evolve which have prevented the diminution of denominational ideology from leading to more dramatic ecumenical consequences.

The denominational amalgamations that have occurred in the ecumenical process in America illustrate the importance of organizational congruence rather than the similarity of doctrinal traditions. The joining together of the Lutheran churches of different national origins was relatively little impeded by either organizational or doctrinal difficulties. The divisions which persisted related to distinctive liberal and fundamentalist orientations within the different traditions. This, perhaps, is now the dominant line of ideological cleavage in American Protestantism, although it has only limited organizational expression.[9] Presbyterians and Congregationalists, too, had originally little but their ecclesiological distinctiveness to keep them apart, but historical circumstances have not brought them closer together—perhaps largely because there was no language gap, which, in closing, could also reduce other, more substantial differences. American denominations have not come nearer together precisely because the ideological defenses of their separateness have been organizational rather than doctrinal, and usually these have not been more than distantly dependent on a transcendental belief system. Among religious, as among secular, institutions, organizations *per se* acquire their own *raison d'être,* independent of their pristine ideals, and hence evolve their own organizational defenses, even in the face of loss, unclarity, obscurement, supercession, or duplication, of primary goals and original ideologies.[10]

The transcendent belief systems of different denominations were, from the outset, necessarily at a discount in America, as compared to Europe, since denominations were unable to press their claims not only to superiority, but also to the monopoly of truth. The assumptions of migration were not only of religious liberty, but inevitably of religious tolerance—a condition which, in the spirit if not in the letter, was established only very much more slowly and more recently in Europe, even in England. Since the uniqueness of ideology could only be pressed for circumspectly, the denominations in America became more reliant on other ideological defenses, which were organizational rather than transcendental. In time, there were no substantive areas of ideological difference to defend: What was defended were persisting organizations.

Obviously, there were general status correlates of religious denominationalism, but real as these were in a society where the existence of classes was often denied, they were far less explicitly recognized than, for example, in England, and were unbuttressed by stratificational ideologies. In America, class-consciousness has been limited; class differences (in contrast to more individualized distinctions of status) have always been vague.[11] Mobility in its various forms—diurnal, geographic, and social—has been sufficiently extensive to prevent the rigidification of class barriers. The denominations have been differentially distributed in the various regions and have taken on different status connotations in different areas.[12] For all these reasons, the hardening of socio-religious correlates has never occurred. Doctrinal distinctions have not been really useful as elevated defenses of firm social class orientations. Individual churches have catered to families of congruent ethnicity (of steadily diminishing significance) or congruent social status, but the denominations as such have not provided ideological defenses or distinctiveness of religious practice for distinct social classes. The correlation has been more that of local status group and denominational allegiance, than of a national social class and its denominational expression, which was much more the case in England.[13]

Oligopoly and Ecumenism

Allegiance to a specific organization may, of course, be strong, even without the claim to transcendent truth for its ideology. The points of distinction between churches need not be pressed, and the warrant of one, as against another, steadily ceased to be much canvassed, particularly with the development of community churches in new urban areas. The major denominations became increasingly brand-images for but slightly differentiated products. Yet brand-images also have their functions in stimulating a logic of competition for organizations.[14] As monopolies and combines have discovered, the multiplication of brands may expand the total market far beyond the market-response were only one homogeneous commodity available. The denominations, too, have no certain monopoly: Homogeneity of larger denominations might lead—perhaps *is* leading—to the emergence of new movements offering a faith really, or apparently, different from an ecumenized Protestantism.[15]

American denominations, despite the slightness of ideological differences, and despite the comity principle inspired in the 1880's and '90's by Washington Gladden,[16] have stood in the relationship of "fair competition" with one another. That competitiveness itself reflects one of the primary secular values of American life. Religious competition occurs between large, rather similar organizations which have undertaken similar large-scale operations for the mobilization of support, the maintenance of premises, services, facilities, a good public image, and the promotion of evangelism. The very possibilities of expansion in the United States stimulated denominational growth, and the formal equality of religious movements—a natural corollary to the formal equality of men—allowed sects rapidly to become denominations (and forced churches to become denominations).[17] The tight molds in which Nonconformists were set in England never applied to American Protestantism.[18] Just as there was a strong personal myth of social mobility (and quite a strong reality), so there was a possibility of denominational mobility in the expanding society, and hence of increased similarity of denominations. In England the myth taught men not to expect to get ahead, but rather to know their place (even though many did get ahead), and denominations likewise knew their place—the measure of social, and religious, distance from one another.[19]

Paradoxically, the likeness of American denominations may not operate as a spur to that ecumenism which might appear to be predicated by the logic of the situation. Similarity may itself partly arise as a consequence of competition on more or less equal terms, in the maintenance of similar activities. Ecumenical developments may appear more likely than in Britain, since American denominations are more alike in style, have enjoyed more formal equality of operation, and have long had fewer ideological differences than the Church of England and the Free Churches in Britain. The English

Nonconformist denominations have, in the past, proudly maintained their difference from the Anglican Church, and, in reflection of that, from one another.[20] But competition also has a logic, and for a commodity with as little relevance to everyday American life as religion, competition may function to maintain the interest and the affiliation of a wide clientele. Ecumenism might be a debilitating development in the American situation, whereas oligopoly controls the fierceness of competition but offers the stimulus of familiar competitive responses. Thus, although, in this case, competition may not do much to improve the product—which is too diffuse a commodity for improvement to be readily measurable or even visible—it may promote the buoyancy of the market, as the existence and the activity of one church sustains another. In England, ecumenical conversations have embraced a wider span of denominational positions, and this has been possible precisely because there was no effective competition between denominations: The Established Church and the Nonconformists had different reference groups; there were profound differences in structure, style, and social affiliation, and hence complementary strengths—or truer, complementary weaknesses—made ecumenism attractive. In America, where the process of amalgamation has been so much more rapid in the business field, distinctive ideological commitment of denominations so vestigial, and communal churches common, much more rapid ecumenical development might have been expected. In England, with its persisting social distinctions and doctrinal differences among the Established Church and the Nonconformists, extensive ecumenical discussions have been a consequence of poor church attendances and low memberships. Ecumenical interests have been given an urgency lest, in delaying, as one churchman has put it, there should be a marriage between corpses. In America, the very strength of the churches, despite the relative insignificance of doctrinal positions, may have retarded the speed of amalgamation.

The Functions of Religion in America

American churches function as voluntary associations, and voluntaryism may itself account for much of their institutional resilience, with membership and attendance figures which are very high when compared to the churches in Europe—especially Protestant Europe —where churches were for so long either "official," or reactions against the official. American churches have for a long time operated more as distinctly social and charitable institutions than have churches in Europe, but they have always seemed to be—except in periods of evangelistic fervor—only mildly spiritual. In contrast with England, where so few remain in the churches, but where those who do appear to be highly committed, American churches seem almost casual—affirming a vague ideological orientation, rather than a deep spirituality, and affirming it largely through social activities which have little specifically to do with spiritual values as such.[21] Thus, there are sometimes literally *dozens* of different social activities in the church program—a phenomenon known only to a very much lesser degree in Europe. Such social involvement creates a sense of belonging to a community in a society in which high mobility (of all kinds) makes a deep community attachment difficult to achieve as a purely spontaneous, unorganized growth of the sustained life of the people of a neighborhood. The churches become surrogate communities, based on the will for togetherness (the essence of voluntaryism), rather than on an ecological premise of shared participations, or on well-known, deeply laid, and firmly held common ideological principles. The demand for togetherness is evident throughout American society, but in churches and in church-promoted enterprises it sometimes even appears as a goal in its own right. Almost on a note of congratulation, two ministers, writing of the coffeehouses currently fashionable as church ventures, report that in the coffeehouse, "No one goes it alone. Everyone is sitting with someone. Each person is related. Those who come in are quickly joined by someone."[22] Someone . . . anyone . . . this is, for a European, a rather behavioristic description of what "being related" means; it becomes a conscious, almost manipulated thing, too much of a sociologist's definition, and too little of a community reality.

The religious remnant in England sometimes entails the broad involvement by churchgoers in one another's lives or a deep commitment to moral values; in America the very general nature of religious activity implies only segmental participation, the operation of interest groups, and that form of togetherness to which theologians do not hesitate to deny the status of *koinonia*.

The impersonality and near-anonymity of American togetherness permits even moral concerns to be detached from moralistic attitudes of mind. In Europe, such moralism is still evident; men are still aware—often censoriously—of being their brother's keeper. The indifference of Americans to many facets of individual behavior and belief (speech habits, dress, degrees of casualness)—not entirely concealed by the mechanical civility and bland friendliness of secondary relationships—implies to those from more traditional societies an indiscriminate quality and lack of depth in community feeling. Strong community sense has, often, its own insularity and narrowness, of course; the lack of it in urban America adds a considerable dimension to the individual's freedom—but the lack of censoriousness is often also the lack of concern. American conformity has been widely remarked, but it is often the conformity induced by organizations and mass media, rather than something rooted in the shared concerns of communities, and mediated by local involvements. As an urban phenomenon, it exists within a context of ultimate indifference which does not participate in the type of common values on which traditional conformity rests.[23] The do-good activities which the churches facilitate, and which some theologians deplore, are indeed often only ways of going through the motions, and often only the monetary motions at that. It is as if individuals seeking community and its joys had not been sufficiently socialized in community life to do more than prize it as a make-belief of putting up bunting and having potluck suppers—just as they might prize a medieval monument, pulled out of the sustaining context in which it could acquire real meaning.

Even so, this form of association appears to fulfill some functions —of identification, of reassurance concerning ultimate meanings and purposes, however little they need to impinge on everyday life. The church may be reassuring men that they need worry no more about those ultimate anxieties, may be acting as a gentle cowpox inoculation to ward off a stark confrontation with smallpox. It is easy for theologians to be contemptuous of the use of the church for these ends, but they are time-honored functions, and in a democracy it is hard to deny that this appears to be what the people want from their religion.[24]

Given the generality of the ideological commitment of the churches, it is difficult to ascribe to them a significant intellectually expressive function. They do perform significant functions for the individual at the emotional level: They are the agencies of emotional release and control, solemnizers of the life cycle and its associated traumas. They provide the context for institutionalized joy at baptisms and weddings. Of more importance—both in the Christian scheme of things, and in a society which has neutralized the effect of almost every other affliction—is death, a less controllable and more traumatic challenge at the level of meaning. Traditionally, Christianity solemnized death, conferring meaning upon it, both for those facing death and for those suffering bereavement. With an eschatology which commands less expressible and vaguer belief, the churches today function by concealing death, beautifying it, sentimentalizing it in acceptable ways, at least for the assuagement of the grief of bereavement, if not for the man who faces death.[25] The paradox that those comforted in bereavement cannot take comfort from this same tacit conspiracy of silence in regard to their own eventual death is perhaps the central dilemma of American Christianity. The church can comfort, but it cannot deeply reassure.

These "therapeutic" activities, the social programs, the attempt to create community, and the provision of opportunities for charitable undertakings are the conspicuous features of contemporary American churches. In some respects, all of these activities provide comfort and relief for believers, which we may take to be the functional bedrock not only of religion in America, but of institutionalized religion everywhere. In a voluntaryistic society, and despite the growth of civil religion, the operation of the churches is largely therapeutic at the individual level. It is a society which has in the past decade manifested great concern about the use of tranquilizers by adults, marijuana and LSD by the young, and escapist television by a wide stratum of society. The demand for anodynes to deaden the abrasive pains of life in the affluent society appears to be not so very different from the demand in societies with much more dramatic and manifest levels of material misery.

Pragmatic Values

It is no accident that Christianity has acquired new pragmatic aspects in America. A commonplace claim in the earlier decades of the nineteenth century was that religion was good for business, that it ensured right-mindedness in politics, that only in its name could justice be done. And if education in America escaped its ministrations in far greater degree than occurred in Europe, that was simply the recognition of the primacy—not the totality—of the secular claims of the state and an assertion of the superior virtue of voluntaryism. Today, one reads that "happiness is going to church"; and not only at the fringe with Mary Baker Eddy, New Thought, and the new meditation cults, but nearer to the center with Norman Vincent Peale, and in a multitude of sermons, one learns that religion provides power for everyday living, success, health, wealth, and achievement.[26] Above all, one sees that the churches offer themselves as "welcoming," "friendly," and problem-solving. The ideas, put like this, are alien to the European mind, taken for granted as they may be in America.

In this sense, American Christianity performs in a sophisticated way, with an objectified, universalized rationale, some of the primary functions of religion. The churches respond to the demand for psychic reassurance. Among simpler peoples, such demands included bodily healing and protection from witchcraft. In a more advanced society, physical healing is available—on the pragmatic test—from more reliable sources, and among a sophisticated public, the explanations of evil are less subject to particularization. It is not personal miracles which are demanded, but rather the realization of a principle in which whole categories of evil can be demonstrably nullified. Again, religion has to prove its secular value, in providing power for people to maintain their ordinary activities—not by the diffusion of moral principles, but by the operation of a benevolent God. The demand has an obvious continuity, except in expression, with that of the Singapore spirit-cultists who demand that the gods change their luck, or the Brazilian Umbandists who seek advice from possessed priestesses, or the Africans who seek protection from witches or evil spirits.[27] The causal principles of science are accepted, but the belief in a benevolent force, which if not actually "intervening" unnaturally, can nonetheless be harnessed for the individual's need, is basically very similar. The system of thought is more rational, the explanations more logical, but the demands are much the same. The gods have a clientele only so long as they have a reputation for providing, if not full salvation, then immediate evidences of a better life. When liturgy is no longer part of a distinctive cultural tradition—great or folk; when it is neither really indigenous nor a primary concern of a society's intellectuals; and when worship ceases to be an act whereby a real community (whether ecologically or ideologically defined) recreates itself in solemn fashion, then the old nexus of, "We love him because he first loved us" (which is not far from, "You need our praise and sacrifice, therefore answer now our prayers"), quickly reasserts itself.

Only when the church group is itself a community, or when it is drawn from a stable social community, can we expect religious activity to acquire significance for communal well-being. When a church is voluntaryistic, composed entirely of self-selected, impersonally-related, and segmentally-associated individuals, it is more likely to manifest the search for purely personal gratifications. It becomes, then, an aggregation of those who need one another as a context for personal gratifications, whether their demands are social approval, the acquisition of status, or the exercise of power. Typically, such a church draws together those seeking opportunity for relatively impersonal do-gooding and for verbally objectified, but actually subjective, get-gooding. The impersonality of the context ensures that the goodwill projected and the charity received are disinterested; thus, it both protects individuals from affective involvements for which advanced industrial society does so little to prepare them, and it accords to the forms of other social activities. In its impersonality and quality of rationalization, this activity differs from that in less-developed nations, but in its pre-occupation with comfort and spiritual therapy, it represents one of the primary core concerns of religion in all human societies.

It is, of course, perfectly understandable that this function should persist in the churches. Religion is not, in the last analysis and in its functional operation, amenable to the type of rational principles on which other institutions have increasingly come to be organized. It remains the repository of emotional and evaluative orientations. It is concerned with the institutionalized expression of emotions which men otherwise have found difficult to control—awe, grief, dejection, guilt, alienation, and the need for love and reassurance. Traditionally, many of these feelings were also vented in violent form—typical of mourning ceremonies, for example, among aboriginal peoples, from New Zealand to North America. Religious socialization has been one agency in the subordination and neutralization of such passion. This passion was once anger against the gods; it was highly personalized, and the development of religion has been partly evident in the reduction in its vehemence of expression. But the strength of the response appears to be intimately associated with its particularism, and it seems difficult for the evocation of such emotional strength to shift from personal to universal levels. In the new breed of ministers, in the civil rightists, there is perhaps an evidence of the universalization of this passion, as there has been in other religious social reform movements, but for the mass of men it has been easier to feel emotional outrage for personal disabilities and to direct it at deities and persons, rather than at social systems.

Community Institutions

In urbanized America, where the stable, local, and slowly-formed community—which is still the basic unit of European, and all traditional, societies—has become rarer, there are fewer spontaneous community resources to satisfy the deeper emotional needs of men. The churches remain one institution which fulfills that function, but in America they increasingly lack the supportive community structure which they enjoyed in the past. In consequence, not only are the churches more needed than they were, but they are also less well circumstanced to perform one of their important functions. One response to this situation has been the extraordinary multiplication of associational activities in American churches, in the attempt to create a sense of community participation. And yet, because of the prevailing mobility and impersonality, and because it exists in a value system where achievement orientation, universalism, affective neutrality, democracy, tolerance, and anti-discrimination are stressed,[28] a church needs to acquire a universal validity in order to be accomodated to the social milieu. In this value context, a church cannot be so highly particularistic as the churches in the past, (and those in the more traditional, European setting). Similarly, their professional men, in a society where role specificity is the logic of work organization, cannot effectively continue to play roles with the degree of diffuseness which characterized religious functionaries in the past. Yet, the particularism of operation and the diffuseness and affectivity of the functionary's role have been an integral part of the function of religion, a necessity for effective operation at the personal and stable community level. And even in advanced society, men live their lives at the parish level, and demand these things still. The impersonality, role specificity, and affective neutrality of the rational social organization of modern America appear to be the focal points of the spontaneous rebellion against bureaucracy and lovelessness articulated among the contemporary hippies. The lack of affection, approval, and reassurance, and of opportunity to claim status and receive recognition of worthiness, is widely held to be an important causal factor in the incidence of crime, deviance, violence, corruption, and the widespread expression of loneliness and isolation which, in America, appear to exceed those of all other societies.[29] The decline of churchgoing in Protestant Europe and the lower incidence of social pathology perhaps reflect the extent to which the structure which was once supportive of church operation is still, in some measure, capable of fulfilling some of its traditional functions, without widespread participation in church activities, as a part of the long-sustained practice of stable community life. The growth of churchgoing and of crime and deviance in America manifests, perhaps, the extent to which widely felt needs are unsatisfied within the society.

The social institutions in which man realizes his ultimate and common gratifications are the community-based institutions of the family, religion, and recreation. (These institutions stand in contrast to societal institutions—economic, judicial, political, military, educational—which, while providing gratifications, are more largely concerned with wider spheres of regulation and organization, and with the means, rather than the ends, of life.[30]) None of these institutions, which together once regulated emotional gratifications and facilitated the operation of other institutions, today functions in a co-ordinated and coherent way. None of them is amenable to the degree of rationalization possible in other institutional areas, even though all of them have made adjustments in this direction, and religion, which relies very directly on its communal bases, has long maintained central hierarchies. The shift from *apparently* spontaneous institutionalization at the local communal level to partially rational, bureaucratic operation, has been uneasily effected and has always led to de-institutionalized responses.

In recreation, which in the entertainment and holiday industry has gone furthest toward acceptance of the rational, economic model, there are persistent attempts to re-create spontaneity and to break the monopoly of institutionalized provision. Innovation and amateurism abound, sometimes using commercial agencies, sometimes not. But since the business ethic has penetrated the area, innovation is quickly exploited—amateur groups are professionalized, sub-cultural expression is taken over and exploited for mass-media audiences or for tourism. Recreation, more than any other area of human activity in modern America, is open to spontaneous expression and to the charismatic, although charisma is subject, as ever it was, to routinization and now, also, to commercialization.

The fragility of the family in contemporary society is evident in the high incidence of marital instability, the extent of sex stimulation and illicit sex, the technologically nearly-perfected break of the nexus between copulation and conception, and flourishing sub-cultures for sex deviants, especially (but not exclusively, as periodic small-town scandals make evident) in large cities. The gratifications of marriage and family life are less exposed to commercial exploitation than are recreational activities, and innovation is impeded by the strength of moral taboos which partly justify themselves by reference to biological imperatives. But some gratifications traditionally provided in association with marriage and kinship—sex, comradeship, age-group identification—are drawn into the more readily rationalized arena of recreation. The church, too, is threatened by extra-institutional demand for, and supply of, its functions (particularly in the growth not only of Christian sects, but also of new cults that may not even explicitly claim to be part of the Christian heritage), and by the growth of secular activities which partially, and in uncertain ways, are thought to serve as substitute-religions. In the past, the church in traditional societies has been especially sensitive to such developments, and has had the means of suppressing them. (This has been so not only in the matter of pursuing heretics, but also in controlling entertainment, such as the prohibition of theaters, and formerly of cinemas, on Sundays in England, and the licensing of public houses.) Yet, conspicuously, in the American case, with its openness to all these developments, the main stream of Christian denominationalism has not only not lost the capacity to mobilize its votaries, but has strengthened its organizational hold on them.

Though frequently subject to innovation, religious institutions, unlike recreational activities, have traditionally been resistant to it. Asserting the timelessness of its truths and the divine warrant for its institutions, Christianity has had difficulty in conscious adjustment. Now, in a climate of extensive innovation, the churches have accepted the use of new technical methods to present their message and to recruit a clientele, particularly by mass-circulation press, radio, television, institutional fund-raising, and bureaucratization. The use of the new techniques has undoubtedly affected the goals in the service of which they were harnessed. The older organizational ideologies (the ecclesiologies of the different denominations) have lapsed, as the churches have steadily transformed their participants into an audience, as denominational bureaucracy has partially reduced congregational and episcopal polities to mere external shells, with synods and conferences as "fronts" for activities increasingly dictated by bureaucratic imperatives.[31]

If the denominations have thus lost distinctiveness of doctrine, so, in general, Christianity, with the impact of scientific and social scientific insights, has lost general theological plausibility. The "death-of-God" theology is the denial of the meaning of all theology: Christianity at large is threatened with the loss of its transcendent ideology. Religious change may suddenly be conscious and deliberate, but it is as yet haphazard, unco-ordinated and differential, not only among denominations, but within them. And yet, in spite of all this, the churches persist and, in America, affiliation to them grows: a process clearly unrelated to the decline of the general Christian, or specific denominational, ideologies.

Nor can this growth be related to the process of bureaucratization and nationalization, which even religious institutions have experienced in industrial society. There is indeed a limit beyond which religion cannot be reduced to rational procedures. Since religion is concerned with end gratifications, it cannot adopt as a final model for its practice the economy-efficiency criteria which dominate other social institutions in modern society, even if such calculations have increasingly characterized the organization of religious denominations. The persistence of high rates of church affiliation and attendance in America appears to be related to functions for which no alternative agency exists—the function of the surrogate community, and the supportive context for individuals in an increasingly depersonalized, rationalized, and bureaucratized society. Historical circumstances have conferred these specific functions upon the churches in America; in Europe community breakdown has proceeded less far, and community functions still appear to be performed in stable social groups.[32] The persistence of distinct historical and cultural traditions within smaller regional and national groups may also have prevented men from feeling the need for other agencies. Men's need in societies of slower growth and change may find less direct articulation. So, we may hypothesize, the general erosion of Christian belief has, in Europe, had direct consequences for churchgoing and religious affiliation not evident in America.

Comfort Functions and Social Protest

The churches in America have been aptly described as fulfilling a "comfort function," serving particularly as a family surrogate, "as a substitute for the void experiences in the lives of the unmarried, divorced, the widowed, and the childless."[33] These same investigators of the Episcopal Church concluded "that parishioners deprived of status gratifications in the secular society turned to the church for alternative rewards, for comfort and consolation. . . . Dispensing comfort seems a major function of the contemporary church."[34] The director of a regional church planning office tells us that many pastors are "finding that an ever-increasing share of their work is devoted to counseling."[35] We have seen that this appears to be a major function of all religion in practice. Among Western nations, the demand for it appears to be especially acute in America, or to be fulfilled by non-church agencies to a much lower extent.

The "death-of-God" theology in America has been accompanied by a critique of the churches by some American theologians, sharper than anything which has occurred within the churches in Europe. There these theological ideas have—or had, until they were popularized by Bishop Robinson—been largely left to the clergy. There is a striking contrast between Protestant Europe with its empty churches and a low temperature of theological debate within, and the United States with its full churches and the intense internal criticism of the churches by religious intellectuals. Obviously America is a society which, in its puissant role in world affairs, feels its radical tensions more deeply than do European countries at the present time. The demand of the new theologians is for the church to play a positive part in the social, economic, and political sphere— an ideal which could no longer be realistically entertained by the Protestant churches in Europe. The position scarcely needs documentation.[36] The demand is made with few scriptural supports, but with a strong assertion of the public moral duty of Christians (of which the Scriptures say little) as distinct from their private moral practice (of which the Scriptures say rather more). But as Glock, Ringer, and Babbie comment, these critics "call upon the church to lead, but provide no convincing evidence that church members stand ready to follow."[37]

Religious movements remain politically active for relatively short periods. The revolutionist tradition within Christianity—and it is a rather dubious tradition if this-worldly action is implied—did not last very long, although it has periodically and ephemerally recrudesced. The evidence for simpler societies where revolutionary religion does sometimes occur suggests that such movements, if they persist, either transform themselves into political parties, or revert after a time to therapeutic comforting functions which appear to be more truly characteristic of religious practice.[38] The transformation of religion into politics is part of a process of rationalization. The ultimate rationalization might seem imminent, once the death of God has been proclaimed, and the search for redemption from worldly woes or other-worldly fears abandoned. But salvation is a persistent pre-occupation of religion, and this appears to be what the contemporary American clientele demand, even if their secularity requires a more this-worldly salvation and reassurance than is traditional. On the evidence, one simply cannot agree with Winter when he says that "the ministry of the church in and for the world has been transmuted into a private pre-occupation with . . . emotional problems."[39] There has been no transmutation. Emotional problems, or their physical correlates, have always been the stock-in-trade of religious practice. Even in the more rational West, the record of dominant religious movements has been of support for governments (largely true even of English Nonconformists), of occasional social (but not political) reform, and, as a major concern, of an effort to bring unto Him all who have suffered and are heavy-laden. The politicization of religion, on the other hand, would be a transmutation, and it might lead to the alienation of the church's clientele without the prospect of there being another clientele ready to accept this orientation under religious auspices. It is not without significance that churches which have engaged in radical political action in contemporary America, in association with the Industrial Areas Foundation, have done so in support of a distinct conflict philosophy alien to the dominant Christian tradition, and under the direction of Saul Alinsky, who is a non-Christian. What the churches share with him are not religious beliefs but civic concerns.[40] The American laity predicate their church activity on a belief in God (however vaguely held) and the need to worship him (however perfunctorily performed), in the expectation that his much emphasized benevolence will continue to be manifested, here and hereafter, and will offer comfort and consolation for the deprivations which necessarily occur in a highly hedonistic society.[41] Yet in so many of its traditional concerns, the church has become highly apologetic—to the laity for enjoining moral behavior and to the new theologians for not engaging in the political and social action which they demand, but for which the laity has little inclination.[42]

What Bishop Robinson publicly said, and what other theologians have subsequently said even more loudly, were things which have been discussed in the privacy of learned theological journals for years. They were the doctrines which the priests kept from the people, but they do not appear to have been widely accepted by so very many priests. Those who have lost faith—or so radically changed it that laymen believe that they have lost it—stand in a precarious position. They may seek to change the charter of the churches to which they belong; they may abandon their positions and their stipends; or they may maintain discretion concerning private opinions and public pronouncements. In a democratic society, with high publicity values, secret theology is almost as difficult as secret diplomacy, and in a society with an appetite for the sensational and high rewards for the publication of new thoughts, the dubious diplomacy of the past is hard to maintain. But it has been noted that the ordinary congregational or parish minister, who most keenly feels the pressure of the laity's demands, has been less responsive than those without such localized commitment to the politicization of the church.[43] It has been the seminary professors, the campus ministers, and the younger men who have shown themselves most vigorous in political causes.[44] The parish minister's concern is necessarily with the deprivation experienced among his immediate clientele. Although the form in which this deprivation is manifested and the type of solace it seeks may not commend themselves to the theological intellectuals, the parish minister may be able to do more for the relatively deprived in the affluent society than for those suffering more absolute deprivation in remote places. It is a function to which the clergyman has been called; it is well exemplified in the Scriptures; it is traditional in Christianity, and in most religion as practiced; it meets the needs of ordinary men and women who are prepared for, and who seek, the church's ministrations, and who provide the churches and their ministers with their financial support.

II

Lay demands for comfort and spiritual therapy, the call of the "new" theologians for the social commitment of the churches to (usually) radical causes, and the obligation to maintain and run church organizations are all laid on the clergy. Ministers are, in many ways, the equivalent of professionals in other institutional orders, but they are also in some respects more than professionals, and in others, less. The gratifications of religion, unlike those of economic, educational, political, judicial, and other institutional spheres, are available at the level of the local community. The local religious functionary offers salvation that is complete, and grace or counsel as abundant, as that which the hierarchs of the religious system could offer. In this sense the clergyman may claim to be much more than the local lawyer, doctor, or teacher, whose skills and authority are necessarily rationally co-ordinated in societal scale. In this sense, the clergyman is more than a professional. In other ways, his career opportunities and professional independence are, for reasons inherent in the difference between communal and societal institutional orders, considerably more restricted than those of other professional men. The process of secularization, however, has led to the increasing proximity of the ministry to the model that applies to other professions. In America, the ministry is commonly regarded as a profession, and ministers themselves often so regard it. This occurs with both the secularization and de-limitation of the clerical role, but it is also a way of enhancing ministerial claim to status. Since sacred status, as such, has steadily diminished in its social significance, the clergy, in their search to retain social status, have readily accepted the successful model of the secular professions as appropriate to their case.

A certain tension is inherent in this shift of significant points of reference. Although status can be effectively claimed only in secular terms, which are the terms of achievement, technical competence, and monetary success, ministerial roles do not lend themselves to developed levels of technical expertise and, at the same time, the ministerial role appears to be best defended when certain spiritual functions can be claimed to be indispensable and irreducible to other more technical and matter-of-fact procedures. These tensions concerning non-rational functions in an increasingly rationalized social system obviously parallel the tensions between communal and societal institutions. The state of religion in a society cannot be understood without regard to the organization, status, and functions of its ministers.

The loss of functions by the clergy has been a universal tendency in Christendom in the past two centuries. In Europe, the clergy have lost educational, magisterial, and sometimes even political functions. With the growth of new and more specialized professions, they have seen the diminution of their therapeutic and counseling functions. If sin is really serious, it passes, as crime, to the lawyer; if maladjustment is urgent, it passes, as illness, to the doctor or the psychiatrist. In America, the religious functionary has acquired other roles which distinguish him generally from most of his European counterparts, and have led to professionalization of the ministry. In Europe, the ministry is still endowed with a sanctity lacking in America, and is regarded as a "calling," a vocation that transcends merely professional commitment. Leslie Paul, in his recent official report on the clergy of the Church of England, felt it necessary to explain at some length that if he called the clergy a "profession," he intended no offense by this—sociologically justified, though theologically inadequate—characterization.[45] In America, the point would not need to be made. The growth of social concerns in American churches, the fact that the clergy are not drawn from elite strata (as Anglicans were until the very recent past), and the acceptance of rational systems of training similar to those of other professions have led to the acceptance of the idea that the ministry is to be regarded as a profession, in many respects like others. This is an aspect of the surrender of religious institutions to rationalization. The idea persists that the clergy have a stronger ideological commitment than inheres in other professions, but this is weak in comparison with attitudes which prevail in Europe.

We may take the principal characteristics of a profession to be the control its members exercise in (sometimes institutionalized) admission to its practice, the institution of regulated, approved training, the emphasis on a regular career, a professional ethic, a fiduciary element in role performance which the professional ethic protects, a highly expert role which can be specified, a high degree of role autonomy, control of the institutional context in which the profession is practiced, and a high degree of colleague-group solidarity and some agency for its expression. Not all of these characteristics have equal salience in regard to the ministry, but we may briefly consider the more important among them, and the extent to which the ministry in America—in passing comparison with England—has come to be characterized by these professional attributes.

Control of Entry and of Training

American pluralism of ideological commitment and liturgical practice has obviously weakened the ministry's control of entry to the profession by its practitioners. Such pluralism has existed in Europe, too, but the continuance of established churches has facilitated the persistence of a sense of control within the entrenched national churches. The avowed equality of men and of religious faiths in America has created abundant opportunity for free entry into the profession through new or marginal religious movements. Since the denominations have tended to make less and less claim to any monopoly of truth, the Protestant ministry has not been able to employ organizational ideology to sustain professional identity.

There has grown up, of course, some consensus about which denominations have acceptable standards of orthodoxy, although this consensus has always been hazy at the fringes and subject to change. It has, nevertheless, provided some vague sense of professional standing which has found expression in the growth of the transference of denominational allegiance by Protestant ministers. Yet such professionalism has been held in check, at the ideological level, if not at the existential level, by Protestant ideology. The assertion of the priesthood of all believers has been a firm tradition within Protestantism, strongly qualifying clerical claims to a monopoly of even liturgical performance. This commitment to an ideal amateurism has undoubtedly retarded professionalization, which in other ways has been strongly promoted in the American ministry. The liturgical revival, and the re-creation of a priestly expertise, even in traditionally rather anti-liturgical churches, may be partly prompted by the desire for fuller professional status among ministers.[46]

Approved training has been institutionalized in the church longer than in other professions, but the growth of pluralism, in destroying the unity of belief, also destroyed the unity of the vocation. At the Reformation, the monopoly of training for an arcane, dramatic performance was destroyed; subsequently, the assumption of preaching activities by laymen and the growth of independent congregations broke the monopoly of control of training for professional practice. Highly diversified standards of training still prevail within Protestantism, even though a common measure of educational attainment has now become regularized among the principal American denominations. This standard had declined perhaps until the 1930's,[47] but since then a general pattern of university education followed by a three-year period of seminary training has become established. But this trend of longer and more rationalized training is no more than has become common in American society generally. In a country where hairdressers are certified, it would be astonishing were ministers not—yet not all ministers are. Those in marginal movements have credentials which frequently deny—on good traditional grounds—the relevance to religious practice of rational criteria of educational proficiency. Such cases apart, the *relative* loss of educational pre-eminence by the ministry over the course of three centuries has militated against a high professional standing. The recovery of graduate status by the main-stream Protestant denominations has been no more than participation in a widespread social trend in which even quite lowly occupations have shared. Even though the distinctive specialist training tends to be given in the three-year seminary period—a short time for a profession—its relevance to the actual tasks which a minister is to perform in the modern world is far from conspicuous.[48] Despite the deficiencies in respect to training, the ministry has conformed, at least in the outward and visible procedures, to the pattern instituted by a regular profession.

In other professions the strength of the individual's commitment is manifestly re-inforced by self-interest, opportunities for status and stipend. Among the ministry these orientations may not be so readily made manifest. Thus, much turns on the normative compliance of the individual to the Christian faith, and, decreasingly, to its denominational expression. But now some seminarians enter theological education without clear convictions or after entering become uncertain about their convictions. The loss of a sense of dedication in a professional is always a serious matter. It is difficult to say whether the aspect of professional defection or the loss of religious commitment might be most serious for the clergyman, but whatever the significance, theological seminaries have become places where significant numbers not only are not yet dedicated to the idea of the professional career, but also are not sure that they accept the values and purposes for which the profession is practiced.[49]

Ministerial Career-Orientation

"Humility forbids ambition, but zeal encourages achievement" is the piously casuistic way in which Father Fichter alludes to career orientation among the clergy.[50] The ministry appears, both in America and England, to enjoy much the same social esteem as the professions generally. Most entrants are, however, sons of fathers who have less than professional status. It appears that about 22 per cent of Catholic priests may be said to be intergenerationally upwardly mobile. Of a large sample of seminarians of the major Protestant denominations, 9 per cent were the sons of clergymen, and 14 per cent of other professionals. Allowing for some non-responses and doubtful cases, it appears that about 70 per cent were upwardly socially mobile.[51] Only 52 per cent of the Protestant seminarians assessed themselves as upwardly mobile in relation to father's occupation. According to usual ratings of the ministry as a profession, this appears, however, to be an underestimate. On educational comparisons, the extent of upward movement was even more pronounced. Among Protestants the degree of occupational succession is higher than in most professions; among Catholics there is a high incidence of relatives in the religious calling.[52]

Social mobility and achievement orientation are part of the dominant values of American society, but such ends have not traditionally been sought by the servants of God. Christian ideals have been toward posthumous social mobility, the earthly counterpart of which has, ideally, been the life of the saint, the man of faith, or the sanctified person. Fichter, again, sees an accommodation between traditional ideals and contemporary secular values when he avers that if the priest performs his social roles "with that degree of excellence that the role permits and demands, he cannot help but acquire higher social status."[53] American ministers do, in fact, manifest considerable status-striving. "It is the unusual minister who has no concern for his career and for the standards of promotion set by his denomination," is the judgment of one investigator who has devoted many years to the study of the ministry and the church.[54] The early mobility of entry into a higher profession persists, and the pressures of American society stimulate the further search for success. Traditional differences of denominational faith are surrendered as ministers pursue personal success goals, rather than devote themselves wholly to dedicated role-performances (moreover, the two frequently stand in some degree of conflict[55]). There is a pattern of shifting denominational allegiance, from less to more highly esteemed denominations; thus, the shift tends to be from the Baptist, Disciples, and Methodist, to the Presbyterian, Congregational, and Episcopal churches.[56] "High prestige congregations are especially likely to receive social climbers of different denominational backgrounds.[57]

In responding in this way, ministers manifest a more typically professional orientation than a dedication to a calling which transcends professional claims. Status, stipend, and security have come increasingly to dictate the character of the ministerial career pattern. We are told: "One clergyman decided to change to the Methodist Church because he liked the security offered by a system of guaranteed job-placement by a Methodist Conference. . . . Another minister left the same denomination because the transfer from parish to parish, with the consequent uprootedness in family life and severing of community ties, made him insecure."[58] In England, it would be scandalous for a minister to leave the denomination which embraced his faith (leaving aside a number of interdenominational developments most of which, even so, entail no abandonment of the minister's denomination of origin). Clearly, American ministers more nearly approximate branch managers who, while retaining their profession, move from one corporation to another, than men dedicated to distinctive tenets which they believe to be articles of truth. As long ago as the 1920's, the Presbyterians noted that 38 per cent of their accessions to the ministry over a five-year period had come from other denominations. In 1951–52, the Presbyterian Church, U.S.A., acquired 372 ministers from other denominations and lost 209 to them. Over a five-year period, the Congregationalists acquired about 40 per cent of their intake of ministers from other denominations. Even in the "small, relatively homogeneous Baptist General Conference, as of about 1950, one third to two fifths of the pastors had received no training in its schools; by 1958, rapid denominational growth had raised this proportion to one half."[59] The disappearance of ideological distinctiveness among the Protestant denominations has obviously facilitated the development of professionalism in the American ministry.

The clergy have not, however, ever evolved more than a rudimentary professional ethic of their own. What they have enjoyed has been an elevated version of the ethic supposedly binding on all the company of the faithful—less differentiated in Protestantism than in Catholicism, of course. What there is of such an ethic is embedded in Canon Law in the Catholic church, and thus not really amenable to the normal process of professional control. In Protestantism, the ideological position of each denomination has tended to define the activities and requirements of the ministry, especially where a distinctive ecclesiology has been prominent. Those more general prescriptions which prevail among Protestants appear to be predominantly injunctions in restraint of "poaching," amounting to genteel rules about not taking the bread out of one another's mouths.[60] Despite the ease of transfer of allegiance by individual ministers, the different denominations are still sufficiently organizationally distinct, and the ideological rationale of their distinction and of the minister's calling still sufficiently strong, to prevent the development of a full professional ethic. The proclamation of such an ethic would, of course, almost suggest that the Christian faith itself was not strong enough to ensure Christian conduct on the part of its supposedly most committed members.

The Ministerial Role

The professional role normally involves a strong fiduciary element: The clientele put their concerns into the trust of the professional they hire. This circumstance is evident in the confessional and counseling function, and, among many Protestant denominations, in the appointment of a minister whose performance cannot be adequately evaluated beforehand. But the diffuseness of the minister's role reduces the significance of this fiduciary element. There is little possibility of objectively measuring ministerial performance or the product of clerical labor. There is a low consequentiality of religious confidences, especially in a social context in which religion has lost its relevance for everyday life. There is less drama in the clergyman's role than in that of the doctor or the lawyer, who is consulted in situations of greater seriousness. Man's extremity is less likely, today, to be the clergyman's opportunity, than that of the medical or legal practitioner.

The specific expertise of the minister is not easily defined. Liturgical practice is evidently the distinctive professional claim of the Catholic priest, but even with renewed interest in liturgy, this is, ideologically, a difficult specialism for Protestants to claim. The role is in fact diffuse precisely because it operates in a community context and has steadily surrendered almost all its more specialized functions to other professions as they have emerged. Those aspects of the role which are most demanding in time and effort are often those which are least visible, and we know from various studies that the clientele demand that ministerial performance should be focused on those aspects of the role which they can see and can evaluate.[61] Those engaged in an occupation with a diffuse role, however, have difficulty in claiming the role-autonomy which a profession normally enjoys. The exposure of the ministry in America to the control of the hierarchy—churchly, or denominational and bureaucratic—on the one hand, and to the lay clientele on the other is well documented. That no precise criteria of measurement are available for the assessment of the ministerial performance; that those aspects of the role which *are* evaluated are largely publicly performed; that public success rests less on objective trained skills than on subjectively appreciated personality factors; and that the erosion of denominational ideologies has reduced the certainties of role-justification are all circumstances limiting the claim to professional expertise and role-autonomy.

The increasing division of clerical labor is, perhaps, in part an attempt to promote the full professional qualities of the ministry, as well as to grapple with increasingly complex social circumstances. The demand for more specialized education is a typical one for a group seeking to claim professional status. The demand is currently made for the ministry—specialization in such fields as Christian education, pastoral counseling, preaching, church administration, youth work, and more post-graduate study. Group ministries are the logical consequences of such developments—a heightening of colleague group solidarity, and an attempt to overcome the disadvantages both of the diffuse role and of its function of distributing affectivity in a society which is highly characterized by affective neutrality.[62] The expectation among the would-be reformers of clerical education of being able to rely more and more on scientific and social scientific skills, technology, and a "rational" division of labor, is an indication of the secularization of religious practice. Obviously, such developments have consequences not only for the clerical profession, but also for the comfort functions of the church. A more bureaucratic structure, of the kind which such specialization creates, will also have implications for the degree to which clergymen will be willing to regard broad social and political issues as having anything to do with their role or their mission.

Professional control of the institutional context is less clear-cut in the case of the clergy than of other professions. In hierarchically ordered churches, the clergy in some respects *are* the church and control its premises and institutions, although this is hierarchic control, rather than control vested in a body of professionals as such. In congregationally ordered churches, the clergy are in a much less effective position to dominate their local clientele in the running of the church, and in a denomination with conferential or synodic government, there is a shared participation of clergy and laity and a superimposition of denominational specialists.

Colleague-group solidarity hardly prevails among the ministry in the way in which it prevails in most professions: The organizational groupings, with their vestigial ideological justification, remain too strong for effective cross-denominational associations of the ministry to establish themselves except at the local level, or even for the acceptance of one common designation for the professional role (priest, clergyman, minister, preacher, pastor). Although many ministers transfer denominational allegiances and are often careless of denominational distinctions of doctrine, the denominations *per se* retain distinctive corporate identities strong enough to prevent the emergence of an effective national association of religious functionaries.[63] Without making explicit the terms of a professional ethic and the assumptions of achievement orientation concerns about status, security, and stipend, as well as those involving role-performance (which could be achieved only with difficulty in face of traditional ideological distinctions), such colleague-group solidarity could hardly find organized or overt expression.

III

The Profession, the Organization, the Clientele

It is evident from the foregoing that in many respects the ministry in America has adopted characteristics of a profession which have not been espoused by the clergy in England. It has done so by adopting rational criteria of training and performance, where these have been applicable, at times even at the cost of the distinctive traditional and charismatic elements of the ministerial role. The circumstance of competition between like organizations has, in Protestantism at least, facilitated the adoption of a model more characteristic of the modern work-order than of the religious sphere of activities. The routinization of training, of career structure, and the substantial, if not total, acceptance of career orientation have made the ministry more comparable to other occupations. The ancient claims to be the highest calling are not completely abandoned, but even in the Catholic case there has been a certain accommodation to the values of the temporal order. The acceptance of the professional model has perhaps operated to reduce denominational distinctiveness which today may rely more on organizational structure than on specific doctrinal and liturgical distinctions. Denominations, like other organizations, acquire survival goals, which maintain an institutional framework. Although these goals have anchorage in ideological distinctions, they draw less and less upon ideology for guidance to denominational practice, faith, or professional personnel. The brand-images have their ultimate referents in faith and liturgical traditions, but in an age which has seen an end of ideology and of mythology, these referents, even among those who are supposedly strongly committed, become very ultimate concerns indeed. Survival goals are associated with the occupancy of organizational positions. Where, except perhaps for a small nucleus of denominationally-committed laymen, there is easy transfer from one church confession to another, and where this is also true of the personnel, it seems likely that it is the higher personnel who most strongly identify with the organization and who have keenest commitment to its survival. The interests of higher personnel may be threatened by amalgamation (they may, of course, also be enhanced by it in certain circumstances). Where a threat is seen, the ideal of organizational survival may be more strongly promoted. In England, the shortage of ministers has persisted for more than a decade and grows steadily more acute; thus, the abundance of vacant statuses has perhaps diminished the threat to the personnel of the churches, and it is conspicuously they, and not the laity, who have promoted widely divergent, but simultaneous, ecumenical conversations.[64]

In summary, it appears that the ministry in America has moved as near as its distinctive role orientation will permit to the style of a profession. Like other professions, it is increasingly embodied in a bureaucratic system. And yet, the clergy, more than other professionals, depend on diffuse role-relationships, and have less technical expertise with which to be independent of the clientele's demands for counseling and therapeutic functions. It is of this more professionalized clergy, in more bureaucratized churches, that, despite its close dependence on its clientele, the prophetic function is demanded by those theologians who believe that otherwise Christianity is ideologically bankrupt. But the tolerance of a stable and affluent society for the prophetic role is limited, and the whole secular trend of institutionalization is contrary to it. Prophets arise in times of social distress, and distress in contemporary society appears to be widespread. But it is not the distress of communities, or of the society as a whole, which functions perhaps more perfectly than ever before. The current distress is that of highly atomized individuals, whose non-rational demands are unaccommodated in an increasingly impersonal, rational system. The problems are personal problems, demanding individual, affective solutions. Neither the enhanced efficiency of bureaucracies with their increasing reliance on technological devices, nor the call of the prophet for societal renewal appear to address themselves to problems of this kind. Prophecy itself is, perhaps, too much an ideological procedure for an organizational society. The clergy have lost the authority to undertake a prophetic role, and prophecy stands in stark contrast with the new professional style that the ministry has steadily adopted and the growing bureaucracy in which it is entrenched. The clergy have little freedom to coerce their clientele, whose patronage appears to depend on the persistence of the consolatory functions of the church. Participation tends to be segmental, with the church as the location for diverse interest groups that are involved in a wide range of organized activities. For most of these groups, neither religion nor the ancillary activities are more than peripheral facets of their lives. Thus, the church cannot be more than a half-effective surrogate for community and an inadequate base for community enterprise. There is no evidence of a "significant relationship between religious affiliation and theological sensitivity."[65] The general press of the cultural milieu has had far more pervasive influence on the psychic life and personality of believers than the feeling-tone or teachings of any particular denomination.[66] Men are induced to join a denomination not for its doctrine, but for some of the organized activities that it sponsors.[67]

Religious denominations are traditionally committed to a system of transcendental beliefs and to procedures of worship. Practice probably outlasts faith, and de-mythologizing has also begun to erode belief without, as yet, conspicuously affecting ritual. But denominations have evolved substitute ideologies that defend the organization as such, and the more committed laymen still have some denominational feeling,[68] even if it appears to be more of an organizational than a theological loyalty. Christian principles, as well as denominational creeds, have been replaced by the survival goals of particular movements. Thus, "the goal of 'making the world Christian' . . . becomes the 'building of two thousand new churches in the next decade.' The goal of 'winning people to Christ' becomes . . . 'getting our fair proportion of the population increase.' "[69] The organizations stand in competition one with another.

National churches necessarily tend to support the values of the societies in which they are established. The absence of a religious establishment in the United States, however, has not meant that all denominations were nonconformist, but rather, that all have conformed to American values. Few, if any value differences have remained among them. And this has not only affected matters such as patriotism and nationalism, but, with acceptance of the achievement orientation, pragmatism and materialism of American life, it has also brought a more pervasive conformity in their operation. Denominational pluralism, although it has offered Americans "the religion of your choice," has not in fact offered effective differences in intrinsic religious commitment, so much as the choice of brand-allegiances. And brand-loyalty has become notoriously weak. It is to these conformist and relatively homogeneous groups that bureaucratization occurs, ecumenism is canvassed, and the clarion call for prophetic nonconformity is given. If, as we have suggested, traditional religious institutions are essentially community-based,[70] and if they need to fulfill comfort functions to satisfy their clientele, each of these influences, were it successful, might, in its own way, sound the death knell for the churches.

REFERENCES

1. Will Herberg, *Protestant, Catholic, Jew* (New York, 1955); Peter L. Berger, *The Noise of Solemn Assemblies* (New York, 1961); Harvey Cox, *The Secular City* (New York, 1965); see also, Langdon Gilkey, p. 137 above.

2. Will Herberg, *Protestant, Catholic, Jew*; Talcott Parsons, *Structure and Process in Modern Societies* (Glencoe, Ill., 1960), pp. 295–321.

3. See the study of W. Wildrick Schroeder and Victor Obenhaus, *Religion in American Culture* (Glencoe, Ill., 1964). For persisting differences within denominations, see Charles Y. Glock and Rodney Stark, *Religion and Society in Tension* (Chicago, 1965), esp. Chapter 5.

4. See Daniel Callahan, p. 339 above.

5. The classic dichotomy of church and sect, drawn essentially from European history, was elaborated by Ernst Troeltsch, *Die Soziallehren der christlichen Kirchen und Gruppen* (Tübingen, 1912). It has passed, often with too little regard for the important differences of social circumstances, into the sociology of American religion. On social aspects of denominationalism in England, see Evelyn Douglas Bebb, *Nonconformity and Social and Economic Life, 1660–1800* (London, 1935); Wellman J. Warner, *The Wesleyan Movement in the Industrial Revolution* (London, 1930); Robert F. Wearmouth, *Methodism and Working Class Movements in England 1800–1850* (London, 1937); K. S. Inglis, *Churches and the Working Classes in Victorian England* (London, 1963); and David A. Martin, "The Denomination," *British Journal of Sociology*, Vol. 13, No. 1 (March, 1962), pp. 1–14.

6. Alasdair MacIntyre, *Secularization and Moral Change* (London, 1967), p. 68.

7. These values of American society are discussed in rather more general terms in Robin M. Williams, *American Society: A Sociological Interpretation* (New York, 1961), pp. 417ff. Among the distinctively American values that Williams discusses are achievement, success, activity, work, efficiency, practicality, progress, material comfort, equality.

8. For the case of Judaism, see Marshall Sklare, *Conservative Judaism* (Glencoe, Ill., 1955), pp. 90–98, 129–32; and Stephen Steinberg, "Reform Judaism: The Origin and Evolution of a 'Church Movement,'" *Journal for the Scientific Study of Religion,* Vol. 1 (Fall, 1965) pp. 117–29. For the way in which the rabbi's functions have approximated the model of the Protestant minister, see Jerome E. Carlin and Saul H. Mendlowicz, "The American Rabbi: A Religious Specialist Responds to Loss of Authority," in Marshall Sklare, *The Jews* (Glencoe, Ill., 1958), pp. 377–414.

9. The extent of diversity of theological beliefs among the laity of various denominations has been documented by Charles Y. Glock and Rodney Stark, *Religion and Science in Tension.* One example of their findings indicates, for instance, that among Congregationalists in their sample, 40 per cent had no doubt that Jesus was the divine Son of God; 28 per cent had some doubts, but felt that Jesus was divine; 19 per cent felt that Jesus was a great man but not a Son of God more than all men were the children of God; and 9 per cent thought that Jesus was only a man. Among Methodists, percentages responding in these ways were 54 per cent, 22 per cent, 14 per cent and 6 per cent; and among Episcopalians, 59 per cent, 25 per cent, 8 per cent and 5 per cent. Asked to respond to the assertion, "There is a life beyond death," of Congregationalists, 36 per cent said that this statement was completely true; 40 per cent said that it was probably true; 21 per cent said that it was probably not, or definitely not, true. Among Methodists the percentages of these responses were 49 per cent, 35 per cent and 13 per cent; and among Episcopalians, 53 per cent, 31 per cent and 13 per cent.

   That denominations hold together in the face of such diversity of doctrinal commitment indicates that these voluntary associations rely more on organizational bases of cohesion rather than on ideological bases; that doctrinal and ideological orientations have receded in significance even in movements which have as their primary *raison d'être* the proclamation (and dissemination) of true doctrines; that doctrine is relatively unimportant in determining values. Glock and Stark provide evidence that the dominant doctrinal cleavage is no longer represented in organizational structures, but lies between liberal and fundamentalist positions which, in considerable measure, cut across the various denominations (albeit unequally). Although this divergence in belief represents widespread heresy from a traditional point of view, it has little effect in the operation of the denominations: It represents a theological, but not a sociological, division, which in the *Gestalt* of modern religion is apparently of little consequence.

10. For discussion of this phenomenon in the context of other institutions, see Philip Selznick, *TVA and the Grass Roots: A Study in the Sociology of Formal Organization* (Berkeley and Los Angeles, 1949); Burton R. Clark, *Adult Education in Transition: A Study in Institutional Insecurity* (Berkeley and Los Angeles, 1956); and Burton R. Clark, "Organizational Adaptation and Precarious Values," *American Sociological Review,* Vol. 21 (1956) pp. 327–36.

11. This vagueness of class-consciousness is the obverse of the strong orientations toward social mobility, and the assumptions of equality (even

though ideals of equality and social mobility are somewhat contradictory one of another). The American ideology was that class distinctions did not exist in the United States. This is reflected in the approach to class of early American sociologists (for example, Giddings and Cooley) who emphasized its subjectivity. See Charles H. Page, *Class and American Sociology* (New York, 1940).

12. The evidence presented by Herbert W. Schneider (*Religion in 20th Century America* [Cambridge, 1952]), illustrates the absence of clear correlates of socio-economic status and denominational allegiance. The Christian Scientists (24.8 per cent of their members), Episcopalians (24.1 per cent) and Congregationalists (23.9 per cent) had the highest proportions of those assessed to be upper class. The Roman Catholics (66.6 per cent), Baptists (68 per cent) and Mormons (66.3 per cent) had the highest proportions of lower-class persons among the members. The Congregationalists, with the lowest proportion of lower-class members, had, nonetheless, more than 33 per cent of its members drawn from this class (p. 228). An indication of the significance of regional variation might be seen from comparing the findings of W. R. Goldschmidt, "Class Denominationalism in Rural California Churches," *American Journal of Sociology*, Vol. 49 (1944), pp. 348–55; with Lloyd Warner, *Democracy in Jonesville* (New York, 1949), pp. 153ff.

13. For an example of the association of local socio-economic status and church membership, and for the importance of socio-economic status for religious attitudes (in contrast to denominational affiliation, which was less clearly associated with religious attitudes), see Russell R. Dynes, "Church-Sect Typology and Socio-Economic Status," *American Sociological Review* (October, 1955), pp. 555–60. See also N. J. Demerath III (*Social Class in American Protestantism* [Chicago, 1965]), who suggests that within particular denominations the lower class may find sect-like, and the upper and middle classes, church-like, elements that appeal to them. It seems highly unlikely that this would be true either of the established church or of Nonconformist churches in Britain.

14. Not only is competition favored in the United States, but—and a European can only wonder at it—competition is advertised as a value in its own right, and as something that protects consumers. See, for example, the contemporary advertising of the Brand Names Foundation, Inc., New York, and their booklet, *What Kind of Future Do You Want?* Non-commercial institutions in America appear to stand in much more overtly competitive relation than is the case in Britain, and employ more direct pecuniary means in the competitive process: American universities offer a prime example.

15. See William McLoughlin, p. 45 above. The growth of new movements has provoked the comment of churchmen for some time, of course. See, for example, Harlan P. Douglass, "Cultural Differences and Recent Religious Divisions," *Christendom*, Vol. 10, No. 1 (Winter, 1945), pp. 89–105; and Charles S. Braden, "Why Are the Cults Growing?" *Christian Century*,

Vol. 50, Nos. 2–5 (Jan. 12, 19, 26, and Feb. 2, 1944), pp. 45–7, 78–80, 108–10, 137–40.

16. For a brief discussion of the operation and eventual failure of the ideals of comity, see Lyle E. Schaller, *Planning for Protestantism in Urban America* (New York, 1965), pp. 96–112.

17. See H. Richard Niebuhr, *Social Sources of Denominationalism* (New York, 1929); Earl D. C. Brewer, "Church and Sect in Methodism," *Social Forces,* Vol. 30 (1952), pp. 400–08; Walter G. Muelder, "From Sect to Church," *Christendom,* Vol. X, No. 4 (Autumn, 1945), pp. 450–62; and Oliver R. Whitley, "The Trumpet Call of Reformation" (St. Louis, 1959).

18. The tightness of the denominational molds of English Nonconformity emerges from a number of studies. It is particularly well brought out, for example, even for the various schisms within Methodism (the nonconformity of which was initially far less explicit than that of other Free churches), in Robert Currie, *Methodism Divided* (London, 1968).

19. Achievement-orientation was, obviously, implicit in the migration of Europeans to America, which was seen as a "land of opportunity." The ideology and the realities of social mobility are discussed comparatively in Seymour Martin Lipset and Reinhard Bendix, *Social Mobility in Industrial Society* (Berkeley and Los Angeles, 1959).

20. For a more extended discussion, see Bryan R. Wilson, *Religion in Secular Society* (London, 1966).

21. In 1855, Philip Schaff, a shrewd German assessor of American religion, wrote that it was "more Petrine than Johannean; more like busy Martha than like pensive Mary. . . . It expands more in breadth than depth. It is often carried on like a secular business, and in a mechanical and utilitarian spirit. It lacks the beautiful enamel of deep fervor and heartiness, the true mysticism, an appreciation of history and the church; it wants the substratum of profound and spiritual theology, and under the mask of orthodoxy it not infrequently conceals, without intending or knowing it, the tendency to abstract intellectualism and superficial rationalism." Philip Schaff, *America: A Sketch of Its Political, Social and Religious Character* (ed. Perry Miller) (Cambridge, 1961), p. 95.

22. Richard E. Moore and Duane L. Day, *Urban Church Breakthrough* (New York, 1966), p. 113.

23. Obviously what has been summarily described here is of highly differential incidence in American (as in European) society. What appears to be truer of America, however, is that the instrumental values: universalism, affective neutrality, achievement-orientation, mobility, and pragmatism—all of which are attributes of work activity in modern society—have been more influential throughout social and community life, and particularly in the urban environment that has been so rapidly expanding.

24. These characteristics of religion in suburban churches in America are noted by Martin E. Marty, *The New Shape of American Religion* (New York, 1958), pp. 100ff.

25. For a discussion of the symbolism and ritual associated with death, see W. Lloyd Warner, *The Family of God: A Symbolic Study of Christian Life in America* (New Haven, 1961), pp. 155–259; a more polemical discussion is to be found in Jessica Mitford, *The American Way of Death* (London, 1963), which is more concerned with mortuary practice. The embarrassment caused by death and the dilemma of bereavement in a society where the sanctity of Christian ideals has been lost will be found in Geoffrey Gorer, *Death, Grief and Mourning* (London, 1965).

26. For a full account, see Louis Schneider and Sanford M. Dornbusch, *Popular Religion: Inspirational Books in America* (Chicago, 1958).

27. On Chinese spirit-medium cults, see Alan J. A. Elliott, *Chinese Spirit-Medium Cults in Singapore* (London, 1955); on Umbandists, see Candido Procopio Ferreira de Camargo, *Kardecismo e Umbanda: Uma interpretação sociológica* (São Paulo, 1961); and Richard W. Brackman, "Der Umbanda-Kult in Brasilien," *Stadenjahrbuch*, Vol. 7, No. 8 (1959–60), pp. 157–73. On African witchcraft see, for example, John Middleton and E. H. Winter (eds.), *Witchcraft and Sorcery in East Africa* (New York, 1963).

28. Religious denominations are necessarily discriminatory in distinguishing their own members from outsiders. In an ecumenical age this point is less well taken, and in the democratic ethos of American society it has been somewhat eroded. It is readily asserted, quite outside of any Erastian context, that the commitment of the church(es) is to serve everyone, even though this idea is quite alien to the underlying assumptions of most denominations. See, for example, the bearing of the comment by Charles Y. Glock, "Afterword: A Sociologist Looks at the Parish," in Walter Kloetzli, *The City Church—Death or Renewal* (Philadelphia, 1961).

29. For a discussion of the "crimogenic" society, see John M. Martin and Joseph P. Fitzpatrick, *Delinquent Behavior: A Redefinition of the Problem* (New York, 1965). See also Robert K. Merton, *Social Theory and Social Structure* (Glencoe, Ill., 1957), pp. 131–94.

30. The distinction that is introduced here relates to the level at which institutions perform their vital functions. Although many social institutions operate locally—for example, political and educational systems—their higher functions are fulfilled through agencies which operate for the state itself. In Christianity, however, full salvation is always available locally (even if the church is centrally organized). The virtue of pilgrimages has lingered on, but the highest saintliness may be manifested anywhere. In religious systems in which an important central location for worship has existed, we can take it that this was in itself an attempt to make manifest the communal character of the entire religious body, as for example in the pilgrimage in Islam, and the centralization of temple worship in Judaism. A somewhat similar function may be performed in the temple rituals in contemporary Mormonism.

31. See, for example, the study by Paul M. Harrison, *Power and Authority in the Free Church Tradition* (Princeton, 1959).

32. British community studies give considerable indication of the persistence of community values: see, in particular, Michael Young and Peter Willmott, *Family and Kinship in East London* (London, 1956), as an indication of this in Britain's largest urban area. See Norbert Elias and J. L. Scotson, *The Established and the Outsiders* (London, 1965), for a semi-suburban community in a Midland city; and Margaret Stacey, *Tradition and Change* (London, 1960), for a market town. Although the processes of change are evident in all these studies, in none do they appear to have eroded community values in the way described even for small towns in America, where the strong image of community life has been found to have little accord with reality, for example, by Arthur J. Vidich and Joseph Bensman, *Small Town in Mass Society* (Princeton, N. J., 1958).

33. Charles Y. Glock, Benjamin B. Ringer and Earl R. Babbie, *To Comfort and To Challenge: A Dilemma of the Contemporary Church* (Berkeley and Los Angeles, 1967), p. 68.

34. *Ibid.*, p. 205.

35. Lyle E. Schaller, *Planning for Protestantism in Urban America*, p. 201.

36. But see, as particularly cogent examples, Harvey Cox, *The Secular City;* Gibson Winter, "Theological Schools: Partners in a Conversation," in Keith R. Bridston; and Dwight W. Culver, *The Making of Ministers* (Minneapolis, 1964), pp. 157–71.

37. C. Y. Glock, B. B. Ringer and E. R. Babbie, *To Comfort and to Challenge*, p. 7.

38. To take but one example, even a movement as radical as Congolese Kimbanguism returned, despite recrudescing revolutionism, to curing, witch-finding and similar concerns, See Efraim Andersson, *Messianic Popular Movements in the Lower Congo*, Studia Ethnographica Upsaliensia (Almquist and Wiksells Boktryckeri, 1958).

39. Gibson Winter, *The Making of Ministers*, p. 162.

40. For a brief discussion of the Industrial Areas Foundation, and of Christian opposition to it, see Richard E. Moore and Duane L. Day, *Urban Church Breakthrough*, pp. 65–80.

41. C. Y. Glock, B. B. Ringer and E. R. Babbie, *To Comfort and to Challenge*, in their thorough survey of Episcopalians provide documentation of those social groups who are likely to feel relative deprivation in a hedonistic society.

42. The shamefacedness of the church in contemporary society has been commented on by Peter L. Berger, "A Sociological View of the Secularization of Theology," *Journal for the Scientific Study of Religion*, VI (Spring, 1967), pp. 3–16:

An example of quite a different kind might be found in the style of the new coffee-house movement. "The coffee house is, in appearance, religiously neutral." The denomination's (perhaps Christianity's) "cherished position does not receive any special push. . . . A good case in point is 'Koinonia' coffee house at the University of Connecticut. On campus, religious views are seldom mentioned, and never given a forum. When 'Koinonia' first opened, its leaders were afraid to mention religion. After many weeks of programming, the leaders reasoned that a 'Christian' viewpoint had *at least as much right* to be heard as the variety of secularist viewpoints that were being presented by speakers and folk singers." John D. Perry, Jr., *The Coffee House Ministry* (Richmond, 1966), pp. 47 and 101 (my italics). The goal of the coffee-house is described as "to create a true model of pluralism" (p. 101) which seems a long way from the precedence that Christianity has traditionally claimed in society. The acquisition of the styles of the contemporary culture becomes a goal for the church, and the provision of the opportunity for men to express themselves accords with the American assumption that men have good inside them, given the chance to express it. It is an idea which has little pedigree in Christianity.

43. Benjamin B. Ringer and Charles Y. Glock, "The Political Role of the Church as defined by its Parishioners," *Public Opinion Quarterly*, Vol. 18 (1954–55).

44. Phillip E. Hammond and Robert E. Mitchell, "Segmentation of Radicalism —The Case of the Protestant Campus Minister," *American Journal of Sociology*, Vol. 71, No. 2 (September, 1965), pp. 133–43. Ernest Q. Campbell and Thomas F. Pettigrew (*Christians in Crisis: A Study of Little Rock's Ministry* [Washington, D.C., 1959]), found that it was younger ministers, and those recently arrived, who were more likely to defend their denomination's pronouncements on social and political issues. The longer a minister had served his congregation, the less likely was it that he would support desegregation during a crisis. Similarly, the more the church was involved in organizational concerns—a membership drive, fund-raising or a building program—the less likely was the minister to take a stand on this issue.

45. Leslie Paul, *The Deployment and Payment of the Clergy* (London, 1964). The Anglican Bishop of Southwell has recently denied that the ministry is a delegation of function or a convenient division of labor. "It cannot be conferred by human appointment, nor can a man choose it by his own will," F. R. Barry, *Vocation and Ministry* (London, 1958), p. 7. Kenneth Slack, "Ecumenism as Failure," *New Christian* (October 20, 1966), p. 15, reviewing Bryan R. Wilson, *Religion in Secular Society*, finds "religious professionals" a phrase with a "pejorative flavour."

46. Bryan R. Wilson, *Religion in Secular Society*, pp. 136–37, 156–60.

47. The estimates made by May for 1929–30 for Protestant theological seminaries suggest that between 47 per cent and 57 per cent of entrants were college graduates. A significant decline in the proportion appears to have occurred between 1872 and 1886. After 1930, the proportion appears to

have increased. See Mark Arthur May, *The Education of American Ministers,* Vol. 3 (New York, 1934), pp. 68ff.

48. For a strong critique, albeit from a rather particular conception of the ministerial role, see Gibson Winter, *The Making of Ministers.*

49. This point is commented on by James M. Gustafson, "The Clergy in the United States," *Dædalus,* Vol. 92, No. 4 (Fall, 1963), pp. 724–44.

50. Joseph H. Fichter, *Religion as an Occupation* (Notre Dame, 1961), p. 171.

51. J. H. Fichter, *ibid.,* p. 62; Keith R. Bridston and Dwight W. Culver, *Pre-Seminary Education* (Minneapolis, 1965), pp. 220, 223.

52. J. H. Fichter, "The Religious Profession," *Review of Religious Research,* Vol. 1 (Winter, 1960), pp. 89–101.

53. J. H. Fichter, *Religion as an Occupation,* p. 137.

54. Charles Y. Glock, "Afterword . . . ," p. 183.

55. For a discussion of the conflict between role-obligations and career-prospects in a diffuse and affective role, see Bryan R. Wilson, "The Teacher's Role: A Sociological Analysis," *British Journal of Sociology,* Vol. 13, No. 1 (March, 1962), pp. 15–32.

56. Robert Lee, *Social Sources of Church Unity* (Nashville, 1960), p. 93.

57. David O. Moberg, *The Church as a Social Institution* (Englewood Cliffs, 1962), p. 255.

58. Robert Lee, *Social Sources of Church Unity,* p. 91.

59. David O. Moberg, *The Church as a Social Institution,* p. 255; Robert Lee, *ibid.,* p. 90. With such extensive transfers of personnel, the speed of American ecumenism seems even less impressive than that in Britain, where transfers on anything like this scale are quite unknown.

60. See the two papers: Paul Hanly Furfey, "The Code of the Catholic Clergy," *Annals of the American Academy of Political and Social Science,* Vol. 297 (January, 1955), pp. 64–69; and Nolan B. Harmon, "Ethics and the Protestant Ministry," *ibid.,* pp. 70–75.

61. Samuel W. Blizzard, "The Minister's Dilemma," *Christian Century,* Vol. 73, No. 17 (April 25, 1956), pp. 506–10. Charles Y. Glock and Rodney Stark, *Religion and Society in Tension,* Chapters 6 and 7, pp. 123–50. The items most frequently demanded of their minister by the respondents of Schroeder and Obenhaus were "a good personality . . . warm, friendly, outgoing person," the ability to preach a good sermon, and exemplary conduct. W. Wildrick Schroeder and Victor Obenhaus, *Religion in American Culture,* pp. 186–89.

62. Expectations of this kind of development are sketched out by Lyle E. Schaller, *Planning for Protestantism in Urban America*, pp. 220ff. Even the lay volunteers in the coffee-house activity of the church should be trained in personality theory, the psychology of religion and group dynamics, according to John D. Perry, Jr., *The Coffee-House Ministry*, p. 89. Demands for this type of expertise and the exposure to courses on such subjects stand in marked contrast to the education of the clergy in England, where the psychology of religion and the sociology of religion are only now, and very tentatively, being introduced into the curriculum of theological education, and even then as strictly academic and abstract disciplines.

63. On the similarities of doctrine held among ministers of different denominations, see Robert Lee, pp. 84–85.

64. For a discussion, see Bryan R. Wilson, *Religion in Secular Society*, pp. 125–78. See also Ian Henderson, *Power without Glory: A Study in Ecumenical Politics* (London, 1967).

65. W. Wildrick Schroeder and Victor Obenhaus, *Religion in American Culture*, p. 156.

66. See, for a particularly vivid example of this, the study of American graduates among whom the Roman Catholics were shown to manifest the traditional attitudes of the Protestant ethic rather more fully than their Protestant contemporaries. Andrew Greeley, *Religion and Career* (New York, 1963).

67. Robert Lee, *Social Sources of Church Unity*, p. 86; N. J. Demerath III, *Social Class in American Protestantism*, p. 93.

68. C. Y. Glock, B. B. Ringer and E. R. Babbie, *To Comfort and to Challenge*, p. 186.

69. Oliver R. Whitley, *Religious Behavior: Where Sociology and Religion Meet* (Englewood Cliffs, 1964), p. 123. See also Donald L. Metz, *New Congregations: Security and Mission in Conflict* (Philadelphia, 1967), for a penetrating analysis of these problems as they confront newly established suburban churches.

70. Some of the new religious cults are, of course, not community-based at all, but capitalize on the impersonal milieu in which modern man in mass society must live. They make a virtue of highly impersonal associations—usually, be it noted, as the appropriate context for therapeutic activities. These "adjustment movements," however, fall outside of our purview.

EDWIN S. GAUSTAD

America's Institutions of Faith:
A Statistical Postscript

I

FOR MANY, to speak of faith's institutions is to speak of faith fossilized, frozen, and hopelessly irrelevant. When talking about "religion
in America," it is less embarrassing to suppose that this vague entity
has little if anything to do with Baptists or Lutherans or Catholics or
Elijah Muhammed. Organized religion is what one apologizes for,
not what one writes essays on.

Yet, as the authors in this volume recognize, the institutions of
faith in America possess the "traditions, resources, personnel" that
ultimately make religion in America worth talking about at all. Understandably, however, many writers are loathe to enter the denominational morass for fear of never finding their way out. Or, they
succumb to a more modern fear that "equal time" will not be given.
They read or remember that there are about two hundred and fifty
denominations in America, and clearly there's no time for that sort
of thing—so they pass on. But pluralism need not mean pandemo-
nium.

Pluralism is, of course, not new in American life, however much
the clichéd character of the word today would suggest otherwise.
The seventeenth century provided variety enough with Huguenots
in Charleston, Anglicans in Tidewater, Virginia, Catholics in St.
Mary's City, Swedish Lutherans along the Delaware, Quakers and
Presbyterians farther up the river, Dutch Reformed in Manhattan,
Puritans in New England, Baptists and Heaven-knows-what-else in
Rhode Island. Current, wide-eyed comment about pluralism must,
therefore, mean something more than mere variety.

Two additional implications, at least, are normally present. First,
pluralism is more than a word for Protestantism's wondrous pen-

chant for a seemingly endless spawning of new sects and divisions. Despite Lord Baltimore's early colonizing adventures, Protestantism pervaded the British colonies of North America from 1607 until well into the nineteenth century. And notwithstanding the remarkable diversity, a working harmony was often achieved, especially in the decades of the early national period. From at least 1850 on, however, Protestantism faced—and generally feared—the swelling ranks of Catholicism and Judaism. One then heard not calm discourse about pluralism, but rather strident cries about anarchy, popery, and shattered destiny. So pluralism today is a broad term, including not only the varieties of Protestantism, but also those of Judaism and Catholicism, and indeed of secularism as well.

Second, the term pluralism today carries no pejorative tone, perhaps not even a neutral tone. The word generally implies that this post-Protestant or even post-religious era is not to be deplored, feared, or fled from, but embraced and preserved. Pluralism is good, variety is nice, diversity is our chief national asset. Though value judgments have all but disappeared from academic prose, it is still possible to extoll the virtues of pluralism, the glories of diversity.

Even in America, nonetheless, pluralism has its limits. The institutions of religion are not scattered into hundreds of meaningless fragments. While the ecclesiastical patterns may bear some resemblance to a crazy quilt, the design is not totally devoid of meaning; moreover, some of the colors are beginning to run. Ten denominational families or traditions of Christendom account for 90 per cent of all church membership in America. And if the Jewish population is included, we account for 94 per cent of the total number with religious affiliation (see Table 1). Already pluralism begins to be more manageable.

The ten major traditions are Roman Catholic (46.25 million), Baptist (23.5), Methodist (14.25), Lutheran (8.75), Presbyterian (4.5), Christian (4.25), Episcopal (3.5), Eastern Orthodoxy (3.25) Latter-Day Saints (2), and the United Church of Christ (2). Judaism belongs in this list too, but since membership figures present special problems, it is necessary to speak of Jewish population rather than religious affiliation. These eleven groups, then, encompass all but about 6 per cent of institutional religion in America. In view of their magnitude, a word about each is appropriate.

Since 1850, Roman Catholicism has been the largest institution of faith in America. While membership figures can be endlessly (and fruitlessly) debated, it should only be noted that Catholic parishes follow a broadly inclusive principle in reporting membership. (In contrast, for example, Orthodox synagogues report only adult males; Baptist churches only "believing"—that is adult—members.) But that Catholicism is America's leading denomination cannot be doubted.

In addition to an impressive membership, Roman Catholics support the largest parochial-school system in America: over five million pupils in elementary and secondary schools. More than three hundred colleges and universities in the United States receive major support from this Church. Monastic establishments, less obvious on the American than on the European scene, are nevertheless a significant presence. There are more than 180,000 nuns in the nation—rather bewilderingly separated into about five hundred orders; more than one third of the Catholic priests in America, also, are members of some religious order.[1]

The Catholic family is about twice the size of the largest Protestant group, the Baptists. Yet, the number of Baptist churches is about four times that of the Catholic churches. Why? First, one

Table 1[2]

Major Denominational Families in America

Family	Membership (1965)	Per Cent of National Population
1. Roman Catholic	46,246,000	23.8
2. Baptist	23,631,000	12.2
3. Methodist	14,280,000	7.4
4. Lutheran	8,793,000	4.5
5. Presbyterian	4,418,000	2.3
6. Christian	4,268,000	2.2
7. Episcopal	3,411,000	1.8
8. Eastern Orthodox	3,160,000	1.6
9. United Church	2,070,000	1.1
10. Latter-Day Saints	1,969,000	1.0
Total	112,246,000	57.9
Jewish Population	5,600,000	2.9
Total	117,846,000	60.8

Inclusive church membership, all groups in the United States, in 1965 was 124,682,000. The ten listed above, together with the Jewish population, constitute 94 per cent of all those having any religious affiliation.

must recall the differences in membership accounting noted above; second, the nature and function of the local church in the two traditions varies greatly. While the Catholic edifice tends to serve many hundreds many times per week, the Baptist structure will often hold a few dozen for only an hour or two per week. Thus, many a Baptist church might in Catholic terms be a mission or a chapel or, in Spanish days, an *asistencia*. And though Baptist membership data can be endlessly debated too, no doubt remains that the Baptist family is Protestantism's largest in America.[3]

That size is due in part to the strong attraction the Baptist tradition has for the American Negro. Ironically, that denominational family which is most integrated in the whole (at least one third of the 23.5 million Baptists are Negroes) is but rarely integrated in its several parts. The last Federal Census of religion (1936) showed that 67 per cent of all Negro church members were Baptist (another 25 per cent were Methodist, leaving less than 10 per cent for all other denominations). While mobility, disillusionment, the Black Muslims, and a growing secularity may have altered this percentage, Negro Baptist churches and Negro Baptist leaders—for example, Martin Luther King and Adam Clayton Powell—still occupy prominent positions on the contemporary scene.

The other member of the family chiefly responsible for its notable size is white: the Southern Baptist Convention. Established in Georgia in 1845, this group has enjoyed phenomenal growth, particularly in the twentieth century. Almost one half of all Baptists in America (and there are about thirty groups) belong to this one Convention. Still predominantly "Southern" in outlook and geographic scope, this branch has moved beyond the boundaries of region. Current growth rate (1.7 per cent) is now only slightly higher than the growth rate of the national population (1.3 per cent).

Thanks to a 1939 merger, much of the Methodist family, more nearly united than the Baptists, gathers under a single organizational umbrella. "The Methodist Church" accounts for more than ten million of Methodism's 14.25 million total, with three large Negro bodies contributing almost three million more. A merger with the Evangelical United Brethren Church, now under way, will bring another three quarters of a million members into the family. (Only a predominantly German ethnic background has kept EUB from joining the Methodist household long before now.) After that merger, Methodism will still not be the largest Protestant body. It will, however, be by far the largest group participating in the significant discussions relating to a new American church: the Consultation on Church Union (see Table 2 below).

Before proceeding with the denominational families, it is appropriate at this point to comment on the religious affiliation of the Negro—appropriate because that affiliation is chiefly within the three groups named above. The Baptists continue to dominate, as

Table 2

Principal Mergers 1939–1967

Constituent Bodies	Resulting Body	Date
Methodist Episcopal Church; Methodist Episcopal Church, South; Methodist Protestant Church	The Methodist Church	1939
Congregational Christian Churches; Evangelical and Reformed Church	United Church of Christ	1957
Presbyterian Church, U.S.A.; United Presbyterian Church of North America	United Presbyterian Church in the U.S.A.	1958
American Lutheran Church; Evangelical Lutheran Church; United Evangelical Lutheran Church	The American Lutheran Church	1960
United Lutheran Church; Augustana Lutheran Church; Finnish Evangelical—Suomi Synod; American Evangelical Church	The Lutheran Church in America	1962

Consultation on Church Union (1962—)

Constituent Bodies	Resulting Body	Date
United Presbyterian Church in the U.S.A. Presbyterian Church in the U.S. Episcopal Church United Church of Christ Christian Churches (Disciples of Christ) Methodist Church African Methodist Episcopal Church African Methodist Episcopal Zion Church Christian Methodist Episcopal Church Evangelical United Brethren	No name yet chosen	No date yet named

Figure 1[4]

Negro Church Membership in America
1965

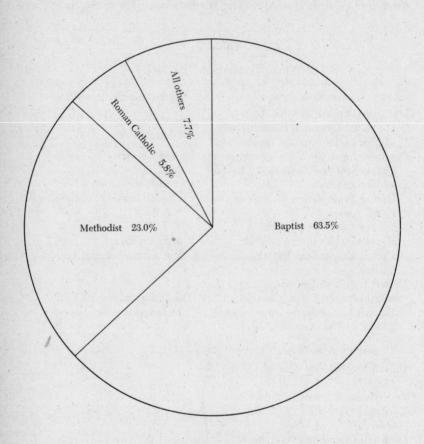

All others 7.7%

Roman Catholic 5.8%

Methodist 23.0%

Baptist 63.5%

Membership in millions

Negro Baptists	7.66
Negro Methodists	2.75
Negro Roman Catholics	.75
All others (estimated)	1.00

they have for more than one hundred years. About two thirds of all Negro church members are Baptists, the vast majority of this number being found in one of two Conventions: the National Baptist Convention of America (approximately 2.75 million members), or the National Baptist Convention, U.S.A., Incorporated (approximately 5.5 million members). Three million Negro Methodists are divided among four major groups: African Methodist Episcopal (about 1.25 million), African Methodist Episcopal Zion (over 1 million), Christian Methodist Episcopal (about .5 million), and the controversial "Central Jurisdiction" of The Methodist Church (over .3 million). Baptists and Methodists together account for four fifths of the total Negro church membership. Roman Catholicism, having made great gains among American Negroes since World War II, is the only other denomination with a sizable Negro membership: about .75 million. All other groups, including small pentecostal sects, the Black Muslims,[5] and predominantly "white" ecclesiastical bodies,[6] probably would not exceed one million in total number (see Figure 1).

America's nearly nine million Lutherans have most dramatically reversed the rules of that all-American game of divide and disappear. From some twenty-four distinct organizations at the beginning of the present century, Lutheranism has reduced its diversity to three major entities: the American Lutheran Church (over 2.5 million), the Lutheran Church in America (over 3 million), and the Lutheran Church–Missouri Synod (almost 2.75 million). Having conquered divisions due largely to varied ethnic origins and immigration patterns, Lutheranism stands ready to make a more powerful impact on American culture.[7] In the political arena, as will be noted below, this is not now the case.

Presbyterians, like the Baptists and unlike the Methodists, remain divided, North and South, along lines that hardened just before the Civil War. Unlike the Baptists, however, the northern branch of Presbyterianism (U.S.A.) is far larger than the southern (U.S.). And in 1958, northern Presbyterianism did consummate a merger with a small Scottish communion to form the United Presbyterian Church, U.S.A.—a body now comprising more than three fourths of all the nation's Presbyterians. The southern church of about one million members is the only other significant group, and family ties —despite organizational division—are still rather strong.[8] A blood kinship is heartily acknowledged, and a unity in purpose is often evident.

Such a sense of kinship is found less often today in the two major branches of the "Christian" tradition: the Disciples of Christ and the Churches of Christ. Though originating in America only a little more than a century ago and breaking apart only a half-century ago, the two groups have moved further from each other. The Disciples (2 million), who demonstrate a strong ecumenical orientation, have recently moved in the direction of greater denominational unity. The Churches of Christ (2.25 million), who avoid all interdenominational involvements, have continued to cherish the utter autonomy of separate congregations. Thus, to speak of "family" here is to talk more of Alexander Campbell and the traditions of the past than of *rapprochement* and the promise of the future.

Episcopalians in America, like Roman Catholics, enjoy a single ecclesiastical structure; in these instances, then, "family" and "organization" become synonymous terms. Though seventh on the list of the "top ten" (see Table 1), the Protestant Episcopal Church has for most of its history exercised an influence out of proportion to its numbers. The Anglican Church in colonial America made its voice heard in politics, education, and economy—vying with Congregationalism as prime mover in colonial affairs. The Revolution temporarily tumbled Anglicans from their eminence, but by the middle of the nineteenth century the climb back to prominence had been made. Unlike most other groups cited in Table 1, the Episcopal Church does not numerically dominate any given area of the country; rather, its presence is felt via wealth and prestige in every region.

Eastern Orthodoxy has been beset, as has Lutheranism, by ethnic diversity and organizational division. Unlike Lutheranism, Orthodoxy has not yet reversed this proliferation. Still too new to a disestablished environment, still too attached to Old World politics, the Eastern Churches confront an Americanization process already completed for most other ecclesiastical bodies. The Greek Archdiocese of North and South America (1.75 million) is the largest unit within this family, but Russian, Syrian, Rumanian, Bulgarian, Ukranian, and Carpatho-Russian groups also enjoy sizable membership. Notwithstanding such symbolic actions as participation in presidential inaugurations, Orthodoxy stands largely aloof from the political and cultural life of the nation—though its rich colors add brilliance to that crazy-quilt pattern of American religion.

The United Church of Christ is the modern form in which traditional Congregationalism now appears. A colonial giant, Congregationalism was badly outdistanced in the nineteenth century by such front-runners as the Baptists and the Methodists. In the present century, Congregationalism began to recoup its relative numerical loss by setting out on a deliberate ecumenical path. In 1931, Congregationalists merged with the "General Convention of the Christian Church" and in 1957 with the "Evangelical and Reformed Church." In the decade since that last merger, the United Church— as its title hints—has actively sought and promoted church union of far broader compass than any yet attained.

The tenth family noted in Table 1, like the sixth, is a product of America's own religious fecundity. The Church of Jesus Christ of Latter-Day Saints, though originating in the East (New York), is today primarily a phenomenon of the West. And in the "Utah Church" (1.75 million), as the principal member of the family is sometimes called, the geographical particularity that prevails is unrivaled by any other religious group in America.[9] Utah and the contiguous counties in Nevada, Idaho, and Wyoming are indisputably "Mormon territory," often to the extent that entire counties are devoid of any other church or sect. Such regionalism may be compared with, but not equaled by, the Baptist concentration in the Southeast, the Lutheran majorities in the Midwest, and the Catholic dominance in the Northeast and the Southwest.[10]

Finally, Judaism constitutes one of the nation's major religious families, though the "family" designation is even more complex here. There are not only denominational differences (Orthodox, Conservative, Reform), but differences between the Jew identified as such on religious grounds and the Jew identified on other grounds. Statistical data are generally given in terms of Jewish population (note Table 1), not synagogue membership. The population figure is clearly too large for Judaism, but a membership figure of adult males (for example, 205,000 Orthodox Jews in 1964) is just as obviously too small. The academic mind is happy to conclude that the truth "is somewhere in the middle"; greater precision is elusive.[11]

Judaism, like Mormonism, has a geographical concentration too. In general, it is urban; in particular, it is in the Northeast. One half of the nation's Jews reside in five counties in New York and eight in New Jersey. One third of the Jewish population lives in New York City itself. After New York (14.06 per cent) and New Jersey (5.27 per cent), the states with the greatest percentage of Jewish citizens are Massachusetts (4.54 per cent), Maryland (4.22 per cent), Pennsylvania (3.87 per cent), Connecticut (3.68 per cent), California

Figure 2[12]

Major Denominational Families in 1965

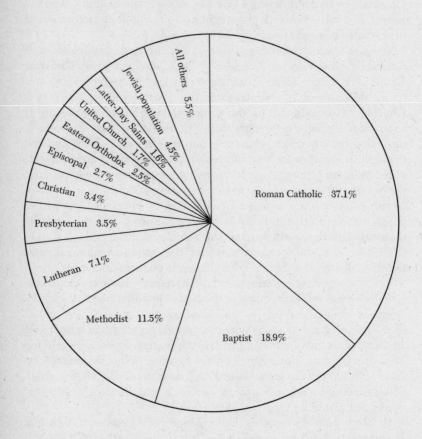

Total inclusive church membership, 1965

124,682,000

(3.48 per cent), Illinois (2.85 per cent), Rhode Island (2.69 per cent), and Florida (2.27 per cent).

America's religious patterns can, therefore, be understood largely in terms of these eleven families (see Figure 2 above), all standing within the Judeo-Christian tradition. Buddhism (especially Zen), Hinduism (especially Vedanta), and Islam are present, but are statistically insignificant—as are the cults that draw on or pervert these traditions. The Black Muslim movement may constitute an exception to the above, but its relationship to world-wide Islam is tenuous at best. It stands more as a rejection of Christianity as the white man's religion than as an embrace of the "five pillars" of Islam.

Even the eleven major families may a decade hence be reduced in number. The most dramatic reduction on the horizon would result from discussions related to the Consultation on Church Union. Stemming from a suggestion offered in 1960 by Eugene Carson Blake (then Stated Clerk of the United Presbyterian Church, U.S.A.; now president of the World Council of Churches), the Consultation has moved deliberately, perceptively ahead in its effort to create a church "truly Catholic, truly evangelical, and truly reformed." With the publication of "Principles of Church Union" in 1966, the cooperating denominations attracted others to active participation.[13] By mid-1967, the number of full participants had grown to ten denominations, including all or part of five of the ten families under discussion (see Table 2).

Should the Consultation be successful, the resulting church of at least twenty-five million would be the largest Protestant denomination in the United States. The two major Protestant groups not participating at present are the Baptists and the Lutherans. (One half of the "Christian" family is in the Consultation—the Disciples; the other half—Churches of Christ—remains outside.) It is conceivable, then, that in the next decade, America's Protestantism will be arranged into three major divisions: Baptists, Lutherans, and a "United Church."

II

We have been considering the basic data of America's institutions of faith—at least 94 per cent of them. The second and harder question, of course, remains: What do these facts mean? If 125 million Americans are members of a church or synagogue, what difference does this make to them, or to their neighbors, or to the world? How much culture is molded by 23.5 million Baptists? How much personal behavior is altered by the convictions of 46.25 million Catholics? How many needs of the individual or of the society are met by millions of Presbyterians, Lutherans, Methodists, and Mormons? The academic mind, in addition to finding truths always in the middle, likes to raise questions it cannot answer. And these fall rather neatly into that category. Yet, some meaningfulness in membership can be suggested here.

The 125 million church members (64 per cent of the total population) may be that and nothing more: mere names on a roster. That much membership is nominal is hardly surprising, whether the subject of discussion be church, club, or political party. What may be surprising is that even more adult Americans than this 64 per cent identify themselves as attached in some way—if only by sentiment or preference—with a particular denominational tradition. Remarkably, more than 96 per cent somehow, in some degree, relate themselves to the major religious traditions of Judaism or Christianity (see Table 3). To some, it is equally remarkable that church membership in America has steadily increased, not declined, over the course of the last one hundred years—and even longer (see Figure 3).

Table 3[14]

Religious Preferences in America, 1957

(civilian population, 14 years old and over)

Family	Number Identifying Themselves	Per cent of population (adult)
1. Roman Catholic	30,669,000	25.7
2. Baptist	23,525,000	19.7
3. Methodist	16,676,000	14.0
4. Lutheran	8,417,000	7.1
5. Presbyterian	6,656,000	5.6
6. "Other Protestant"	23,678,000	19.8
7. Jewish	3,868,000	3.2
8. "Other Religion" (includes Eastern Orthodoxy)	1,545,000	1.3
9. No religion	3,195,000	2.7
10. Religion not reported	1,104,000	0.9
Total population 14 years and over	119,333,000	100.0

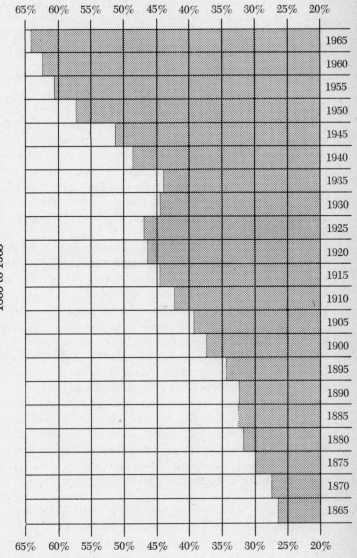

Figure 3[15]

Percentage of National Population with Religious Affiliation
1865 to 1965

Furthermore, a sizable degree of involvement is evident and is in part measurable. For example, church attendance is the pattern for nearly one half of the nation in any "typical" week. (In 1955 and 1958, the percentage was as high as 49 per cent.) According to Gallup polls, attendance in church or synagogue has in the past generation never fallen below one third of the total population of the country. Catholics are the best churchgoers (68 per cent), Protestants a poor second at 38 per cent, and Jews poorest with 22 per cent. Among Protestants, Lutherans have the highest rate of attendance (43 per cent), Episcopalians the lowest (31 per cent). The higher the level of education, the greater is the likelihood of church attendance. And the secular city may not really be so secular, for the greatest level of church attendance is in urban centers of one-half million or more inhabitants. Fewer citizens attend church in the West than in any other region of the nation, but even western America's record of attendance (33 per cent) looks excellent when compared with the Anglicans of England (7 per cent) or the Lutherans of Sweden (3 per cent).

The voluntary principle has often been cited as the defining feature of American religion. Nowhere is that principle more severely tested than in the matter of financial support—and regularly the test is passed. In 1966, the principal Protestant groups collectively contributed about three billion dollars to local and benevolent causes. (The highest per capita giving was by the Free Methodist Church of North America—$358 per member—as compared, for example, with that of the Methodist Church—$59 per member.) Another billion dollars were expended for the construction of religious buildings in 1966. Jewish philanthropy flows through a myriad of federations, services, and appeals, an estimated two and one-half billion dollars having been raised by this minority in the quarter-century from 1940 to 1965. The contribution of America's Catholics has been such as not only to support their churches, schools, seminaries, and hospitals at home, but also to provide, in the 1960's, approximately one half of Catholicism's total missionary budget around the world.

To be sure, commitment, relevance, and involvement cannot be established solely by data on church preferences, church attendance, and church support. Such evidence can only warn against accepting easy generalizations regarding "nominal" religion; the burden of proof begins to shift, and the defining of terms begins to be more refined.

The major question remains: what of the churches' influence in American society, what of their cultural leadership, what of their social pecking order? Again, much rests upon subjective guesses and casual hunches. A folk humor, sometimes translated into humorless propositions, avers that as one moves up a socio-economic scale, he automatically shifts his affiliation from Baptist (or whatever) to Presbyterian to Episcopalian to Unitarian (or whatever). The joke and the proposition have to change names from one part of the country to another, from one period of time to another. Social status does vary according to time and place. In one region, the power structure is Baptist; in another, Dutch Reformed; in another, Roman Catholic. In one era, the intellectual leadership is Unitarian; in another, Presbyterian; in another, Jewish. In one town, the economic stratum served by the Salvation Army may in another be served by Episcopalians. Pecking orders there may be, but the names and numbers constantly change: Only the name of the game remains the same.[16]

One measure of cultural impact may be essayed in the political realm. To examine the religious affiliation of the members of the present (Ninetieth) Congress and the current governors is to suggest some degree of cultural contribution on the part of the several denominations. There is, of course, an element of religion in America which regards increased cultural involvement as a sign of decreased spiritual integrity. But without passing judgment on that thorny

Table 4[17]

Political Leadership in America, 1967, by Denominational Family

Senate	House	Governorships
1. Methodist 24%	1. Roman Catholic 22%	1. Methodist 20%
2. Episcopal 15%	2. Presbyterian 17%	2. Roman Catholic 18%
3. Roman Catholic 13%	3. Methodist 16%	3. Episcopal 16%
4. Presbyterian 12%	4. Episcopal 12%	4. Baptist 12%
5. Baptist 12%	5. Baptist 10%	5. Presbyterian 10%
6. United Church 6%	6. United Church 5%	6. United Church 10%
7. LDS (Mormon) 4%	7. Jewish 4%	7. Lutheran 6%
8. Lutheran 3%	8. Christian 3%	8. Christian 4%
9. Unitarian-Universalist 3%	9. Lutheran 2%	9. LDS (Mormon) 4%
10. Jewish 2%	10. LDS (Mormon) 1%	. . . .
(all others 6%)	(all others 9%)	(no others)

125

issue, it is still possible to measure the degree of political leadership provided by or offered to the major religious traditions (see Table 4 above).

Looking first at the United States Senate in 1967, one quickly notes that one fourth of the Senate is Methodist. Since Methodism represents only 6 per cent of the national population, this denomination's political involvement is clear. Similarly, Episcopalians account for 15 per cent of the Senate's membership, but for only 2 per cent of the national population. Similar disproportion prevails for the Presbyterians (12 per cent of the Senate), for the United Church (6 per cent), and for the Mormons (4 per cent), all of whom have percentages of representation four times as great as their population ratio would warrant. The prize in this regard is held by the Unitarians who, though less than one tenth of 1 per cent of the population, account for 3 per cent of the Senate membership. Baptist and Jewish representation in the Senate (12 per cent and 2 per cent respectively) is about equal to their population ratio. But Roman Catholics (13 per cent) and Lutherans (3 per cent) are underrepresented, while Eastern Orthodoxy is totally absent from the Senate list. This pattern of underrepresentation persists in the case of Eastern Orthodoxy and to a lesser extent in the case of Lutheranism.

In the 435-member House of Representatives, Roman Catholicism has the largest denominational bloc, with ninety-six Catholic Congressmen. This proportion, 22 per cent, is almost precisely the fraction of the national population which is Catholic. There are, however, seventy-one Presbyterian Congressmen, five times as many as some sort of "religious re-apportionment" would allow. The next largest group is Methodist (sixty-nine), two and one-half times as many as their population ratio. Episcopalians (fifty-three) have six times as many Representatives as sober statisticians would predict, and the United Church (twenty-three), five times as many. Again, Baptist (forty-three) and Jewish (sixteen) membership in the House, as in the Senate, is about what their ratio within the national population would suggest. The same is true of the Christian Churches (seventeen) and of the Mormons (nine). Lutheranism (ten) has less than one half its legitimate expectation, while Eastern Orthodoxy (two) is once more woefully deficient.

Among the fifty governors, only nine denominational families are represented—all from those listed in Table 1. The only one missing from the top ten is, as now may be expected, Eastern Orthodoxy. Also, none of the fifty governors is Jewish. There are ten Methodist governors, nine Roman Catholic, eight Episcopal, six Baptist, five each for the Presbyterians and Congregationalists (United Church), three Lutherans, and two each for the Disciples (Christian) and the Latter-Day Saints (Mormons). From these data, four observations can be made.

First, denominational size and political affluence show no close correlation. The groups mentioned in Table 1 are surely and repeatedly represented in both Houses of Congress and in the states' gubernatorial mansions as well. But the order and magnitude of their representation shows considerable disarray. The largest group in the Senate is third in the country, while the Senate's second largest group is the country's seventh. Similarly, the group that ranked second in the House ranks fifth in the nation, while the fifth-ranking group in the House ranks second in the nation.

Second, while 36 per cent of the general population is not affiliated with any church or synagogue, that percentage drops sharply in the political world. In the House those who report no religious affiliation are less than 1 per cent, in the Senate just 1 per cent, and among the governors, it is 0 per cent. In view of this situation, the 36 per cent of America's non-affiliated may argue that it is the most underrepresented minority in the country—even more neglected than Eastern Orthodoxy. And the cynical aspiring politician, studying Table 4, might argue that he should either be a Catholic or a Methodist, or, failing that, then a Unitarian—unless he were running for governor.

Third, while America's entry into the post-Protestant era (or even a post-Christian one) is widely acclaimed, the political stratum of American life does not appear to have entered that era. Eighty per cent of the Senate, 78 per cent of the governors, and over 70 per cent of the House is Protestant (in all cases, Mormons, who do not consider themselves Protestants, are not included in these totals). This heavy Protestant dominance is due, as has been noted above, to the disproportionate representation enjoyed by certain Protestant groups: namely, Methodists, Presbyterians, Episcopalians, and Congregationalists (United Church).

Fourth, Lutheranism and Eastern Orthodoxy still suffer some degree of cultural isolation. The fourth largest religious family in America, Lutheranism lags far behind smaller Protestant groups. Its low representation in the House of Representatives is particularly surprising; of those states where Lutheran population is heavily concentrated, only Minnesota sent a significant delegation (three) of Lutherans to the House. The explanation lies, of course, in the ethnic, linguistic, and organizational diversity that has not only divided Lutherans from one another but, to some degree, separated Lutherans from the surrounding culture. Since that complex of problems is now being resolved, Lutheran political participation is almost certain to rise sharply in the years just ahead.

Alone among the top ten, Eastern Orthodoxy is unrepresented either in the Senate or on the governor's roster. In the House, it is represented for the first time in 1967. Ethnic differences among the Orthodox are often compounded by competing political and ecclesiastical loyalties, both at home and abroad. Also, the "Eastern" of Eastern Orthodoxy is more than a convenient title: It is a reminder that the later Roman and medieval periods, the Renaissance, the Reformation, and the Enlightenment are not parts of its heritage. Understandably, both Orthodox laity and clergy sometimes find dialogue with their "Western" neighbors frustrating and difficult. Until, in something like the pattern of Lutheranism, Orthodoxy begins to conquer its internal divisions, it is not likely to conquer its cultural insulation nor its politically dis-enfranchised status.

The wave of rapidly growing pentecostalism and other "Third Force" movements has yet to leave its mark on the political shorelines. Seventh-Day Adventists elected their first Representative in 1966, while Churches of God, the Church of God in Christ, Assemblies of God, Nazarenes, and Jehovah's Witnesses have yet to make even that modest debut. Many of these groups are, of course, small when compared with those listed in Table 1; together, however, the denominations named in the previous sentence had in 1965 a membership of about 2.5 million—placing them as a group ahead of both the Latter-Day Saints and the United Church. While these Third Force movements share some common elements in purpose and approach, it is misleading to treat them as a single-minded entity. And it is their many-mindedness which directly affects their social responsibility and their cultural impact.

The same may be said of American religion as a whole, and surely of Protestantism in particular. Cultural impact does appear to be related to unity of purpose if not to uniformity of organization. Today's ecumenical trend is, therefore, among other things an agonizing response to the impotence which fragmentation and incessant schism bring. Or if not that, it is a counterthrust directed against a type of ecumenicity either feared or deplored. Within American Protestantism, three co-operative agencies endeavor to speak for more than a single ecclesiastical tradition. Of these three, the National Council of Churches of Christ is by all odds the most significant. With a current membership of forty-two million, the National Council includes all or part of the seven Protestant families cited in Table 1. (Neither the Latter-Day Saints nor, of course, the Roman Catholics are included among the Protestants, and neither group is within the Council; Eastern Orthodoxy, on the other hand, is in the Council, or at least about three fourths of its total membership is.) More Baptists and Lutherans are outside the National Council than are inside; nevertheless, that ecumenical body can operate in the name of about two thirds of all America's Protestantism.

The National Association of Evangelicals, with a membership of about two million, demonstrates a markedly conservative theological orientation. Among its affiliates are such groups as the Free Methodists, the Evangelical Mennonite Church, the Ohio Yearly Meeting of Friends, and—largest of all—the Assemblies of God (a half million members). The third co-operative agency, the American Council of Christian Churches, stands politically far to the right of the National Association of Evangelicals. This group also sets itself deliberately against the basic direction of the National Council. Its quite modest membership is drawn from a dozen or so groups, ranging in size from the General Association of Regular Baptist Churches (121,000 members in 1960) to the Fundamental Methodist Church (1,000 members), and ranging in ideology from fundamentalism to the Militant Fundamental Bible Churches—of which there were thirteen in 1960 (see Figure 4 below).

Apart from politics, what other kinds of cultural force are exerted by America's denominations? Answers are neither easy nor uniform. And the response will often depend on the special aspect of culture under examination. Is it music? Consider the power of the Lutheran's tradition of great music or of the Negro Baptist's blend of jazz, hymn, and folk song. Is it art? Note the leadership manifest in Catholicism, both East and West, especially in the Benedictine direction of a liturgical renaissance. Is it education? Try to write American history without attention to the Presbyterian and Congregational stimulation and support in this area of national culture. Is it literature? Consider the remarkable flowering of Jewish letters, particularly in the last thirty years. None of these cultural catalysts bears much direct relationship to family size or to financial contribution, and none lends itself to unarguable measurement. But all of them—including the family size, the financial contributions, the

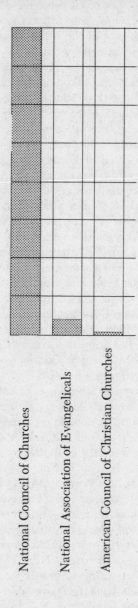

Figure 4[18]

Protestant Cooperative Organizations in America
1960

National Council of Churches

National Association of Evangelicals

American Council of Christian Churches

Membership in Millions

stated preferences—show religion in America to be now, as in the past, intimately tied to what goes on in synagogue and church, in synod and conference. One cannot, after all, ignore everything that transpires under parochial labels and family names even though these do, on occasion, appear as a stumbling block and an offense to all.

REFERENCES

1. See the *Official Catholic Directory 1966* (New York, 1966), fold-out chart.

2. These data are to be found, though not in this form, in Constant H. Jacquet, Jr. (ed.), *Yearbook of American Churches 1967* (New York, 1967), pp. 198–210.

3. The Baptist "family," to be sure, includes some twenty-nine groups, but four fifths of the total membership is in only four groups: the Southern Baptist Convention (10.75 million), the National Baptist Convention, U.S.A., Inc. (5.5 million), the National Baptist Convention of America (2.75 million), and the American Baptist Convention (1.5 million).

4. *Ibid.;* see also C. H. Jacquet, *Yearbook of American Churches 1967*, and Joseph H. Fichter, "American Religion and the Negro," *Dædalus,* (Fall, 1965).

5. C. Eric Lincoln in *The Black Muslims in America* (Boston, 1961) estimated the membership as "more than 100,000" in 1960. But the vigor of that membership, which is mainly young and male, gives an impression of even greater size.

6. The Protestant Episcopal Church, for example, has about eighty thousand Negro members (out of a total membership of about 3.5 million), the Congregationalists or United Church about forty thousand (out of a membership of two million). See Harry V. Richardson, "The Negro in American Religious Life," *American Negro Reference Book,* ed. John P. Davis (New York, 1966).

7. With one exception, the other Lutheran bodies are quite small. The exception is the rigorously conservative Wisconsin Evangelical Lutheran Synod which in 1964 reported a membership of 358,000.

8. All other Presbyterian bodies in America together have a membership of about 150,000.

9. There are only two major Mormon groups, the "Utah Church" having nine tenths of the total membership. The Reorganized Church of Jesus Christ of Latter-Day Saints has fewer than 170,000 members, with three other tiny schisms accounting for a total of about 5,000 members.

10. See E. S. Gaustad, *Historical Atlas of Religion in America* (New York, 1962), fold-out map.

11. See Morris Fine and Milton Himmelfarb (eds.), *American Jewish Yearbook 1965* (New York and Philadelphia, 1965), p. 23. The relative strength of Orthodox, Conservative, and Reform sentiment in America may be partially gauged by a three-city study reported by Alvin Chenkin in the above volume. One half to two thirds of those interrogated expressed a preference for Conservative Judaism over the two competing "denominations." In Camden, N. J. (1964), the indications of preference were as follows: 8 per cent Orthodox, 66 per cent Conservative, 22 per cent Reform. In Detroit, Mich. (1963), this was the response: 17 per cent Orthodox, 49 per cent Conservative, and 26 per cent Reform. In Providence, R. I. (1963), it was 16 per cent Orthodox, 56 per cent Conservative, and 24 per cent Reform. *Ibid.,* p. 145.

12. See note 1, above.

13. An annual *Digest* of the proceedings of the Consultation on Church Union provides the best means for staying abreast of this rapidly changing movement. Such *Digests* (from 1962 on) are available from the Executive Secretary, Box 69, Fanwood, N. J. See also the *Consultation on Church Union: The Reports of the Four Meetings,* and the *Principles of Church Union,* both printed in Cincinnati (Forward Movement Publications, 1966).

14. Bureau of the Census, "Current Population Reports," Series P-20, No. 79 (February 2, 1958). On a voluntary basis, the Census Bureau in 1957 asked a designated sample of the nation's population (over fourteen years of age), "What is your religion?" Responses, of course, do not imply membership or attendance, but they do imply at least a self-identification with some specific religious tradition. (The sample included 638 counties and independent cities; responses were obtained from about 35,000 households.)

15. See Gaustad, *Historical Atlas of Religion in America,* pp. 110–11, and elsewhere.

16. Appendix A to Herbert W. Schneider's *Religion in 20th Century America* (Cambridge, 1952; rev. ed., New York, 1964) treats "Religion and Class Structure." Though the data are now twenty years old, they do reveal in the immediate postwar period relationships between religious affiliation, on the one hand, and economic class, education, political preference, and union membership, on the other hand. Regarding the economic status, Roman Catholics and Baptists manifest a similar distribution; each group has about two thirds of its membership in the lower economic stratum. On the other hand, "the Presbyterian, Episcopal, Jewish, Congregational, Christian Science, and Reformed groups exceed their 'upper-class' quotas." *Ibid.,* p. 264 (rev. ed.).

17. This table is based on a poll conducted by the staff of *Christianity Today,* a fortnightly journal published in Washington, D.C. For identification of

the religious affiliation of individual Congressmen, see the issue for December 9, 1966, pp. 276–77.

18. See C. H. Jacquet, *Yearbook of American Churches 1967*, for data on the National Council; data on the National Association of Evangelicals and the American Council of Christian Churches was provided by those bodies.

CONTEMPORARY ISSUES

LANGDON GILKEY

Social and Intellectual Sources of Contemporary Protestant Theology in America

WHAT KINDS of sources are there of a mode of thinking—in this case, contemporary American Protestant theology? There are, first of all, deep, often unconscious sources. Germane to the whole historical context within which that thinking takes place, such sources, as the presuppositions of that cultural time and place, determine the mode of thinking by conditioning it unconsciously, giving it its shape as "contemporary" and "American" thinking. On the other hand, there are "sources" that are, to a limited but still real extent, consciously appropriated and chosen. These are points of view, systems of categories, and ways of approaching material that a thinker finds more congenial than other available modes of contemporary thought. He adopts them more or less freely as tools and aids to his thinking. Both sorts of sources, generally held presuppositions and more or less freely adopted sets of categories, determine the character and structure of a man's thought; both must be discussed if the sources that have shaped his thought are to be tracked down. Our concern in this article is to describe only the "secular" sources of current American theology; we shall not, therefore, discuss the influences of such "religious" sources of theology as Scripture, ecclesiastical or dogmatic tradition, or religious experience.

American theology has, of course, not been conducted in isolation from Western culture generally. The most fundamental social and intellectual factors that have shaped American theology are those that have determined the character of thought everywhere in the West. These general presuppositions of modern theology have in turn helped to make the more specifically secular disciplines and concepts so intensely relevant to recent theological inquiry; they have also in large part caused the conflicts in recent decades

137

between the older, orthodox forms of Protestant religion and the newer liberal forms.

(1) The first of these is the broad influence of science, as it had developed in the early-seventeenth century and was spread abroad in the Aufklärung of the later seventeenth and eighteenth centuries. Under this influence, recent Protestant theology has generally agreed or, better, conceded (with the early liberals, this was voluntary, but with many conservatives involuntary) that matters of fact within the space-time continuum are to be determined by scientific inquiry—whether it be through the natural, historical, or social sciences—rather than by revelation. No "religious truth" was, henceforth, regarded as embodying objective information about the age, structure, or inner workings of the observable universe. This vast shift forced by modern science in turn led to a complete reinterpretation of what religious truth is. Such truth was subsequently regarded as purely symbolic in character, a human expression in propositional language of some deeper pre-propositional or not-yet-thematized level of experience: of religious consciousness (Schleiermacher), of moral insight or postulation (Ritschl), of existential depth (Tillich), or of existential encounter with God in his acts (Brunner, Reinhold Niebuhr). In no case was such truth considered divine information of various sorts. Modern theologians (with the possible exception of that complicated being Barth) have regarded theology as reflection on religion, and thus as the very human and fallible *result* of religious faith or experience rather than as the sacred *object* of religious faith, that is, as an authoritative exposition of divinely revealed truth. What the further relation to philosophical reflection of this sort of symbolic religious truth might be has been widely debated; in any case, recent American theology has completely accepted this assessment of itself as a system of symbols communicating no objective "matters of fact." Clearly the burning question of the status, meaningfulness, and verifiability of such a system of symbols, referent in some sense to reality and yet establishing no matters of fact, was bound sooner or later to arise, as it has uncomfortably in the most recent theology of the last decade.

This change with regard to the status and character of Christian doctrine has in turn caused some of the deep tensions within American religious life. For many Christians still regard the religious truths of their faith as divinely revealed propositions about "matters of fact" set down in an infallible Scripture. Consequently, unable or unwilling to comprehend the newer understanding of the symbolic character of religious truth, such Christians tend to insist that everything the Bible says about the early history of the earth, man's creation and fall, and the events of Israelite and early Christian history is simply and literally true because it had been revealed as propositions by God. Thus, they regard scientific hypotheses and attitudes that contradict these doctrines as dangerous. They distrust the "liberal" and critical religion of the seminaries, viewing theologians and (most) pastors as anti-Christians. A separation, previously unknown in this form in Christian history, has arisen between the intellectual representations of the faith and its simpler, less educated or less sophisticated adherents, in many cases a separation between pulpit and pew. In the last hundred years, American religion especially has been plagued by this tension between the liberal view of religious truth and the older conservative understanding. In some cases, the proponents of the latter view have become radically defensive, even fanatical. But for most church people, only confusion, a sense of uneasy distrust, and sheer lack of understanding have resulted when they hear their leaders propounding a view of religious truth that they do not recognize from their own religious upbringing and the necessity of which they do not as yet comprehend—though one suspects their children will.

(2) The second presupposition of all modern theology stems from nineteenth-century culture in which the historical character of human experience and thought, including the religious, was first stressed. Religious truths were considered to be relative to their culture, and therefore subject to change, development, and, in principle at least, irrelevance and abandonment. Even the sacred Scriptures and tradition were thus *historically* studied and interpreted in Protestant theology. Scripture and tradition came to be regarded as a reflection of man's historical experience and historical self-interpretation, rather than as containers of timeless truths.

Again this change has produced many tensions within American church life. The admission that important doctrinal statements in the Scriptures (for example, the Creation myth, the Story of the Fall, the Virgin Birth, the miracle accounts, the ascension, and the return on the clouds of glory) reflect more the particular viewpoints and cosmology of early cultures than infallible truths, and that they must be appropriately translated out of these literalistic images into "modern" concepts has made many devout Christians feel unhappy and distrustful, or at least alienated from the intellectual leadership of the churches. In the more confession- and creed-oriented churches (Lutheran, Calvinist, and especially Roman Catholic), many laymen have been profoundly shocked by the notion that the historic creeds of their church may be, in part, expressions of faith relative to the time in which they were written. The sense of the historical relativity of ideas and beliefs is one of the most pervasive themes of our cultural life. But this does not mean that it has penetrated into every level of our culture, nor that it has been able to qualify the ultimacy of our deepest and most strongly felt convictions. Many of the most severe disagreements in both the political-social and the religious dimensions of American life originate because some elements of the population accept the historical relativity of America's most fundamental ideas, while others cannot conceive of such an admission.

Two important corollaries follow from the application of this historical and relativistic viewpoint to the sources of religious truth: (a) no unequivocal divine authority appears for theological reflection, not even one embodied in Scripture or tradition; and (b) a theology, to be vital, must speak in the categories and in the accents of its own historical period. As a result, recent theology, most certainly in America, has had a very ambiguous and vacillating relation to secular culture. On the one hand, it has been unsure of its indigenous authorities or criteria, lacking, as has been noted, any clear, definite, divinely imparted authority in either Scripture or tradition. It has consequently felt uncertain and anxious about *how much* "secular" thought it could safely embrace. Paradoxically, doubt about the certainty, the clarity, and, therefore, the inviolability of the indigenous sources and norms in Scripture and tradition has created a fear of outside influences that did not exist before Scripture and tradition were relativized; if the home authorities of theology become shaky, then foreign influences had best be kept clear of the house. As a result, neo-orthodox theology tried for a period to free itself completely from the influence of "worldly" thinking. On the other hand, all modern theology, in order to be historically relevant, has found itself forced back into the secular culture to discover appropriate categories and attitudes with which meaningfully to address its own time. Its sense of its own historicity has thus pulled contemporary theology away from secularity in fear and, at the same time, toward it in expectation. Much of the recent, rather violent, seesawing of theology in relation to "the world" and its ways of thinking, and a good deal of the present ambiguity among theologians about the relation of their thought to its "social and intellectual sources" stem from this tension created by historicism.

(3) A third general influence, beginning with the Renaissance and continuing apace since then, has been the this-worldly emphasis of modern culture, its concern with this life and its fulfillment rather than with life beyond death. Correspondingly, the central axis of religious concern has shifted, most especially in American religion, from the matters of ultimate "salvation," of judgment or justification before God in eternity, and of heaven or hell, to questions of the meaning, necessity, or usefulness of religion for this life—be it for self-fulfillment and self-integration, for ethical norms and moral efficacy, for "meaning in life," for self-affirmation, or for what the existentialists call "authentic existence." Clearly, with this shift in emphasis, the relevance for theology of such secular disciplines as psychology, sociology, political theory, and ethical philosophy has greatly increased.

(4) Along with this latter shift from, so to speak, eternity to the present has come a corresponding shift in Christian ethical concern from personal holiness to love of the neighbor as the central obligation, if not the essence, of Christianity. Consequently, recent Christian ethics has been far more concerned with a man's attitudes and behavior in relation to his neighbor in the social community than it has been with the problem of his personal vices—except where these may affect other people.

There is no question, of course, but that the New Testament itself regards love for the neighbor as the basic ethical quality of the Christian's life on earth. While this quality always remained present in Christian ethical thought and striving, two other concerns tended frequently to replace it as determinations of a good Christian: the demand for the purity of doctrinal belief, and the demand for personal holiness (or, more specifically, freedom from vice) in order to appear spotless before the throne of grace. Under a multitude of influences, gradually maturing, these two latter concerns have tended in recent centuries to recede—at least among the more serious and thoughtful Christians—so that love of the neighbor has become again the accepted ethical desideratum of a full Christian existence.

Two comments might initially be made about this development. First of all, it represents, in this writer's opinion, the greatest single advance in recent church history (if it may be called an advance, since it is also a return to what was surely the gospel's

141

original intention), giving to Christianity the possibility of becoming the creative force in human affairs it should always have been. Secondly, this significant shift has caused perhaps the deepest tension within present-day American church life. For many devoted Christians, the commands to keep their beliefs free from doctrinal error and their personal lives free from vice remain as the fundamental requirements of valid Christianity. To such persons, problems of property, minimum wages and economic security, race relations, war and peace, and slum clearance are not "religious" at all. They concern neither correct belief nor personal vices. Consequently, such people would rather be seen in a White Citizens' Council meeting than be caught in a bar. When, therefore, they find pastors and theologians, who *also* question the absoluteness of Christian beliefs, calling upon them to support and even to encourage social and economic reforms, integration, disarmament— not to mention withdrawal in Viet-Nam, they again feel alienated form their own leadership. They suspect, not infrequently, that the relativizing of doctrine and the encouragement of reform together from a left-wing plot against true Christianity. Thus do fundamentalism, pietism, and right-wing sociological political ideas frequently coalesce against "liberal religion," both doctrinally and socially, to create the vast misunderstandings and tensions in American church life today.

When one searches for the sources of this significant shift in ethical ideals from personal holiness to love of the neighbor, one finds them multiple indeed. Little credit can be given to the confessional or sacramental churches or to the evangelical revivals of the eighteenth and nineteenth centuries. Rather, it was originally the radical sixteenth- and seventeenth-century sectarian movements— the Socinians, the Mennonites, and the Quakers—that, scornful of dogmas and sacramentalism alike, stressed brotherly love, justice, and peace as the primary Christian ideals. But the dominant influence effecting the shift surely came from the growing humanitarianism of Western culture generally, a secular movement, with Christian roots to be sure, but one that has over the decades prophetically challenged the churches which had forgotten their own major task. This humanitarian spirit, a spirit concerned with the welfare and comfort of man on earth, matured slowly during the eighteenth and nineteenth centuries. It received perhaps its first strong expression in Enlightenment deism, in the revolutionary movements devoted to bettering man's estate, and in utilitarianism.

It found vivid expression in Kant, for whom human perfection, moral and religious, meant simply and solely treating every other person as an end and not as a means; the early Hegel re-affirmed it in saying that the essence of Christianity is its gospel of love; and then it re-appeared in more radical guise in Feuerbach for whom man's fulfillment comes not in religion at all but in service to the community of mankind. The entire tradition of socialist thought, Marxist and non-Marxist, moreover, embodies this spirit: The goal of history—the deepest purpose of creative human existence—is the building of a society based on cooperation, justice, peace, and universal brotherhood. Most thoughtful writers and thinkers of the nineteenth century, religious and non-religious alike, accepted this as the most adequate statement of the measure of human obligation—and regarded any other set of moral norms as hopelessly misguided.

Under the impact of this growing mood, which itself began to result in many early social reform movements, Christian theology experienced a corresponding shift. The experience of religious wars fought over doctrines and of the persecution of free thinkers and heretics combined with the new sense of the relativity of doctrine to make any mistreatment of another man "for the sake of orthodoxy" seem demonic in the extreme. The same spirit now tended to see the ideal of personal holiness for the sake of individual salvation—especially in one callous about his neighbor's welfare—as a form of transcendental selfishness that could hardly be called Christian. A large section of nineteenth-century Christianity argued that the Christian man has been called neither to preserve pure doctrine nor to get himself into heaven, but to build on earth the Kingdom of God, a community in which human welfare replaces material gain and political power as the end of man. Consequently, the holding of slaves and their mistreatment gradually came to be viewed as a greater sin than swearing or doubting the Trinity. Later the same judgment was applied to those who paid low wages, forced unhealthy or dangerous working conditions, or made large profits from slums and monopolies. A Social Gospel evolved in which Christianity was viewed primarily as an agent of the reform of society and so of history rather than as a gospel of individual salvation in the next life. Although in the last forty years many elements of this older Social Gospel have dissipated, especially its explicit socialist categories and its buoyant optimism about progress, this emphasis on service to one's fellow man through social reform, as love ex-

143

pressing itself in the social forms of brotherhood, justice, and peace, has *not* receded. Not only every major theologian but also every major church body here and abroad has accepted as valid this estimate of Christian perfection. In any case, it is again evident that the study of social and psychological structures becomes very relevant indeed to a modern theological ethic so oriented.

These are, then, the most significant presuppositions of modern theology everywhere. Many, if not all, of these fundamental assumptions of modern culture have important roots in the religious tradition they, in turn, have recently influenced from the outside. The church and the world, the sacred and the profane, have historically illustrated neither a simple union nor a simple opposition, but a dialectical relation that corrects and refreshes both. Perhaps in this sense a purely "religionless" or "secular" theology would cease to be of interest or of real help to a world that had itself totally determined what that theology had to say.

American theology, however, not only illustrates these general characteristics of modern theology; it also has its own special style because of its peculiar cultural environment, an environment with specific attitudes toward life and toward the place and role of religion in life. Thus, while the general characteristics of modern theology have led the theologian to view with great seriousness his surrounding secular culture, the peculiar characteristics of American existence have greatly influenced *how* the American thinker uses these secular sources and influences and *how much* they determine his thinking. These characteristics have tended, moreover, to accentuate the relationship of American theology to American culture. Thus, Americans have made secular influences *more* important as sources for theology than they have been elsewhere. Four decisive characteristics of the American *Geist* in relation to religion are evident.

(1) The first is what might be called the principle of the "unity of American culture," the manifest harmony between the secular and the religious elements of the society, with the consequent interpenetration of each by the other—the secular influencing the religious and the religious the secular. Numerous commentators have pointed out that the antipathy characteristic of present-day Europe on the part of the wider culture to the church and its traditions, its beliefs, and its ethos is not nearly so evident in America.

To be "religious," even in a secular way, is, except among the higher intelligentsia, generally affirmed in the United States where our major religions are accepted as creative, if harmless, elements of national life. Perhaps this sense of harmony between the secular and the religious exists because there has been little fear of overt domination by religion in such a religiously pluralistic society; as Professor Krister Stendahl has pointed out, one can accept and love a tradition if it is not a threat to one's freedom. In any case, as a result of this general principle of unity and harmony, American religious thought has more quickly and more thoroughly accepted and used secular cultural ideas and categories than has European theology. Throughout its history, it has been consistently more "modernist," "evolutionist," "empiricist," "psychoanalytic," or "socialist" in its character than has Europe. To Europeans this greater unity of theology and cultural influences has seemed to be the syncretistic heresy of American theology; to Americans it has appeared to be a factor making the relevance and health—or "success," if one prefers—of religion greater here than they are abroad. The creative possibilities for both society and the church of this union of the religious and the secular are obvious; its dangers, in terms of a national American religion, are equally real if not so immediately apparent to all of us.

(2) From almost the beginning of American history, religion in the United States has been regarded as a personal and inward phenomenon rather than as an ecclesiastical—institutional—phenomenon. Although religion here has always exhibited a strong communal character, evident in the great sense of "fellowship" among members of a congregation, religion for Americans is, nevertheless, a qualification of a man's inward life and of his own moral behavior, if it is anything at all. It is not primarily an attribute of an objective institution or tradition. Religion is not something that comes to a man from an objective institution that possesses and communicates grace; rather, the institution is formed by the voluntary association in fellowship of religious people. In this characteristic, America clearly shows the dominance of the free-church tradition over its religious life. This emphasis in turn explains the kind of unity between the secular and the religious that has been achieved in America. Except for those elements of "civil religion" referred to by Professor Bellah, this unity has not been achieved through a political concordat between church and state, for, since the Revolution, American political institutions have been deliberately separated

from objective religious institutions. Rather, the unity has been achieved through the inwardness of the individual citizen who in his work is active in the secular realm, but, in theory at least, is continually refreshed, reborn, and motivated by an inward personal religious existence derived from his church life. At least this is the way Americans *look* at religion, even if objective ecclesiastical "works" have taken marked preponderance over inner religious experiences and beliefs in the present relatively secularized church life.

American theology has tended to be interested in neither traditional formulations nor systems of doctrine. Those intellectual elements of religion that buttress and preserve the institutional structure of the church—the hierarchical or priestly, the liturgical, and the dogmatic—have been de-emphasized or ignored in America in favor of inward, personal, and activist elements. This emphasis on inward personal rather than objective institutional religion has caused American theology to be more concerned with expressing and enhancing the feelings, the experiences, and the activities connected with individual religion than with pursuing the traditional intellectual problems of theology for their own sake or with formulating Christian truths into systematic form, both of which it has tended to distrust as too much oriented to the objective institutionalizing of religion. When creative theological formulations have appeared in America, as they surely have, they have been directed to "doing" religion rather than to giving to religion systematic intellectual form. Dogmatic or ecclesiastical theology for its own sake has seldom been a characteristic of American theology. American religious *life* has been vastly creative of new forms and new vitalities; it has influenced and will continue to influence European religious life tremendously. Its emphasis on fellowship within the congregation's life, on participation by the laity in the support and direction of the church, its emphasis on the relevance of Christian existence to the secular life and to the social problems of the surrounding community, all of these have been exported creatively to other lands. But on the level of new theological points of view or creative *intellectual* formulations of religion, it has been and will perhaps remain primarily receptive to European influences, though America's closer touch with the secular spirit and with secular disciplines may in the future raise some interest across the water in American theological reflection.

In the light of this history, it is ironic that at present the main characteristic of American church life is its strong institutional flavor. The immense energies, money, time, and devotion that are poured into American church life are spent, on the whole, on developing and furthering the institution itself: whether it be the membership and plant of the local church, or the growth and influence of the wider denomination. How is this explained? With the growth of "secularity," the activist elements of American religion have remained—but now they no longer concentrate on religious conversion or on saving a soul from vice (both goals would horrify the modern resident of a new suburban development). Thus, the emphasis on personal religious experience and on personal ethical behavior has tended to lessen dramatically in the modern secular mood. Traditionally unconcerned with sacrament, theology, or hierarchy, the vast churchly energies and monies of Americans have been spent on the "church" itself. In recent decades this has created in this least of all ecclesiastical cultures a new species of ecclesiasticism, one stripped of all the dogmatic, priestly, and sacramental elements that have characterized other kinds of ecclesiastical systems. As of now, the variety of American church life has little theological, liturgical, pietistic, or even Biblical content, but it is nonetheless burgeoning with air-conditioned sanctuaries, ladies' and men's societies, large Sunday-school plants, "holy name" baseball teams, and innumerable suppers and dances. It is a "religious" institution of immense power, wealth, and prestige, but one characterized largely by secular values such as recreation, sociability, and sporadic good works in the community. The social value of such an institution is undoubted in our mobile, rootless, suburban culture. Whether it has any real *religious* character—whether it manifests a presence of the holy in its midst or offers a higher ethical standard for man's daily life—is something else again.

Another way of describing this same characteristic is to point to the "pragmatic" character of American religion and to the theological reflection stemming from it. If religion is an affair of the individual person, then its significance lies in what it does in the person's life—how it affects his character and behavior on the one hand, and his resultant attitudes toward life on the other. American theology has avoided purely theoretical issues and problems; its energies have been directed toward results, and these primarily in the ethical field. The creative theologians in America (Edwards excepted) have generally been ethicists: Gladden, Rauschenbusch, the Niebuhrs—and one may soon be able to add the present advocates of the "worldly gospels." Consequently, American theology has given to world theology not new formulations of doctrine but its insight into religion's social and psychological relevance. In America, then, the "this-worldly" tendency of modern theology has generally been greatly accentuated by an innate ethical pragmatism. Religion is viewed as primarily a moral and social-communal matter, relevant to the enactment of good in the lives of men and the wider social community. Again the positive possibilities of the influence of religion on American society are obvious; but concomitantly there is a vast danger of national messianism, if this understanding of religion as merely providing motives for doing good for and to others gets harnessed to the expanding national interest.

(3) A third characteristic of American religion has been its almost total acceptance of the social, secular context of life. American religiosity has traditionally viewed the state, the community, the marketplace, the farm, and the family as fundamentally innocent, and even as revelatory and redemptive in character. The "world" has seldom been for the American a "fallen" place—a place of misery, sin, and frustration, a place from which either the wise, the good, or the religious man might legitimately seek to escape or flee. Thus, monastic religious communities have never flourished (until recently) on American soil. Most separatist sectarian groups, who initially regarded the world and its ways as evil, have in the end acquiesced and become, like most other citizens, normal, middle-class Americans. To the American mind, the free democratic community of their country is "God-given." Blessed by a special benevolence of Providence, it remains a haven from the evil ways of the world's other societies. America has seemed to be a nation with a destiny under God that will lead all of mankind to a better life. Thus, American religion has never conceived of itself as being opposed to the world around it. In fact, much of what God was doing in history would, in the American view, be expected to appear in the social and political history of American life. The explanation for the happy and creative harmony between religion and the secular lies here; as does the deepest root of the ever-present danger of a national messianism.

Two explanations for this peculiar attitude of American religion to its social environment are evident. First, American culture and, consequently, American religion have their roots not in the medieval period but in the Enlightenment. According to Enlightenment thought, human society could function according to its innate na-

tural laws if it could be freed from the control of irrational historical traditions, upheld by "priests and kings." These natural laws,
like the laws of nature recently discovered by Galileo and Newton,
were God-given and so creative of the good life for man; a society
founded on them, rather than on arbitrary tradition and privilege,
would be an innocent, creative society, one in which the God-
given destiny of the human race might be expected to achieve
fulfillment. Secondly, America functioned in the eyes of those who
came here as a veritable "promised land," as a haven of rescue and
opportunity out of the darkness of the oppression, the frequent
starvation, and more frequent underprivilege that they had experienced in traditionalist Europe. Many immigrants experienced on
entrance into American life a kind of secular salvation—however
hard they may have been treated on arrival. And the common success story that later followed, for the next generation if not for the
first, validated over and over this religious assessment of the social
environment of American life. For these two reasons, therefore,
American religion has looked benevolently if not idolatrously on
its secular environment, and has more often than not found itself
blending unconsciously into that environment far more than most
forms of Christianity have.

(4) The fourth character of American religion, following from
these three, is its inherent "secularity." It has been, as has been
noted, united in its thought patterns to the secular life around it,
and it has been oriented to "doing" in that life. From its Puritan
beginnings through its revivals to its present social and secular
gospels, its whole existence and drive have been within the orbit of
personal experience and behavior enacted within the God-given
American environment. More than a sacramental, an ecclesiastical,
a dogmatic-confessional, or a transcendentally directed faith, its
face has been toward the actual world in which men live and act.
Again, religious grace for Americans has not been a power latent
within an ecclesiastical institution that possesses its own unyielding dogmas and standards and that communicates its grace to the
secular world outside it. Religion has been, rather, an experience
and a quality of the people who are *in* the world; thus, the church
is made up of people formed *by* the world. Theoretically and hope-
fully their religiousness in turn influences the world. If one then
adds to this traditionally socially-oriented character of American
religion the present predominantly secular mood of American
society as a whole, one finds at least a partial explanation for the

most apparent trait of American religiosity today, namely, its "secular" character. Manifested in both America's church life and its current theology, this characteristic is less evident in all forms of traditional church life in Europe.

By a "secular mood" is meant, first of all, the prerational sense, virtually universal in the urban elements of American culture, that reality, truth, and value lie solely in the observable world of nature, society, and man, and in no sense beyond it; and secondly, a cultural spirit in which, as a consequence, no transcendent dimension appears at all, and in which none is thought to be necessary. Man's life is not felt to be set within any wider framework than the one nature and community provide for him; its fulfillment requires not help from divine grace but only the application of his own powers of mind and will in the social context. In such a mood, religion tends to be translated exhaustively into ethics or communal values. Any sense of the reality of God's presence and actuality is reinterpreted into the creative possibilities latent within the human community and in the wider social process. To be sure, as any Jew is aware, present-day American culture reveals Christian remnants, like classical columns in a modern Italian city. Nevertheless, the content of these, insofar as they are social phenomena, is apt to be neither religious nor authentically Christian; they have little reference to either the transcendent dimension represented by the symbol of God or to the historic origins and teachings of the faith in the figure of Jesus. Like the prayers at a political convention or at the start of a southern football game, they represent a "Christian secularity."

This secular mood has vastly influenced the American religious thought of the last decades. Modernism, as the late-nineteenth- and early-twentieth-century attempt to translate Christian perspectives and values into current secular concepts and ideals, always had a larger hold on American theology than it did on European, and it was far more extreme in the United States than it was in Europe. Even the neo-orthodox reaction against modernism, which will be noted later, retained in America far more of a sense of responsibility for and relevance to the secular social scene than it did in Europe. Neo-orthodoxy attempted to combat the secular mood by re-introducing into American religion the nearly lost dimensions of the transcendent, of the sense of the sinful and the tragic in human social existence, and by witnessing to the deeper resources of forgiveness and grace beyond the natural bonds and values—as well as the crises and predicaments—of human community life. For a variety of reasons, this theological effort has now run its course, and a new era has begun. The most potent cause of its demise was the continuing power of secularity in America's national consciousness, rendering the older "Biblical" motifs, myths, and symbols which neo-orthodoxy sponsored almost meaningless to the laity, and arduous if not ultimately unreal to the preacher and the theologian who sought to work with them.

The current movements of American theology are, then, almost all in a secular direction. The more radical ring accepts this mood *in toto,* proclaiming the "death of God" in our time and the consequent need for Christian faith and for theology to proceed— without reference to God—in building itself entirely around the figure of Jesus and his call to service in the world. Whether such a greatly reduced theology is viable or even Christian remains to be seen. Still, it has revealed to an astounded and often shocked church and society how profoundly a deep secularity has entered into the heart of an American culture that regarded itself as religious.

Although most current American theology is not so radical, it, too, has a decidedly "secular" orientation. It seeks above all to make the symbols of religious language intelligible in terms of secular experience and secular discourse. In plotting out new forms for the church, it emphasizes the task of the church within the secular world and in the midst of its problems. While elements of religious transcendence are maintained, they are, in intention at least, not allowed to remain separate from the ordinary day-to-day lives of men. The peculiar genius of American religion may prove very creative in this situation. Although European culture is, if anything, more secular than the American, the European church and its theology tend to remain locked within the chapels and the castles of the religious establishment. They may retain the transcendent element in religion, but this religion is unrelated to and, consequently, unheard by the culture surrounding it. American religion, on the other hand, faces the problem of retaining a *religious* dimension in its now secularized church life and theology; it is by no means certain that such a churchly tradition can continue to be fruitful if it loses all touch with its trans-cultural sources.

As has been noted, on the level of specific and concrete intellectual influences, America has had primarily a receptive relation with Europe. The ethically and socially oriented character of American theology has been indigenous, although the conceptual tools with which its characteristic patterns of thought were worked out have not been. Thus, in the liberal period before World War I, the influences of Kantian-Ritschlian value-centered theology, Hegelian idealism, Spencerian and Bergsonian evolutionism, and the historicism of Troeltsch were predominant. Correspondingly, when neo-orthodoxy dominated the general American theological scene (from the early thirties until the early sixties), the predominance of ideas of European origin continued. The influences of Kierkegaard, of Buber, and later of Heidegger—mediated through such continental theologians as Barth, Brunner, and Bultmann—provided most of the intellectual categories with which American theologians of a generally neo-orthodox stripe (the Niebuhr brothers, Paul Lehmann, and David Roberts, for example) reinterpreted their liberal and Biblical heritage. American Biblical theology was fed by such European Biblical scholars as Eichrodt and Von Rad in the Old Testament, and Schweitzer, Dodd, Cullman, and, of course, Bultmann in the New. Correspondingly present-day New Testament scholars receive most of their stimulation, if not their ideas, from such current European leaders as Käsemann, Bornkamm, Fuchs, and Ebeling.

Even among the radicals, for whom European neo-orthodoxy has died along with deity, it is still from Europe that the main intellectual impetus has come. Only in this case the tradition to which they appeal is that which has declared the disappearance of the transcendent and, in its more radical forms, of all traces of the Divine. This tradition begins with Hegel, continues in Feuerbach and Marx, and reaches its apogee in Nietzsche and Freud. All forms of present "religionless Christianity" look to the potent and oracular writings of the German martyr Bonhoeffer for their most authentic inspiration.

In each case, the American spirit has contributed to these European influences a sense of empiricism, of social relevance, and of a this-worldly secularity. The creative role of American theology has been, in general, to re-fashion for usage in the technical and secular world ideas that had been created inside the European religious establishment. Although most of the categories of American religious thought—Kantian, idealistic, evolutionary, existentialist, "Biblical," and so on—arose on European soil, many of them, filled in America with a new vitality and relevance, have traveled back to Europe where they have in turn exercised enormous, if still barely recognized, influence.

In this sense Paul Tillich could be said to be a personal embodiment of American theology. Armed with a magnificent set of typically European philosophical and theological categories, he crossed the water to America only to find, as he often said, not that his categories changed, but that he was in this atmosphere forced to think more concretely, more empirically, and more for the sake of actual life, its problems and its possibilities. Too "liberal" and "secular" to be influential in Europe during its neo-orthodox days when all use of philosophical language and cultural categories seemed to be a betrayal of Biblical faith, Tillich appeared in the liberal American scene as the representative of the *classical* tradition in Christianity. As he always wished, he stood "on the boundary" between Europe and America, mediating the influence of each to the other. Although he formed no school of followers, he became the most continuously fruitful and stimulating figure in American theology in this century.

Philosophical influences on theology are always exceedingly complex. This complexity exists partly because the influences of philosophy are always present in theology in some form or other; and partly because they vary greatly according to the prevailing attitudes of both philosophy and theology, making the influence in some periods overwhelming and in others minimal. For example, from the turn of the century until the late twenties, liberal theology was oriented self-consciously toward its culture, while philosophy was, in turn, either idealistic or evolutionistic; philosophy, consequently, had a direct and determinative influence on theology. One thinks at once of such important American theologians as E. S. Ames, E. Brightman, E. Lyman, D. C. McIntosh, H. N. Wieman, and C. Hartshorne, all of whom used philosophy directly in their religious thinking. When, however, in neo-orthodoxy theology turned inward toward its own Biblical and traditional sources, and when philosophy was, as in the thirties and forties, generally either naturalistic or positivistic, philosophical influences on theology not only weakened but in many cases were vigorously repudiated. Yet even here, existentialism appeared to give a real if unacknowledged conceptual basis for most neo-orthodox theology. Certainly in the same theological tradition, pragmatism had vast influence on the understanding of both theological truth and ethical obligation.

Since roughly the end of the 1920's until quite recently, the most important philosophical influence on American theology has been unquestionably that of process thought, centered on the later works of Alfred North Whitehead, who, unlike Tillich, became a systematic philosopher *after* he reached these pragmatic shores. The two most distinguished recent American philosophers of religion, H. N. Wieman and C. Hartshorne, took their main philosophical concepts directly from Whitehead and applied them with some changes to theological matters. Since their time there has been a steady stream of first-class theologians, including such important present names as B. Meland (also influenced by William James), D. D. Williams, B. Loomer, S. Ogden, and J. Cobb, stemming from this process school, the center of which has been the University of Chicago.

The University of Chicago is in itself worthy of mention in an article on "American" theology because in its relatively brief history it has been the center of the only two recent indigenous schools of theology of which this writer is aware. At the turn of the century, in its early period, several crucial figures on the faculty, notably W. R. Harper, E. D. Burton, J. M. P. Smith, Shailler Matthews, Shirley Jackson Case, G. B. Smith, and Edgar J. Goodspeed, sought to apply the historical and sociological methods to the study of the Scriptures, church history, and the development of doctrine, and to the problems of systematic theology. Being the first concerted effort to apply "secular" methodologies to religious materials, their work had enormous influence on American religious studies. Later, in the twenties, a change took place in the Chicago "school." Under the influence of Wieman and Hartshorne, the categories of process philosophy replaced those of the historical-sociological method as the main tools of interpretation. Nevertheless, the basic modernist approach remained, for in this case, too, a secular philosophical system, designed to integrate into a coherent unity all facets of the learning and life of the world at large, was used as the conceptual framework within which traditional Christian symbols and concerns were re-translated in order to make them both intelligible and relevant to modern experience. Both forms of "Chicago" theology demonstrate, then, the principle of the unity of the cultural and the religious that is an American characteristic. One should add, however, that there has been one "un-American" aspect of process theology, namely, its overriding concern for the intellectual or philosophical formulation of religious thought and its frequent indifference to the life and activity of religion itself.

During a somewhat later period, from the 1930's until the 1950's, neo-orthodox American theologians, who found their main centers at Union Seminary and Yale, were influenced by quite different intellectual sources. Here Reinhold Niebuhr may be taken as the most distinguished and illuminating example. Influenced by Marxist thought in his early social analysis, his sense of the inevitable dissonance of man's communal and personal existence drove Niebuhr to more purely theological categories, which he found not in liberal American theology but in neo-orthodox Europe. Gradually the Augustinian view of political and social existence supplemented that of Marx. Then the existential insights of Kierkegaard and of Buber, combined with the rediscovery of the "Biblical view" and of the Reformation, partly from his own study of the prophets and the Gospels and partly from the influence of continental theology, provided him with a set of "Biblical-mythical categories" with which he sought to understand the paradoxes and mysteries of man's historical existence. Supplementing these central theological sources were influences from Freud, Nietzsche, and Dewey, and from countless social, anthropological, and psychological scientists.

Niebuhr is, therefore, typically American in three senses. First, the main intellectual categories of his thought stem from European sources, both ancient and modern. Second, he was driven to these categories not by dogmatic interests but rather by his own predominantly *social* concerns and the demands on thought that he felt arose from a careful analysis of secular society. Third, influenced himself by the intellectual forces of the secular culture, he gave to the traditional Biblical and theological ideas he received from Europe a more historically vital, socially relevant, and "secularly oriented" character than had any European. Of all great indigenous American theologians, he more than any other has mediated the influence of continental Europe into the American context; and yet ironically, this mediation occurred precisely because his thought is typically American, because it is more vividly involved in the secular social scene than that of any other recent American theologian. Again, the principle of the unity of culture and religion and the principle of a this-worldly, ethical concern are illustrated by Niebuhr, but with an entirely different set of intellectual and theological categories than were represented in process theology.

Like Tillich, Niebuhr is also important because he illustrates not only the impact of secular concepts and attitudes on American theology but also the reverse influence, namely that of a theologian on the thought patterns of secular culture itself. Both Tillich and Niebuhr have contributed a sense of depth to the American interpretation of existence. While Tillich's insights have stimulated a number of psychological and sociological thinkers, Niebuhr's thinking has effected changes in the fields of social and political theory, international relations, and the philosophy of history.

A brief summary of the character of Niebuhr's influence is difficult. Suffice it to say that American social thought had been dominated by a pragmatic attitude toward social matters and toward history itself, an attitude in which "meaning" was almost exclusively conceived of in terms of visible progress, concrete improvements, and the gradual eradication of serious problems. Correspondingly American attitudes toward social matters tended to equate a moral view of human affairs with an idealistic one. Since the "good" was understood solely in terms of concrete social improvement, the possibility of and the sanction for a moral approach to society tended to vary with the strength of one's confidence in concrete progress. Hence, as in liberal religion, the moral man came to be identified with the optimistic man; the realist about society and history, with the cynical and the self-interested man. Such a view of social matters fitted well with the abounding optimism of the early-twentieth century; but it contained few resources for a period in which the complexity and the ineradicability of social problems seemed suddenly apparent—in short, when history revealed itself as suffused with both the tragic and the demonic. In such a period, hope for immediate concrete solutions is apt to appear inane and to falter; if social morality is based on optimism, this morality will falter too—or else refuse to look at the problem and become fanatical. The thrust of Niebuhr's message during the thirties, the forties, and into the fifties, a message that was heard not only by the "religious" but also by the "secular," was that realism about history did not connote cynicism but was, on the contrary, a healthy precondition for a more creative morality. As he urged in books, articles, and sermons, history is not so easily amenable to our good intentions as we had thought. It is infinitely complex, morally ambiguous, and frequently tragic. Nevertheless, despite this proximate realism, there are deeper dimensions to human existence to be reached neither by scientific inquiry nor by rational calculation, but by faith. These dimensions are in turn expressed in the religious symbols of creation, judgment, forgiveness, and renewal. Through faith these symbols provide the bases for a moral, serene, and even hopeful participation in such a problematic history. More than any other thinker, Niebuhr has prepared the once overly optimistic American intelligentsia—and this is the only group he has directly touched—for the present complexities and frustrations of America's national existence.

In the most recent period, philosophical influences other than Kierkegaardian existentialism have become important in theology. At its first appearance in the logical atomism of Russell, in the Wittgenstein of the *Tractatus,* and in the positivism of the Vienna Circle and of A. J. Ayer, language philosophy seemed to be too antithetical to the interests of theology to make very much affirmative impress on theologians dominated by either process metaphysics or neo-orthodox existentialism. But gradually under the guidance of the later Wittgenstein, Wisdom, Austin, and a host of others, ordinary language philosophy has become increasingly genial to more than merely scientific forms of discourse, while the plausibility of metaphysical construction and the power of existentialism have waned. More and more theological formulations have come to be influenced, if not wholly determined, by the methods, aims, and limits of language analysis. Examples of this use in theology come from the writings of Paul Holmer of Yale, Frederick Ferré of Dickenson, John Hick recently of Princeton, and, on the radical left, Paul Van Buren of Temple. Although the origin of language philosophy lies ultimately in Europe, and especially in England, at present it dominates American philosophy departments and has been *the* philosophy taught most younger theologians since 1950. One can, therefore, only expect its influence to be on the rise in American theology. Language philosophy itself has undergone very radical changes in its short career so that its future course is ambiguous. Consequently, it is difficult to predict what the long-term effects of this movement on theology will be. The probabilities are that, with its present almost "metaphysical" bent, it may well become a creative tool for clarifying the structure, logic, and purpose of religious discourse.

The other contemporary influence of philosophy on American theology comes from phenomenology. This influence takes two forms, one of relatively long standing and the other much more recent. The phenomenological existentialism of Heidegger has been introduced into New Testament interpretation through the vastly important work of Bultmann. The main categories with which many younger New Testament scholars seek to "demythologize," that is, to comprehend in modern language the content, the significance, and the limits of the Christian gospel, are derived ultimately from Heidegger. The important "new quest for the historical Jesus," both here and in Germany, finds its justification in a Heideggerian understanding of Jesus' relation to and relevance for our time. Heidegger's direct influence has been less in the field of systematic or ethical theology than in the field of New Testament hermeneutics; still, such familiar Heideggerian phrases as "self-understanding," "being-in-the-world," and "authentic existence"[1] pop up everywhere in theology, even in the most unlikely places.[1] The thought of at least one major contemporary theologian, John MacQuarrie of Union Seminary, is explicitly shaped by this influence. Thus, Heidegger's phenomenological method with its existentialist content has, in the immediate post-neo-orthodox period, had a determinative role to play.

A second, more recent, influence of phenomenology on theology concentrates on the method of phenomenological description, originated by Husserl, exemplified in Heidegger and Sartre, but for present purposes most helpfully developed by the late Merleau-Ponty and especially by Paul Ricoeur. In America this concern with phenomenological method as a tool in religious studies began, probably, in the history of religions with the significant work of Joachim Wach and Mircea Eliade and their pupils. Wach used this method to isolate and define the intrinsic character of religious experience as a whole. Eliade, on the other hand, used phenomenological description of primitive religious activities and symbols as a means of exploring the character of archaic and Eastern experience, and of discriminating within that experience the interrelations of the sacred and the profane. This method soon revealed its usefulness for constructive theology. Recent radical theology (God-is-dead theology) has so pointedly raised the question of the viability and meaningfulness of any sort of religious discourse that theology has been forced away from its Biblical and metaphysical moorings toward an examination of concrete modern experience in order to find there the bases for contemporary religious discourse. The methodology of phenomenological description is showing its usefulness in such an effort. By this means, the dim backgrounds or horizons of concrete experience can be analyzed with some intellectual integrity, and the functions and meanings of religious symbols in thematizing that experience can be demonstrated. In the immediate future, the main philosophical influences on American theology will most probably be those of the tradition of process thought, language philosophy, and phenomenology—with the continual possibility that American pragmatism, especially in its Jamesian form, may make a strong reappearance.

As has already become clear, secular disciplines other than philosophy have been important sources for American theological thought. And as with the philosophical influences, fashions of influence also seem to vary here with the times. In the first forty years of the century, for example, American theological reflection found itself wrestling with two central problems—both of which had been raised by or within the secular cultural environment. The first set of problems revolved around the disturbing implications for religious belief of the new scientific cosmology and especially of evolution. In trying to re-interpret their faith in the face of this challenge from natural science, theologians at the turn of the century became interested in the physical and biological sciences; they sought and found there the main categories—primarily, of course, that of "evolutionary development"—with which they re-interpreted the Christian tradition. During the same period, the prestige of those sciences made the "empirical" method, even in its most stringent forms, a preferred approach to theological truth. The second problem that concerned early-twentieth-century American theology was that of economic justice. In this connection, democratic, socialist, and Marxist categories appeared predominantly in many theological and religious writings—for example, those of Rauschenbusch, Fosdick, and the early Niebuhr. In each case the spiritual crisis of the time arose in relation to some particular secular discipline; theology turned, consequently, to that discipline to find the categories relevant to the solution of its own theological or religious crisis.

The same pattern repeated itself during the middle decades of the century. After World War II, personal problems of alienation from a conformist and technological civilization came to the fore in American secular life. Theology correspondingly turned from a concern with scientific developments and with outer social structures to a concentration on inner disorders. Theologians became greatly influenced by various forms of psychoanalytic theory. Freudian, Jungian, Rankian categories appear in their writings, and the models and concepts of Horney, Fromm, Riesman, and Theodore Whyte tended to replace those of Darwin and Spencer, Marx and Laski. With the demise of the theory of progress during the postwar period, moreover, questions were again asked about the meaning and direction of history; and so the writings of Spengler, Toynbee, Dilthey, Troelstch, and Collingwood became the other favorite "secular" sources for theological thought. During this neo-orthodox period, therefore, theologians were wrong in thinking they could pursue an autonomous enterprise based only on the Biblical word and indifferent to the secular disciplines. To be sure, they no longer built their concepts on scientific categories, and they eschewed metaphysical systems. But just as theology fed on existentialist philosophy, so also did it thrive on psychology and the study of history, for its own deepest concerns, no longer cosmological, involved the turmoil of man's inner life and the patent chaos of his outer history.

The mood of American culture has again shifted, this time moving once more toward the sphere of external social problems. Reflecting this shift, the secular subjects intriguing to theologians have also changed: Christian ethics is currently less interested in problems of neurosis and self-acceptance than it is in those of the relation of affluence to the Protestant ethic of work; of automation to the Christian responsibility for full employment; of delinquency to the ideals of order and self-expression; and of slums to the question of human dignity; not to mention issues raised by the "sexual revolution" and LSD. Overshadowing all these current social crises has been the civil rights movement—of enormous concern to the leadership of the churches and of vast significance in the deep reappraisal of the failures and the new tasks of American religion. In general, then, theology has responded to the present domestic crises by turning its attention from the inner man to the inner city, by shelving its psychological studies for those of sociology—as the very influential sociological writings of Peter Berger, Gibson Winter, and Harvey Cox show on the one hand, and as the even more significant growth of urban training centers for pastors and theologians in our cities demonstrates on the other. As Martin Marty has remarked, true to the traditional American belief that the Divine works as much in and through our history as through the ecclesiastical means of grace, many current American religious thinkers, having become dubious about any transcendent deity, are inclined to look for an epiphany of the Divine in the protest movements that crowd our city streets.

Recently, it must be added, another "secular" source for theology has appeared prominently: the use of literature as a direct source of theological reflection. For both Thomas J. J. Altizer and William Hamilton, literature can function much as the Bible once functioned for theology: as an authoritative basis for ideas in Christian theology. If Saul Bellow is "optimistic" in *Herzog*, then theology should be optimistic too; if William Blake has an eschatological vision of the death of God in his poem "America," then this vision is a valid basis for theological proclamation.[2] It has, of course, long been recognized by critics, both secular and religious, that any significant literature has important theological implications; no one doubts that many literary works explore deep religious problems and express religious and even Christian symbols and attitudes with more power than can either theology or preaching. This, however, is not the same thing as saying that secular literature can or should be an originating and self-authenticating *source* for theological concepts, or that it provides criteria for determining the rightness or the contemporaneity of theological reflection. To maintain this is, of course, to deny any trans-cultural origin of essential religious notions and to regard as valid a theology growing directly out of the cultural consciousness itself, as expressed in art, literature, and science. This new role for literature bespeaks, therefore, the method implicit in the present radically "secular theology" and the current disenchantment with the traditional sources and authorities of classical theology. Thus, in this view, the theologian becomes a kind of amateur literary critic just as once he had been a second-class natural scientist or metaphysician—a role which seems in either case to auger little staying power.

American theology in the last half-century has, then, received substantial help from a number of secular disciplines ranging from the physical sciences through the social and psychological sciences to the humanities and the arts. These bewildering changes of intellectual partners reveal, however, one continual characteristic of American theology and its relation to its "sources." They show that American theology has been socially involved first with regard to intrinsic concern, and then, as a consequence, with regard to the formation of its own fundamental categories of thought. The evidence indicates that the intellectual shape of recent American theology has been determined in each decade by the character of the crises then current in the wider secular milieu.

This repeated pattern of involvement in secularity has not been characteristic of European theology. The influence of contemporary social and intellectual crises in the community has been present, to be sure, in European theological writings too. But this has been a submerged influence, hidden between the lines, peeping out from behind the main categories, and discussed openly only in footnotes. Since the presence in theological writings of secular categories has been regarded with suspicion by the more isolationist theological methods of the continent, the reader has to dig out these influences from under a good deal of traditional Biblical and theological language. By contrast, in American theological writing, the influence of "secular" categories has been direct, almost blatant. Marxist concepts, Freudian images, and sociological structures appear on the surface, lying on the page next to Biblical and traditional notions, or replacing them by some mode of translation. Thus are the American themes of the unity of the secular and the religious, of the social involvement of the religious in the secular again revealed in the relation of American theology to its sources.

It is, therefore, no surprise, nor in spirit anything radically new, that a totally "secular" theology devoid of any "religious" or transcendent elements has now appeared in the United States. The new form of this theology does, however, reveal a change in the character of American secularity. In the period of nineteenth-century liberalism, this secularity was so imbued with the sense of immanent creativity, it could unite with religious convictions about God's purposes in the world without overwhelming loss to either partner. American secularity has now become more radical; finding little meaningful beyond the immediate natural and social environment, this mood in theology enforces a much more stringent restriction on theological language, denying the possibility of any transcendent reference at all if theology is to be meaningful.

In this most recent theology, social crises and movements, as well as philosophical themes, have again played a major role in the formation of theological concepts. There is no question but that participation in the civil rights movement and the sudden "plunge" into the urban and poverty problems have had an invigorating effect on these current theological reflections, providing most of the positive ethical content to the God-is-dead theology and fundamentally transforming current thought about the nature and task of the church. Civil rights is a social movement in relation to which positive Christian commitment has been both obligatory and creative, a movement whose moral issues have been clear and unambiguous, and where the action of dedicated groups has begun to have an observable and obviously healthy result. Consequently, much of America's most recent radical theology, informed by participation in this movement, has understood its religion solely in the ethical terms of love and service, commitment and self-giving, and creative and hopeful action. Since these ethical motives fortunately do spring up within liberal hearts, both Christian and non-Christian, Negro and white, the theological reflection that eventuates from them tends to be humanistic and optimistic. Where is the need for God if man can by dedicated activity in the secular realm solve his own problems? Why do we need to talk of sin, guilt, forgiveness, and the question of meaning if moral action for and in the world serves our brother and fulfills our own existence?

Such questions have made sense in relation to the past history of this particular social issue. I suspect, however, that the further development of current crises in American life may foster other kinds of theological reflection. Any social movement (for example, that of labor), as it leaves a situation of total repression and takes on social power, becomes more ambiguous in its moral character; power both corrupts the new wielders of power and also reveals the ever-present ambiguity that has always been latent within them. The civil rights movement is already experiencing this fateful ambiguity in its internecine struggle over the issues of non-violence versus violence, and of integration versus "Black Power." But above all, the crisis of American action in Viet-Nam, in which American religion will, one trusts, become more and more involved in the days ahead, reveals the tragic and sinful dimensions of all worldly action, even action with the best intentions. In such a situation, an innocent, well-intentioned "affirmation of the world to save the world" on the part of American power is *not* to follow the pattern of Jesus at all, but rather the familiar, and perhaps dangerous, pattern of American national messianism. Theological reflection on the Viet-Nam crisis—where action is undertaken not by the oppressed but by those who have power, and in the case of the United States by those who are mighty—will find relevant some of the older theological categories descriptive of sin and guilt within all active social involvement, categories expressing the need for communal repentance, forgiveness, reconciliation, and meaning beyond the ambiguity that is consequent to everything that man does. It would be personally more gratifying to be able to predict that American theology will take an optimistic form based on creative domestic social action, than to look forward to the return of a classical theology because of a dreaded tragedy in our streets at home or in international affairs. But I fear that we shall not have to live very long for the demonic as well as the creative possibilities in all of us to reveal themselves, and then, as has been the habit of American thought, the present humanist stance of much American theology may well change again.

What are the creative elements as well as the dangers of the peculiar kind of theology and religiosity that is American? First, it is evident that American religion and American theology exhibit a striking involvement with their cultural surroundings, an involvement that is a matter not only of ethical concern but even more of intellectual interchange. No theological tradition in history has been so much influenced by the secular categories that surround it— and correspondingly no form of church life has so wholeheartedly participated in the communal life of its culture. Consequently, American thinkers have elaborated more than other forms of Christianity the relevance of their religion to the problems of culture; in parallel fashion, American clergy have participated more than most in the social crises of American life. Theology, thus, has had a relevance and a vitality in American life unmatched in the rest of Christendom, where the secular is more secular, the church more traditional, and the separation between the two, the irrelevance of the one to the other, more apparent. Since, moreover, one cannot but believe that the strength of the secular spirit—the sense of the autonomy and meaningfulness of natural life and of historic community—will grow rather than diminish in Western and possibly in world culture, the creative influence of the peculiarly American form of Christian thinking may increase in the years to come.

On the other side of the ledger, the dangers of this amalgamation of culture and religion are equally apparent. In a powerful culture aware of its own idealism and self-conscious about its message for the world, the identification of its deepest religious convictions with the particularity of its cultural ethos presents the ever-present danger of nationalistic spiritual pride and fanaticism.

How does such a culture deal with alien social concepts and standards if it thinks that the activity of God is inevitably involved with its own cultural destiny? How can it see its own partiality and its own faults if it identifies the divine righteousness with its own point of view? How can it bear the frustrations of its ideals and the challenges to its power and security if the meaning of all existence is equated with the success of its own way of life? The danger of older forms of religion based upon transcendence—a transcendent gospel and an other-worldly ethic—has always been that such a gospel has been irrelevant to the ordinary life of men, leaving in that cultural existence a vacuum to be filled with other faiths. But the danger of a "worldly" gospel, as in America, is that this gospel might find itself associated too directly with the security, the welfare, and the permanence of the culture with which it is married. In such a case, a message of transcendent judgment, of transcendent mercy, and of transcendent hope is the only requisite for a healthy religious and theological life. Such a message is difficult in this secular age—but this difficulty does not at all demonstrate either its invalidity or its irrelevance to the health of America's common life.

Finally when one tries to survey the present relations of American theology to its secular sources, one can feel only a certain guarded optimism about the immediate future in theology— certainly more than a couple of years ago, and certainly more than in Europe where the separation from its culture increasingly frustrates the creativity of theology. First of all, thanks to the God-is-dead theologians, there is a new sense of the importance of theological questions, a new concern for fundamental issues, and a new desire to think things out creatively from the very beginning, for ourselves and for our own age. There is at present a new openness to cultural influences and a new sense of total involvement in the world's life—both of which have been *the* creative factors in American theological development. And yet increasingly there is the sense that a *purely* secular gospel is of no real help. Intellectually, humanism in a Christian garb lacks the means with which to understand creatively and to deal creatively with the turbulent secular social scene; existentially, total involvement in the world in a Christian way requires deep and treasured Christian resources that a merely secular religion might squander. Thus, more than at any time in the last half century, there is a sense of a needed dialogue between the sacred and the profane, the religious and the cultural, between the theologians and the reflection that stems from secular sources.

One should add that at present the vigorous forms of philosophy, ordinary language philosophy and phenomenology, seem to be open to usage in theological contexts. Unlike most speculative metaphysics, moreover, their usage in theology does not seem, at least from this vantage point, to predetermine the character of the theological thought that results; they seem to offer to theology helpful methods rather than autonomous and competing visions of reality. All of this may sound too optimistic, and perhaps it is. But if one compares the present situation with the rather moribund neo-orthodox scholasticism of fifteen years ago, and the frustration with regard to creativity of five years ago, when only critical and historical works seemed possible in theology, one can only feel good about the present and its possibilities.

One last word. It might seem from this account that theology was merely a piecing together of secular sources and nothing more. This was not at all the intention. In the first place, the origins of many of the concepts adapted creatively by theology from its cultural setting lie in the religious tradition that theology seeks to interpret. The very creativity of secularity derives in part from its continual relation to an autonomous and strong theology. But more important, as even a secular gospel centered on the figure of Jesus shows, any creative theology ultimately draws its strength from its own sources. This spiritual strength becomes explicit when it is re-expressed for each new age in "secular" categories relevant and appropriate to its time and task. But unless its message springs from these indigenous sources, theology has little with which to perpetuate its own life in time and even less to offer the world in which it seeks to live.

REFERENCES

1. See Paul Van Buren, *The Secular Meaning of the Gospel* (New York, 1963).

2. For the first, see William Hamilton's article, "The New Optimism from Prufrock to Ringo," *Theology Today*, Vol. 22, No. 4 (January, 1966); for the second, Thomas J. J. Altizer's "William Blake and Role of Myth in the Radical Christian Vision," *The Centennial Review*, Vol. 9, No. 4 (Fall, 1964).

MARTIN E. MARTY

The Spirit's Holy Errand: The Search for a
Spiritual Style in Secular America

IN THE religious revival of the 1950's and the social revolution of the
1960's, formal, theological, and ethical obsessions crowded out spiritual concerns. In the process, *spirituality* as a term was abandoned,
especially by academic religionists.

During the 1950's, when people spoke of a "revival of religion,"
metropolitan newspapers enlarged their sections devoted to religion. For a decade, the press gave attention to the material expansion of institutions. It dutifully reported on the building of churches
and synagogues and chronicled the growth of religious bodies and
the rise in attendance at rites. By the end of the decade such reporting had begun to pall on both newspapermen and their readers. Few look back to the years of the purported revival as a time
of spiritual increase in the United States.

During the 1960's, the newspapers again portray the decade's
religious preoccupations. Today, "a revolution in religion" has come
to be a front-page topic. Ethics and theology receive first attention.
Newspapers report clerical involvement in civil rights activities, denominational statements on housing and poverty, theologians' demonstrations against the war in Viet-Nam. Radical and epochal
changes in the thought of Christian and Jewish leaders are related
in columns devoted to Vatican II and denominational assemblies.
The death-of-God theology merely climaxes a sequence of stories
through which the public has become aware of the unorthodoxies
of Bishops John Robinson and James Pike, of the forward look in
Harvey Cox's *The Secular City*, and of the frank secularity and
worldliness of much academic theology.

Urgent issues of theology, ethics, and the social forms of the
church so preoccupied the elite and the avant-garde of the religious

communities that they tended to ignore "the spiritual dimension" of both individual and collective life. Paul Tillich, America's most prestigious theologian in these decades, spoke of "the almost forbidden word 'spirit'" and worked heroically to bring discussion of the term into sophisticated academic theology and philosophy: "Should and can the word 'spirit,' designating the particularly human dimension of life, be reinstated? There are strong arguments for trying to do so; and I shall attempt it." But even Tillich despaired of the attempt to resuscitate the adjective *spiritual;* it "is lost beyond hope."[1]

Despite the disinterest or the despair of academic religionists, concern for the spiritual did not, however, disappear. It went underground and became the property of adherents of America's folk, lay, civic, or societal religion. With or without formal leadership, a search for a spiritual style in America goes on.

Evidence of an Ongoing Search

When people detail their reasons for pursuing the religious quest, they usually speak of psychological and moral situations relating to what Tillich called the "unity of power and meaning" denoted by the term *spirit.* The same sociological surveys that find the majority of Americans professing belief in God and affiliating with church and synagogue find only a minority expressing any interest in theology or concurring with their church's major ethical positions. Although academic critics find the churches' theological quest earnest, and their ethical renewal reasonably impressive, they find missing any articulation of the profoundest features in "the particularly human dimensions of life."

While religious institutions abdicate their roles in spiritual development as they face apparently more urgent concerns, the search becomes informal and, one might say, para-religious. It is manifest in the interest shown best-selling books like Pope John's *Journal of a Soul,* Dag Hammarskjöld's quasi-mystical *Markings,* Teilhard de Chardin's tantalizing glimpses of a spiritual human future, and even the slangy rituals of a book of prayers like Malcolm Boyd's *Are You Running with Me, Jesus?.* People make heroes of the Albert Schweitzers and pay attention to a Paul Tillich or a Martin Buber for their "style" even where they cannot share their substance. On the more popular level, they seek to spot authenticity and sincerity in television personalities and rate Billy Graham among the ten most admired men in the nation. The majority of Americans criticize the Supreme Court's rulings against public-school prayer. The public has some nebulous and vestigial sense that devotion "belongs" for the development of psychological and moral dimensions of personality.

The search for a spiritual style in today's America—whether expressed in popular support of religious institutions or in rejection of these institutions by the academy; whether revealed in the literary culture's tastes or in the popular culture's causes and preferences —need not be described as obsessive or urgent. The political establishment gains most support when it invests in projects that enable people to travel faster and farther, that make things explode, that increase the Gross National Product. But the "spiritual" underground supplies an undertone to the noisier features of national life. Its members express uneasiness about psychological and moral drift or anarchy, about *anomie* and disintegration. They speak of a desire to see life transformed, the *charisma* of leaders transferred to followers, and roots given to personal and public life.

Disappearance of the Transcendent

Once, spiritual man was seen to be the one who stood before the *mysterium tremendum*. He maintained a direct or clearly mediated access to a transcendent order or being; he had some contact with the primal depths of a universe that both terrified him and pronounced perpetual benediction on his doings. Today, this transcendent order has disappeared from consciousness. Any new quest by people who have experienced the disappearance of transcendence must take place in the empirical world. Their quest would eventuate from Merleau-Ponty's affirmation: "Because we are present to a world, we are condemned to meaning."[2] The spiritual person, in this case, would be the man who lives out the terms of condemnation creatively. Spirit, to quote Arnold Come's theological definition,

is . . . man in the fullest possible actualization of what he is in his heart. Man as spirit is "the forceful and indeed purposeful individual," man at his most personal level, wherein the totality of all the dimensions and capacities and contents of his life (soul) are brought to conscious unity in realization.[3]

With this definition, discussion of spirit need not be restricted to certain formal religious objects or creedal propositions.

The advance guard of American theology approaches sustained discussion of spirituality only in the context of the phrase *holy worldliness* (or its converse, *worldly holiness*), abstracted from Dietrich Bonhoeffer's attempt to find a nonreligious expression of the Christian faith. The phrase *holy worldliness* shocks an America accustomed to hearing preachers advocate the "holiness" of a realm set apart and associated with transcendence. The public has come to feel that religious leadership has deserted traditional theological, ethical, and spiritual beliefs. As the custodian of a kind of supernaturalist sub-culture, the clergy had been expected to summon rhetoric to advocate religiousness and a spirituality based on it. With their vested interest in transcendence and cosmic order, they could provide models for sainthood. They could stand for morals, law, and order.

Theologians now tell Protestants, Catholics, and Jews that people in these religions must advance the cause of "secularization." They must purge the world of its mythical, superstitious, and—in a dramatic usage of the term—*religious* vestiges. They assert that the future belongs to "God's advance guard," and that much in the past must be overcome if life is to be made more human. They testify in Congress against proposed constitutional amendments that would permit saying prayers in the public schools. Leading racial demonstrations, they break laws and disrupt order. Some of them speak of the "death of God" and put in a good word for the atheist.

All these public perceptions of the roles of clerical leadership bear directly on the search for a spiritual style. If they are accurate, the clergy *is* leaving behind and *wants* to leave behind an approach that obtained for three and a half centuries. The theological and ethical leaders may be making this change in order to retrieve for themselves some part in spiritual definition in the future. Until their activities and motives are made more clear, however, it will be possible for opponents to exploit their positions and for others to see in these positions contributions to spiritual drift and anarchy.

The New Setting in Secular America

Americans have consistently been considered a future-oriented people. They have often repudiated history, tradition, the European past. Pragmatic, optimistic, and now industrially or technologically adept, they have chosen a secular mode of existence. In their practical daily lives, "the world has become an entity rounded off in itself, which is neither actually open at certain points where it merges into God, nor [undergoing] at certain observable points the causal impact (*ursächlichen Stoss*) of God."[4]

Practical godlessness does not presuppose a formal repudiation of the old ways in theology, ethics, or spirituality. Norman Birnbaum has an insight into the mixed character of American life when he observes that the typical American is a Calvinist who has neither fear of hell nor hope of heaven. The Calvinism may be gradually slipping away, but it symbolizes an element of the past that cannot be shrugged off lightly. Sociologist J. Milton Yinger has seen the transition as a development of a "laymen's ecumenicalism, a folk effort," independent of religious professionals. The public redefines its religion "while disguising or obscuring the process by holding, somewhat superficially, to many of the earlier religious symbols."[5]

Americans are caught, then, between the "religious" and the "secular," between the divergent directives from the religious institutions and leaders of the past and those of the present. Father John Thomas, S.J., commenting on an extensive religious survey made in 1952, admits that the findings lend "considerable support to the contention that the frame of reference within which modern man defines the essential human dilemma has lost its transcendental referents," though roughly half the adult population "still regards the churches as representatives of a transcendental point of view." Sociologist Gerhard Lenski also concludes that in general "a transcendental faith is gradually being transformed into a cultural faith."[6]

The "Calvinist" side of this new man, this American who has neither fear of hell nor hope of heaven, is nostalgic. This man looks back, as his father before him looked back, to a society and a religious context in which spirituality grew out of an agreed-upon frame of reference. He expects religious institutions today to propagate something of that earlier context's assumptions. He feels cheated when religious leaders want to lead him away from those assumptions.

The Spirit's Holy Errand in American History

Ralph Waldo Emerson could hardly be seen as a spokesman of America's colonial orthodoxies, yet he was typically nostalgic about one feature of colonial life and was concerned about what would replace it.

What a debt is ours to that old religion which, in the childhood of most of us, still dwelt like a sabbath morning in the country of New England, teaching privation, self-denial and sorrow! A man was born not for prosperity, but to suffer for the benefit of others, like the noble rock-maple which all around our villages bleeds for the service of man. Not praise, not man's acceptance of our doing, but the spirit's holy errand through us absorbed the thought. . . .

And what is to replace for us the piety of that race? We cannot have theirs; it glides away from us day by day.[7]

Because of what he held in common with those who earlier had known "the spirit's holy errand," Emerson today sounds as archaic as they. His "piety," or spirituality, glides away too. Many today could more easily relate to the colonial covenant than they could to Emerson's transcendentalist Over-Soul. But in his time he was able to help give the contemporary "image of the free individual cosmic significance." If the "old Calvinism which in his youth hung like a benediction over New England, holding each man down to *his* place with the weight of the Universe," was gliding away, Emerson "pronounced the same benediction over his fellows."[8]

Most contemporary Americans are not, of course, direct spiritual heirs of colonial New England. The Roman Catholics, Jews, and continental Protestants who immigrated after the middle of the nineteenth century would have found little congenial in New England village life. But consciously and unconsciously, by historical study and by osmosis, they share its general outline. More important, most of these later immigrants lived in sub-communities or enclaves that reproduced the essential feature in the life of the original covenanted community. Human personality and spirituality were still measured according to standards shaped by belief in a transcendent order. Beneath the sermons of oligarchical clerics or the constructs of the founding fathers, in the diaries and simple accounts of daily life, formal religious concerns seem less obsessive than they do today. Real infidels were rare, but disaffection was common; many were "nothingarians" in religion. One quiet dissenter addressed his clergyman:

We have heard your animadversions upon our absence from Sabbath meetings, and humbly conceive if you wish our attendance there, you would make it worth our while to give it. To miss a sermon of the present growth, what is it but to miss of an opiate? And can the loss of a nap expose our souls to eternal perdition?[9]

But if disaffection was common and dissent widespread, it was easier then for people to be aware of what it was from which they were dissenting and how radically they desired to dissent. At the base was what verged on an ontocratic order, to use Arend van Leeuwen's thoughtful term. In it, man's spiritual life grew out of an understanding of the cosmos in the context of a total order of harmony between temporal and eternal, human and divine.

The sense of a quasi-metaphysical setting was pervasive. It was not restricted to churchgoers. Almost ten times as large a percentage of the population is affiliated with religious institutions today as was at the end of the colonial era. All forms of society were given a sacral dimension. A theocratic foundation underlay or a theocratic penumbra surrounded these institutions. Toleration-minded pluralist colonies like Roger Williams' Rhode Island, or Catholic colonies like Maryland, hardly differed in this respect from the homogeneous and organismic society advocated by John Cotton in Massachusetts.

Oscar Handlin has written of this archetypal American experience:

Every event had a deep meaning. The ministers were rationalists who had faith in the power of logic to resolve the most difficult theological problems; and the people had to think matters through for themselves when they could not depend on habit. . . .

Indeed nothing that occurred in the world was simply a random event. Everything was the product of the intent of some mover. A tree did not fall; it was felled. When a monstrous child was born or a school of porpoises seen, that was a sign of something designed. Life was full of signs and portents which indicated the direction of events and the intentions of the forces at work in the universe. . . . In the pilgrimage of life, man cautiously made his way, examining every incident for clues to his destiny.

. . . The second generation had not so much lost this sense as transformed it. . . .

They too, although in a different way, were moved by a conviction of the grandeur of their destiny.[10]

The quest was communal. As Yale President Ezra Stiles put it for a later generation: "We must become a holy people in reality, in order to exhibit the experiment, never yet fully made in this unhallowed part of the universe, whether such a people would be the happiest on earth."[11]

Not many in subsequent generations held to a pure Puritan vision in which people "could find cosmic issues in a sneeze."[12] But when they replaced this with their first formal "secular" experience, with what is often called the American Enlightenment, one constant remained. A sense of cosmic order and purpose still conditioned philosophy (not theology), laws, manners, character, "holiness." "The Heavenly City of the Eighteenth Century Philosophers" offered the spirit a new home. The deists maximized the sense of congruity between what was perceived in nature or reason and the ultimate order of things; they did not doubt that order's existence and meaning. They were confident about a Supreme Being or First Cause or Grand Architect of the Universe, the accountability of man, the assuredness of rewards and punishments. They shared with the theologues much of what had been implied in the term *Providence*, though they were beginning to translate it *Progress*. Thomas Jefferson and Thomas Paine, seen as the radicals of the later period, differed less than they thought from their orthodox opponents.

In the nineteenth century, Protestant evangelicals, the newly-arriving Roman Catholics, and the romantic and transcendentalist spokesmen witnessed transformation, but a transformation that maintained continuity with the previous periods. They did not perceive a fundamental breach with the earlier order of things. This order could be perceived in Scripture, in creation, in Over-Soul. The westward movement in the early-nineteenth century was marked by revivalist agitations. Yet during that era, when muscular Christianity seemed most appropriate, only belief in cosmic threat or salvation as the source and norm of spiritual values prompted revivalists' bold appeals for conversion. In the minds of many later Protestants, the evangelicalism of this frontier and early industrial period becomes fused with colonial religion and represents the mythical "good old days."

The Unitarians, in departing from and reacting against colonial Puritanism or their contemporaries' revivalism, did not depart from the sense that human spirit was in discourse with the Spirit. Foreign visitors like de Tocqueville noticed with surprise the manifest spirituality of this materially successful egalitarian nation: "There is no country in the world where the Christian religion retains a greater influence over the souls of men than in America."[13] Neither denominational competition and entrepreneurial expertise revealed in the founding of new sects and movements nor the Civil War could break the fundamental unity of order and purpose. For later Americans, Abraham Lincoln stands as a representative of an

American spirituality that could be nurtured outside the established denominations.

Ralph Henry Gabriel noted of these years that Americans affirmed "that beneath society, its customs and institutions, a law exists that men did not make. . . . For the individual it establishes the principles on which to found a beneficent and constructive life. For society it institutes an order within which persons may grow in understanding and virtue."[14]

Throughout the transformations of the nineteenth century—the replacement of Providence by Progress, and the general weakening of unity as America became conscious of her pluralism—something of this transcendent and unitive cosmic order survived. The nationalism of Manifest Destiny and the economic and religious creeds associated with Social Darwinism may have inverted much of the earlier value systems, but they were not fundamentally unsettling. The most radical modernistic theologies tended to be overt theistic systems; theologians were supremely self-confident concerning the order out of which spirituality grows.

The Loss of the Cosmic Sense

What Protestant competition could not do to evangelicalism, what Roman Catholicism could not do to Protestantism, what Judaism could not do to Christianity during the peak periods of immigration, the onset of industrial life began to accomplish. Eventually, "instead of finding their democratic faith in supernatural religion, Americans . . . tended to find their religious faith in various forms of belief about their own existence."[15]

Only now are Americans becoming aware of the profound transformation of values that occurred during the nineteenth century. Perry Miller suggested that around 1815, when textile mills opened in New England, a business civilization came to be "the dominant theme of American history" at the expense of other value systems. Today a serious thinker like Clarence Ayres can contend that "it is [the] technological continuum which is the locus of truth and value."[16] Nineteenth-century prophets began to notice that the business community kept many of the old symbols and used them ideologically, but the business continuum had become the locus of truth and value. Professor James Ward Smith was only a little overconfident in his writing of the obituary for the old:

From 1620 to 1914 American thought was marked by a persistent optimism that courses of action can be justified by sweeping cosmic theories. Even our "pessimists," who deplored the actual course of events, retained the optimistic conviction that they understood ultimate truths which enabled them to judge and to condemn. . . . No single fact about American philosophical thought since 1914 is more important than the loss of confidence embodied in this "cosmic sense." . . . The cosmic sense of American philosophy was, while it lasted, universally religious in tone.[17]

According to Walter Lippmann, little survived the collapse of the single cosmic sense in personal, political, and philosophic life. But Lippmann did not stop talking about the spiritual; indeed, he called for a humanistic value system, "the religion of the spirit."

In an age when custom is dissolved and authority is broken, the religion of the spirit is not merely a possible way of life. In principle it is the only way which transcends the difficulties. . . . The religion of the spirit does not depend upon creeds and cosmologies; it has no vested interest in any particular truth. It is concerned not with the organization of matter, but with the quality of human desire.[18]

Such an envisioned humanistic religion of the spirit shares space with creeds and cosmologies in America's mixed religious history. The search for a spiritual style continues.

Professional Disinterest and Suspicion

No doubt the informal search will continue to be met with some disinterest and even suspicion on the part of academic theologians. *Spirit* has become an almost forbidden word because it eludes precise definition. As a category, it is notoriously evanescent. In 1888 Lord Bryce complained, "To convey some impression of the character and type which religion has taken in America, and to estimate its influence as a moral and spiritual force, is an infinitely harder task than to sketch the salient ecclesiastical phenomena of the country."[19]

What is more, as the academicians are well aware, resort to "the spiritual" can serve as escape from responsibility into narcissism, from community concern into self-seeking. Thus, John Dewey commented: "What is termed spiritual culture has usually been futile, with something rotten about it."[20] It is little wonder that the quest for a spiritual style goes on so informally, with few guides, or leaders, or norms.

In the best of circumstances, the effort is difficult and complicated. Questions come to mind: Is it legitimate to try to isolate American spirituality? Is the United States at present sufficiently homogeneous to support such an isolation? American ties to the history of spirituality in Europe, in the West, indeed, in Hebraic and Hellenic culture are fairly obvious. Yet, at the risk of seeing the quest perverted along nationalist lines, there are reasons to discern elements of uniqueness in America where the technological culture has developed most rapidly and where religious institutions have remained strong.

Although the search is complicated by many features of the American environment, few have as much import as the transition from rural to urban life, from a pre-industrial to a technological society. Authors of the manuals of spirituality have always tended to echo British bishop Samuel Wilberforce's father, who congratulated the son for turning down an urban see. Only in the country would he have been able to cultivate "devotional feelings and spirituality of mind."[21] Pastoral imagery haunts the counselors of piety; the monastic model of contemplation and withdrawal seems to remain normative in traditional texts on religion. But few Americans know such pastoral solitude. America has few contemplatives and does not know what to make of those it does have. Moreover, withdrawal is difficult in an activist, pluralist, interactive society paced by mass-media communications.

Critics of religion, both within and outside denominations, charge that American religion—voluntaryistic and competitive as it is and must be—is too political, too compromising, too institutionally self-seeking to provide room for spiritual development. The burdens of administration and the pressures on leadership are such that spiritual depth would be misunderstood and discouraged if not structurally ruled out. These familiar complaints further complicate the quest for spirit.

But most problematic of all features is the radical change in spiritual styles. "Humanist concerns now embrace the divine. Both speak the same language." The theologians have abolished the transcendent. Ernest Gellner writes:

There is a sense in which the old conflict between religion and disbelief, profound though it seemed, was a parochial matter. The two sides often agreed on the kind of world they lived in: they just disagreed about one special feature of it. One side added an item—albeit an important one—to the cosmic inventory: the Deity. The other side refused to countenance this addition. One side considered the hypothesis of the Deity to be the best, or the only, or the obligatory hypothesis, required for the explanation of the other features of the world. The other side considered the same hypothesis to be inadequately supported or refutable, or objected morally to any hypothesis being made obligatory. But clearly, this disagreement presupposed a certain consensus about the world which was to be explained—and, in fact, there often was such agreement.

That particular struggle is over—partly because we are told that the Deity has ceased to be an hypothesis at all. Just what It is instead is obscure and varies a good deal with intellectual fashion.[22]

Now, Gellner adds, more fundamental conflicts are before us. Divines and humanists form alliances for or against racial harmony, war, scientific understanding, or spiritual expression.

Models, Events, Features

Despite all these complications, Americans are beginning to make their way with some creativity in their quest for a spiritual approach without a cosmic reference. Such an approach needs personal models to fill the roles saints played in earlier pieties. Such models, in the form of a number of charismatic world citizens, have begun to be appropriated: Pope John, Dag Hammarskjöld, Albert Schweitzer. Depending upon tastes and predilections of various sub-groups, names like Gandhi, Martin Luther King, Adlai Stevenson could be added to this list. The newer "world-oriented" clerics and lay leaders in Protestantism have made much of Dietrich Bonhoeffer as a spiritual figure, both for the secular manner of his later theologizing and for the way he sealed his life with a politically problematic kind of martyrdom. Roman Catholics have done the same with Alfred Delp, S.J., another ranging theologian and concentration-camp victim. Following the injunction of one manual to "seek a city saint," some have paid attention to John F. Kennedy, who infused a pragmatic approach with idealist imagery.

Events serve the same function as persons do in the quest for spirituality. Civil rights marches are often seen as "epiphanies"; service groups like the Peace Corps offer "revelatory" experiences. Just as the Civil War still seems to reach certain almost mystic chords in Americans' natures, so the chaos and ceremony following John F. Kennedy's death serve as a paradigmatic event for the new spirituality. H. Richard Niebuhr speaks of revelatory activity as "an event that so captures the imagination of a community that it alters that community's way of looking at the totality of its experience. It is an event that strikes the community as illuminatory for understanding all other events."[23] In this case, the Kennedy death was revelatory in secular America: It enlarged the spiritual range and scope of both horror and ceremony as affirmation. American Jews, perhaps for generations to come, will see the experience of Auschwitz and other death camps as determinative for their spiritual value systems, though they may remain divided over the issues of relating Auschwitz to a Lord of history, a transcendent scheme or activity.

An interesting feature of the new search is the ability of its participants to live with pluralism. So much of the old spiritual style (Perry Miller's pre-1815 or James Ward Smith's pre-1914) depended upon homogeneity, upon assent to all details of a cosmic system. Today, many draw spiritual sustenance from synthesists whose fundamental vision they cannot share: Paul Tillich or Teilhard de Chardin, Arnold Toynbee or Lewis Mumford, William Ernest Hocking or F. S. C. Northrop, Erich Kahler or Pitirim Sorokin. With a syncretism or eclecticism born of necessity, many have learned the "merits of borrowing" from such figures. The Christian ecumenical movement and the interfaith concord advocated at mid-century played its part: Pope John was probably the first Catholic pontiff looked to for specific spiritual leadership by Protestants, Jews, and others.

Certain substantive features in the new spiritual style are becoming apparent: a native *charisma* in the personal model of spirituality, coupled with a sacrificing life; an at-homeness in the world paired with a certain "otherness" or personality secret; a willingness to accept the terms of life "on the boundaries"—between epochs or value systems. Significantly, whether these heroes and models believe in a transcendent order or purported access to a transcendent being is considered irrelevant. Some of them are theists; some are not. Some have a clarified synthetic sense of cosmic purpose; others make their way existentially and in the face of the absurd—the example of Albert Camus' acceptability in American academic and religious circles comes to mind at once. Traditional American spirituality would have found the question of transcendence, metaphysics, and cosmic order all-important.

An Agenda for the Future

That traditional view was based on what Walter Lippmann called "The Great Scenario," inherited from the past and compounded of elements from the cosmic drama revealed and portrayed in the Bible. No such scenario is the common property of

Western men or of Americans in particular today. Lacking a scenario, Americans can still look ahead and envision certain determinants of the future of spirituality in secular America. What would help to give a more substantive plot to what is now an informal and vague quest?

The theologians would suggest that the public must first forego Emersonian nostalgia, not because they are ungrateful to the fathers, but because they see the emotion to be uncreative. Americans have consciously, deliberately, and consistently regarded the "secular," technological, problem-solving, pluralist life as liberating and life-enhancing. Should they wish to regress to the metaphysical, pre-industrial, homogeneous religious and community life of their forefathers, they would have to pay prices they obviously are unprepared or unable to pay. In Bonhoeffer's terms, they would have to move mentally and spiritually from a kind of maturity to adolescence. If they borrow only a memory of the old piety without becoming aware of its detail, they are in danger of using it ideologically to the impoverishment of the spirit.

Purge of nostalgia need not imply destruction of tradition or jettisoning of history; rather, it helps introduce critical history. After examination of detail of the old piety, the "merits of borrowing" from it can be reexplored. In a famed address at Columbia's bicentenary some years ago, J. Robert Oppenheimer discussed spiritual malaise at a time when "orders disintegrate as well as bind. . . . Diversity, complexity, richness overwhelm the man of today." So? "Each . . . will have to cling to what is close to him, to what he knows, to what he can do, to his friends and his tradition and his love, lest he be dissolved in a universal confusion and know nothing and love nothing."[24] The "old piety" certainly lived on in many ways in Bonhoeffer, Pope John, and Tillich among the Christians, and in Buber and Rosenzweig among the Jews. Moreover, this did not inhibit them from being at home in the secular world.

Critical examination of tradition leads to a constructive exposition of a basis for life-style today. The public might legitimately expect theological leaders to clarify the implications of the growing reluctance to discuss transcendence, the readiness to forget metaphysics, and the willingness to live with pluralism. Such clarity on the part of theological and ethical thinkers would necessitate radical change in the status and position of leaders in religious institutions. The reforms of Catholicism inaugurated by Vatican II and the pronounced ethical involvements of Protestants and Jews in current social issues may make many religious leaders unpopular, but they have also increased these leaders' credibility as sacrificial and spiritually compelling agents of change. In advocating "holy worldliness," theologians have suggested that material life and spiritual life are not incompatible. Religion means not withdrawal from but exposure to the world of men and things. Ecclesiastical leaders are trying to suggest that "the church as institution" and "the church as community of the spirit" are not mutually exclusive but rather represent polar functions. They will become persuasive to the degree that the institutions are seen to be reforming and self-sacrificing, and their leaders freed for authentic service and personal expression.

In the wild pluralism of American life, the search for a spiritual style appropriate to the secular setting will inevitably issue in wild experiment. At any moment such experiment may seem very "unspiritual" and plotless. Yet from it a new language of the spirit could evolve. Today, there are advocates of ESP, Psi-phenomena, and LSD. In search of spiritual expression, people speak in tongues, enter Trappist monasteries, build on Jungian archetypes, go to Southern California and join a cult, become involved "where the action is" in East Harlem, perceive "God at work in the world," see Jesus Christ as the man for others, hope for liberation by the new morality, study phenomenology, share the Peace Corps experience, borrow from cosmic syntheses, and go to church.

The Role of Particular Communities

Within this pluralism, the greatest responsibility will lodge for some time with the institutions serving the two thirds of the American population that is formally affiliated with religious groups. These institutions have traditions, resources, personnel. They experience the most dramatic problems at a time of change. Living between old and new styles, they have shared the real benefits of neither. Until recently, they have been content to be repositories of safe cultural and civic religions. A measure of societal religion may be necessary for knitting a complex democratic society. But in taking refuge in compromise and utility, the churches often sacrifice their potential as agents of spiritual development. Some observers of this civic religion have compared it to the status of Antonine Roman religion as Gibbon described it:

The various modes of worship which prevailed in the Roman world were all considered by the people as equally true; by the philosopher as equally false; and by the magistrate as equally useful. And thus toleration produced not only mutual indulgence, but even religious concord.[25]

Such concord is no small benediction in pluralist America. Its occasion, however, suggests the difficulty of developing spirituality out of civic religion. It is safe, compromising, bland, unembarrassing. Almost all the religious sub-communities in America have given evidence of their ability to share life in a free society—to accept its terms, to gain its ear. Many responsible religious leaders are concerned by the spiritual barrenness of individuals and the lethal measure of the culture as a whole. Out of traditions, their resources, their partly disciplined community life, they are trying to speak words of judgment, of the future, of hope.

These people may lose favor in certain quarters. They are trying to be taken seriously "by the philosopher" and not to be immediately useful to the magistrate. In the process, they may be able to extricate themselves from the web of cultural expectations. If they do, they can produce an exceptional model, moment, or thought as a contribution to man's spiritual quest. Lippmann hoped the contributions that had once been "the possession of an aristocracy of the spirit" could be seen as a possibility for all men. Profound spirituality is rare and belongs to the exceptional man. But all men can profit from clarification of the context out of which "spirit" grows—man in the fullest possible actualization of what he is in his heart. Seen in this light, spirituality would contribute to—but need not compete with—the deserving theological and ethical preoccupations of today's responsible Americans.

REFERENCES

1. Paul Tillich, *Systematic Theology Volume III: Life and the Spirit, History and the Kingdom of God* (Chicago, 1963), pp. 21-30.

2. Quoted by Huston Smith, *Condemned to Meaning* (New York, 1965), p. 17.

3. Arnold B. Come, *Human Spirit and Holy Spirit* (Philadelphia, 1959), p. 72.

4. See Karl Rahner, "Wissenschaft als Konfession?" *Wort und Wahrheit*, Vol. 9 (November, 1954), pp. 811-13.

5. J. Milton Yinger, *Sociology Looks at Religion* (New York, 1963), pp. 36, 67ff.; see also, David Martin, "Towards Eliminating the Concept of Secu-

larization," *Penguin Survey of the Social Sciences 1965*, ed. Julius Gould (Baltimore, 1965), p. 171.

6. John L. Thomas, S.J., *Religion and the American People* (Westminster, Maryland, 1962), pp. 67, 229; Gerhard Lenski, *The Religious Factor* (New York, 1961), p. 54.

7. Ralph Waldo Emerson, "The Method of Nature," *The American Transcendentalists*, ed. Perry Miller (New York, 1957), p. 66.

8. Sidney E. Mead, *The Lively Experiment* (New York, 1963), p. 94.

9. *New Haven Gazette and Connecticut Magazine*, October 9, 1738.

10. Oscar Handlin, *The Americans* (Boston, 1963), pp. 65ff.

11. In John Wingate Thornton, *The Pulpit of the American Revolution* (Boston, 1860), p. 487.

12. Daniel J. Boorstin, *The Genius of American Politics* (Chicago, 1953), p. 44.

13. Alexis de Tocqueville, *Democracy in America*, Vol. 1 (New York, 1954), p. 314.

14. Ralph Henry Gabriel, *The Course of American Democratic Thought* (New York, 1956), p. 14.

15. Max Lerner, *America as a Civilization* (New York, 1957), p. 715.

16. Perry Miller, *The American Character: A Conversation* (Santa Barbara, California, 1962), p. 23. For Ayres, see Robert Theobald, *The Challenge of Abundance* (New York, 1961), p. 122.

17. James Ward Smith, *The Shaping of American Religion*, eds. James Ward Smith and A. Leland Jamison (Princeton, 1961), pp. 402, 404.

18. Walter Lippmann, *A Preface to Morals* (paperback edition; Boston, 1960), p. 327f.

19. James Bryce, *The American Commonwealth*, Vol. 2 (New York, 1959), p. 487.

20. Quoted in Norman Foerster, *Image of America* (South Bend, Indiana, 1962), p. 104.

21. Quoted by K. S. Inglis, *Churches and the Working Classes in Victorian England* (London, 1963), p. 8.

22. Ernest Gellner, *Thought and Change* (Chicago, 1964), pp. 194, 206.

23. H. Richard Niebuhr as paraphrased by Van A. Harvey in *The Historian and the Believer* (New York, 1966), p. 253.

24. *The Reporter*, January 13, 1955.

25. Boorstin, *op. cit.*, p. 135.

THOMAS F. O'DEA

The Crisis of the Contemporary Religious Consciousness

DURING TIMES of religious crises, existence tends to be experienced in terms of its manifold contradictions. People have neither the noetic capacity to integrate an organized outlook nor the psychological ability to achieve a sense of meaningful participation in their society. In recent decades, this condition has come to characterize the outlook of strategic strata in Western countries. It represents a severe crisis of Western religious consciousness. There is much in the present situation that is not new; unbelief, ambivalence, and the temptation of nihilism have characterized religious crises in the past. The inherently close but fundamentally incompatible relationship between faith and doubt is a permanent and perennial characteristic of the religious experience. Yet the conditions of Western man today present this perennial and abiding element of crisis in a new setting—a dynamic and secularized society embodying a scientific world view. This new setting alters radically both the meaning of the perennial crisis and the modes of handling it available to men. At the same time, the combination of perennial and novel elements creates a genuinely new human situation and justifies speaking in terms of the crisis of contemporary religious consciousness. Still, this crisis is experienced differently by people from different social backgrounds, cultural traditions, and religious faiths. But whatever be the differential incidence and different degrees of involvement in the crisis among the various groups in America and the West, the democratization of higher education brings the crisis and involvement in it to ever increasing numbers.

For a sociologist to attempt an analysis of this crisis is to undertake a task that transcends the conceptual tools of his profession, however useful they may prove in certain respects. Behind any analysis of this kind lie an individual experience, a particular perspective, a personal vision. The overview of any writer on this topic will reflect both his professional and his personal biography, his own individual confrontation of and mode of adjustment to the basic elements of the crisis. In the present case, it reflects not only two decades spent in the scholarly study of man's historical and social existence, particularly in relation to his cultural productions and his religious concerns, but also a life lived in a time of war and revolution, of chaotic violence and routinized extermination, of rising expectations and increasing anxieties, of promise and unprecedented threat to man's future. Intellectual and sociological analysis alone can delineate the elements of crisis; this will be attempted with soberness and objectivity. But the configuration they assume will reveal the significance that the analyst sees in them or attributes to them, a significance that expresses not only objective reality but the author's relation to the world. What is attempted here will be a reasonable and open-minded exposition of one sociologist's view of the contemporary religious crisis, eschewing both the smug flattening out of disturbing implications that some social scientists mistake for objectivity and the overdramatic wallowing in catastrophe of certain of their intellectual critics.

Five aspects of the contemporary religious crisis, each of which deserves more attention than can be given it within the scope of this article, will be investigated: (1) the range and variety of crisis experiences; (2) the perennial elements of the religious crisis; (3) the urgency of the contemporary situation; (4) the available modes for confronting the crisis; and finally (5) the problem of relevance for organized religion today.

I. *The Range and Variety of Crisis Experiences*

Let us begin by describing in ideal typical, and somewhat foreshortened and stereotyped terms several kinds of people recognizably suffering in one way or another from the implications of the religious crisis.

We start with a bright Italian-American student on the campus of a Catholic college. Reared in a traditional Catholic home, he attended a parochial elementary and high school and is now in his junior year of college. He is a major in the humanities or the social sciences and has read widely, especially in serious modern thought and literature. He strongly identifies with Catholic intellectuals critical of the tenor of American Catholic life, with progressive theologians, and with the so-called "liberal" party at Vatican II. He champions ecumenism and liturgical revival within his church and is generally sympathetic to new departures in religious thought and action. He considers the problem for people like himself to be that of developing a contemporary and relevant Catholicism that remains, at the same time, true to itself as the bearer of an authentic hierophany. He sees the religion of his parents and, even more, that of his grandparents as "folk" Catholicism, once a protective cocoon for a living religious tradition and experience but now thoroughly dysfunctional for people like himself. He thinks that his fellow students who take refuge in conservative politics or in a combination of conservative politics with a preconciliar Catholicism are practicing an ostrich-like obscurantism, forgivable in aging priests but lamentable, if not reprehensible, in his contemporaries. To him, many of his older clerical teachers and pastors, and possibly his bishop, vary from well-meaning but ineffectual religious conservatives to religious neanderthalers. Beneath this posture—as genuine and authentic as possible for him—there lurk both anguish and dread. He experiences genuine crises of meaning and the real threat of meaninglessness.

We leave the Catholic college and go to a nearby secular campus. Here we see a young man, Jewish by descent, who was brought up in a socially mobile family in which religious teaching, religious atmosphere, or religious concern was at a minimum. He has taken courses in history and the social sciences. In college he has discovered that he is a Jew, not in the sense that he had somehow always known it, but in a new way. He has discovered that there exists a religious, an intellectual, and a legal tradition in which the term *Jew* takes on new meaning for him. He puts on a yarmulke, perhaps even begins to grow a beard, learns Hebrew—or rediscovers the value of some he reluctantly learned in childhood—becomes meticulous concerning dietary regulations and the proper observance of the Sabbath. His secular friends, also of Jewish background, ridicule him somewhat good-naturedly for his "Jew-cap" and his interest in "pilpul," but they nevertheless sense something significant in his behavior. Moreover, they feel that his behavior relates them to him through some unvoiced bond. He is not always sure what he believes about the God of Abraham, Isaac, and Jacob, but his mentors assure him that with faithful observance in terms of what have been called "action symbols" the rest will somehow take care of itself. Beneath this posture—as genuine and authentic as possible for him

—there lurk uncertainty and nervousness, which sometimes issue in inner desperation, sometimes in outer aggressiveness.

In a nearby school of theology we observe a young American Protestant from a small town in the Middle West. He is a candidate for the degree of Bachelor of Divinity. Although he studies the traditional subjects prescribed for such a course, he is intensely interested in protest movements, especially those which he thinks involve an ethical challenge. He is aware of the current theological situation in American Protestantism, and he is confused by it. The "obsolescence" of the Social Gospel, the "contributions" of neo-orthodoxy, the "challenge" of the new Death-of-God theology affect him, but often leave him groping for a sense of direction. He is not sure what he believes, but he has maintained the notion that through the Christian idiom in some way, and within the context of the churches somehow, he can and will find the path to the experience that will relate him significantly to life. He participates in protests against the war in Viet-Nam and joins the marches for civil rights. In these activities he may meet the two young men sketched above; if he does, he will experience a momentary but exhilarating epiphany of ecumenicity and solidarity. Through it all, he looks for a more profound epiphany—a showing forth of the divine for which he still uses the sacred name of Christ. He is not certain he believes in God or what belief in God really means; nor is he clear about what Christ means to him. Still, he hopes for the authenticity of his goal and is convinced of the genuineness of his search. Beneath this posture—as genuine and authentic as possible for him—lurk self-diffusion and anxiety, which at times throw him into fits of depression and at others provide him with the energy for heroic action.

There are many other types of young people seeking significance in action, in politics, in psychedelic drugs, in sexual experimentation. All of them are touched in some way by the contemporary crisis that has so deeply affected the relevance and significance of traditional and institutionalized religion today. But let us look for a moment at the older generation.

In a sizable city in a southwestern state there is a banker—head of a medium-sized commercial bank—who belongs to a family long prominent in the region. The population has grown greatly in the last two decades, and his position in the community has become less visible, less secure. Moreover, in the nation as a whole, changes in corporate business, in the tax structure, and in the role of government in economic life have created a new world in which he does not feel at home. Politics have changed, and the international situation reveals a world in which he feels strange and more than a little afraid. Changes in the relationship of the races have instituted a world he never made, one that he finds difficult to understand. His daughter returns from college—and not an eastern college either—with ideas on all these topics and even on the relationships of the sexes that bring home to him the frightening quality of his newly recognized status as stranger, as outsider. He is sure of one thing, one stable element in his life—his membership in the United Presbyterian Church. He has been its constant supporter, although irregular in attendance. His Presbyterianism has always been part of his selfhood, alongside his bankership, his Republicanism, and his family lineage. He has also been attracted to conservative politics, in which he has sought some defense—at least symbolic—of a better day. One morning a couple of years ago, he picked up his morning paper to find that the Stated Clerk, the highest elected officer of his denomination, had been arrested on a civil rights picket line. The world he was holding together so precariously threatened then and there to come apart. Fortunately for him, he found a local schismatic Presbyterian church that combined fundamentalist religion with radical-right politics. He now finds his refuge in this group. With this man we can speak less of a posture than of a condition, but it is a condition that draws near to the edge of the void that can threaten human consciousness when one is out of step with a world one cannot understand.

In an eastern city there is a Roman Catholic pastor who has served a local church for thirty years, first as curate and then as parish priest. He is an Irish American. Graduating from the diocesan seminary of his day, he learned little sophisticated theology, and soon after ordination found himself so involved in the practical tasks of his pastoral assignment that he had little time for theology at all. Throughout the years he found his parish to be a bastion of traditional belief surrounded by what seemed like a sea of indifference, unbelief, and even aggressively anti-religious sentiment. He lived through the local repercussions of the Spanish Civil War. He and his parishioners saw that war as the struggle of the forces of unbelief against a Catholic nation and culture. His non-Catholic neighbors who had other associations with Spanish history than those of the Irish-Catholic memory saw different values at stake in the Iberian struggle. He experienced the 1930's as an increasingly "red decade," and during the forties saw his country an ally of militantly atheistic and anti-religious Soviet Russia. He was aware of the reality of danger to his faith and to the world in which his own variety of that faith had been at home. In the early 1950's he rejoiced temporarily in the exorcism of the threat by the late Senator Joseph McCarthy. The calm of the late fifties under a conservative president was a relief to him. He received some ambivalent satisfaction in 1960 with the election of a member of his church to the highest office in the land and the end of the last shred of the stigma of his second-class citizenship, but he was quite aware that the outlook of the new President was perilously close to the secular liberalism that had threatened him all his life. Then came Vatican II, which reversed the basic religious tone in which he had been reared and which had been reinforced in his adult experience on almost every crucial issue. It looked to him as though the Catholic Church was indeed being Protestantized. He continued to obey his superiors, grateful when they put the brakes on this *aggiornamento*, as they frequently did. He is really not sure what to make of it all. Questions from his parishioners—a new phenomenon in his parish—irritate him, especially those on birth control. He fears the apostasy of the young. He still believes—believes in the Nicene Creed, believes that he offers Christ to the Father in his morning Mass. But it becomes harder and harder to relate these beliefs to the world about him—even to the church about him. Sometimes, like T. S. Eliot's magus, he "would be glad of another death." To him, the world seems to be approaching chaos—what the ancient Hindu writers called the "confusion of castes." He, also, seeks some succor in right-wing politics, but his troubles are deeper, and his surcease must be sought elsewhere. He manages to maintain the traditional posture, but within he is a baffled and defeated man.

This list could be prolonged with profit. We could consider the Mormon youth who, uneasy in the religion of his forebears, is searching for a new stance by rebelling against the symbols of the older provincial orthodoxy or by embracing them with an over-determined rigidity and a heightened defensiveness. Or the southern youth at the northern university who embraces a new liberalism in hopes of finding both an outlet for the moral conviction imbibed from a Christianity in which he can no longer believe, and a way of entering and participating in the larger, unprovincial, intellectual world. Yet for him, beneath this genuine and useful posture, lurk real guilt for his revolt against his fathers and his deviance from regional loyalties, and resentment of any condescension involved in his acceptance by his new northern friends. We might also consider those young people who seek meaning in new secular ideologies that offer themselves as the psychological, functional equivalents of religion. Or we might continue to examine the older and more established who seek in professional identifications and activities sufficient self-definition and expression to keep the inroads of the current crisis at a distance.

All of these represent people who are trying to live in and cope with change—change in society, change in thinking and styles of life, change in education, in community structure, in the churches. The younger ones are looking for a self-definition with which to face life; the older ones are clinging to an old identity rooted in circumstances and beliefs, habits and values now being rendered irrelevant. Other elements beside the religious crisis are involved in these personal predicaments. Personal crises are always to be found in times of social change; but in this time of exceptionally rapid social change they are more numerous and more significant. Moreover, beneath the contemporary identity crises hides the void created beneath the institutionalized assumptions by the religious crisis itself. These little stereotyped biographies, those described and those suggested, are idiosyncratic and selective refractions of the spiritual history of today. They are as real a part of the present crisis as the explicit anxieties of the intellectuals who attempt to formulate and meet the problems involved on the explicit conceptual level.

These representative biographical types—representative, of course, in the Emersonian rather than the statistical sense—not only mirror the spiritual condition of our time; they also reflect the history of America. Immigration and assimilation, westward expansion, industrialization and urbanization, the communications revolution, and the increasing democratization of education on all levels have all affected the American milieu. Each American religion seems at present to occupy its own half-way house in which defense of its traditions and its vested interests is found in short-term adjustment to a severe situation for which no final solutions are envisaged. The biographies of all Americans reflect the profound uneasiness of the religious communities.

Moreover, the different religious traditions place different emphases upon the role of ideas in religious life. Consequently, intellectual issues affect some groups more directly than they do others. Because Catholicism continues the Patristic and medieval synthesis of religion and culture and emphasizes the central significance of intellectual assent in the act of faith, it is most vulnerable to the pressures of intellectual scepticism and conflicting ideologies. Protestantism, though deeply affected by the challenge of intellectual research, study, and theorizing in philosophy and Bible study, has faced modernity with less defensiveness, though hardly with fewer debilitating consequences. Moreover, the residual effects of Protestantism's earlier unofficial establishment in America has made it, on the whole, far less defensive before the challenges of modern life. In American Judaism, the substrate of ethnic identity and the abiding centrality of the family have enabled many to accept any ideological, philosophical, or religious position and to remain in some sense Jews. Thus, within these three traditions, the identity crisis and the religious crisis are likely to be differently related and to assume different forms. For those of secularist background—an old and honored tradition in the history of America, the progressive impetus of traditional conceptions appears to share in the general crisis and to offer little to the on-coming generation in its search for identity and meaning.

II. *The Religious Crisis: Its Perennial Elements*

The primal crisis of religious consciousness is revealed, albeit covertly, in religious myth, the earliest and most holistic form of religious expression. Myth, to use the terminology of Theodor Gaster, translates reality into ideal terms, and preserves the momentary experience by giving it duration. Myth, moreover, is the affirmation by man that he is at home in his world—that he belongs, a being among the many beings, in the orderly and meaningful world of his experience. Yet myth is the obvious product of consciousness and imagination—the creation of a being who has already eaten of the Tree of Knowledge and has, thereby, disrupted a psychic, primal harmony with reflection, questioning, and doubt. Myth reveals itself to the modern scholar as a meaningful assertion made in the face of a potential threat of meaninglessness. It can be inferred, in a manner analogous to that by which Freud posited the existence of unconscious motivation, that there existed for mythic man a potential crisis of consciousness; this became the setting for myth-creation and for an assertion, through myth and ritual, of "faith" in a world of meaning. In the face of possible doubt, myth declares man's relationship to and significance in the world of his experience.

But man not only related himself to the world of his experience; he also attempted to exert control over elements of his surroundings.

According to L. S. B. Leakey, some two million years ago *Homo habilis* made and made use of tools. As man slowly extended his control over nature, he increased and multiplied, and according to the modest standards of his time proceeded to subdue the earth. Alongside this growing mastery and intricately related to its later stages, mythic apprehension and expression made way for logical conceptualization and rational discourse. Men broke through the enchanted garden of the mythic world.

Earlier man had made a peculiar kind of relation to his total situation: He apprehended it and responded to it as "sacred" through ritual and myth. Man's success in developing his control over nature and his consequent development of new forms of social existence introduced and enlarged areas of experience from which the sacred quality was removed. In thought, as in action, manipulation produced a world more and more shorn of its emotional and projective character. The fruits of these developments are to be seen in the agriculture and engineering, the administrative and legal structures of the ancient empires, and the growing sophistication technologically and strategically of the conduct of war. They assume a new quality, however, in the peculiar religious experience of the Hebrews. By positing the existence of a transcendent God, the Hebrews demythologized the earth, thereby emancipating man from the magic circle of older religious world-views. Whatever may seem the mythological character of the Bible to modern man, Biblical religion stands in stark contrast with myth in its genuine form. Moreover, the rationalizing implications of men's thought and effort reached their manifest expression in Greek philosophy. Socrates showed men how to overcome myth, demonstrating that they could achieve a new freedom through the positive power of self-knowledge. His contribution was joined to those of the Hebrew Bible by the Fathers of the Christian church. In a great creative adjustment, they brought into being the religious core of the cultural epoch of European civilization.

Yet Biblical religion and Hellenic rationality could not do away with the primal crisis involving the simultaneity and incompatibility of faith and doubt that lay at the core of religion in its mythic form. Three instances sufficiently demonstrate the way in which this basic crisis comes to the surface of man's consciousness in the Hebrew and Hellenic contexts. Within the Hebrew Bible is an odd book whose inclusion in the canon has long perplexed the pious and puzzled the scholarly. The ruminations of Qoheleth—known as Ecclesiastes, the Greek transformation of his name—present an example of religious crisis. They show that the emancipation from myth together with its positive religious achievements uncovered and revealed more fully the crisis elements primordially lurking at the core of man's religious experience. Uprooted from the closed community of his forebears, Qoheleth lived in the wider world that trade and war had created. Under the conditions of Jewish life in the early Hellenistic period, he spoke to men as individuals facing intimately the problem of meaning.

Qoheleth's religion reflects his confrontation of the threat of meaninglessness and cosmic aloneness that lay concealed behind the mythic assertion of earlier religions and the belief and hope in a relation to a transcendent God of his Hebrew forefathers. He sees a world characterized by movement without genuine change, effort without authentic profit. Events are predetermined, but their reasonable comprehension remains forever impossible. All values are negated by their opposites, just as life eventually is by death. The facts of life contradict the optimistic Hebraic idea that retribution from God inevitably overtakes evil and that goodness is repaid in prosperity. Neither character nor works affect one's fate. Before the incomprehensible frustrations and enigmas of human life, Qoheleth cries, "A vapor of vapors! All is vapor!" But he does not despair completely. Rather, he seeks to find happiness in a kind of anemic vitalism, by enjoying the day-to-day experience of living itself and avoiding the restlessness and unhappiness inevitably involved in straining after religious peace and certitude. What Qoheleth sees and recommends to others is the little life of modest ambitions in a disenchanted world.

The mythic assertion concerns itself with the problem of meaning, to which the problem of evil is central. Biblical religion attempts to handle the problem of evil even more optimistically than had many older mythic views. "Right will protect the blameless life, but sin overturns the wicked" (Prov. XII:6). Qoheleth's disenchantment challenges this view, but it is questioned most seriously and most poignantly in the Book of Job. In this great inconclusive classic of theodicy, a righteous man is overwhelmed by disaster and subjected to the taunts of his conventionally righteous associates. The Book of Job fails to answer the question of how the facts of existence can be reconciled with the reality of divine justice or the existence of a benevolent Providence. Job expresses faith as his solution. Although based upon despair and resignation, his is a faith nevertheless capable of asserting unshakable trust and genuine hope. Through Job's suffering there is brought into existence the religion of the "twice born." Unlike Qoheleth's mild, this-worldly resignation and his acceptance of a naïve natural enjoyment of life, Job finds the stance of faith as the mode of conquering meaninglessness and aloneness.

Nihilism remains a constant potential of religious thought and feeling. With the broadening of human experience and the rationalization of thought, nihilism threatens increasingly to come to the surface. Its most impressive surfacing may be seen at the beginning of the Christian era in the religion of the Gnostics.

The Gnostics, various as they were, saw a world from which men were fundamentally estranged, a world produced by an evil or, at best, a neutral and inferior creator. Men must find emancipation from this world through esoteric knowledge of a hidden god and his ways. Man's was not a disharmony of body and soul because of sin, but an ontological dualism rendering him an acosmic being, radically alien in and alienated from the world. Gnosticism represents a desperate faith driven to find an answer to its severe disarticulation with existence in an escape to a god who is himself alien to the world of human experience in the most fundamental way.

Doubt was not unfamiliar to Jeremiah and the Prophets, nor to deeply religious men of all ages who plumbed the depths and discovered the religious crisis for themselves. But doubt was confronted and resolved by incorporating it into a larger affirmation of faith. God may chastise men, he may even appear to desert them, but he was ultimately just; God was God.

The Christian church accepted the conviction of classical antiquity from Plato to the Stoics that the world was a *cosmos*, a knowable order, and that there existed a fundamental harmony between this order and man's nature. It brought together this conviction with its Hebraic antecedents. God was thought to reveal to mankind knowledge of himself and of the path to salvation. The harmony of microcosm and macrocosm transcended the world; man's ultimate place was determined by his eternal relationship to God. Peter Lombard (1100/1164?) in his *Four Books of Sentences*, which from the thirteenth to the sixteenth century was the most important single work in European religious education, said that man can achieve knowledge of the invisible things of God "through creatures visible and invisible. For he was aided by two means, namely by nature which was rational and by works performed by God that truth might be manifested to man." Christianity succeeded in burying for centuries the possibilities of radical nihilism to which Gnostic religion had given expression. But doubt came to plague Christianity as its late medieval resort to inquisitorial and authoritarian repression sadly testifies. The elements of crisis continued to lurk beneath the surface throughout the ages of faith themselves.

First to be doubted was the second of Peter Lombard's propositions—that God had performed works that truth might be made manifest to man. The first proposition—that nature was rational and that rational man was, therefore, at home in the world—stood up longer. Religious doubt in early modern times did not, by and large, transgress the cosmological and human limits of earlier Christian views. Progress replaced Providence; perfectibility through grace gave way to perfectibility through effort. The city of man belonged in the world of nature. History was no longer a religious drama but a natural process.

But pessimism—and behind it the threat of meaninglessness, of spiritual nothingness—continued to lurk beneath the surface of an optimistic revolt against other-worldly religion. Even Descartes, who saw in science the instrument to make man the "master and possessor of nature," and who dared to turn doubt into a method, toyed with the Gnostic hypothesis that an evil genius might have created the world. By joining subjective and objective in an ontological argument for God's existence, he found his personal and intellectual solution and, concomitantly, the necessary basis for his world-view. In Hume's philosophy, secularized optimism was itself seriously challenged. Human reason was not self-sufficient, but rested upon premises beyond proof. Kant answered Hume, but in a way that undermined once and for all a comfortable acceptance of such premises as self-evident. Earlier, Pascal had faced, as a Christian, the implications of man's aloneness in the new world that science and philosophy were making known. He saw a silent universe that did not answer man's cry or longing, but remained alien and indifferent to his aspirations. Before the incomprehensible immensity of that world Pascal was frightened. He came to see man's aspirations rooted in reasons beyond reason and made his wager on a hidden God who was still the God of Christianity. Yet he retained the classic pride in man's capacities—a thinking reed superior thereby to a universe that might at any moment crush him.

Science has revealed to man a world with which he has no inner resonance; it has trained him to a stance toward the world which makes lack of mystic response "natural," "proper," and "objective."

Moreover, the scientific study of man himself has revealed a historical and ontological relativity concerning all human accomplishments and productions—whether in thought or in life. Cultures and societies stand revealed as "compromise formations" formed from competing interests, points of view, and cognitive perspectives upon the world of experience. Entities of limited durability, they are destined to pass away. Indeed, individual identity itself is seen to be problematic, highly dependent upon circumstances; most cherished spiritual achievements rest upon a potential void. Social science has rediscovered in a new idiom the older mythic insight into the relation of primal order to primal chaos. But is modern man able to make an act of faith and an assertion of resonance comparable with that made in myth and in Jewish and Christian religion? While these developments characterized the emerging modern consciousness, Christianity tended to become either a culture religion raising no fundamentally disturbing questions or to remain in a spiritual ghetto in militant opposition to developing modernity. Kierkegaard experienced this alienation, this estrangement from the world of being; he sought escape in an act of faith more desperate than the wager of Pascal. Nietzsche saw nihilism, "this weirdest of all guests," standing before the door of his century and the world standing before man as a "gate to deserts stretching mute and chill." Projecting himself in his parable of the madman, he proclaimed, "God is dead. God remains dead. And we have killed him."

Modern developments bring the perennial latent crisis to actuality and in a setting shorn of traditional compensations. Modern men appear to make two fundamental responses within the general tradition. Following Job (and Pascal and Kierkegaard), they attempt to posit an act of faith; or like Qoheleth, they seek in mundane experience—not just daily trivia but this-worldly experience seen in the this-worldly frame of reference of the Enlightenment, often seasoned with Christian elements—satisfactions of an ante-penultimate character. Thus is revealed the neo-Christianity and the neo-Stoicism of today. Both accept the deeper substrate—the reasons beyond reason of Pascal—in one form or another. Man has aspirations, he displays an effort after the ethical, but he is not part of a cosmos with whose immanent logos he can feel any sustained and dependable kinship. He is a stranger creating meaning out of his own estrangement. His reflective acts reveal his naked aloneness in a nature that is purposeless. He clings to values that lack all ontological support. Existence is seen, by some, as absurd; man, once the capstone of creation, is but a futile passion. Men struggle with their absurdity and, in accepting it, attempt to transcend it.

The cosmic backdrop of medieval Christianity or of Enlightenment unbelief has dropped away and with it the resonance between subjective orientation and objective setting upon which all cultures have ultimately rested. The lurking primal crisis of the religious consciousness is unveiled for modern man. He may either accept it with faith or with stoic resignation, or attempt to avoid it in the busyness of less than ultimate pursuits. Writing in the nineteenth century, John Henry Newman told how Napoleon responded to his excommunication by asking, "Does the Pope think that the muskets will fall from the hands of my soldiers?" Newman commented that a few years later the muskets literally did fall from the hands of the Emperor's troops on the plains of Russia. Men who consider themselves in some sense "religious" have smiled at this story. Yet how many modern men could make such a statement as Newman's in today's world? This was the point of view of the prophets, of the evangelists, of the Fathers, of the Reformers. Its practical disappearance marks the end of an epoch and heralds a form of the religious crisis unique in the history of Western man. Nietzsche's guest stands in our midst.

III. *The Religious Crisis: Its Contemporary Urgency*

Genuine religious experience issuing in authentic faith and wholeness of spirit and combining with contemporary relevance has become increasingly rare and difficult. Consequently, this age lacks relevant religious exemplars. Today, as in past ages, most men adhere to religions by a more or less uncritical acceptance of what is established. But conventional religion has always depended ultimately upon the existence of the profound and authentic religious experience of its *megalopsychoi*—the great souled ones. Without that, even conventional religion falters. It draws its strength from the past, which it does little to preserve at the deeper psychological level. In this situation, institutional religion displays two kinds of irrelevance. Either it has maintained some significant personal meaning for its adherents, but has lost a relationship to man's larger history; or it struggles to attain historical relevance and exhibits little personal significance for ordinary men. Seen in itself this represents a severe and advanced form of religious crisis, but when viewed in the total setting of modern man a new urgency and even desperation is brought to light.

Men have achieved the technical capacity to alter the conditions of human life to an extent that was undreamed of even twenty years ago, but these very men in the advanced industrial countries are unable to go beyond piecemeal and contradictory programs in shaping these conditions. Ivan Karamazov commented that without God, everything is possible. Modern man has experienced to his sorrow what this can mean. But it is also true that without God nothing is possible; man can now also experience what this means. In the development of technology a great bureaucratic structure has been elaborated. All men, except the "culturally deprived," fit into this structure; they have become parts of a great social machine. The social relationships and institutions formed to enable men to control the world of nature have become a second nature controlling them. Modern man finds himself consuming in order to work, reversing the ancient causal formula; in a hundred ways he adapts himself to the social leviathan he has brought into being. Mastery over nature has become objectified into a social structure that controls all men. The capacities of technology for humanizing life have not been realized. As the irrationality of such a situation becomes more evident, the possibility of a rational understanding of the human situation and of programs based upon this understanding recedes beyond the grasp of the immense intellectual establishment. In fact, this establishment has become increasingly integrated into the great machine as the provider of the trained personnel which it more and more requires. Among the peoples of the world not simply discord but potential chaos threatens continually. In the West, the problem-solving mentality, the product of science and pragmatic effort, finds itself capable of solving any problem, but without the reservoir of world-view and value-orientation that would define and attribute priority to needs and aspirations of contemporary men. The problem-solving mentality reigns supreme, but it does not rule. Rather, it adapts itself to the initiative of circumstances and the caprice of events. The use of reason in the broad service of life retreats before the mind of modern man to join the powers and principalities of myth and the God of the Bible. Without an orientation to being, modern man cannot put himself together into a whole. Having lost transcendence, he finds himself without practical leverage in effectively changing his world. Without God or his memory in Enlightenment philosophy, he no longer knows what it means to be man, and hence, cannot utilize his enormous capacities to humanize the conditions of his life. The irrational, affluent societies of the advanced industrial countries begin more and more to resemble the society projected in the imagination of Auguste Comte—a technocracy dominated by the organizers of industry and knowledge. Today, however, the military must be added. In the present Comtean condition, the three religious traditions play the role of the "religion of humanity," often shedding even their partial and truncated transcendence for a common "civic religion." In a world that cries out for authentic transcendence and genuine community, the trumpets of conventional religiosity give forth the sounds of uncertainty. Enlightenment philosophers naïvely hoped that by crushing the "infamy" of supernatural religion and liberating men from the tyranny of a supernatural city of God, men would be free to construct a humane, this-worldly city of man. These hopes threaten to become as remote as Jeremiah's and Newman's Yahwistic notions of a divine and providential lord of history. In this situation, certain people, the more stubborn, the more sensitive, or the more disturbed, attempt to assert a measure of freedom and transcendence in sheer refusal—combating the absurd with the absurd. Their efforts, confused and confusing, assume a bewildering variety of forms.

Since the establishment of Charlemagne's Empire, Christianity has provided the noetic integrator and the spiritual sustenance that made possible the rise of Europe as a sociological and historical reality. It provided convictions in terms of which man could act and judge action, develop discourse, and project self-realization. Today man lives on the echoes and memories of that situation. In the face of current opportunity and contemporary urgency, most people are unable to believe with the depth and fervor that would provide direction to their thinking and motivation for their actions in meeting the demands of modernity. Nor are they able to disbelieve with the genuineness, conviction, and vigor that would produce the creative negation that might eventuate in a new and positive human orientation. In the past, the recalcitrance of nature, human and nonhuman, separated ideal and real. Today, inability to form the ideal with reason and conviction leaves man controlled by circumstances, despite the enormous capacities of his technological rationality.

IV. *Modes of Adjustment to the Religious Crisis*

Some men avoid the contemporary religious crisis by relying upon an enlightened and sophisticated common sense. Accepting older values as humanly self-evident although without ontological foundation, they leave questioning to those whom they consider esoteric and impractical. Scientific research, human understanding, human rights, abolition of hunger, the "Great Society" are all ideals derived from the older situation. Although they still seem adequate, it is sometimes noticed that these old war cries no longer stir the troops, especially the young recruits, as they once did. Other men stay within the safe confines of academic disciplines and professional pursuits. They do not question fundamentally the implications of their methodology, their results, or their functions. Within particular institutions petty authoritarianism may be practiced to keep out dangerous thoughts likely to infect the young and untried. Such behavior is by no means peculiar to religious institutions. The resulting fragmentation of intellectual and spiritual life passively abets the developing crisis situation.

How, in fact, is the crisis to be met? Concern for the religious quality of contemporary life or belated urges to return to the classics in education appear almost the gestures of a bored and defeated complacency. Obviously, spirituality today needs its authentically relevant exemplars, and reason its humanly relevant embodiment. The history of religious crises suggests certain solutions.

It would be possible to institutionalize religion in the old way with some functional equivalent of a church presiding over society, yet reasonably accommodated to its needs. Here the model in history is the medieval church; in philosophy, Plato's *Republic* and *Laws*. New generations would be brought up within a culturally sanctioned "right reason"; a genuine, if strait-jacketed, transcendence would offer satisfaction to men's religious needs. Yet the church discovered it needed inquisitions, and Plato foresaw the need of a Night council. This solution did not prove viable in more appropriate historical conditions; it had to break up or eventuate in tyranny. Post-Tridentine Catholicism attempted to institutionalize a version of this solution within its own ranks. That, too, proved of ambiguous value and has been abandoned by Vatican II. The solution of such an institutionalization of religion is virtually closed for it would entail serious spiritual regression.

The present situation of pluralism of religions in a secular society could be prolonged and primacy given to secular values. While superior to the first solution, this half-way house offers no final escape from the current predicament. The present religious communions continue to transmit the spiritual heritage with varying degrees of profundity and success. The present religious dialogue continues to place before men the reality of the religious challenge. But the old heaven and the old earth have irretrievably passed away. The language of religion remains ambiguous and confusing. Sometimes it points the way to deeper spiritual realities; other times it beguiles its listeners with obsolescent memories.

Attention might be shifted from religious confrontation to the attempt to utilize the findings and methods of the social sciences in constructing secular communities and developing secure ego-formation among children. The conscious development of family life, friendship, and local community might attack the problem more successfully. Yet such a program requires value-consensus on both a small and a large scale. In quest of value-consensus, men would encounter all the problems of the current religious crisis head on. Matthew Arnold could appeal to love and urge men to be true to one another. A few years ago Archibald MacLeish could propose love as the final solution in his dramatic reworking of the Book of Job. But it appears a remnant of the Western religious tradition that by itself does not promise to generate either its own motivation or justification.

A possible solution could also be found in the new nationalisms. Yet the Communism of the Chinese, the nationalism of the Arabs, Africans, and Asians, the Zionism of Israel, and the sense of mission of America and France are also half-way houses of ambiguous value. While any rational philosophy will recognize the just demands of the secular community and its proper claims for individual support, it must provide for individual consciousness and effort. Nationalistic reasons beyond reason contain dangerous possibilities as history has so unmistakably demonstrated.

The current attempt to find meaning in the ultimate admission of absurdity could provide still another solution. Here many follow the injunction of Joseph Conrad—in the destructive element, immerse—and seek significance in the sheer experiential quality of experience. The possibilities are great, ranging from the ascetic, crypto-Christian action-mysticism of T. E. Lawrence to the newer, less confined "holiness" of Saint Genet. In these terms, all escapes from the limited world of contemporary consciousness, all plunges into the unconscious are seen as possibly productive of spiritual worth. Sexual experience, available to the poorest of the underprivileged as Ernst Toller once observed, becomes a favorite area for experimentation, though by no means the exclusive one. New drugs promise new possibilities. Extreme experiences lived at a heightened intensity substitute for and replace the religious experience. It is difficult to see at present the ultimate significance of this important current development. It alone does not appear capable of effecting spiritual and cultural metamorphoses.

V. *Religion and Relevancy Today*

To rediscover the relevance of his heritage, man must achieve authentic transcendence and genuine community. Institutionalized religion must contribute to this goal to the best of its capacity. To be relevant today, religion must translate into a contemporary idiom the "foolishness of the cross." By synthesizing joy and tragedy in a new way, man could become at home in his world, even while remaining forever a sojourner and a pilgrim in the midst of his fondest, this-worldly achievement and values. Religion must nourish and sustain an interiority that makes external relationship and accomplishment possible. But this interiority must never lose itself in its products; it must be able to find its own way among the many ways it creates in the world. To be relevant today, religion must support those human aspirations that cry for fulfillment in terms of the modern technological capacity. It must become relevant to the effort toward a more abundant life for man. It must teach not only the appropriateness of justice, wisdom, fortitude, and courage, but it must also bear witness to a faith, hope, and charity rendered relevant to the new world man has made and the new man whose promise it contains. Institutionalized religion and institutionalized learning must strive to beget honesty and transmit seriousness in facing problems, eschewing fixated ideologies and petty interests. Then, spirit and reason will find their own embodiment, for one may still hope that the spirit bloweth where it listeth. Let men learn, in the words of Dag Hammarskjöld, to become recipients, out of humility, and to be grateful for being allowed to listen, observe, and understand.

EMIL L. FACKENHEIM

On the Self-Exposure of Faith to the Modern-Secular World: Philosophical Reflections in the Light of Jewish Experience

I. *A Contemporary Reversal of Traditional Fronts*

EVER SINCE the Age of Enlightenment there has been a tension between the traditional religions of the West—Judaism and Christianity—and the secular world then beginning to emerge: its science, technology, economics, politics, and, in general, its attitude toward life. And since the modern-secular world would not go away and could not be wished away, its effect on orthodox belief was one of crisis—whether orthodox belief declared itself under total siege, ventured the odd sortie, or even undertook a wholesale assault on the alien territory and in so doing became itself transformed. By now, this crisis has existed for so long that it has become a permanent condition of religious belief in the modern world; and most of the recent talk about a brand-new religious crisis in our own age merely reflects the permeation of the old crisis into nearly all parts of modern society. Among the factors responsible for this recent development are the fast pace of modern technology, the rapid growth of the secular city, and two world wars fought in one generation.

A new crisis, or at any rate a new dimension of the old crisis, has nevertheless made its appearance in the present generation. This is indicated by a remarkable current reversal of traditional fronts among those professionally competent to consider the estate of religion. Believers now exalt secular "relevance" and "celebrate" secular culture at the precise time when some former protagonists of secular culture look beyond it or even despair of it.[1] Sociologists occupationally geared to the here-and-now take the long view of secularism and the religious crisis,[2] while theologians (whom one would expect to take the long view) see the most startling, not to say apocalyptic, upheavals in the mid-twentieth century.[3] Christians, traditionally far more suspicious than Jews of the secular world and all its works, now seek total self-exposure to it, whereas Jews, long dwellers in the secular city and in love with secularist-liberal ideas ever since these had been instrumental in securing their emancipation, now warn Christians lest too uncritical a self-exposure to the secular world issue in total surrender.[4] Most startling of all, at the precise time when some agnostics have become cautiously open to traditional religious claims, they are told by some Christian theologians that, in the mid-twentieth century, "God is dead."[5] When has such a battle cry ever issued not from the lips of a self-declared "anti-Christ" such as Nietzsche, but from those espousing, and insisting on continuing to espouse, the Christian gospel?

This essay seeks to bring philosophical reflection to bear upon the present reversal of traditional fronts; yet, written in the perspective of Judaism and Jewish experience, it is essentially within rather than above the battle. In a case such as the present, partisanship is inevitable; a phenomenon such as "the present crisis of religion" eludes, in the end, any wholly objective appraisal. A statistician can measure church or synagogue attendance; he cannot measure the depth of a religious commitment. A psychologist can uncover the neurotic etiology of spurious religion, but that of all religion only on the prior dogmatic assumption that it is all spurious. A sociologist can correlate religious behavior with social forms, but can see it limited by the "laws" of these forms only after having denied the freedom of both God and man. Philosophy, like the social sciences, has limits in this area that cannot be transcended. Philosophers seek universal conceptual clarification, including that of religious concepts. They may possibly even venture beyond the logical and linguistic forms of religious belief into its substance, and seek to decide what can and cannot be believed. They cannot, in any case, *qua* philosophers, descend from the realm of the universal into that of the particular in order to decide what tenable beliefs are, in a given situation, live options. Such a decision can be made not by the philosopher who rises above the situation but only by the man who lives in it. And this is a particular man whose experience is partial and fragmented.

Ever since the Jew became modern, he has existed, as it were, between Christianity and secularist liberalism. If a believer, he has shared with Christianity the Biblical God; and if not, at least a regard for a religious tradition to which he owes his survival. With secularist liberalism he has shared the ideals that have produced democracy and his own emancipation; so far as these are concerned, even orthodox Jews are secularist liberals. The conflict that came to exist *between* these two forms of modern belief and life has contributed to a religious-secularist conflict *within* Jewish existence. The one conflict still exists, and so does the other. In any contemporary reversal of traditional fronts, the Jew is obviously not an impartial bystander but rather a participant; his stance, whatever its nature, is informed by his Jewish situation.[6]

This first experience has been joined, if not overshadowed and dwarfed, by another in this generation. The one experience the Jew has lived with and assimilated for nearly two centuries; the other is, as yet, wholly unassimilable. The events that are associated with the dread name of Auschwitz still pass human comprehension. But they have shaken Jewish existence to the core, even when they are uncomprehended. They call everything into question: for the believing Jew, for the unbelieving Jew, for the Jew who is neither believer nor unbeliever but merely asks unanswered or unanswerable questions. Only one thing is as yet clear. The Jew may not authentically think about religion, or its modern crisis, or the goods and ills of the modern-secular world as though Auschwitz had not happened.

II. *On Dietrich Bonhoeffer's Christian Confrontation of a "World-Come-of-Age"*

The present reversal of traditional fronts in Protestantism may be said to originate with Dietrich Bonhoeffer's *Letters and Papers from Prison*,[7] written in a Nazi jail and concentration camp in 1943-44 prior to his execution. This is an oversimplification historically, but not poetically. These documents were written in a country which, once the heart of Western Christendom, was then in the grip of demonic, anti-Christian powers; and by a member of a church which, alone among German churches, clearly opposed these powers, in the name not of modern humanism but rather of the ancient gospel, brought by neo-orthodox theology to new life. The man who wrote these documents did not only die a martyr; he suffered this death because he had given his Christian witness a political expression by participating in a plot on Hitler's life. No more dramatic example can be found in this century of what has since come to be the basic issue at stake in the current reversal of traditional fronts: *the radical religious—in this case, Christian—self-*

exposure to the modern-secular world and all its works. The example is all the more compelling because it occurred in a country in which Christianity, since Luther, has been prone to cut off the "inner" world reserved for Christian conscience from the "outer" world, handed over to Machiavellian princes and autocrats.

No less dramatic than the occasion and the author of the *Letters and Papers from Prison* are those of its passages—terse, radical, though, as will be seen, in the end profoundly problematical— which were destined to be the most influential. The confrontation between Christianity and the modern-secular world demanded in these passages is indeed radical. The modern-secular world is taken as it takes itself, and as such confronted; and what it is confronted with is not weak, diluted apologetics, but rather the pristine Christian gospel.

For the present purpose, Bonhoeffer's crucial passages may be summed up in four basic affirmations. First, the modern-secular world has "come of age." Its science, politics, morality, even its philosophy and religion stand in no need of God as a "working hypothesis," in terms of which they must be explained.

Secondly, the "autonomy" of the modern-secular world rules out any honest Christian recourse to "the so-called ultimate questions —death, guilt—on which only 'God' can furnish an answer." Thus is rejected any Christian use of "the existentialist philosopher and the psychotherapist" who "make it their object first of all to drive man to inward despair, and then it is all theirs." For "whom [do such efforts] . . . touch? A small number of intellectuals, of degenerates. . . . The ordinary man who spends his everyday life at work, and with his family . . . is not affected. . . ." Modern-secular man exists *"etsi Deus non daretur."*

Yet, thirdly, while even the Christian ought to live in this god-less world, he lives in it "before God." God is no longer needed as a crutch. Everywhere he is confronted by faith and love.

Fourthly and finally, to confront God in faith is to find him in the midst of life, not merely at such of its margins as guilt and death. And to speak of him to secular man is not to "speak ill of . . . his worldliness" but to "confront him with God at his strongest" rather than at his weakest point. Far from letting "this world be written off prematurely," the Biblical God—in the New as well as in the Old Testament—focuses his primary concern not on other-worldly salvation, but on this-worldly life.[8]

Their radicalism lends these affirmations a tremendous liberating power. Swept aside is all apologetic nineteenth-century halfheart-edness—toward the scientist, the secularist reformer, the agnostic moralist, each of whom used to be told that he stood in need of religion, no matter how much his thought and his life gave the lie to this story; it was to be replaced by a radically honest self-expo-sure. Swept aside, too, is the halfhearted Christian testimony that used to define itself in alien terms—the terms of a world for which it could still perform some useful function, or the terms of philoso-phies still left with a gap of some kind. This was to be replaced by a testimony to a God who, ever-present to man, can confront mod-ern-secular man as surely as his less secular ancestors. Radical, modern-secular honesty is united with radical Biblical authenticity.

A Jew's Jewish affirmations may differ from Bonhoeffer's Chris-tian ones. Yet the Jew is bound to be moved by them and, indeed, become deeply involved. For one thing, the profane-sacred, tempo-ral-eternal dichotomy has always been alien to Judaism and Jewish existence; and Bonhoeffer opposes it because of Hebraic inspira-tion. For another (as has been said), modern Jewish existence has been exposed to special strains because of the modern conflict be-tween secularist liberalism and Christianity. But, when more closely considered, Bonhoeffer's affirmations are, in the end, profoundly problematical; and, as will be seen, what is problematical about them is augmented in the thought of his disciples.

Two questions are left hanging in mid-air. First, who is the God to be *confronted,* and how is he related to the "God-hypothesis" to be *discarded,* the hypothesis through which things were once *explained?* Although this may seem an abstract theoretical question, it is, nevertheless, inescapable. What if Bonhoeffer's modern-secu-lar man were to reject—indeed, were in all honesty *obliged* to reject—the God with whom Christian testimony confronts him as a mere myth of bygone ages, now in need of demythologization? As will be seen, this question haunts Bonhoeffer's theological disci-ples.

The second question is even on the surface not abstract and theo-retical only. Who is Bonhoeffer's "man-come-of-age," happy in his secularity and free of guilt? Is he an ideal man as pictured by Spi-noza, Kant, or Hegel? But that man is himself only an ideal. Or is he an actually existing man? Doubtless he is this latter, for he alone is an "ordinary man who spends his everyday life at work, and with his family." It is a tragic irony, however, that Bonhoeffer should have cleared this man of guilt at the precise time when he became implicated, all around him, in a guilt without historical precedent: not only when his "work" was to drive gas-chamber trucks or to fight Hitler's war, but also when it was merely to clean the streets—and hold his peace. Bonhoeffer aimed at two great goals: a gospel found in the midst of life and joy rather than merely in death and guilt; and the protection of the secular man against religion-inspired slander. A nearly incredible lack of realism made him fail to rise to what would have been not slander but judgment—of "ordinary" Christians and secularists alike.

Clear-sighted witness, apostle of Christian self-exposure to the secular world and himself martyr to his cause, Bonhoeffer nevertheless failed wholly to grasp—almost no one to this day has succeeded in wholly grasping—the monstrous evil in the actual world about him. This painful truth, in retrospect inescapable, cannot escape his Jewish reader. In a concentration camp filled with Jews subjected to every imaginable form of torture, Bonhoeffer writes that Protestants must learn about suffering from Catholics.[9] No mention is made in the *Letters and Papers* of Jewish martyrdom.

III. *On the Self-Exposure of Faith to the Secular City*

The ambiguities implicit in Bonhoeffer's affirmations become explicit among those of his British, American, and Canadian disciples who currently demand radical Christian self-exposure to the modern-secular world and all its works. This current Christian demand is producing a Jewish reaction that, while sporadic, is possibly highly significant. Time was when even orthodox Jewish believers would ask of Christians a more wholehearted acceptance of those secular-liberal ideals that have separated state and church, established the equality of all citizens, and emancipated Jews. Now that some leading Christian thinkers urge precisely that, they are warned against abandonment of the Biblical God by Jews not all of whom are self-declared believers.[10] One could not altogether blame Christian thinkers if they felt that, so far as Jews are concerned, they can never do right.

This present Jewish stance is due not to greater Jewish religious firmness but to recent Jewish experience. At a time when Christian thinkers are becoming aware of the gap between the modern Christian church and the modern-secular world, Jewish thinkers are becoming aware of the bond between Judaism and Christianity, even when their commitment to Judaism is problematical.

Only in recent decades have Jews had occasion to realize fully the bonds they have with Christianity as well as with secularist liberalism. In the heydey of nineteenth-century optimism, the Western Jew was apt to throw in his destiny wholly with secularist liberalism "abroad" even if he remained an orthodox Jew "at home,"[11] and to have no very positive relation to the forces of Christianity except insofar as these, too, threw their weight behind liberal ideals. But what if secularist liberalism were to become wholly omnipotent? Would it remain liberal? Could it be counted on to respect the Jew's right to his Jewishness, of which it had little appreciation, and to his Judaism, of which it had less? Might it, in fact, even be perverted into a demonic pseudo-religion and deny the Jew's very humanity?

Some of these questions have *in abstracto* been present ever since, after the French Revolution, the Jew was requested to surrender his public Jewishness "abroad" (if not his private Jewish faith "at home") as the price of his emancipation. In the mid-twentieth century, these questions have assumed a reality of which no wild imagination could have dreamed in the nineteenth. Soviet secularism seems bent on a policy designed to dissipate both Jewish culture "abroad" and Jewish faith "at home." And the Nazi secularist pseudo-religion of blood and soil has succeeded in the physical destruction of one third of the world's Jewish population. These two events must, under no circumstances, be viewed as in the same class, and can be so viewed only by indiscriminate cold-war warriors. They have, nevertheless, had the common effect of making many Jews view secularism with newly critical eyes. The modern Jew has been obliged to look to secularist liberalism for the recognition of his humanity in the past. The momentous and fearsome events of the present have made him wonder whether, if to anyone, it is not to the Christian that he must look for the recognition of his singled-out Jewish condition.[12] Indeed, may contemporary events not indicate that secularist liberalism itself stands in secret need of Biblical inspiration for its liberalism? If bereft of this inspiration, or subjugating and thus perverting it, may secularism not become illiberal and totalitarian, or even a demonic pseudo-religion?

Such fears are obviously not felt by those Jews who grasp the opportunities offered by the secular city for surrendering their Jewishness in the faith that such a surrender will make them "simply human." But despite statistics concerning assimilation and inter-

209

marriage, their response to the secular city does not represent what must be called mid-twentieth-century American Jewish normative behavior. To the astonishment of many, the normative American Jewish response to the events of this century has been a reaffirmation, if not of Judaism, at least of Jewish group-survival. (In the light of the dynamic of present Jewish life, it is the Jewish intellectuals whose intellectualism has led them to surrender their Jewishness who are out of step, not the community which they have abandoned.) The causes of this reaffirmation are complex: among others, a flight from the anonymous society of megalopolis to the community—such as it is—of suburbia; loyalty to the martyred European millions which, once aroused by plain need, refuses to vanish; a new seriousness about Judaism among formerly perfunctory believers; and even a new openness to Jewish religious resources among formerly confirmed secularists. All these responses, from a minimal commitment to Jewishness to a maximal commitment to Judaism, imply some degree of criticism of the modern-secular world where before there was little or none.

In the light of this experience, how will a Jewish reader react to such a work as *The Secular City?*[13] On first reading he may well seem to be perceiving messianic signs. Has he come upon a genuinely Christian-Biblical effort to make peace with those liberal-secular ideas with which the Christian forces have been at odds too long—an alienation of which the Jew has been a special victim? There is such an effort, and it aims at peace not with a mere abstract idea of secular freedom but with its actual carriers in the secular city: social mobility and big-city anonymity, cultural pluralism and pragmatic scepticism, and an open marketplace governing religious beliefs as much as all else. Their acceptance, moreover, is by a faith far more Hebraic than Hellenic in inspiration: a faith which will not freeze a past world into permanence, nor divide reality into an all-important heaven and a worthless earth. *The Secular City* seeks a worldly God who speaks *into* the here-and-now; not a conservative God confined to the past, but a God of the present who is geared to the future. Jewish faith has, since Biblical times, sought a worldly God of the present and the future; and it is largely by dint of circumstances not of their making that modern Jews have been split into those seeking the old God, but able to find him only in seclusion from the modern-secular world, and into those embracing the modern-secular world, but unable to find the old God in it. Are unprecedented opportunities now in the making for a tripartite secularist-Christian-Jewish dialogue in which what is at stake is the word of the old Biblical God for the modern-secular world?

This may indeed be cautiously affirmed, no less because of events in Alabama and Mississippi than because of events in theological seminaries. A Jew's duty is to bring Jewish experience to bear on his participation in the tripartite dialogue. Part of so doing, however, is to express caution to Christians lest an indiscriminate self-exposure of faith to the modern-secular world end in surrender.

The Secular City justifies caution. No single item of the work will strike a Jewish reader more forcefully than its failure—twenty years after—to come to grips with Nazism. The work warns in a general way against the dangers of the modern-secular world; yet such is the degree of its infatuation that it has no room for Nazism in that world. Nazism is a mere "throwback to a lost tribalism." What an insult to any tribe ever in existence. And what a staggering failure to grasp that Nazism, far from being a mere falling-out-of-step innocuous to all who are *in* step, is, alas, a distinctly modern phenomenon. How, except for modern anonymity and modern technological quantification, could Nazism have engaged in its grisly mathematics of mass-murder? So blithely is *The Secular City* in love with the virtues of modern secularity that it is able to commit this enormous tautology: "When a political leader makes religious or totalitarian claims, when a Hitler or Stalin tries once again to assert himself as the pure expression of the *Zeitgeist* or the dialectic, free [*sic*] men recognize this as an affront to their deepest convictions about politics."[14] As if the question raised by Nazism were not precisely why Germans preferred slavery to freedom, and even "thought they were free"[15] when in fact they were slaves. Moreover, for long and crucial years, even "free" Western leaders—both Christian and secularist—appeased Hitler not only as the lesser evil to war but also as the savior of Western civilization from Communism.

The Secular City comes to grief over Nazism not because of moral blindness but rather because, like Bonhoeffer, it fights on one front and ignores the simultaneous need to fight on another. It fights for the recognition of the challenge of the liberal secular-city dweller to the religious believer, in particular to the rural believer. It fights, too, against all religious efforts to reduce the former to a guilt or despair for which there is neither need nor cause. It ignores the real *grounds* for despair and guilt—among secularists and believers alike. Is there no guilt in an America well-fed in the midst of world-wide starvation and with enough arms to destroy the human race? And no despair in the secular city even if guilt can be shut out? Not if those novelists are to be believed who discover meaninglessness in busy suburbia as well as in the slums. American "pragmatic man" may waste "little time thinking about 'ultimate' or 'religious' questions," and be able to live "with highly provisional solutions."[16] But only the idolization of pragmatism can shut out those ultimate moral dilemmas of the present time in the light of which all the provisional solutions must be groped for; or fail to notice that it is precisely when his actual needs are filled that pragmatic man falls either to restlessly inventing ever-new unneeded needs or to asking the desperate and utterly unpragmatic question: "What is the use of use?"[17]

The secularist must find his own way out of the dilemmas of the secular city. The believer—Jewish and Christian—must surely seek the word of the ancient Biblical God as it applies to the modern-secular world. Such a search, if it remains for the Biblical God, will not result in a surrender to secularism, if only because the Biblical God *judges* the world—the modern-secular world as much as any other—even as he accepts it in love.

The Secular City, to be sure, does not surrender. It culminates in the attempt to speak "in a secular fashion" of God, sociologically, politically, and even theologically. It is, however, virtually left without speech. So deeply is the work impressed with the novelty of modern-secular man as to see virtually no continuity between him and the whole preceding human species. Hence, it cannot hear a divine voice from the past in the present and is faced with a future that is wholly open.[18]

Less reliance on sociology and more metaphysical discipline might have prevented such a hollow outcome. Following an old and shopworn doctrine harking back to Auguste Comte, *The Secular City* views metaphysics as primitive guesswork about the universe the necessity of which disappears with the rise of science. In fact and at its best, metaphysics is radical thinking about the totality of human experience. As such, it helps see in perspective all changes, including those in the human social condition and those that the believer may affirm about the Divine. The famous passage (Exodus 3:14) that *The Secular City* translates as "I will do what I will do"[19] assuredly contains no ontological information about the divine nature. But neither does it command an openness to the future so total as to fragment the One God of Israel into as many "moment-gods"[20] as there are historical moments. The Hebraic believer confronts the future with a present knowledge coming from the past; the word from the past is judging justice and accepting love. He who revealed himself to Moses as "I shall be who I shall be" may disclose himself in the future by yet unknown names. He will be the same already-known "I."

IV. *On the "Death" of God*

But what if a truly uncompromising self-exposure of faith to the modern-secular world *ipso facto is* surrender to secularism? We have noted Bonhoeffer's failure to clarify the relation between the "God-hypothesis" that is to be discarded, and the Biblical God who is to be confronted. Its nemeses are the current so-called "God-is-dead" theologies.

The expression covers a variety of different and possibly incompatible assertions. The first is purely metaphorical: not God is dead in our time but merely human belief in him. This latter is dead not so much because men no longer, in fact, believe, but rather because the legitimacy of belief would have vanished even if belief were still widely alive.[21] Modern science has demythologized the world of fact, thus disposing of the need for a God-hypothesis; and modern philosophy—it is linguistic empiricism, mostly Oxford-inspired—has reduced the meaning of the word *God*, as employed by the believer, to a mere expression of emotion. The believer imagines that the assertion "God exists," although not necessarily demonstrable, nevertheless refers to an objective truth. Philosophy disposes of this illusion. The believer's statement is not "about the world," but merely about his own attitude toward the world.

The philosopher may or may not find this attitude legitimate; on his part, he is clearly incapable of himself adopting it. How, having acquired knowledge, can he return to innocence? How, having unmasked the word *God* as a mere projection upon the world, can he ever again adopt an attitude dependent on the belief that a truth beyond his mere attitude is disclosed in it? Belief in God, then, is dead among the scientifically and philosophically enlightened; and it would never have been alive among previous generations had they been blessed with our present enlightenment. As for God himself, he is not dead. He was never alive.

There is nothing either new or startling about these assertions

—except that they should be made in a theological work, *The Secular Meaning of the Gospel.*[22] Here they are the more startling because what is aimed at is not a return to pre-neo-orthodox liberalism but rather a position that has incorporated neo-orthodox Christian insight. What is here wanted is not the Sermon on the Mount and the ethical-preacher Jesus, but the Christ on the Cross and the Easter. How can this goal be attained when the Father and the resurrection have both fallen prey to a demythologizing philosophy?

The goal cannot be attained. The Christ, Son of the Father, becomes the "man free toward others"; and the Easter becomes his "contagious" effect, in the first instance upon his immediate disciples, and at length upon the Christian church.[23] One need not raise obvious historical objections to this reduction, nor ask embarrassing questions as to how the "contagious" effect of the Christ compares with that produced by other charismatic figures, not all of them admirable. It suffices to point to an internal contradiction upon which *The Secular Meaning of the Gospel* suffers inescapable shipwreck. The secular gospel is "freedom-toward-others," *total* in the Christian only when it is *secular,* when it is freed of faith in the Father. This freedom, then, supersedes that of the Christ himself, who was *not* secular but believed in the Father. And yet it is faith in the Christ that makes the secular Christian free. *The Secular Meaning of the Gospel* is secular, to be sure; but it cannot be gospel. It is a surrender to secularism.

More important than this surrender is why it should have been thought necessary, at least on the grounds that are here offered. It is, to begin with, highly questionable whether even in the minds of Biblical authors God ever was a hypothesis needed for the explanation of fact. A myth such as creation does not, after all, *explain* anything. Nor is God in the Bible ever accepted hypothetically only, as a mere assumption in need of confirmation and capable of refutation. The prayed-for rain may confirm him; it confirms not his existence, but merely his mercy, even as lack of rain evidences not divine non-existence, but merely divine refusal. Linguistic empiricists resort with tiresome repetitiousness to Elijah at Mt. Carmel.[24] But their reflections are thoughtless as well as tiresome. Is it really imaginable that an Elijah—of all prophets—would have become one of the priests of Baal if fire had consumed not his sacrifice but theirs? That the Jew's faith, at any rate, is no hypothesis is shown by its very survival; if empirically refutable, it should stand refuted a thousand times. And must a Jew really remind a Christian of Paul's view of faith as the evidence of things not seen? Or that the "fool who says in his heart that there is no God" (Ps. 14:1; 53:1) is a fool not because he lacks eyes and ears, but because he lacks the eyes and ears of faith?

Does philosophy reduce faith to a mere expression of emotion, or, in any case, to a mere attitude toward the world without access to objective truth? Only when it begs the main question from the start. Empiricism accepts as objective "data" only what is accessible to a detached—unbelieving—observer; thus the objective realm is confined to "the world," which in turn is empirical data and the hypotheses needed to explain them. On these grounds, faith certainly reduces itself to a mere attitude toward the world. But empiricism does not understand faith as faith understands itself. In its own self-understanding, faith is a committed confrontation of the world, not a detached observation; and in this confrontation of the world, it is receptive of a God who speaks in and through the world. Faith, to be sure, is a "subjective attitude"; but because it is a *believing* attitude, it takes itself as receptive of an objective truth accessible only in the believing attitude and inaccessible otherwise. Linguistic empiricism poses as a refutation of faith; in fact, it merely takes its stand outside the circle of faith, in a circle of its own in which the word of God is not heard and only "data"·are given. As for *The Secular Meaning of the Gospel*, it does not follow an inexorable imperative of intellectual honesty when it leaves the circle of faith. It merely confesses its atheism.

The Secular Meaning of the Gospel reduces affirmations made from within the circle of faith to affirmations made from without. "God-statements" dissipate themselves into "man-statements": "God loves me" means no more than "I feel secure."[25] This reduction evidently follows for one who has moved outside the circle of faith and judges faith by the standards of agnostic empiricism. The reduction is totally fallacious, however, within the circle of faith itself. The believer who stands before God does *not* "feel secure." He is, on the contrary, exposed to the most radical of all insecurities. When the revelation of divine love breaks into this insecurity, it comes as the absolute surprise that the Divine who in his glory does not need him should yet choose to need him, and that he, the believer, should in all his unlovableness nevertheless be loved. That this revelation is inaccessible to the detached observer is not strange but expected; his reduction of "God-statements" to "man-statements" has cut him off from God.

215

The surrender of *The Secular Meaning of the Gospel* to secularism, then, is sadly unnecessary. There is, in any case, no need for it on the grounds of either empirical science or linguistic philosophy.[26] A Jewish reader will have a special sense of sadness; for the surrender here carried out cuts off ties that have existed between Jew and Christian through the centuries. Few New Testament passages are more alien to Jewish faith than the following: "For it is the God who said 'let light shine out of darkness' who has shone into the hearts to give the light of the knowledge of God in the face of Christ" (II Cor. 4:6). Yet even here Jew and Christian, at odds over "the face of Christ," still share the God who speaks. This bond is destroyed when *The Secular Meaning of the Gospel* reinterprets the passage so as to eliminate God.[27]

In its self-exposure to the modern-secular world, can Christian faith come upon deeper challenges than those faced by *The Secular Meaning of the Gospel?* Is it faced not only with the long-obvious threat of externally opposing forces, but also with a threat from within? Or, to stay with the previously used image, is Christian faith challenged not only to *abandon* its own circle for the secularist circle external to it, but also to *transfigure* itself radically, so as to become absorbed by the secularist circle without remainder? With this question we come upon a far more profound Christian self-exposure to the modern-secular world, and at the same time one far more dangerous. *The Secular Meaning of the Gospel* merely abandons the Biblical God for an atheistic humanism. *The Gospel of Christian Atheism*[28] literally affirms and indeed wills the death of the Biblical God; and its affirming and willing produces the spectre of idolatry.

The Gospel of Christian Atheism revels in sweeping generalizations and unsubstantiated assertions,[29] as well as in a dialectic which, while at times the Hegelian movement of spirit which transfigures what it negates, is at other times merely incoherence made into a theological virtue. But rather than pounce on such vices, one must attend to its central virtue, a radicalism than which one bolder and more extreme it would be difficult to imagine. Here the central theological issue left hanging in mid-air since Bonhoeffer is confronted head-on and dealt with in a manner that leaves no room for ambiguity or compromise. *The Gospel of Christian Atheism* is a work which itself must be confronted head-on, if only to be uncompromisingly rejected.

For all its lack of intellectual discipline, the work states its central thesis with admirable clarity. The spirit of the modern-secular world is most clearly expressed in modern speculative philosophy; this is neither simply indifferent to Christianity nor simply hostile to it. Modern speculative philosophy—and the whole modern-secular world—are the dialectical result of Christianity, as well as its dialectical negation. Its result: only the Christian God incarnate in the world has made possible "profane" modern worldliness. Its negation: only as modern worldliness negates the transcendent otherness of the Biblical God, so as to appropriate it into total immanence, does it, *qua* worldliness, become complete. This movement is already, in principle, complete in modern philosophy—above all, in Hegel and Nietzsche; for here the "death" of the transcendent God is effected by means of an immanent self-elevation of thought toward divinity. If the movement is as yet incomplete in the modern-secular world as a whole—if at the present time there is a chaos in which the old Christian values have already vanished while new, post-Christian values have not yet emerged, it is in large measure because Christian theology has opposed modern autonomous-godless thought in the name of the transcendent God, when to transfigure itself into just that mode of thought, and hence to accept the death of the transcendent God, is in truth its inescapable destiny. Christian theology must therefore accept and even "will" the death of God—anyhow occurring in the midst of Christendom "in our time, in our history, in our existence,"[30] and in effect write a third testament. The Old Testament knew only the alien, transcendent, externally commanding Father. He became the Son, incarnate and immanent, in the New Testament. It will be left for the third testament to come dialectically to deny the Son's resurrection to transcendence, and along with it the Father who makes this resurrection possible. This step will lay "faith . . . open to the most terrible darkness"; yet in precisely that darkness will it "be receptive of the most redemptive light." And the redemption-to-come will be the "full and actual presence of the Christ who is a totally incarnate love."[31]

Such, in brief, is *The Gospel of Christian Atheism.* In this essay, it calls for both a philosophical and a Jewish response. This response must begin with noting the work's totally inadequate grasp of Hegel, more obviously even than Nietzsche its philosophical patron saint. Hegel *does* transfigure Christian faith into autonomous philosophical thought. He does *not* in the process produce the death either of God or of the Christian faith. Hegel's philosophy rests on two crucial presuppositions: on the one hand, the faith which receives the descent of God into Christ; on the other, the ascent of modern secularity to freedom and autonomy. Its task is to reconcile these two presuppositions in the form of philosophical thought, and yet so to reconcile them as not to destroy them. Thought transfigures secular and religious life into a union of *thought;* but it also *re-instates* them in that creative difference in which they exist *in life.*[32] If taken at his full word rather than selectively made use of, Hegel lends no support to *The Gospel of Christian Atheism.* On the contrary, he anticipates the move taken in that work and rejects it.

But there is, of course, ample precedent for the kind of selective reading of Hegel that takes a left-wing turn and denies transcendence. It is instructive to consider the fate of nineteenth-century left-wing Hegelians. Their denial of Hegelian transcendence led them to seek an absoluteness immanent in actual humanity; yet in the process of this search virtually every left-wing Hegelian accused his predecessor of dissipating concrete man into an unreal abstraction. This process may be said to have culminated in Marx and Nietzsche, both left-wing Hegelians in a wider sense. Scorning the spurious "freedom" of Feuerbach's "abstract" humanity, as well as the "mere idealism" of "utopian" socialists, both men sought an *actual* humanity *absolutely* free, in the one case in the future classless society; in the other, in the future "Overman." But with what success? In retrospect, Marx's dialectical socialism is far more utopian than "utopian" socialism. As for Nietzsche's Overman, he is a mere myth, and one far more unreal—and dangerous—than all those transcendent deities that he was meant to replace.

Nietzsche assuredly is not a proto-fascist. He is, however, a reckless and apocalyptic mythmaker, divorced from reality as all apocalyptic mythmakers are. Americans have only lately discovered Nietzsche. Now that some American theologians idolize him, they stand in need of a warning from someone who never has had to discover him behind false stereotypes. Karl Loewith, lifelong German student of Nietzsche and author of a classic study of him as far back as in 1935, writes in 1956:

He is still close to us, yet already quite remote. . . . [In his case] the question of . . . the historic responsibility of all public thought, speech and writing is inescapable. For in the case of Nietzsche it is undeniable that he wished from the beginning to be effective through his writing and be as philosopher a "physician of culture." Thus in the end he sketched a world-historical program designed for "great politics.". . .

And he coined maxims with an unheard-of harshness and recklessness of which in his personal life he never was capable, maxims which entered into public consciousness and then were practised for twelve years. Among these were the maxim of the dangerous life, of contempt for sympathy . . . , of a decisive nihilism of action, according to which that which already falls is yet to be pushed down.[33]

What responsible secular philosopher of the age of Auschwitz and Hiroshima would utter the Nietzsche-style demand to "abandon all those moral laws which the Christian Church has sanctioned"?[34] It seems strange that theologians should embrace Nietzschean apocalypticism when secular philosophers—Sartre and Camus come to mind—have abandoned all reckless human aspirations to an immanent divinity, leaving man with a responsible but finite freedom.

But perhaps this is not strange. Theologians, after all, cannot let go of infinity and divinity, even if the search for these is at the cost of a reckless antinomian disregard for morality. Is this disregard necessary? And is the search successful? It is tempting to contrast the goal of *The Gospel of Christian Atheism* (which is to lay hold of concrete present worldliness) with its actual result (which is the apocalyptic dissipation of everything concrete and present into what Hegel would have called a "night in which all cows are black"). One is all the more tempted to dwell on this result because apocalyptic nihilism is not uncommon among present post-Christian writers, who respond to our present despairs with the indiscriminate surrender of all those things in the present which must under no circumstances be surrendered, but, on the contrary, loved and nurtured.[35] But we must turn at once to what in the context of this essay is the crucial theological issue: between any possible form of Jewish faith and this Christian (or post-Christian) theology—possibly the most radical anti-Judaic theology ever nurtured in the bosom of the Christian church.

Why must *The Gospel of Christian Atheism* accept and even "will" the death of God? Not because modern belief in God is no longer genuine; the work would attack it as reactionary even when it was genuine. Nor because God is ruled out by modern science and empiricist philosophy; the work cares little about science and less about empirical evidence. The death of God must be willed because "God . . . is the transcendent enemy of the fulness and the passion of man's life in the world, and only through God's death can humanity be liberated from that repression which is the real ruler of history."[36] In short, it is the Lord of Israel whose otherness—and hence lordship and divinity—is the enemy; and only as Christianity rids itself of this Jewish element can it consummate the salvation aimed at ever since the time of its origin, but until now unconsummated because of its failure to emancipate itself from Judaism.[37]

Such views must produce from a Jew one fundamental question. Who is this hostile God, foe of human freedom and source of every repression? He is not and never has been the authentic God of Israel: not in the Hebrew Bible, not in the rabbinic writings, not in the history of Jewish religious thought until this day. He is not the God of the psalmist when he "delights" in the divine commandments (Ps. 119:47); not the God of the rabbinic sage who declares that "when the Torah came into the world freedom came into the world" (*Midrash Genesis Rabba, Wayyera* LIII 7); not the God of the ordinary Jewish worshiper who daily proclaims that it is in his love that God gave commandments to Israel. The enemy-God is a caricature. The authentic God of Israel is he who in his transcendent otherness does not need man and yet chooses to need him; who in his love makes man free and responsible, and thus as commanding demands a free response. He is, in short, a God of grace. But must a Jew tell a Christian about grace?

From time to time this would appear to be necessary. In the perspective of Judaism, Nietzsche's titanic war on the Biblical God is not a modern necessity, inevitably waged in behalf of human freedom. It is the nemesis manifested in this parson's son of an age-old Christian—or is it pseudo-Christian?—blindness to a grace that is manifest in the commandments, to a grace that does not diminish or vanquish human freedom but rather augments and, indeed, establishes it. This same nemesis is manifest in *The Gospel of Christian Atheism*.[38]

V. On the "Eclipse" of God

Philosophers have always been demythologizers.[39] More to the present point, the Bible demythologizes when it reduces nature to the un-divine product of a divine Creator that is intended for human use. (It has been plausibly argued that modern science and technology are Biblical in inspiration when, rather than contemplate nature with a religious awe, they subject it to experimental "torture" and technological control.) But while the Bible demythologizes the creation, it does not demythologize a divine word that may enter into it, in order to be present for man in and through it. It is the possibility of just this presence that the modern-secular world calls radically into question; and when the question is given an unequivocally negative answer, modern secularity has turned into secularism.

The essence of secularism may be formulated as an answer to one of the questions left hanging by Bonhoeffer. Suppose a secularist experienced, with or without the witness of a Bonhoeffer, the presence of the "confronting" God: Would he believe in him? If he were an unrepentant secularist, he would "explain" the confronting God as the mere unconscious projection of his subjective "experience." This explanation, moreover, would encompass in principle all similar experiences throughout human history. Secularist man may or may not deny "the existence of God." He is, in any case, cut off from his presence. According to his lights, man—every man—is radically and inescapably alone.

Faith does not radically expose itself to the modern-secular world if it avoids the challenge of secularism. Yet self-exposure to secularism involves a risk without precedent in the history of faith. When faced with false prophets, an ancient prophet recognized the possibility and the risk that he himself might be false. When faced with secularism, modern faith recognizes the vastly more shattering possibility that all human witnessing to a divine presence ever made might have been based on a radical illusion: the possibility that man is, as secularism holds him to be, radically alone.

The modern believer dare not ignore this possibility, lest his self-exposure to the modern-secular world fail precisely when it is most serious. Yet dare he embrace the possibility as actuality? This would be to surrender to secularism. The modern believer walks on the "narrow ridge" of total risk.

On this ridge the great modern theologians have been walking for nearly half a century. To give one example, whatever questions may be asked about the "positivism" of Karl Barth's neo-orthodoxy,[40] it does not ignore secularism but arises from self-exposure to it.[41] To give another, Martin Buber's *I and Thou*[42] is not a mere homily that expresses its author's experience of a "divine Thou" and ignores the secularist objection that such experiences are in principle illusory. It confronts the secularist objection and repudiates it. *I and Thou* does not refute a Feuerbachian secularism that makes all I-Thou relations human. Faith can neither refute secularism nor itself be proved. The work does bring about, however, a significant confrontation; from this, it emerges that Biblical openness to a divine presence and the unyielding solitariness of secularism are both equally unprovable and irrefutable. They are, in this sense, rival faiths.

Secularist unbelief dissipates the present divine Other into a projection of human feeling. Belief on its part takes human feeling as the mere by-product of an actual encounter with Divinity: Only if man is "withdrawn" from the encounter is he left with mere feeling. Secularism asserts that belief deifies the projection of feeling. Faith retorts that secularism deifies its withdrawal from God; it holds that to repent of his secularism a man must not in his withdrawn state cast about for "religious experiences," but rather "turn" away from his self-absorption and toward the God who speaks.

This self-exposure is in principle adequate[43]; it bears witness to the "confronting" God while, self-exposed to a secularism that would "explain" away belief in this God, walking on the narrow ridge of risk. It falls short, however, in at least one crucial particular. Committed to the thesis that God speaks constantly,[44] *I and Thou* stakes all responsibility for "hearing" on a human "turning." But the weight of such a responsibility was too great even in Biblical times. In the modern-secular world it is intolerable.

But perhaps the greatest achievement of Buber's career is the steadfastness with which it moves from an original resort to romantic illusions toward an ever-greater realism. About thirty years after *I and Thou*, Buber writes:

Let us ask whether it may not literally be true that God formerly spoke to us and is now silent, and whether this is not to be understood as the Hebrew Bible understands it, namely, that the living God is not only a self-revealing but also a self-concealing God. Let us realize what it means to live in the age of such a concealment, such a divine silence. . . . It would be worthier not to explain it to oneself in sensational and incompetent sayings, such as that of the death of God, but to endure it as it is and at the same time move existentially toward a new happening, toward that event in which the word between heaven and earth will again be heard.[45]

This statement is made in direct response to Sartre's atheism, but in indirect response to all modern secularism and, in anticipation, to all the "God-is-dead" theologies. Faith stands here self-exposed to all the evidence that secularist unbelief might cite against it in the contemporary world; yet it remains faith because it continues to listen to God even if, there being no hearing, there may be an "eclipse of God." An eclipse does not destroy the sun; moreover, it is temporary. A faith which accepts a divine eclipse listens even in a time of silence, in the trust that the divine word will again be heard.[46]

Can such a faith endure in the present age? This is an as-yet unanswered question. The contradictions in which this endurance must prove itself today are nearly nowhere confronted. In this age, there is celebration of the freedoms of the secular city, coupled with dread of its emptiness. Democratic tolerance coexists with unprecedented violence and with the spectre of universal disaster. Modern man is torn between an at-homeness in a secular world exalting human autonomy, and flights from both into an apocalyptic nihilism. The listening endurance of faith will have to exist steadfast *in* this world, exposed at once to its marvels and terrors.

The Jew is singled out for special contradictions. In America he enjoys a freedom and security unparalleled in his history; yet he is but twenty years separated from the greatest and as yet uncomprehended Jewish catastrophe. His trust and joy in the modern-secular world cannot but coexist with radical distrust and profound sorrow. Authentic Jewish religious witness in this age must both face up to Auschwitz and yet refuse a despair of this world which, wholly contrary to Judaism, would hand still another victory to the forces of radical evil. Insofar as he is committed to Jewish survival, the Jew has already taken a stand against these forces. But survival-for-survival's-sake is an inadequate stand. The Jew can go beyond it only if he can reopen the quest of Jeremiah and Job, who for all their agony refused to despair either of God or the world.

VI. *Despair, Silence, Waiting, Interrogation*

Is there an authentic Jewish enduring of the contradictions of present Jewish existence? Is it giving rise to a quest, to a listening, indeed, to an interrogating of God which, born of faith, may itself bespeak a Presence while as yet no voice is heard? Perhaps one must not look to philosophers or even theologians. Perhaps one must look to a novelist whose heaven-storming shatters conventions and literary forms.[47] Elie Wiesel's *Night* is no mere speculation upon imagined darkness. It is an eye-witness account of the most terrible actual darkness, by a man who experienced it when he was a fourteen-year-old boy. In this document—the document of our time of the impact of radical evil on Jewish faith—we read:

One day when we came back from work, we saw three gallows rearing up in the assembly place, three black crows. Roll Call. SS all round us, machine guns trained: the traditional ceremony. Three victims in chains—and one of them, the little servant, the sad-eyed angel.

The SS seemed more preoccupied, more disturbed than usual. To hang a young boy in front of thousands of spectators was no light matter. The head of the camp read the verdict. All eyes were on the child. He was lividly pale, almost calm, biting his lips. The gallows threw its shadow over him. . . .

The three victims mounted together onto the chairs.

The three necks were placed at the same moment within the nooses.

"Long live liberty!" cried the two adults.

But the child was silent.

"Where is God? Where is He?" someone behind me asked.

At a sign from the head of the camp, the three chairs tipped over. . . .

I heard a voice within me answer. . . :

"Where is He? Here He is—He is hanging on this gallows. . . ."[48]

The hero of *The Accident* has listened to Sarah, former "SS whore" who has been forced into every degradation conceivable by a satanic imagination.

I shouldn't have listened. I should have fled. . . . Whoever listens to Sarah and doesn't change, whoever enters Sarah's world and doesn't invent new gods and new religions, deserves death and destruction. Sarah alone had the right to decide what is good and what is evil, the right to differentiate what is true from what usurps the appearance of truth.[49]

The Town Beyond the Wall ends with a legend. Man once was granted by God his request for a temporary exchange of places. The request granted, he immediately assumed omnipotence and refused to return to his place. In the years or centuries or eternities following:

The past for one, the present for the other, were too heavy to be borne. As the liberation of one was bound to the liberation of the other, they renewed the ancient dialogue whose echoes come to us in the night, charged with hatred, with remorse, and most of all, with infinite yearning.[50]

In *The Gates of the Forest*, Gregor remains in an inconclusive argument with the Hasidic rabbi.

Gregor was angry. "After what has happened to us, how can you believe in God?"

With an understanding smile on his lips the Rebbe answered, "How can you *not* believe in God after what has happened?"[51]

Yet Gregor reaches an affirmation, or the fragment of an affirmation, or the fragment of a fragment.

"Whether or not the Messiah comes doesn't matter; we'll manage without him. It is because it is too late that we are commanded to hope. . . . The Messiah isn't one man, Clara, he's all men. As long as there are men there will be a Messiah. One day you'll sing, and he will sing in you. . . ."

At the appropriate moments Gregor recited the *Kaddish,* that solemn affirmation, filled with grandeur and serenity, by which man returns God his crown and sceptre. He recited it slowly, concentrating on every sentence, every word, every syllable of praise. His voice trembled, timid, like that of the orphan suddenly made aware of the relationship between death and eternity, between eternity and the word.[52]

REFERENCES

1. In addition to the works discussed in this essay, see John A. T. Robinson, *Honest to God* (London, 1963); Pierre Berton, *The Comfortable Pew* (Toronto, 1965); William Kilbourn (ed.), *The Restless Church* (Toronto, 1966). I select these works from among many because of their wide popularity in their respective countries. *The Comfortable Pew* is a critique of the church that was commissioned by the Anglican Church of Canada, and *The Restless Church,* a response commissioned by the same body.

2. For an excellent example, cf. Milton Himmelfarb, "Secular Society? A Jewish Perspective," this volume, pp. 220-36. The reader may form his own judgment as to the extent to which Himmelfarb's "long view" is inspired by contemporary Jewish experience.

3. "God has died in *our* time, in *our* history, in *our* existence." (Thomas J. J. Altizer, in *Radical Theology and the Death of God,* by Altizer and William Hamilton [Indianapolis, 1966], p. 95.)

4. Cf., for example, H. Jonas, "Heidegger and Theology," *The Review of Metaphysics,* Vol. 18, No. 1 (1964), 207ff. (reprinted in: *The Phenomenon of Life* [New York, 1966], pp. 235ff.); E. Borowitz, "Bonhoeffer's World Comes of Age," *Judaism,* Vol. 14, No. 1 (1965), pp. 81ff.; and my own "A Jew Looks at Christianity and Secularist Liberalism," *The Restless Church,* pp. 86ff. Cf. also, A. Wolf (ed.), *Rediscovering Judaism* (Chicago, 1965), by a group of writers united by their concern to seek out the classical sources of Judaism in their confrontation with the modern-secular world.

5. Cf. *infra,* Section IV of this essay.

6. I have attempted to view the confrontation of Christianity and secularist liberalism from the standpoint of contemporary Jewish experience and faith in the article referred to *supra*, n. 4.

7. Dietrich Bonhoeffer, *Letters and Papers from Prison* (London, 1953).

8. *Ibid.*, pp. 163, 146ff., 163ff., 160, 157ff.

9. *Ibid.*, p. 111.

10. Cf. the articles listed *supra*, n. 4. Professor Jonas warns Protestant theologians against undue reliance on Heidegger's secularistic ontology, even though he finds it "awkward . . . to act as . . . defender of the cause of Christian theology," being both a Jew and "a mere child of this world."

11. Here and *infra*, I allude to a famous post-French Revolution slogan, according to which the Jew was to be permitted to remain a Jew "at home" —in the privacy of a purely religious conscience—on condition that he become "a man abroad," that he purge all remnants of Jewish national-cultural life from his public-secular existence. In pluralistic North America this artificial and illiberal dichotomy never took hold.

12. This statement is not, I think, the product of mere romantic optimism. I must, however, mention in passing that during the thirties Jews then in Germany, this writer included, were wont to make a saint of any Christian showing the slightest signs of resistance to Nazism; for example, of so questionable a figure as Cardinal Faulhaber, solely because he spoke up in behalf of Old Testament Patriarchs. (Cf. G. Lewy, *The Catholic Church and Nazi Germany* [New York, 1965], pp. 111, 276.) In those dark days it was a simple human impossibility to recognize enemies on *all* sides; and it would appear to be no accident that it took twenty years for works to appear that fully document the grim truth that while Nazi anti-Semitism is, of course, anti-Christian in essence, both this anti-Semitism and the attempted genocide in which it culminated would have been impossible except for centuries of Christian anti-Semitism; indeed, without considerable cooperation of Christians not all of whom were nominal. I trust I am not uttering a Jewish view only when I assert that the confrontation of this grim truth, now begun in some Christian quarters, is one of the major tasks of Christian thought in this generation.

13. Harvey Cox, *The Secular City* (New York, 1965).

14. *Ibid.*, pp. 3, 26ff.

15. This is the title of a book by Milton Mayer (Chicago, 1955), which gives a portrait of ten Germans, all of them decent people and Nazis.

16. Cox, *op. cit.*, p. 63.

17. An expression used by the nineteenth-century Jewish Hegelian Samuel Hirsch, in his critique of the utilitarian destruction of Roman religion in the later Roman Empire. With respect to religious pragmatism, there is an uncomfortable resemblance between the modern-secular world and the

Roman Empire as viewed by Hegel himself: uncomfortable because Hegel sees Rome's all-encompassing utilitarianism as the source of its destruction.

18. Cox, *op. cit.*, Part IV.

19. *Ibid.*, p. 268.

20. Cf. Martin Buber, *Between Man and Man* (Boston, 1955), p. 15. For the interpretation of the Exodus passage, cf. Buber's *The Prophetic Faith* (New York, 1949), pp. 28ff., and his *Moses* (New York, 1958), pp. 52ff.

21. The claim that belief can no longer be genuinely alive is logically distinct from the claim that it is no longer intellectually legitimate. The latter claim is presently under review; the former will be discussed in Section V of this essay.

22. Paul Van Buren, *The Secular Meaning of the Gospel* (New York, 1963; paperback edition, 1966).

23. *Ibid.*, for example, pp. 121ff., 132ff., 137ff., 141ff., 151ff., 163ff.; pp. 133ff., 137ff., 152ff., 168ff.

24. The fashion was started by J. Wisdom's "Gods," *Proceedings of the Aristotelian Society* (1945-46). Cf. also Van Buren, *op. cit.*, p. 68.

25. Van Buren, *op. cit.*, p. 68. From this reduction it follows that "today, we cannot even understand the Nietzschean cry that 'God is dead,' for if it were so, how could we know? No, the problem now is that the *word* 'God' is dead," *ibid.*, p. 103.

26. That linguistic philosophy need not necessarily involve an empiricism destructive of Christian faith is illustrated, for example, in D. Evans, *The Logic of Self-Involvement* (London, 1963).

27. Van Buren, *op. cit.*, pp. 198ff. The elimination is followed by this incredible statement: "The fact that the *language* of our interpretation of Jesus and Easter is different from that of Paul does not preclude the possibility that our *meaning* and Paul's may be the same" (italics ours).

28. Thomas J. J. Altizer, *The Gospel of Christian Atheism* (Philadelphia, 1966). Cf. also *Radical Theology and the Death of God*, by Thomas J. J. Altizer and William Hamilton; referred to as *RT*, *infra*.

29. Cf., for example, *RT*, p. 95: "We shall *simply assume* the truth of Nietzsche's proclamation of the death of God . . ." (italics ours).

30. *RT*, p. 95.

31. *RT*, pp. 20ff., 157.

32. This is argued in detail in *Peace Between Faith and Philosophy: The Religious Dimension in Hegel's Thought*, scheduled for publication in 1968 by Indiana University Press.

33. *Gesammelte Abhandlungen* (Stuttgart, 1960), pp. 127, 129, 130.

34. Altizer, *The Gospel of Christian Atheism*, p. 147.

35. Cf. Robert Alter, "The Apocalyptic Temper," *Commentary* (June, 1966), pp. 61ff. Alter's article is an outstanding critique of the "savagely comical apocalypse in vogue in American fiction."

36. Altizer, *Gospel of Christian Atheism*, p. 22.

37. In fairness, it must be added that *The Gospel of Christian Atheism* in no way follows the kind of crude anti-Jewish line that attributes whatever is found inconvenient in Christian ethics and theology to Jewish influence. Cf. Altizer, *op. cit.*, p. 45: "It is . . . Christianity that has reduced human existence to sin and guilt, confronting a broken humanity with a wholly other God who demands total submission to his numinous and judgmental power." If the "wholly other" God is Jewish, then this Jewish God has been essential to Christianity until the time of his "death."

38. The section just concluded is not intended as a comprehensive critique of the "God-is-dead" theology. I may, however, say in passing that I am puzzled to find William Hamilton in close association with Altizer. His ethically inspired optimism (and consequent repudiation of such writers as Ezra Pound); his intense concern with actual human suffering; his stance of "waiting for God": these and other themes would appear to associate him far more closely, on the one hand, with *The Secular City* and, on the other, with the doctrine of the "eclipse" of God (cf. *infra*, Section V); they would also appear to make the expression "death of God" in his case not readily intelligible. Cf., for example, *RT*, pp. 37ff., 157ff.; also William Hamilton, *The New Essence of Christianity* (New York, 1966), especially pp. 44ff.

39. On the theme of this section, cf. also my "On the Eclipse of God," *Commentary* (June, 1964), pp. 55ff., reprinted in *The Star and the Cross*, ed. K. T. Hargrove, R.S.C.J. (Milwaukee, 1966), pp. 227ff.

40. Cf. Bonhoeffer, *op. cit.*, pp. 126, 148.

41. Those currently inclined to dismiss Barth's neo-orthodoxy as being in the end merely old-fashioned orthodoxy might find instructive his *From Rousseau to Ritschl* (London, 1959), a work showing a far deeper penetration of Hegel than is shown by those who invoke Hegel in their argument for the death of God.

42. Martin Buber, *I and Thou* (New York, 1958).

43. The brief summary of Buber's teaching just given is based, as well as on *I and Thou*, on other writings, notably those collected in *Between Man and Man*. The adequacy of Buber's teaching, here merely asserted, is argued for in my "Buber's Concept of Revelation," in the forthcoming *The Philosophy of Martin Buber*, eds. Schilpp and Friedman (La Salle, Illinois).

44. Buber, *I and Thou*, pp. 75, 77, 99, 118ff.

45. Martin Buber, *Eclipse of God* (New York, 1952), pp. 89, 91.

46. Altizer refers to the possibility of a divine eclipse (*RT*, pp. 10, 107, 126); but despite much pondering, I cannot conclude that he has seriously considered it. Cf. *RT*, p. 126: "Buber asserts that the Jew can be safe in a time of God's eclipse because he exists in an eternal covenant that cannot be annulled by an act of man. The contemporary Jew can experience the contradiction of our existence as a theophany. However, not existing in an eternal covenant with God—if only because he exists in an Incarnate Word—the Christian cannot know the death of God as a theophany." Is the Jew "safe," and does Buber consider him so? Is a divine eclipse a theophany? Is not the Christian too in a covenant, the question of the "death" of God being precisely what is at issue? Finally, can Christian and Jew be as infinitely apart as is here asserted?

47. At a recent symposium "Toward Jewish Unity," S. Schwarzschild said: "The . . . point which I want to make . . . is a reference to an experience which many of us here shared last summer. . . . It was a gathering in the Canadian Province of Quebec . . . where a number of us, from all over the spectrum of Jewish life, gathered for a week's intensive study and conversation. . . . We discovered something at the end of the week . . . , namely, that the one man who spoke and protested and stormed the heavens and implicated Israel most tellingly for our generation and for our hearts, and for our hopes, and for our tragedy, was not a theologian, nor a professor, nor even a rabbi. The *de facto* High Priest of our generation turned out to be Elie Wiesel." (*Judaism*, Vol. 15, No. 2 [Spring, 1966], p. 157.)

48. Elie Wiesel, *Night* (New York, 1961), pp. 77ff.

49. Elie Wiesel, *The Accident* (New York, 1962), pp. 90ff.

50. Elie Wiesel, *The Town Beyond the Wall* (New York, 1964), p. 179.

51. Elie Wiesel, *The Gates of the Forest* (New York, 1966), p. 194.

52. *Ibid.*, pp. 225ff.

DONALD MEYER

Churches and Families

DURING THE two decades since World War II, the United States has enjoyed a family boom. This boom in domesticity almost certainly fed the postwar religiosity that reached its peak in the late fifties. A remarkably high marriage rate led quickly to a high rate of family formation, and new families locating in the suburbs swelled church-membership rolls and caused hundreds of new churches to be built. In such a milieu, "family life" naturally became attractive to the churches. Family-life agencies prospered, drawing on the skills of psychiatrists, psychologists, educators, sociologists, and lawyers. A considerable family-life journalism flourished. Premarital counseling took on a new self-consciousness. Pastors, rabbis, and priests affiliated with colleges enjoyed heavy business. Husbands, wives, and husbands-and-wives could attend special conferences, belong to special clubs, and go on special retreats.[1]

None of this was thoroughly new, but it occurred in contrast with an ambiguous past: wartime years of family disruption, depression years of bitter stresses working both for and against family stability, and the last decade of "normal" life, the twenties, when popular manners had appeared to suggest a really fundamental and irreversible transformation of inherited ways. By contrast, the postwar era seemed to register a return to familiar norms: high marriage and birth rates, marriage at earlier ages, even a very high rate of remarriage among the divorced. Such statistics certainly suggest that society had re-established its moral foundations if, as countless sages have announced, the foundation of society is the family. The affinity between the church and the family flows in both directions: Both contain basic and permanent drives of the race. Each finds security in the other.

Yet the churches did not regard the postwar family boom as an unmixed blessing. They could not claim convincingly to have been crucial in inspiring it. The family boom could just as easily be construed as expressing potentials severely troublesome to traditional church teaching—time bombs, so to speak, not easily accessible to quick de-fusing. At the same time, certain of these potentials might demand adjustment from the churches rather than resistance. And it is not always easy to decide which is which.

The marriage boom need not have generated a population boom, but it did. From the standpoint of an established birth-control ethic, this in itself posed no problem. In Protestant and Jewish middle-class circles, a somewhat diffuse but perfectly evident consensus had been reached by the twenties: Only so many children as the family could afford were to be conceived, physical and mental health, neighborhood, and schools figuring in the reckoning. Behind the veil of traditional Roman Catholic teachings, Catholic parents came to share the same conviction. Postwar births did include multitudes of infants whose parents could not adequately provide, and these came to figure in religious disputes over government subsidies for birth-control programs in the sixties; but it was the birth rate among prosperous young parents that was impressive. The new birth rate did not appear to press national resources as a whole. From a strictly agricultural and economic calculation, the United States remained a relatively underpopulated country. Social Gospel men of the depression decade had never decried population pressure as an American social evil.

On a larger stage, a kind of embarrassment did impend. Clergymen shared in the spreading postwar anxiety over worldwide population explosion. Ethically, how could we tolerate the American population boom and fail to sanction the population boom in Catholic Latin America? Could ethics justify absorption of the American food surplus by millions of new American mouths as famine once again threatened millions in Hindu India? Richard Fagley's *The Population Explosion and Christian Responsibility* ably canvassed the issues. He suggests that Christian responsibility finds it hard to constrain nationalist, racist, and isolationist potentials in an American population boom in a time of world population explosion. Some senior churchmen, recalling the thirties, were more troubled than others: Christian social ethics tailored to American good fortune had not proved fortunate then.

Geopolitics aside, what was to be made of a population boom based on "choice"? The demographers' data indicated that huge numbers of babies were being born to young parents who knew about choice. In earlier days birth-control advocates had commonly assumed that the general practice of birth control would mean fewer babies, not more. But for a good many years after 1945, it was impossible to tell whether or not the new generation of parents wanted big families. In 1958, P. K. Whelpton concluded, after completing a statistical analysis, that the large number of first births had been three times as significant a factor in the postwar birth rate as large families. Whelpton observed that it could not then be determined whether large families were on the agenda.[2] It now appears that they were not. The fertility rate of 1957 proved to be the postwar peak, and after a few years of modest decline, it began to decline more sharply in the sixties. Not so much more babies as earlier marriage, earlier babies, and an earlier end to having babies proved to be the pattern.

This analysis illuminated somewhat the meaning of the family boom. Rather than easing issues about the boom, however, it merely refined them. The ethical case for birth control had never been used to persuade people not to want children. Birth control had been used and justified simply because it helped people to have no more children than they wanted. But a population boom could evidently be based on children who were wanted and who could be afforded, at least in the immediate future. The American population boom was not yet a population explosion, and American resources seemed sufficient for a doubled or even trebled population, but these local and temporary circumstances merely postponed the ethical urgency. Sooner or later, ethics would have to consider issues of population control far more difficult than those yet confronted. Obviously all the churches—and not just the Roman Catholic—would prefer "later" rather than "sooner," for what if ethics had to consider counseling against parental impulse itself? What if ethics lost its major argument for marriage?

The reasonable assumption of widespread acceptance of contraception makes the population boom interesting. Before Pope John, Roman Catholic response to the population boom, both in the United States and the rest of the world, followed a course that clearly showed an overriding concern with sexuality. Practically the only time respectable Roman Catholics spoke as utopian social revolutionaries was when they explained how the contraceptively-unrestrained billions of the future were to be fed.

Contraception was, of course, the central subject of postwar family ethics, with the dawn of *aggiornamento*. As late as the late fifties, traditional rhetoric still flourished in Catholic circles. In Buffalo, at the Catholic Family Life Conference of 1958, the host bishop excoriated "the ghastly art of infanticide" and advised that it was "better to have six children than for a young mother to become psychotic or neurotic," as though these were the only alternatives in family life.[3] This traditional rhetoric found itself outdated with startling suddenness.

We cannot know precisely how many Roman Catholic families had anticipated a change in teachings. A 1955 study found 33 per cent of Catholic women approving planned family limitation.[4] How many of these assumed that family planning meant planning only by methods disapproved by the church was unclear. The Church itself had urgently promoted awareness of its own approved method after the war, but with undetermined results. Among Roman Catholic mothers, the option of planning had become less theoretical by 1955. The 1955 investigators found that 50 per cent had used birth-control methods not approved by the Church. Among these women, 40 per cent of those attending Mass regularly approved Church-disapproved methods; among those attending Mass rarely or not at all, 83 per cent approved. The study did not inquire whether acceptance of "illicit" methods led to religious non-observance or the reverse.[5] Nevertheless, these figures probably represented a spreading tide of dissent, and Roman Catholic leaders were challenged to respond.

By 1965, a Gallup poll indicated that 78 per cent of American Roman Catholics favored birth-control information being given to any woman who wanted it; 63 per cent believed that the majority of their fellow Catholics wanted the Church to re-evaluate its teachings.[6] In Roman Catholic journalism, *aggiornamento* had released a boiling debate. Church officials might still exalt a "fertility cult," designating a family with eight children Catholic Family of the Year in 1962, and a family with eleven children in 1963, but officialdom often finds itself tending symbols of a dying past while others struggle for the present.[7]

Among Protestants and Jews, the "issue" of birth control had been settled and remained so. The postwar pills and IUD's, significant not only because of their greater effectiveness but also because they shifted control to women, provoked no debates on basic principle. In the 1955 study, the investigators affirmed that "even wives belonging to fundamentalist sects, approved strongly [of planned family limitation], 74 per cent expressing unqualified approval and only 4 per cent unqualified disapproval."[8] One might fault the implications of the word *even*, since it is unclear what differentials had existed before Protestant unanimity swallowed them up. Protestant and Judaic church authority had already negotiated its peace with modern familial contraceptive practice.

But Roman Catholicism had not, and the issue has come to shake the church. The issue of contraception has escalated into the issue of "authority." Any number of lines of reasoning have been proposed for a new teaching sympathetic to contraceptive practices. Few have been able to explain how such a teaching would not contradict the old teaching, which, after all, had been expounded in 1930 through the exalted medium of a papal encyclical, *Casti Conubii*, by Pius XI. Father Hans Küng has proposed that Pope Paul agree, quite simply, that Pope Pius made a mistake. "Everybody makes mistakes."[9]

Why this issue arose in Roman Catholicism remains more important than how it has been and will be resolved in individual cases. Kingsley Davis correctly observed at a 1949 symposium on "Demography and Values," that "although contraception has become a Western folkway, no major religion advocated its use prior to its popular adoption. The common people took it over in the face of almost universal opposition."[10] Davis' use of *almost* may not do justice to those clergy who helped break the ancient prohibitions on contraception. Even more here than in other reforms, such clergy had to fight their own establishments. Davis suggests a process whereby the churches, in order to preserve anything like a pretense to civic significance, had had to catch up with those they presumed to instruct. When to do so and which goals and practices to incorporate have been crucial issues in the history of the churches. In the 1949 symposium, Josiah Russell traced the tension between churches and folkways at least back to the Middle Ages. The churches have stood for order, asceticism, community; the folkways for freedom, abundance, the dignity of the individual.

Protestant and Jewish teaching has reserved contraception for use within marriage. It is not clear, however, that this reservation has been intended by the folkways. Here, at least among Protestants and Jews, church teaching has been faced with the need to decide how far to carry a concession it has already made. Until the early sixties, the issue of early sex had been met in postwar America by early marriage. We have no data demonstrating a distinct increase in premarital sexual intercourse in the period 1945–1960 in comparison with the previous three decades. There are other explanations for early marriage than that it has "contained" sex, but the result has been evident. The controlling comparison is with postwar Sweden, where premarital sex has been widely sanctioned in conjunction with much later marriage than in the United States. In the United States early marriage has meant less premarital sex, but it has also meant more divorce.

One can only say that in the face of this situation church attitudes have been less than straightforward. On marital sexuality, Protestant, Jewish, and some Catholic counselors have by now elaborated a view that can be summed up fairly as a modern doctrine of "sacred sex."[11] Roman Catholic apologists point out that marriage is a sacrament, while celibacy is not. (Although if this has always been the case, it is hard to explain why priestly celibacy has not come under critical review until today.) The ethic of sacred sex is expounded as the medium for deeper discovery and fulfillment of the self in love. Again, one is drawn to think the folkways led and the churches followed. Sacred sex has helped to extricate human values from anxieties about social order. These anxieties in practice have meant the draft of the family into service to the state, the economy, even "the Church"—to almost anything but its own best interests. Sacred sex has softened and sluiced away the anti-sexual attitudes of an ancient priestliness within marriage.

But celebration of married sex has stabilized neither marital nor sexual ethics. It has not been a simple case of pro-sexual folkways demanding sexual carte blanche from the churches. As one pastor-humorist put it: "American Protestants have discovered sex, of course, but they are slightly ashamed of it and prefer to think that their preachers haven't."[12] Here the churches have had to allow the folkways an extended interval of trial and error before offering even the most sympathetic counsel.[13]

In the fifties and sixties, commentators have seemed more apt to deplore rather than sanction youthful marriage. The "causes" of early marriage commonly cited—going steady, indulgent parents, pregnancy—add up to an indictment. The churches teach that every marriage requires responsibility and maturity. But it is difficult to translate the counsel to be mature and responsible into terms directly relevant to teen-age life without directly confronting the sexual issue. Having sanctioned contraception, the churches have lost one important "prudential" argument against premarital sex. Having exalted married sex, they have intensified the problem of advising the denial of sexual impulses. Postwar counsel has centered on problems of teen-age morality. Abstinence for persons twenty, twenty-two, or twenty-five years old and still unmarried is difficult indeed to formulate. When people marry young these difficulties vanish.

Unfortunately the divorce rate of those who marry before they are twenty is twice the average rate. The postwar Protestant and Jewish moralists have had to accept the implications of the modern divorce rate whether they like it or not, and, I believe, the same may be said of Catholics. Catholic teaching has not prevented Catholic laymen from contributing very nearly their share to the divorce rate.[14] We can hardly know how many church counselors have, in fact, preferred to deal with the divorce rate rather than with the issue of premarital sex. Church forces during the postwar period, by contrast with earlier eras, have clearly refrained from attempts to "deal with" divorce by tightening divorce laws. Indeed, after years of futile effort to overcome Catholic opposition, reformers in New York succeeded in 1966 in some easing of the state law which for generations had been the primary cause of the "scandal" of "easy" divorce in places like Nevada. Some Catholics even helped to pass the legislation.[15] During the fifties and sixties, Episcopalians, Methodists, Presbyterians, and Lutherans also loosened the restrictions on remarriage. No longer did they depend on the legal system's practice of designating parties "plaintiff" and "defendant"—that is, "guilty" and "innocent" as in a criminal case.[16] What were more and more of the divorced guilty of? They were too young, immature, unready; but who, if not the churches, had sanctioned these premature marriages? Divorce has come to be seen generally not as a "necessary evil" (for its necessity is not the point), but as a positive good for a man and a woman and, often, their children.

Church temporizing has contributed to perpetuation of an impasse: a legal divorce code without ethical meaning, folkways forced by the code into subterfuge, churches fearful of real reform because of the folkways. Efforts at reform by English churchmen faced by a similar situation have been interesting. In July, 1966, the Archbishop of Canterbury's commission recommended in its report, *Putting Asunder,* that divorces be granted on one, obvious, ineluctable ground: the breakdown of the marriage. Here the logic of personalism, including sacred sex, won due recognition. But, the churchmen said, the determination of breakdown should be made not on the basis of the testimony of the parties involved, but on the findings of a court of inquiry. No one could doubt the churchmen assumed such a court would rely heavily upon church ethics. In November, 1966, a British Law Commission rejected this proposal.[17] The lawyers cited the great cost of such a procedure; clearly they visualized the court of inquiry being thoroughly deliberate in its ability to decide whether or not married persons knew the state of their marriage. The lawyers proposed that the "breakdown" principle be incorporated without inquest by the law, relying on the evidence of the parties themselves through separation and mutual consent over some period of time. It was precisely this that the churchmen did not want. In the United States, even such a frustrated effort as this would be impossible: No church or combination of churches could expect courts of inquiry to represent them. Dismantling America's present artificial system of legal fictions would mean running the risk of neither church authority nor legal difficulty remaining to provide restraint. "Free" divorce would follow and would inevitably mean many more divorces. The chief problem that the churches have not been able to treat remains early marriage. At present, the churches clearly prefer immature marriages and a high divorce rate to mature marriages, a lower divorce rate, and sex for the unmarried young.

In their counsel to the young on sex, the churches' appeal to Biblical texts and simple punitive prohibition has been less overt and more discreet than in earlier eras. Sociological and, above all, psychological arguments count for much more. Of course, the proportions vary. Though Catholic counsel has also been heavily reinforced with sophisticated secular arguments for prudence, it still tends more toward pure religious suasion. This is advanced with the tacit acceptance of the sexual double standard usual in the Latin and peasant communities to which Catholicism evidently remains more allied than to American middle-class Protestantism and Judaism. The gist of the socio-psychological advice is that sex is too dangerous for the young. It may call down community censure or set up dire psychic reverberations. The significant point in this counsel—whether purely religious or prudentially sociopsychological—is that it does not cultivate maturity. Consequently, the counsel is caught by its own logic: Getting married does not necessarily extract from sex all the danger threatening the immature. The one decisive gain in marriage would be the freedom from community censure. Thus, the teaching is a hostage of the mores of the community, which might come to cease censuring sex among the unmarried. Biblical and punitive prohibitions avoid this captivity only to face the possibility of outright collision with the mores.

The most explicit effort to confront the teasing dilemmas, frankly, in counsel for the young has been that of "situational ethics."[18] In its sanction of premarital sexual intercourse in certain cases, situational ethics remains certainly a minority counsel; it has not even been discussed in any organized way at official conferences. Nevertheless, it has become a definite strain in Protestant circles, especially in universities. In Sweden and England, its case has been made at higher levels.

Situational ethics hold quite simply that what counts is responsibility. Two people who are fully aware of the implications of their acts for each other and who accept responsibility for them create their own ethical circle. Responsible for each other, they will not exploit each other. If they sleep together, they protect, may even strengthen, each other's integrity and harm no one.

Situational ethics implies that church teaching should not be hostage to the undeniably pervasive immaturity of the young and the common censoriousness of their elders. The immature are, of course, to be protected; church teaching should, however, promote maturity and discourage censoriousness. Sheltering the weak, churches should also encourage the strong and the bold. Apart from any scandalous conclusions, this implication challenges preoccupation with sheltering lambs, innocence, and doves. Situational ethics admires a certain adventurousness.

Nonetheless, situational ethics remains more the child of older church authority than of a new spirit it plainly regards as worthy and serious. Its updated ethics of premarital responsibility invites an hypocrisy that probably should be seen to follow from the churches' marriage ethics generally. How can an individual have the foreknowledge of consequences and the understanding of the other person that close the circle of responsibility? The legal, not the subjective, fact of marital responsibility sets a further guard against the ill effects of inevitable ignorance and inevitable incomprehension. The churches themselves, the Catholic excepted, have agreed that marriage itself is not a closed system; "responsibility" can mean divorce. At bottom, situational ethics demands that the young and unmarried act even more married than the married. Clearly this does not meet the terms of the questions earnest parishioners bring to a college chaplain.

Still, situational ethics has touched a sensitive point in postwar sexual mores and morals: Should youthful marriage be the primary control upon youthful sexual impulse? A number of reasons—psychological, sociological, economic, and educational—could be cited as to why individuals and the community might prefer later marriage. Are these all to be counterbalanced by the single issue of sex? Situational ethics cleared the way for integrating sexual values with other values.

Situational ethics has not dared to make headway on the implications the pressure of the folkways has for traditional teaching. Perhaps sex was not—or need not be—quite so dangerous as past efforts to control it had assumed. Tacit acceptance of the sexual double standard had always conceded the point. Neither Catholicism nor Protestantism nor Judaism ever troubled much to honor virginity in the bridegroom.[19] The contraceptive science of the fifties offered to females as well a sex less dangerous sociologically. Was it quite certain that psychological prudence alone could sustain the old assumption? Sex might not require the prophylaxis of marriage or of mature responsibility in order not to violate even personalist ethics. Arguments against sex as the undangerous, irresponsible play of the immature might remain, but need not imply the containment of sex within marriage, either legal or in spirit. Sex might be regarded as one of many routes to maturity—like any other kind of education. Perhaps the certain heedlessness essential to a good education was as relevant to sex as elsewhere. Perhaps people learned about themselves and gained strength by learning to take consequences as well as by predicting them. Some of the sexually indulgent unmarried might be regarded as more mature in not getting married than their immature married peers.

Early marriage has been the key to postwar family and sexual ethics. Early marriage may itself testify to the lingering influence of the churches' traditional teaching even as it strains that teaching to the breaking point so far as responsible marriage is concerned. The folkways of unmarried sex press hard but remain confused. Thus far, the churches have not attempted to clarify and purify the folkways, but to temporize in the hope that an unsatisfactory code and rate of divorce are better compromises than a new marital

DONALD MEYER

ethic. If early marriage proves to be the practice of a generation in transition, the folkways will evolve a new premarital ethic with which the churches will then have to catch up. If, on the other hand, early marriage proves to be persistent, pressures to establish an ethical system of divorce would increase, again more in accord with the folkways than with the traditional authority of the church. No doubt this situation is as it should be: On the historical record, the churches have no particular claim to monopolize leadership in these matters.

The young, married and unmarried, have exerted most of the pressure on postwar family ethics. But the family boom has renewed certain problems of long standing for the mature—the feminist mature. It has been difficult for postwar feminists to contemplate the family data with cheerful hearts. The most familiar text is that of Betty Friedan: Woman have sunk back into tradition.[20]

The easiest way to respond to postwar feminism has been to observe that there must not be many feminists: After all, women have rushed to embrace domesticity, not careers. But feminism had never meant principled spinsterhood, as Mrs. Stone, Mrs. Catt, Mrs. Stanton—and Mrs. Friedan—suggest. Even Miss Anthony abjured matrimony not because of principle but for the crusade. Latter-day feminism did have some difficulty deciding which elements of the family boom were discouraging: early marriage, or so many marriages, or such total immersion in marriage? In the *Dædalus* 1964 issue on women, Mrs. Alice V. Rossi criticized the lack of child-care facilities that might help women combine motherhood with jobs and careers. Mrs. Helen Gurley Brown's evangel, explaining how women might control their marital urges until their thirties, had a rather different thrust.[21]

My point here is to note first the tension between the family boom and feminist aspirations, and, second, the indifference to such aspirations in religious circles. It has been a continuing indifference, sharper in Catholic than in Protestant and Jewish life. There has been no reliable stream of sympathy for feminism in any church circles. Since the early nineteenth century and the rise of feminism, churches traditionally have exhorted women, not listened to them and tried to help.

During the postwar years, the well-established discussion—usually in journalism for women—of feminine (not feminist) discontent did not abate. The popular literature of "happy togetherness" constituted a countercurrent in the fifties; Friedan attacked it as a conspiracy. Conspiracy or, more plausibly, another editorial gimmick tied to advertising, the lore of contented domesticity never did emit the buried feeling of discontent so unmistakable in the lore of the feminist. One might dismiss this other lore as trivial. A mild self-pity seems endemic in literate and overorganized societies. Nevertheless, the lore of the discontented housewife cannot be categorized as general restlessness. Its lamentations are too specific and too local, grounded as they are in the very routines of housewifery and motherhood.

It is extremely difficult to tease out of the record of church practices and the exposition of church values just how the churches have regarded this endemic discontent over the years. In *The Positive Thinkers* (1965), I tried to clarify one tactic of spreading popularity in middle-class Protestantism over the past eighty years, that of encouraging a kind of autohypnotic reduction of the power not of the causes of discontent, but of that which feels discontented—the ego. Among Jewish women of the last generation, autohypnotic therapies have probably been less important than the more invigorating recourse of community involvement. Exhortations to willed contentment with traditional feminine seclusion have remained much the most common theme of Catholic counsel. None of these concedes justice or desirability to new roles. All are compensatory.

Now and then guilt has broken through into church consciousness, but not often. "The Church must frankly acknowledge," the Anglican bishops at Lambeth resolved in 1920, "that it has undervalued and neglected the gifts of women and has too thanklessly used their work." But guilt led to nothing. American Episcopalians (male), meeting in national conference in 1964, once again denied higher offices to women. Here the pattern of church versus folkways does not necessarily dominate: The Episcopal clergy were ready to go ahead, the laymen were not.

So obvious a story is usually neglected, yet it has its curiosities. Analyzed in terms of power, Western churches have always been the monopoly of men, but women have been a more faithful clientele than men. The relationship may or may not express something elemental and unchanging. Nevertheless, whatever it may once have been, the relationship in recent times has not been one blithely to be taken for granted. Churchmen have been tempted to assume that the postwar baby boom registers women's free choice of traditional femininity, which it has not done. Many white Americans today are still anti-Negro; even fewer of these still insist upon Negro happiness. It is for Negroes to say if they are content. Similarly, it is for the domestic heroines of postwar America to say if they have been content. The statistics of the family boom are not evidence one way or the other.

The family boom certainly did express a great deal more than feminine choice. Feminist aspirations may have been simply swallowed up not, as Friedan lamented, in feminine retreat, but in a massive shift in masculine priorities. Women always have been seductive, but not more so since 1945. The family boom has expressed, at the very least, willing masculine collaboration.[22]

One way of looking at this is presented in Daniel Miller and Guy Swanson's *The Changing American Parent* (1958). Assuming a profound change in the economy from entrepreneurial to bureaucratic modes of organization, Miller and Swanson correlate a change in family style with this larger change. The formal, impersonal routines of bureaucracy, they argue, relieve men of many anxieties. Men are freed to spend a great deal more of their psychic attention elsewhere, notably in family life. Miller and Swanson clearly indicate that the new model family of the bureaucratic world is much more enjoyable than the family geared to entrepreneurial modes. Paralleling Harvey Cox's similar analysis of bureaucratic modernity generally, in *The Secular City* (1965), the Miller-Swanson approach suggests that postwar domesticity has rested more on masculine than on feminine choices.

The same general conclusion can, however, be reached on more pessimistic grounds. In *Love and Conflict: New Patterns of Family Life* (1958), Gibson Winter interprets the popularity of the family as a function of flight rather than of release from the larger world. "The loneliness of our mechanized way of life creates intense needs for intimacy," and the family has remained the one and only place this intimacy can be had. In his book, Winter seeks to promote a psychological sophistication capable of accepting conflict within marriage in order that real intimacy be achieved.

Which is right? Winter's view is the more conventional, drawing as it does on the long-established habit of lamenting alienation in the world of work. The Protestant Ethic itself had taken this for granted. It admonished the male to prepare himself to be tested in the cold and alienated world, and to return periodically to the family for time-outs. The Social Gospel lamented the alienation, but Social Gospel men aspired to rehumanize the larger world by reforming it according to family-life ethics. Winter concerns himself simply with how family warmth can, in fact, be sustained despite and against the social coldness. The Miller-Swanson-Cox approach draws more original conclusions from the same facts. As against the Protestant Ethic, it assumes that the basic work-world does not require the investment of men's most important energy any longer —seeing no reason why the work-world cannot be left to machines and routine behavior. As against Winter, it reasons that the family is strengthened, not threatened, by the automatism of the work-world.

Empirically, of course, *the* postwar family would melt into a variety of different sorts of families, just as *the* secular city would dissolve into a variety of situations, some of which might be even more entrepreneurial and demanding than ever. But, significantly, these two approaches both link successfully the processes of masculine psychological identity with family life and make it plain that modern society has enabled a much greater overlap between masculinity and femininity and that the locus of this enlarged overlap is the family. (In England, Geoffry Gorer has concluded that contemporary Englishmen love family life even more than English women do.)[23]

In such a situation, loosely held notions about the family being "the foundation of society" would lose coherence. Families might be—as Winter holds—successfully intimate; they might be—as Miller and Swanson hold—successfully abundant; yet in either case families may not prove to be the culture par excellence of "backlash" in the fullest sense. Passively dependent upon the affluence generated by bureaucratic economic processes, they may contribute nothing to keeping those processes going. Actively defensive against any suggestion of impingement upon their haven, they may freeze the society before all families have found security. If churches embark upon collaboration with family impulses, they may find themselves assisting in defensive protection of intimacy, blessing eager exploitation of abundance. In either case, they will have sunk more deeply than ever into nurture of parochialism, exclusiveness, and tame passions interrupted by degrading fears.

The realistic, practical, common-sense rejoinder to this possibility must be obvious: Too many things still stand in the way of successful retirement into familial tranquility. Wars remain to be fought, better machines to be invented, justice to be extended. Perhaps the purest version of this response came from George Orwell in his discussion of Charles Dickens.[24] In Dickens, Orwell discerns the desire for self-contained domesticity to be the goal of competitive middle-class life to which both Winter and Miller-Swanson give credence. Orwell understands the appeal—a "dream of complete idleness," an "utterly soft, sheltered, effortless life," swarming with children—but it disgusts him. Orwell knows that politics is what still counts. Paying tribute to Dickens' artistry in conveying the dream, he nonetheless concludes: "No modern man could combine such purposelessness with so much vitality."

Undoubtedly Orwell is right about politics. No intimate haven nor cheerful suburb is secure, today any more than in 1940 when he wrote. Still, modern men may very well be more intent upon the dream than ever. Churches are not likely to challenge flourishing family life in favor of vigorous politics. They never have. They may, however, find a way to collaborate with the drive of the folkways toward "purposelessness" in such a way as to reclaim them for political vitality, and in doing so, be consistent with at least one part of their own tradition.

Assuming the psychological disaffiliation of more and more men from a bureaucratized work-world and from a bureaucratized politics, the family may indeed sink simply into private life, but it need not. Tacitly, both Winter and Miller-Swanson assume what has been true: The family, far from being the foundation of society, had been until modern times a service agency for society, training people suited to social roles. Becoming its own purpose, perhaps "against," perhaps simply independent of, the social system, the modern family has ceased to be a training ground. It does not, however, have to remain "merely" free. Free to perfect itself, it can well generate standards relevant to a new civic identity. A civic world geared to such yardsticks as nurture, care, growth, help, education, states of consciousness, states of communication, states of intimacy, and shared pleasure would directly express potentials of the new-model family. Such yardsticks have already been applied in scattered areas of the larger world.

But for these potentials to be discerned, let alone grasped and extended, in religious terms, the churches would have to overcome their ancient incapacity to treat women like men—as more than purely traditional beings. Yardsticks of nurture, help, education, and shared pleasure are already socially identified equally with women and men. To restrain women to their traditional spheres while extending such yardsticks to a civic order would call not just for indifference to women, but for an active rejection of women. Today, the folkways do not suggest the likelihood of this rejection. If the folkways rejected feminism in the past, they did so because women as well as men could not abide the thought of women becoming cold in a cold world. The folkways suggest in the modern family a new meaningfulness in life shared between the sexes, and none of the old reasons for leaving the civic order to masculine monopoly obtain in extending this collaboration beyond the family.

To grasp this potential, the churches would also have to discard their traditional sexual ethics. The new meaningfulness in life shared between the sexes emphatically includes sexual rapport and equality. We have no evidence whatever that contraception and premarital sexual relations practiced by people who are members of happy families, harm anyone, let alone society. Only an ethic frankly collaborating with the folkways can begin to confront the problems engendered by early marriage and divorce (as well as adultery and abortion) with compassion rather than with legal, social, and psychological fictions.

These are frankly utopian trajectories. Again, the impracticality of utopia may be obvious on any number of grounds—wars, poverty, inequity, and so forth. Social analysis, however, always feels for the utopian pulse points. We learn about vast and impersonal social forces so as not to be overwhelmed by them. Today, the family may be the one point at which we can feel the utopian pulse clearly. Religion's most important tradition is its claim to the existence of heaven. The vision of the Kingdom of God has been said by some —notably, H. Richard Niebuhr—to have been the inspiration of religious vitality in the United States itself. Perhaps it has. But if so, then the distinction implicit throughout this paper should be made explicit. Religion does not mean the churches.

If religion means "ultimate things," in Paul Tillich's sense, and if ultimate things are not objects or forms but a free activity, an activity reducible to nothing else, then we might find religion in the folkways of the new model family (including its teen-age members). If the churches cannot ally themselves with the folkways, they will remain what they have commonly been: defensive "defenders of the faith," repressive, ascetic counselors of prudence, representatives of immaturity and of indifference to women. They will cater to all that is defensive, fearful, immature and confused in the folkways, inhibiting the utopian, tender, and bold. Sex, a free activity upon

DONALD MEYER

which the existence of societies, including churches, depends, might well be called religious if only to save the function of religion to criticize all blasphemous pretensions to closure and completion and final order. Once construed as a realm of necessity, of pure nature, and socially embodied in the confinement of women, sexuality has been claimed by the folkways as the supreme expression of freedom. This is logical. In identifying themselves with organizations, social systems, ideologies, cultures, styles, and natural laws, men and women mostly lose themselves as individuals in their service to life. They relate to society as children to parents. They surrender their chance for maturity. They possess in their sexuality the vitality no society can afford to shackle—the one irreducible ground of hope for being an individual and becoming mature.

REFERENCES

1. Two useful surveys are Roy W. Fairchild and John C. Wynn, *Families in the Church: A Protestant Survey* (1961); and John L. Thomas, *American Catholic Families* (1956). A few examples of instruction are W. H. and M. I. Morgan, *Thinking Together about Marriage and Family* (1955); J. C. Wynn, *Pastoral Ministry to Families* (1957); Henry A. Bowman, *A Christian Interpretation of Marriage* (1959); Oscar E. Feucht, *et al.*, *Helping Families Through the Church* (1957) for Protestants; Alvin Worth and Clement Mihanovich, *Papal Pronouncements on Marriage and the Family* (1955); Joseph E. Kerns, *The Theology of Marriage* (1964); Edgar Schmiedeler, *Marriage and the Family* (1946); Fulton J. Sheen, *Three to Get Married* (1951) for Catholics; and Stanley R. Brau (ed.), *Marriage and the Jewish Tradition* (1951); Norman Lamm, *A Hedge of Roses* (1966) for Jews. E. S. and W. H. Genné (eds.), *Foundations for Christian Family Policy: The Proceedings of the North American Conference on Church and Family* (1961) contains the transcripts of several lively sessions uniting (Protestant) church spokesmen and "secular" professionals from several fields.

2. W. H. Grabill, G. V. Kiser, and P. K. Whelpton, *The Fertility of American Women* (1958).

3. *Los Angeles Times,* July 17, 1958.

4. R. Freedman, P. K. Whelpton, and A. A. Campbell, *Family Planning, Sterility and Population Growth* (1959).

5. By contrast, T. F. Cooper, *Catholic Fertility in Florida* (1946), found no relation between religious participation and birth-control practice—a finding perhaps even more troubling to "authority."

6. *Los Angeles Times,* January 6, 1965; *Look Magazine,* June 29, 1965.

246

7. Msgr. G. A. Kelly, *Birth Control and Catholics* (1963), a defense of pre-Vatican II teachings; John T. Noonan, *Contraception* (1965); Michael Novak (ed.), *The Experience of Marriage* (1964); William Birmingham (ed.), *What Modern Catholics Think About Birth Control* (1964); on fertility cult, Edward Wakin and J. F. Scheuer, *The De-Romanization of the American Catholic Church* (1966).

8. Freedman, Whelpton, and Campbell, *Family Planning, Sterility and Population Growth.*

9. Joseph Roddy, "The Pope's Unsolvable Problem," *Look Magazine*, December 13, 1966—a remarkable article.

10. George F. Mair (ed.), *Studies in Population* (1949).

11. See Derrick S. Bailey, *The Mystery of Love and Marriage* (1952) and *Sexual Relation in Christian Thought* (1959); W. G. Cole, *Sex in Christianity and Psychoanalysis* (1955) and *Sex and Love in the Bible* (1959); and Jose de Vinck, *The Virtue of Sex* (1966), a popular Catholic statement.

12. Charles M. Smith, *How To Become a Bishop Without Being Religious* (1966).

13. For a direct response to the folkways, see Seward Hiltner, *Sex Ethics and the Kinsey Report* (1953) and *Sex and the Christian Life* (1957).

14. W. J. Goode, *After Divorce* (1956).

15. See *Commonweal*, February 18, 1966, for a notice of the "Committee of Catholic Citizens to Support Divorce Form."

16. See Nelson M. Blake, *The Road to Reno* (1962).

17. *Los Angeles Times*, November 10, 1966.

18. See Joseph Fletcher, *Situation Ethics* (1966); a debate between Fletcher and Father Herbert McCabe in *Commonweal*, January 14, 1966; Richard F. Hettlinger, *Living with Sex: The Student's Dilemma* (1966); and also, L. Kirkendall, *Premarital Intercourse and Interpersonal Relationships* (1964) for a sociologist's exposition. For defenses of chastity, see Evelyn M. Duvall, *Why Wait till Marriage?* (1965); Dietrich Von Hildebrand, *In Defense of Purity* (1962); also E. M. and S. M. Duvall, *Facts of Life and Love for Teenagers* (1956); Simon Doniger (ed.), *Sex and Religion Today* (1953); and Ralph J. Eckert, *Sex Attitudes in the Home* (1956), all more or less updated traditionalism.

19. See the interesting comment of L. Kirkendall, in Genné and Genné (eds.), *Foundations for Christian Family Policy*, p. 93.

20. Betty Friedan, *The Feminine Mystique* (1963). From the rest of the rather large array of attacks on the postwar domesticity see Elizabeth Hardwick, "The Feminine Principle," *Mademoiselle*, February, 1958.

21. Helen Gurley Brown, *Sex and the Single Girl* (1962).

22. See J. F. Cuber and Peggy B. Harroff, *The Significant Americans* (1965), for interesting interview data suggesting a conflict between traditional entrepreneurial "success" and significant marital fulfillment.

23. Geoffrey Gorer, *Exploring English Character* (1955).

24. Orwell, "Charles Dickens," *Inside the Whale* (1940).

WILLIAM A. CLEBSCH

American Religion and the Cure of Souls

IN AMERICA today, public attention focuses on religion when church leaders declare controversial opinions on public policy, participate in protests by oppressed minorities, or openly deviate from established doctrines. The more routine but flourishing engagement of religion in the affairs of a very large proportion of Americans consists in their submitting hurts and hopes to the care and help of pastors. Gauged both by consumer demand and by clergymen's self-evaluation, the chief business of religion in the United States is now—as it probably has long been—the cure of souls. *Cura animarum,* briefly stated, means the use of sacred words, objects, and gestures to help persons overcome spiritual vicissitudes or seize opportunities for personal fulfillment, when they view these problems and aspirations *sub specie æternitatis.*

Through pastoral care, religion is now penetrating American society far more profoundly than through social activism that is aimed at shaping official policies. One is hard put to elaborate that statement convincingly without being interpreted as a social and political reactionary, a religious isolationist, or (worst of all) an other-worldly quietist. The point, however, is not that the formation of attitudes about race relations, open housing, military intervention, the regulation of abortion, and the like lies beyond the effective reach of religion. The point is rather that such attitude-formation itself relies upon relations of confidence between clergymen and their parishioners, and that these relations are established more basically by effective pastoral care than by demonstrations of socio-political sagacity. Laity look to clergymen as men of God who are able to supply holy resources to personal needs, for so clergymen primarily present themselves to laity. Where that ability is trusted by having been tested in experience, "the issues" can be raised with remarkable equa-

249

nimity; where it is distrusted, clerical activism evinces additional distrust and thereby undermines the possibility of pastoral care.

This mental-health boom in American religion is only partly explained by the fact that an unprecedented majority of the United States population reports that it holds membership in organized religion. The persons who enroll in religious congregations do so anticipating that they will benefit from the cure of souls. Pastoral care is clearly the primary activity that parishioners expect from their religious leaders, according to the richest collection of sociological data about religion in contemporary America.[1] Parishioners want their clergy to emphasize "visiting" and "giving people advice," and they are dissatisfied with the impression that their ministers are spending more time preparing sermons than performing any of several other major tasks.[2] Clergymen agree that the cure of souls lays the most valid claim on their working time and energies, yet they express frustration that administrative chores inundate them; successive studies since those by the Russell Sage Foundation in the 1950's bear out the conclusion. The fact that clergymen and parishioners, in considering several distinct ministerial roles, agree on the one which *should* dominate but disagree on the ones which in fact *are* primary implies emphatically that religious professionals are still generalists in our age of specialization. Indeed, considering them as belonging to the helping professions—law, medicine, education, social work, psychiatry, and so forth—clergymen comprise the last remaining general practitioners, save perhaps for the nearly extinct one-room schoolteacher.

The cure of souls in American religion today is one of several interlocking ministerial duties, each of which has its appropriate mode. It is as advocative as preaching is hortatory, worship sacerdotal, catechizing didactic, administration managerial, and living a model life exemplary. The tug of all these multiple demands is leading many American ministers to concentrate on one or two roles. But the roles are mutually supportive, and there can be little doubt that the pastoral role distinguishes the clergyman's special competence in the eyes of persons who turn to him. The best available studies show that half the troubled Americans who seek professional help turn initially to ministers, priests, and rabbis—who altogether number slightly less than the nation's corps of active physicians. Even more arresting than that is the fact that problems referred to religious professionals, again on the testimony of "self-referrals" (persons seeking help on their own initiative), are successfully resolved at twice the rate scored by psychiatrists. Probably the somewhat more tractable personal predicaments go to the cloth, while grave disturbances make their way to the couch; pastors are commonly sought for help in cases of interpersonal friction, grief, moral confusion. Nevertheless, clergymen are today very prominent agents of mental health in America, according to data set out by Gerald Gurin, Joseph Veroff, and Shiela Feld.[3]

It is therefore not surprising that the closest thing to genuine specialization among religious professionals involves the cure of souls. Specialists in pastoral counseling recently formed a national association to set professional standards, regulate practice, and certify practitioners who work almost exclusively in aspects of pastoral care. A major Protestant denomination has planned to deploy pastoral specialists so that no member of a congregation will live more than one hundred miles from a pastoral counseling clinic. Several leading pastoral theologians have stoutly opposed the American Association of Pastoral Counselors, touching off a debate whose outcome is ominous for the future of religion in America. Will the demand for specialized, professional leadership increase, either overreaching or undercutting the traditionally congregational structure of our religious institutions? Or can the general-practice ministry endure and maintain, even by significant transformation, the structure of the major denominations?

On the presumption that the ministry will retain its prominence among the other helping professions while the latter shift from disease orientation to health orientation, the question of specialized or general ministerial activity ramifies into acute problems for the cure of souls. The practical ramifications, too complex to analyze fully here, tend to cluster around a basic, theoretical need for a modern vocabulary of the soul which expresses the ways in which contemporary Americans actually hope and hurt. That vocabulary is needed to replace antiquated spiritual nosologies which were built in the seventh century around the seven deadly sins and seven chief virtues, or in the sixteenth century around man's guilt and God's forgiveness of it. To understand this theoretical need, it is first necessary to ask which elements in the great tradition of the cure of souls remain religiously potent and ministerially viable in modern America, and which ones are largely falling to the other helping professions. My thesis is that the pastoral functions of healing and guiding—with some exceptions that go against the trend—are being effectively captured by medicine and psychotherapy, respectively.

Meanwhile the pastoral functions of sustaining and reconciling remain prominent now and are promising for the future. After elaborating the thesis, it will be appropriate to return to a description of the pastoral profession today, and then to the crisis in the conceptualization of modern spiritual yearnings and woes.

The Erosion of Healing and Guiding in the American Experience

Modern religion inherits four types of the cure of souls from the entire range of Western religion: healing, guiding, sustaining, and reconciling.[4] Healing bodily or spiritual diseases by religious means traditionally employed sacramental anointings, supplications to saints who held prerogative over particular maladies, applications of religio-magical balms, charismatic powers of persons able to exorcise demons and command cures, pilgrimages to shrines, and a wide variety of other distinctly objective procedures. Precisely because of their objectivity, Americans have come to regard such means of healing as miraculous or, worse, merely superstitious. Religious healing flourished while Galen's theories of *dyskrasia* and *eukrasia* (being out of balance and being in balance) held sway, because the four bodily "humors" were believed to be inseparable from their corresponding spiritual tempers. René Descartes' sharp dichotomy between matter and spirit split physical medicine from religion, and after Louis Pasteur medical efficacy became so demonstrable that many moderns have thought religious healing to be occult or even deluded.

Nevertheless, faith-healers claim important followings in most American denominations. Oral Roberts is the ancient exorcist projected onto a television screen, and Mrs. Agnes Sanford proclaims that devout prayer with unshakable belief will work cures where medical remedies have been of no avail. Probably most congregations in the Episcopal Church schedule regular worship services especially aimed at healing. Americans visit the shrines of Lourdes and of St. Anne de Beaupré, which attract, it has been estimated, more pilgrims today than did the most famous medieval healing shrines. The largest American denomination of recent native origin, Christian Science, bases its entire doctrine, discipline, and worship on faith-healing.

Yet for all its persistence, pastoral healing has yet to answer fundamental questions about its dynamics and its limitations. What range of ailments—physical, psychical, or psychosomatic—yield to it? Is the sufficient condition of cure the patient's belief or the healer's power—or, if a combination, in what proportions? Is faith-healing inimical to physical medicine, as Christian Scientists teach, or supplemental, as most hospital chaplains contend, or simply a last appeal for divine dispensation from medically incurable conditions, as some practitioners think? These and related questions are either brushed aside or inconclusively disputed by pastoral theologians in America today. Until they are answered, training in pastoral healing seems confined to the simple indoctrination which prepares Christian Science practitioners or to mere imitation of the master by the apprentice. Meanwhile, the relation of pastoral healing to the medical arts flounders in vagaries. Only clear answers to these questions will allay the frequent charge of charlatanry. Notwithstanding, claims of miraculous cures abound and fascinate many religious folk.

In Europe, religious healing remains a traditional but minor feature of the cure of souls, employing ancient sacramental and liturgical means. But the kind of pastoral healing we are discussing is typically American, even if missionary outreach has spread it to Latin America and Africa. In the closing half of the nineteenth century, several prominent Americans made special use of the teachings of Emanuel Swedenborg, the Swedish scientist who during the Enlightenment conceived of material objects as mere expressions of higher spiritual realities. The elder Henry James joined Swedenborgian doctrines with Fourierist teachings. His interests found institutional embodiment on a less exalted intellectual plane when W. F. Evans, a Swedenborgian minister, joined with Phineas P. Quimby, the mesmerist and mental healer whose influence over Mary Baker Eddy is controverted, in forming a religious movement around constructive thinking as the source of health and creativity. The movement, known by the end of the century as "New Thought," attracted the attention of William James, whose writings on the philosophy and psychology of religion focused sophisticated attention on spiritual healing. This most typical American philosopher grounded faith-healing in pragmatic arguments and also imbued it with intellectual respectability and psychological authenticity in the famous Gifford Lectures of 1901–1902 on *The Varieties of Religious Experience*. New American religions emphasizing faith-healing, like that begun by Mrs. Eddy, commended themselves as returning to pristine Christianity scrubbed clean of accretions. What could be more "American" than religious reductionism granting health and creativity while claiming to be "scientific" because "it works"? Christian Science is justly famous as a church whose one foundation is faith-healing, but the interests and attitudes which made it possible belong to the entire imagination of newly urban and industrial Americans. Health through prayer and right believing enlisted advocates in all the wealthier, citified denominations whose constituencies had escaped the harsh, material realities of agrarian living and manual labor.

Pastoral healing through faith, prayer, and exorcism is more widely practiced than carefully discussed in America today, and its claims offer verification mainly by personal testimonies that medically incurable ailments yielded to spiritual powers. Faith-healing is not only persistent but also, save where explained psychologically, fabulous. But these qualities hardly mitigate American physicians' working monopoly over remedies for diseases and injuries.

Pastoral healing still reflects the important Judeo-Christian notion that when a person has received cure by divine power he advances to a level of spiritual well-being that was unattained prior to his illness and cure. Partly in reflecting on this tenet and partly in reclaiming the Judeo-Christian insistence that man is a psycho-physical unity, some physicians (for example, Paul Tournier) and some pastoral theologians (for example, Seward Hiltner) have brought their theories of faith-healing to terms with leading concepts of psychosomatic medicine. Such theoretical formulations usually tend toward psychological understandings of the cure of souls, and they make pastoral healing ancillary to physical medicine. Chaplains of general hospitals commonly find that their work submits more readily to psychological than to theological analysis. While a very great deal of faith-healing goes on today, it flounders for an explanation of itself which at once goes beyond the old alliances between Christian sacramentalism and Galenic medicine, avoids anti-materialistic spiritualism, and refuses to collapse theological categories into psychological ones. Perhaps only with the adumbration of an alternative theory can pastoral healing come into its own again—if ever.

If medicine in America is supplanting pastoral healing, then the helping professions with psychotherapeutic orientations are similarly invading the arena of pastoral guiding. In all Western religion, the cure of souls has helped men and women discover and do what is just in the sight of God and man. The key philosophical issue underlying such guidance is the question of the identity of, or difference between, divine justice and human justice. The American Puritans ingeniously solved this problem by placing the secret will of God utterly beyond human knowledge and by contending that God's revealed will could be learned by studying Scripture, which, in this view, teaches that what God wills is the welfare of faithful men. This "federal theology" found a new way of equating the good with the advantageous, as Stoicism had done long ago. Swept clean of theological subtleties, the insight yielded the simple, prudent ethics of Franklin: "Honesty is the best policy." Transferred to crude conditions of agrarian America, sobriety kept a man alert to depredation by animal and fire and led to prosperity; eschewing revelry preserved family solidarity on which basic economic functions rested; scarce money, needed for commodities unavailable through tillage and husbandry, must not be dissipated by gambling. The "frontier" revivalists adduced somewhat tortured Biblical sanctions against drinking, dancing, and gambling as the elements of a prudent ethic. But just as the Puritan virtues in Franklin's hands became rationalistic maxims, so frontier virtues carried into cities became petty moralism. While the "Protestant ethic" in America avoided the precisianism of European moral theology, the sweep of American history turned ethics into mere manners. Thereby the conceptual basis of pastoral guiding lost both its theological and its prudential sanctions while retaining an aura of respectability. In this most serious predicament, the cure of souls can do little more than help perplexed men and women choose courses of action that lead to personal and social adjustment. It is precisely that kind of help at which psychotherapeutic procedures excel over the technique of pastoral care.

To be sure, Catholicism, Eastern Orthodoxy, certain kinds of Lutheranism, and Judaism brought to the United States various forms of prescriptive ethics based on the traditional Christian moral theologies or on the Torah and its commentaries. The thrust of American life toward an ethic of adjustment took a very different turn in these denominations. Catholic and Jewish guidance became increasingly cultic and impinged on the common life through ritual and dogma rather than moral considerations—for example, by outlawing the use of contraceptives by Catholics or by forbidding Jews to open their stores on the Sabbath.

What American denomination has developed moral norms that are at once realistic and genuinely religious to guide persons who are perplexed by a welter of new problems such as abortion, divorce, euthanasia, extramarital sexual intercourse, financial manipulation, conscientious objection to military service in cases of intervention? In dealing with confusion over such actions, psychotherapists are more effective than pastoral counselors (unless the latter emulate the former), because they view personal adjustment as a desideratum that is uncluttered by the kinds of norms which religion devised for prior epochs and disappearing social structures.

Guiding as an activity of the cure of souls, like healing, surely persists in America. Faithful Catholics and devout Jews follow prescriptions of personal and social morality as best they can, and many Protestants still abstain from liquor, dancing, and gambling on religious grounds. Many pastors render valued services by lending a patient ear to parishioners who fumblingly talk through their confusions to some workable decision, and others do the same by giving the best advice they can adduce from principles, like love or altruism, that apply variously to various situations. American theologians and ministers avidly discuss ways of updating religious ethics; such proposals are usually tagged "the new morality" or "contextual ethics." But in the end of the day, to expunge the traditional aspects of religion is to cut out the essence of the matter. Pastoral guiding in contemporary America is faltering not from unwillingness to be helpful, but from having found no way of relating the will of God to the welfare of man in a swiftly changing, bafflingly complex, and eudemonistic (perhaps even hedonistic) society. The psychotherapists' advantage lies finally in their being professionally and ideologically unconcerned about the will of God, and thus single-mindedly given to the welfare of their clients.

Of course, decline in the religious construction and maintenance of moral values is by no means total. Doubtless religious interests are more patently and more potently at work in the morality of small, homogeneous communities and in the stricter religious groups than in pluralistic cities and liberal denominations. Glock and Stark have indicated that 15 per cent of the Southern Baptists as against 2 per cent of the Episcopalians they queried thought that "drinking liquor" would "definitely prevent salvation"; yet "practicing artificial birth control" was thought to bar salvation by 23 per cent of Catholics and 1 per cent of Presbyterians.[5] One might surmise that in every instance the reported percentages would have been tripled fifty years ago. Without significant change in official dicta concerning such behavior, it can hardly be challenged that priests and ministers today find in the individual believer's own conscience a primary—not to say infallible—norm for personal morality. Apart from firm data, hard conclusions are not to be drawn, but it may be worth remarking that the means employed in pastoral acts other than guiding are meanwhile becoming more, rather than less, formalized—with, for example, confession, penance, and ritual absolutions of guilt enjoying a renaissance in many Protestant congregations. Moreover, there is an inner logic to the trends by which guiding yields to pastoral reconciling. As formerly *verboten* acts such as divorce, homosexual relations between consenting adults, extra-marital sexual activities, the termination of pregnancy, and subtle forms of euthanasia win increasing acceptance, many people who consider themselves religious judge between optional courses of action which were, as one denominational discipline has said of divorce, never to be whispered about. That pastoral care is less prescriptively and less decisively guiding persons who do these things does not remove these persons from the cure of souls. Having taken decisions upon themselves, they may not need guidance but rather reconciliation with the God whose will is no longer as precisely known to them as it was to their forebears.

Two traditional types of the cure of souls, healing and guiding, fell under the acute influence of the American experience. The agency of healing shifted inward to the client's faith or the pastor's charisma, and these subjective entities (however deeply religious) defied the kinds of analysis and classification which were possible when the sacral agents of pastoral healing were sacramental ointments and benedictions. The criterion of guiding became the client's welfare, increasingly conceived in terms of personal goals that were detachable from specific rules or distinct sanctions such as the will of God. In these respects, the American experience has tended to erode the cure of souls and to transfer healing to the physician and guiding to the psychotherapist.

The Potency of Sustaining and Reconciling in America

Yet precisely because they are men of God professionally concerned with holy things, pastors retain certain advantages over the other helping professions. These advantages appear particularly in the act of sustaining persons whose lives seem to be falling apart because of some ominous disruption (the best example is grief over sudden death of a loved one), and in the act of reconciling persons whose intimate relations have been or are about to be ruptured (the best example is a broken or breaking marriage). As men of God, clergy symbolize eternal securities that are safe from the changes and chances of mortal existence, and they hold office as peacemakers amidst fractious humankind. Put another way, American religion impinges on believers' quests for meaning in life and on their human associations in much the same way that traditional religion touched these areas of human affairs. Roughly to the degree that, both historically and religiously, the human troubles which are amenable to sustaining and reconciling have *not* taken on distinctly American colorations, these aspects of the cure of souls remain viable. And their viability is, in fact, heightened because of the peculiarly congregational aspect of American religion.

While bereavement nicely exemplifies an opportunity for pastoral sustaining, many other experiences can make life seem to run precipitously downhill. Sudden gain of wealth, power, responsibility, new surroundings, and the like can disrupt as powerfully as sudden loss. Religious cure for souls shaken out of "normalcy" requires consolation, perhaps by assurance that God cares, through reciting a familiar verse of Scripture. The pastor can then help his client to find some firm peg on which to hang whatever personal resources have survived the crisis—children, work, friends in similar predicaments, and so forth. Finally, a new style of life must be built out of remaining resources. This classical pattern of pastoral sustaining in Judaism and Christianity exhibits nothing perceptibly American. But the pattern operates most dynamically when the original step is taken with dispatch, when the pastor is quite familiar with the circumstances of the person he helps, and when friends can be summoned to help the bereft person adapt to his new mode of life. The typical organization of American religion, like-minded people bound together by common loyalties into a group in which clergyman and parishioners know one another well, facilitates pastoral sustaining in every respect. Additionally, the pastor repeatedly notifies his congregation that he is available to them in crises as a man of God, and he is expected to present himself on these occasions without waiting to be summoned. By contrast, members of the other helping professions consider it unethical to advertise their services or to pursue their clients. While the lawyer, doctor, psychiatrist, counselor, or teacher may often help people in need of spiritual sustenance, none has built into the fabric of his professional work so many capacities for sustaining as the clergyman.

Similarly, religious leaders solemnize and sanctify the intimate relation between man and wife at matrimony, and that between child and parent at baptism or circumcision, confirmation or *bar mitzvah*. When frictions threaten these associations, it is only natural for clergy to hold powerful means of re-establishing harmony. Both Judaism and Christianity teach that all interpersonal relations involve one's relation to God. Reconciliation of human animosities is a corollary to reconciliation between man and God. Thus, for his parishioners, the rabbi, priest, or minister is an arbiter or peacemaker with authority over enmities that arise between family, friends, neighbors, employers, employees, or other associates. To confess before him guilt for broken human relations is ordinary and natural, and his absolution or assurance of forgiveness is expected to involve repentance and restitution.

It may be that the professional social worker, psychiatrist, or marriage counselor today understands better than most pastors the personal and interpersonal dynamics involved in a failing marriage or a crisis over marital infidelity. The pastor's special capacity to reconcile persons in such cases does not, of course, arise from ignorance, but it may nevertheless abide psychological inexpertness. As one who typically solemnizes matrimony with divine sanctions, the minister symbolizes and can impart resources for forgiveness, renewal, and rededication which, for him and for his parishioners, spring not from themselves but from an abundantly gracious God. Where parties seek reconciliation within the sacral context which the pastor represents, the efficacy of their restored relation can be heightened by the solemnity of its restoration. Moreover, theological concepts—for example, sin, contrition, pardon, covenant, fidelity, love—are obviously relevant to the pastoral work of reconciling, and they furnish a ready vocabulary by which to understand the impingement of transcendant and immanent power upon interpersonal relations.

No peculiarly American feature distinguishes the occasions for or the patterns of pastoral reconciliation, but special resources lie ready to the pastor's hand because of the congregational form of American religion. Familiarity with parishioners, the duty to intervene in their lives on his own initiative, and the capacity to muster assistance from fellow believers give unusual potency to the reconciling aspect of the cure of souls—potency unavailable in such forceful combinations to any other helping profession. Problems in marital or other human relations naturally rank high among the types of trouble which suggest clergy as effective helpers.

Thus, healing persists and fascinates many believers, but its procedures are elusive and mystifying; its theorists and practitioners can enter dialogue with the medical arts only in psychological language. Guiding continues as a pastoral act, but stands almost paralyzed before the crucial question of the relation between God's will and man's weal in a society whose ethics are pragmatic, prudential, utilitarian, and self-fulfilling. But as the American experience drives these two traditionally religious activities into the hands of secular agents, at the same time the congregational shape of American religion undergirds and re-inforces pastoral sustaining and reconciling.

The State of the Pastoral "Profession"

So far it has been taken for granted that the cure of souls belongs to persons trained and ordained (or otherwise authorized) as religious leaders. For the most part that is true, but the assumption tends to belie a strong laic impulse in American religion, past and present. To give this laicism its due place in the cure of souls is also to acknowledge the reluctance in most denominations to regard clergymen as comparable in their professionalism to doctors, lawyers, educators, and the like. Regarded by clients and peers as not a fully professional person, the pastor is hard put to identify himself or his function in American society. Three connected theses may delineate the basic problems of the identity of pastors. First, lay pastoral care, while inevitable and desirable, is no substitute for expert adeptness in the cure of souls by clergymen. Second, American clergy must resist intense specialization in order to increase their pastoral effectiveness. Third, expertness in the cure of souls for the religious "general practitioner" requires new conceptual foundations. Many may dissent from one or more of these assertions, but to discuss them will serve to outline the major crises facing pastoral care in contemporary America.

The American penchant for making political officials servants of the people instead of an elite class carried over into religion from early colonial times onward, and injected a definite laicism into pastoral care. In New England Puritanism, especially after the famous "Half-way Covenant" of 1662, the spiritual nurture of children became a primarily parental duty. Baptist and Quaker protests against any separate order of ministers made every believer a "priest" in his family and congregation, and this conviction commended itself to many American denominations which derived from the more hierarchical European churches. From the beginning, the Methodists in America were organized so that each member placed his spiritual life under scrutiny and guidance of the cell or "class," a practice which extended to the other popular denominations. American Reform Judaism assigned didactic functions to rabbis, reserving much of the cure of souls and some ritual observances for family life. Many American Catholics during the nineteenth century fought to establish lay trusteeship over the temporal affairs of congregations. Although remote to the cure of souls, the struggle over "trusteeism" illustrates how far laicism invaded all varieties of American religion.

Indeed, the responsibility of each believer to encourage and exhort spiritual rectitude in his family and fellow believers is a hallmark of American religion, prompting even today a voluminous literature pleading for "the ministry of the laity." Yet this laic impulse still exhibits—as it has always done—ambivalence. The efficacy of each aspect of the cure of souls hinges on the involvement of a special man of God, and laymen commonly defer to the person whose calling, training, and commissioning authenticate the application of sacred means to personal problems and aspirations. In fact, seminary educators in representative denominations habitually complain that candidates for the ministry rely on their call and commission to make their pastoral care effective, even to the neglect of training which, in this view, alone yields expertness.

Pastoral healing and guiding lack conceptual foundations and clear analyses, a lack which can be made up only by rigorous study of the pastoral tradition and its contemporary relation to the theory and practice of medicine and psychotherapy. If healing and guiding are largely lost from the pastoral repertory, the loss is partly attributable to inexpertness and unprofessionalism on the ministry's part. If religious sustaining and reconciling leave abundant work for pastoral helpers, they nevertheless require prompt diagnosis of spiritual conditions, keen assessment of remaining resources, and thorough familiarity with the available means of sacred cure. Untrained laymen may continue to perform effective acts of pastoral care, but that fact gives clergymen no warrant to avoid the special adeptness which is expected of them as professionals engaged in the cure of souls.

Little of the restlessness which presently infects ministerial ranks in America springs from jealousy that more specialized professional helpers are performing functions which once belonged to religion. Few clergy resent their calling's having lost the honor of representing the community's most learned man. Rather, basic ministerial frustrations arise from concurrent demands for expertise in many areas of work—areas which compete for time and energy but also re-inforce one another's potency. The catechist wants to become a theologian, the preacher a poet, the administrator an executive, the liturgist a thespian, the pastor a psychiatrist, and (compounding the problem perhaps by geometric progression) the exemplar a saint. In any denomination's roster of clergy, virtuosos in each of these roles can be found, and the more traditional churches support monastic orders where specialization is feasible. The firing line of American religion, however, remains at the congregation where versatility is at higher premium than virtuosity, even in parishes that are able to afford the services of several ministers, each with his own special competence. When specialization in one ministerial role minimizes or excludes the others, the mutually re-inforcing power of all roles is forfeited.

The last assertion sums up several previous points, some explicit and some implicit. Opponents of the American Association of Pastoral Counselors feared that specialists in the cure of souls would soon be indistinguishable from psychotherapists or social workers if they gave up preaching, conducting worship, and managing the affairs of congregations. Indeed, the minister does announce by preaching his availability as a helping person. He exhibits his status as a man of God liturgically, and he claims his right to initiate pastoral relations by assuming administrative and exemplary roles. Each interlocking priestly function is weakened when dissociated from the others. Specialization carried to the point of isolation threatens particularly to vitiate the cure of souls. Pastoral care in America today cries for professional expertness *within,* not in place of, the general-practice model of the ministry.

Pastoral expertness awaits, however, the development of a new vocabulary of spiritual strengths and weaknesses. The language inherited by the cure of souls from our Western religious traditions is out of tune with modernity in general, because it emphasizes disease more than health and, in particular, because it blames individual persons more than circumstances for human troubles and credits divine intervention more than human virtues for spiritual attainment. This vocabulary of sin and forgiveness acquired its special Christian denotations during the Reformation when men indeed worried profoundly about their spiritual unworthiness *coram Deo* and wanted, as Luther quite typically put it, "to find a merciful God." Where the formal terminology of the seven deadly sins and seven major virtues persisted, penitential connotations made man accountable for his woes and thanked God for providing respite or surcease. Since the Enlightenment, a few theorists have tried to reconcile traditional religious vocabularies of the soul with the categories of special schools of academic psychology, but always with primary orientation toward disease or weakness as the normal state of the spirit. Steps in the opposite direction were taken by theological liberalism, but the recent theological renaissance in America dwelt upon man's estrangement and isolation from God and humanity, italicized sin and evil, and set a low ceiling on human achievement. Allusion to the writings of Reinhold Niebuhr carries the point.

Meanwhile, certain American philosophers and psychologists have reconceived of the rhythms of human life in terms of personal yearnings and strengths. In their conceptions, turmoils of the human spirit are, to be sure, unavoidable, but turmoil is not taken to be the normal state of affairs. One thinks, for example, of Alfred North Whitehead's "rhythms of education" which progress through the phases of romance, precision, and generalization, or of Erik H. Erikson's description of human growth in terms of three stages: childhood's hope, will, and purpose; youth's competence and fidelity; adulthood's love, care, and wisdom. The contrast of these conceptions with the emphases of serious religious language—laying aside the bromides of help-yourself-to-self-help-preachers—on sins and debilities is jarring. It is fruitful to ponder the appropriateness of Whitehead's or Erikson's conceptualizations to the cure of souls. Surely their penchant for analyzing human strengths expresses the quest of today's American more precisely than does the disease orientation of traditional pastoral theology or of recent neo-orthodoxy. The opportune challenge before the cure of souls today is to hammer out a vocabulary describing how sacral powers contribute to the fulfillment of human personhood.

Contemporary Americans are no less ingenious than anybody else in discovering new forms of personal woe, and the curators of their souls can surely stay busy helping clients over humps. The point of that affirmation which is re-orienting the whole mental health movement today is not a Pollyanna's blindness to trouble but the realization that a "return to normalcy" does little good unless normalcy itself is conceived as a dynamic program of building virtues appropriate to a person's age, circumstances, and spiritual resources. It is demonstrable that American pastors stand in the front ranks of the helping professionals to which people turn for personal help. The increasing demand is for more than restoration to a *status quo ante* which might be typified by the declaration of forgiveness of sins and the exhortation to "Go, and sin no more." The demand is rather for the kind of solace that teaches the bereaved how to hope realistically, for the kind of reconciliation that helps partners in a strained marriage practice a wise love and care for each other and their offspring. The language of hope, will, purpose, fidelity, care, love, and wisdom is religious language at a certain level, no matter how specifically psychological it may also be in the particular use which Erikson makes of it. As the language of pastoral care, from the viewpoint of the client as well as that of the pastor, both levels of meaning express desiderata too long overshadowed in American religion by the avoidance of familiar sins which is the essence of petty moralism. The religious client seeks from his pastor what he rightly expects the pastor to know how to make available: concrete, step-by-step ways of cultivating the special graces needed to live not only with crises but with those routine, workaday rounds that can be even more devastating to joy and happiness.

Proficiency, then—not specialization—in the cure of souls is the goal to be sought by shifting the conceptual emphasis from remedying debilities to that of developing spiritual strengths. Increased pastoral ability is American religion's only appropriate response to its most flourishing function in American society, the cure of souls. That clergymen bear heavy case loads in the cure of souls indeed befits their role as nearly the last general practitioners among this nation's highly specialized helping professions. The practitioner of the cure of souls in America derives his identity from his activity as a helper of persons, not from his rank in a denomination. To those whom he helps, he is eminently accessible. No waiting room deters his client. No fee schedule prompts uncertainty whether the need is acute enough to warrant the encounter. No shame attends having resorted to the agent of divine blessings. To the extent that he thinks in a language about human virtues, the presumption of illness need not befall the parishioner who asks his assistance. In the normal run of things, he is competent in many ways of helping, and his client need not expect frequent referral to a specialist stranger.

Probably the most ominous of many questions facing American religion today is whether it can and will bend its pastoral care toward co-operation with a new search for the achievement of human personhood. The requisition has, I believe, been filed. It awaits action by a profession which presently seems fascinated by matters of public policy to the detriment of its potency in evincing spiritual health, education, and welfare.

REFERENCES

1. Charles Y. Glock and Rodney Stark, *Religion and Society in Tension* (Chicago, 1965).

2. *Ibid.*, p. 149.

3. Gerald Gurin, Joseph Veroff, and Sheila Feld, *Americans View Their Mental Health* (New York, 1960).

4. Definitions of these types are set out and their traditional practice surveyed in detail in Charles R. Jaekle and William A. Clebsch, *Pastoral Care in Historical Perspective: An Essay With Exhibits* (New York, 1967).

5. Glock and Stark, *Religion and Society in Tension*, p. 112.

PLURALISM AND ITS PROBLEMS

WILBER G. KATZ
AND HAROLD P. SOUTHERLAND

Religious Pluralism and the Supreme Court

I

THIS ESSAY examines the pattern of religious pluralism in the United States and the role that the Supreme Court has played in its development. *Pluralism* is a term of many meanings: A society characterized by strife, hostility, and divisiveness may be called pluralistic. In this essay, the term will be used in a sense that expresses hope rather than fear, unity rather than fragmentation. Pluralism, in this sense, describes a society in which there prevails an attitude toward differences that reinforces and contributes to social cohesiveness.

A religiously pluralistic society, then, is one in which the principal religious groups not only claim freedom for themselves, but affirm equal freedom for others, whatever their beliefs may be. In such a society, these groups have also an internal freedom which is reflected in tolerance of criticism and openness to new insights. Individuals are free to doubt and to believe. This freedom is affirmed because of a realization of the need for dialogue, because groups and individuals have a stake—a religious stake—in the freedom of others. The model pluralism is also one in which there is a sensitivity to the differing needs of various groups and a disposition to accommodate these needs. Such a society need not embody perfection; it may contain groups that do not believe in or practice religious freedom. But a society can approximate the model pluralism if such groups are no great threat to freedom, if a trust in the common commitment to religious freedom prevails among the principal groups.

In this essay, the recent work of the Supreme Court will be interpreted as expanding religious freedom and thus creating a legal structure favorable to the maturing of this kind of religious pluralism. This interpretation may be debatable, legally and historically; but however the Court's work is interpreted, the influence of its decisions on American religious culture can be neither ignored nor minimized.

Controversy in church-state matters centers on the First Amendment's cryptic injunction that "Congress shall make no law respecting an establishment of religion, or prohibiting the free exercise thereof." This provision is now held to bind also the state legislatures by virtue of the due-process clause of the Fourteenth Amendment. The historical meaning of the quoted words is at best obscure. But there is general agreement that they were designed to accomplish some kind of separation of church and state. When inquiry is made, however, as to the degree and kind of separation required, agreement disappears—with respect both to historical meaning and to policy objectives. It is here submitted that the Court has made it clear that the church-state separation required by the Constitution is not one that insulates government from contacts with religion, but rather one that maximizes religious freedom through a policy of government neutrality. The Constitution does not limit religious freedom to the freedom compatible with strict separation; it requires only the separation compatible with maximum freedom. (Religious freedom has, of course, its limits, as the courts have made clear in cases dealing with polygamy, blood transfusion, snake handling, and compulsory education.)

The Supreme Court has expanded freedom in two principal ways. It has insisted upon a policy of neutrality that forbids government promotion or sponsorship of religious beliefs. By this insistence, the Court has not merely protected the freedom of those who hold different beliefs; it has protected the freedom of commitment to favored beliefs from being compromised by government sponsorship. In the second place, the Court has also expanded religious freedom by permitting, and sometimes requiring, special provisions to be made for religion where this is necessary to neutralize the otherwise restrictive effects of government's expanding activities.

These actions have not always been viewed as actions expanding religious freedom, nor have the Court's opinions always been couched in these terms. But for the study of religion and American culture, the prime significance of the Court's recent work has been its creation of broadly libertarian structures for the religious pluralism of the future.

II

The outlines of neutrality, the dominant theme in the Court's church-state decisions, began to emerge in 1947 in *Everson v. Board of Education*,[1] the first of the Court's controversial decisions in this area. In this case, New Jersey's provision for bus transportation for parochial-school students was attacked as a "law respecting an establishment of religion" prohibited by the First Amendment. Although the opinion sustaining the statute was primarily a discussion of the limits of separation, it included a statement that the First Amendment requires the state to be neutral—not only neutral toward sects but also neutral toward "groups of religious believers and non-believers."

The meaning of neutrality became much clearer in 1961 when the Court unanimously struck down a historic provision of the Maryland constitution requiring a declaration of belief in the existence of God as a prerequisite to holding public office.[2] The plaintiff was a member of the American Humanist Association who had precipitated the test by applying for a commission as a notary public. In holding that the test oath requirement violated his "freedom of belief and religion," the Court declared, in effect, that the state may not discriminate on grounds of religion, regardless of whether the discrimination favors a particular belief or favors all who believe in God at the expense of non-theists. In this case, the Court departed for the first time from traditional usage of the word *religion*, referring to "religions . . . which do not teach what would generally be considered a belief in the existence of God" and citing "Ethical Culture and Secular Humanism."

In the 1962 and the 1963 cases on public-school devotions, the plaintiffs included both sectarians who objected to the particular kind of worship that was sponsored and secularists who objected to any religious devotions. In all of the cases, the Court held that public-school authorities may not sponsor practices which imply the taking of sides in relation to religion. In the *Regents' Prayer* case,[3] the emphasis was on the impropriety of the Regents' action in promulgating an official prayer, notwithstanding its nonsectarian character and the broad approval given it by Jewish and Christian spokesmen.

In the *Schempp* case,[4] the neutrality doctrine received repeated emphasis. The Court stated a test: To avoid violating the "no-establishment" clause, an action of a public agency must not be designed to promote (or inhibit) religious beliefs or practices. In the words of one of the justices, neutrality requires "the extension of evenhanded treatment to all who believe, doubt, or disbelieve— a refusal on the part of the State to weight the scales of private choice."[5] All but one of the justices considered official sponsorship of daily devotions to be inconsistent with neutrality.

Some of the Court's critics have argued that toleration is all that a religious minority (including those who profess no religion) can reasonably expect. Erwin N. Griswold, for example, wrote in his criticism of the *Regents' Prayer* case:

The child of a nonconforming or minority group is, to be sure, different in his beliefs. That is what it means to be a member of a minority. Is it not desirable, and educational, for him to learn and observe this, in the atmosphere of the school—not so much that he is different, as that other children are different from him? And is it not desirable that, at the same time, he experience and learn the fact that his difference is tolerated and accepted? No compulsion is put upon him. He need not participate. But he, too, has the opportunity to be tolerant. He allows the majority of the group to follow their own tradition, perhaps coming to understand and to respect what they feel is significant to them.[6]

This view is incompatible with the kind of pluralism envisaged by the Court, a pluralism based not on tolerance but on equal freedom. As Mark DeWolfe Howe has said, leaders in the formative period of our government aimed at "converting the liberal principle of tolerance into the radical principle of liberty" and "believed that it might be achieved by prohibiting the governmental establishment of religion and guaranteeing religious freedom to all persons."[7]

The case of the humanist notary made it clear that the protection of the neutrality principle extends to those who do not believe in God. The 1965 conscientious-objector decisions had, therefore, been foreshadowed. Exemption from military service for conscientious objectors has traditionally been predicated on opposition to war stemming from religious training and belief. In 1948, Congress added the qualification that religious belief for this purpose means "belief in relation to a Supreme Being," to the exclusion of moral, philosophical, or other views. But, in *United States v. Seeger*,[8] the Supreme Court held that the exemption covers an agnostic whose opposition to war is based on "belief in the devotion to goodness and virtue for their own sakes, and a religious faith in a purely ethical creed." The Court refused to attribute to Congress any narrow or parochial concept of religious belief, although it seems quite likely that a narrow concept had been intended. The test, the Court said, was "whether a given belief that is sincere and meaningful occupies a place in the life of its possessor parallel to that filled by the orthodox belief in God of one who clearly qualifies for the exemption." Citing an impressive array of theological authorities, the Court stated that its interpretation embraced "the ever broadening understanding of the modern religious community."

Thus far, this section has dealt with the way in which the neutrality doctrine protects the freedom of those who hold a particular belief from governmental action penalizing them or promoting other beliefs. But the promoting of religious beliefs or practices by government would impair also the freedom of those who hold the favored beliefs. The neutrality rule protects the freedom of religious commitment from the devitalizing effects of government sponsorship.

Recent observers of American religious culture have seen that "establishment" can be a threat to free religion even where there is no established church. Peter L. Berger has written of "the religious establishment in America" as the principal threat to the vitality of Christian commitment.[9] The danger is that churches may become captive institutions submerged in a culture religion identified with the American Way of Life. Berger called the public schools "the principal agency representing the politically established culture religion." From this point of view, one can readily see at least symbolic importance in what the Court has done in checking the use of the public schools to propagate this faith.

In this respect, the Court's work can be interpreted as building upon the insights of Roger Williams concerning the nature of religious freedom and the evils of establishment. As Perry Miller has explained, Williams saw religious freedom as more than a set of external conditions. Williams' passionate religious concern made him "an analyst, an explorer into the dark places, of the very nature of freedom. His decision to leave denominations free to worship as they chose came as a consequence of his insight that freedom is a condition of the spirit."[10] Williams saw that persecution not only invades the freedom of the persecuted, but reveals the absence of freedom in the religious commitment of the persecutors. This view of interior religious freedom led Williams to demand a "hedge or wall of separation between the garden of the church and the wilderness of the world." As Mark DeWolfe Howe explains the Williams thesis, the wall protects not merely against possible efforts of government to injure religion, but against government's misguided desire to favor the churches.[11]

Varying reactions of "believers" to the public-school prayer decisions give clues to varying attitudes toward this internal religious freedom. Initial comments of religious spokesmen were largely critical of the decisions. They often interpreted them as restrictions of the religious freedom of the majority and rejected the Court's assertion that free exercise of religion "has never meant that a majority could use the machinery of the State to practice its beliefs."[12] Second thoughts brought many religious leaders to defend the Court and to oppose efforts to nullify its decision by amendment of the constitution. Some of the second thoughts were induced by concern over the peculiar religiosity of many of the demands for Constitutional amendment. They had an almost hysterical quality that seemed to reflect a fear of genuine religious freedom that was masked behind an insistence that religious belief have the support of agencies of government. Church leaders came to see the dangers of civic religion as a substitute for other religious commitment. They came to see government sponsorship of religion as a threat to the prophetic witness of the churches and a threat to religious freedom. According to one witness at the Congressional hearings, "the threat is not the secularization of our schools but the secularization of our religion." The Court's insistence on neutrality came to be seen as a protection against this threat.

Critics of the Court often claim that the prayer and Bible reading decisions are hostile to traditional religion and amount to an establishment of secularism. These claims ignore not only the point just developed, but also the Court's careful assurances that neutrality toward religion does not mean the elimination from public education of all study of religious beliefs and practices. On the contrary, the Court warned:

It might well be said that one's education is not complete without a study of comparative religion or the history of religion and its relationship to the advancement of civilization. It certainly may be said that the Bible is worthy of study for its literary and historic qualities. Nothing we have said here indicates that such study of the Bible or of religion, when presented objectively as part of a secular program of education, may not be effected consistent with the First Amendment.[13]

Educators are beginning to struggle with the practical problems inherent in such "objective" study of religion. The difficulties in maintaining neutrality are formidable. There must be no "teaching for commitment"; the teaching must be "about" religion and not "of" religion. Furthermore, even in a community with a large Protestant majority, it would not be neutral to limit the instruction to beliefs of Protestant churches. There may be even greater difficulty in maintaining neutrality toward traditional religious beliefs and other views of man and his relationships. There is always a danger that teaching about representative faiths (Protestant, Catholic, and Jewish) will carry the implication that this tri-faith pluralism is the American religion, that all good Americans are at least nominally committed to one of these faiths.

Perfect neutrality, however, is not required. In one area, at least, the Court has tolerated what Mark DeWolfe Howe has called "*de-facto* establishment."[14] The Court has refused to upset traditional Sunday-closing laws. Notwithstanding the admittedly religious roots of these laws and the religious language in which some of them are still cast, the Court found that Sunday laws are now designed to serve the secular purpose of providing a uniform day of rest and recreation.[15]

III

The Court has also protected religious freedom by holding that the establishment clause does not forbid special provisions for religion of a type that may be called "neutralizing" aids. These are provisions made to neutralize the restrictions of religious freedom that would otherwise result from government's secular activities. The classic example of such provisions is the chaplaincy program in the armed services. This program is designed not to promote religion, but to promote religious freedom. When the government separates men from ordinary opportunities for worship and pastoral care, it may properly provide substitute opportunities. Such action accords with a policy of neutrality and is therefore not forbidden by the establishment clause. This assertion may be made with confidence although the chaplaincy program has never been before the Court.

Religious exemptions furnish other examples of neutralizing aids. A familiar case is that of the draft exemption of religious conscientious objectors. In the 1918 *Selective Draft Law Cases*,[16] the Court brushed aside a contention that the exemptions were invalid under the "no-establishment" clause, and the recent cases reaffirm this view. This does not mean that Congress might not constitutionally abolish all exemptions for conscientious objectors. The result is that conscription is an area where the effective scope of religious freedom depends upon action by Congress, subject only to a constitutional duty to avoid discrimination.

In certain other areas, however, religious exemptions may be mandatory. This has recently been the Court's ruling with respect to unemployment-compensation laws. These laws provide compensation only for persons willing to accept employment, and for most workers this means willingness to take a job requiring work on Saturday. In 1963, the Supreme Court held that the Constitution requires that a Seventh Day Adventist be exempted from this requirement.[17] This result, the Court said, "reflects nothing more than the governmental obligation of neutrality in the face of religious differences, and does not represent that involvement of religious with secular institutions which it is the object of the Establishment Clause to forestall."

Even more striking is the decision of the California Supreme Court that the First Amendment requires exempting from narcotics laws the traditional use of peyote in religious ceremonies. The court assumed that non-religious use of peyote might be proscribed. The dominant consideration in requiring the exemption was apparently the court's view of the value of cultural pluralism:

In a mass society, which presses at every point toward conformity, the protection of a self-expression, however unique, of the individual and the group becomes ever more important. The varying currents of the subcultures that flow into the mainstream of our national life give it depth and beauty. We preserve a greater value than an ancient tradition when we protect the rights of the Indians who honestly practiced an old religion in using peyote one night at a meeting in a desert hogan near Needles, California.[18]

Exemptions for Sabbatarians are often written into Sunday-closing laws. While these exemptions are not mandatory, they have been upheld by the Court as not involving "establishment." Special exemptions for other religious groups are increasingly common. For example, the recent amendments to the Social Security Act exempt from social-security taxes the members of religious groups that are conscientiously opposed to insurance and that make adequate provision for their own dependent members. These are examples of what Justice Harlan called the "many areas in which the pervasive activities of the State justify some special provision for religion to prevent it from being submerged in an all-embracing secularism."[19]

All of these illustrations show that an insulating type of church-state separation is not required. Avoiding religious controversies is not the prime objective of church-state policy. If all religious exemptions were outlawed, legislative bodies would, to be sure, be protected from troublesome involvement in religious disputes. But this protection would be at the expense of religious freedom. It is for this reason that the Court has held that such insulation is not required by the First Amendment. The Court apparently believes that the health of American religious pluralism is such that issues concerning religious exemptions need not be kept out of the public forum.

Permissible aids for religion are not limited to aids in the form of exemptions, as the case of the chaplaincy program makes clear. But can the use of public funds for education in religious schools be defended as a neutralizing aid, a means of promoting freedom of religious choice? This question is the principal item of unfinished church-state business faced by the Supreme Court. To understand the question one must begin with an impressive fact: the enormous cost of public education. This cost is properly assessed upon all taxpayers, whether or not they patronize the public schools. But the burden of this cost, in the absence of neutralizing aids, greatly reduces the practical freedom to choose a school that combines general education with religious training. The Constitution guarantees the rights to conduct and to patronize religious schools if they meet general standards,[20] but taxes for public education hamper the freedom to enjoy this right. The position taken in this paper is that in a religiously pluralistic society freedom of religious choice is a matter of general sympathetic concern, and that the legal structures for such a society ought, therefore, to permit financial aids to be voted in order to neutralize restraints on such freedom.

Many educational aids have already been provided by both federal and state governments. Among the more important federal statutes are the National Defense Education Act, the Higher Education Facilities Act, and notably the Elementary and Secondary Education Act of 1965. State aids include not only provisions for transportation, standard textbooks, and various auxiliary services, but also appropriations for college scholarships and tuition grants. Aids at the college level raise less controversy than those for elementary and secondary education. Proposals for aid at the lower levels bring out deep-rooted oppositions to private schools in general and Roman Catholic schools in particular.

Even at the elementary-school level, however, there is widening recognition among religious leaders of the strength of the case for government aid as a feature of free pluralism. Dr. F. Ernest Johnson, long an education expert of the National Council of Churches, wrote that he considers opposition to transportation and textbook aid to be unfair and "a conspicuous example of the fact that Americans seem readier to accept the idea of cultural pluralism than to accept its consequences."[21] Recently, Milton Himmelfarb has challenged the "wall of separation" position from which American Jews have traditionally opposed aids to religious schools.[22] He developed the case for government aid not only in terms of fairness and of national educational policy, but also as a means of preserving a vigorous pluralism as a safeguard of freedom.

These views have increasing support because of increasing trust in the commitment of American Catholics to religious freedom. The declaration of Vatican II on this subject and the new openness of Roman Catholicism to other religious groups have combined to create a new climate for American religious pluralism.

The Supreme Court has spoken twice on the subject of educational aids. Twenty years ago, the Court upheld in the *Everson* case the constitutionality of a state statute providing reimbursement of the cost of bus transportation to parochial schools. The Court stated the neutrality rule in language already quoted and said also:

We must be careful, in protecting the citizens of New Jersey from state-established churches, to be sure that we do not inadvertently prohibit New Jersey from extending its general state law benefits to all its citizens without regard to their religious belief.[23]

The same opinion, however, included also a general statement against aid to religion which is often cited by advocates of strict separation. The actual decision in *Everson* can be regarded as settled since the Court voted in 1961 in a similar case not to permit reargument of the question.[24]

It is possible, of course, to distinguish between costs of transportation and costs more directly related to education; many other distinctions might conceivably be drawn. The type of aid provided by the federal education act of 1965 furnishes a convenient focus for considering the general problem. This statute provides that projects submitted by local public-school authorities must include arrangements such as dual enrollment in which children in private schools can participate. Dual enrollment (or "shared time") refers to an arrangement by which parochial-school pupils also attend the public school on a part-time basis. Such arrangements have long been in operation for subjects such as industrial arts and home economics; they have been held constitutional in the only case in which a test has been made.[25] The use of dual enrollment has recently been extended to instruction in sciences, languages, and other subjects not always available in religious schools.

A second title of the education act authorizes grants for textbooks and school-library resources. State authorities receiving funds under this title must give assurances that such books and resources will be provided on an equitable basis for the use of children and teachers in private schools.

Both of these provisions for private schools are questioned by those who are committed to an insulation type of church-state separation. The American Civil Liberties Union, for example, has declared that dual-enrollment programs "present grave constitutional and civil liberties problems under the Establishment Clause . . . because of the substantial benefit that [they] confer upon sectarian schools and because of the joint involvement by secular and church authorities."

Much of the Congressional debate on the education act centered on the so-called "child-benefit" theory, under which it was contended that the bill granted aid only to children and not to religious schools. On this theory, so the argument runs, these aids furnish no precedent for other, more substantial types of aid, such as grants for purchase of scientific equipment. This child-benefit distinction is highly unsatisfactory since all these aids benefit both the children and their schools. All such aids can be defended, however, as neutralizing aids designed to promote freedom in the choice of school.

While prophecy in constitutional law is foolhardy, we hazard the prediction that the Court will not adopt a broad prohibition of programs that help religious schools meet the costs of standard education. None of the bases on which such a prohibition might conceivably be rested seems likely to appeal to the Court. It is highly unlikely that the Court, after its careful exposition of the neutrality principle, will ever take "absolute separation" as a major premise. Nor does it seem likely that the Court will say that separate school systems are so undesirable in a pluralistic society that the establishment clause should be construed as forbidding neutralizing aids. It is also unlikely that the Court will support the claim of opponents of parochial schools that their religious freedom includes freedom from taxes levied to protect freedom of educational choice. Nor is it likely that the Court will follow the fear-inspired logic of those who believe that Roman Catholic attitudes toward religious freedom are still ambivalent, notwithstanding the declarations of Vatican II.

Finally, one may trust that the Court will not consider questions of educational aids to be so hot that they must at all costs be kept off the agendas of Congress and state legislatures. These are issues that can be left to the democratic process because of the healthy vigor of American religious pluralism: a pluralism that is finding its unity in a spreading trust in the common belief in religious freedom.

<h1 align="center">IV</h1>

Decisions of the Supreme Court have here been interpreted as creating a legal structure within which religious life in the United States can move toward a mature pluralism that reflects an active commitment to religious freedom. Discussion has focused on two applications of a general principle of neutrality. The structure created by the Court is partly permissive. Government may aid religion in ways which protect religious freedom in the context of government's own pervasive activities. But part of the Court's structure is restrictive. Government may not take sides in religious matters; it may not promote religious beliefs—either specific beliefs or religion in general.

It is easy to belittle the practical importance of these restrictions. In the public-school cases, for example, did the Court actually add to the freedom of minorities? Did it actually increase the freedom with which beliefs are held by the majority? It is easy to give a negative answer, and it is easy also to criticize the Court's "absolutist" rhetoric. But such judgments miss an important point. The principal importance of the Court's decisions in this field is symbolic. The Court is commending to citizens of a country with many faiths the ideal of an expanding and deepening religious freedom. In doing so, it is not surprising that the Court uses high-sounding rhetoric. As in the cases on desegregation, if the Court succeeds, it will be through its influence on changing attitudes.

It is not impossible that cultural development in the United States will be toward a pattern in which religious life is sustained more by the vitality of inner freedom than by the pressures of social establishment. It is not impossible that development will be toward a pluralism in which minorities are accorded not the grace of toleration but the right of equal freedom. If these developments do take place, future historians may assign some of the credit to the Supreme Court.

REFERENCES

1. *Everson v. Board of Education,* 330 U.S. 1, 18 (1947).

2. *Torcaso v. Watkins,* 367 U.S. 488 (1961).

3. *Engel v. Vitale,* 370 U.S. 421 (1962).

4. *Abington School Dist. v. Schempp,* 374 U.S. 203 (1963).

5. *Ibid.,* p. 317.

6. Erwin N. Griswold, "Absolute Is in the Dark," *Utah Law Review,* Vol. 8 (Summer, 1963), pp. 167, 177.

7. Mark DeWolfe Howe, review of Stokes, *Church and State in the United States, Harvard Law Review,* Vol. 64 (November, 1950), pp. 170-72.

8. *United States v. Seeger,* 380 U.S. 163 (1965).

9. Peter L. Berger, *The Noise of Solemn Assemblies,* (Garden City, N. Y., 1961).

10. Perry Miller, *Roger Williams* (New York, 1962), p. 255.

11. Mark DeWolfe Howe, *The Garden and the Wilderness* (Chicago, 1965), Ch. 1.

12. *Abington School Dist. v. Schempp,* 374 U.S. 203, 226 (1963).

13. *Ibid.,* p. 225.

14. Mark DeWolfe Howe, *The Garden and the Wilderness,* p. 11.

15. *McGowan v. Maryland,* 366 U.S. 420 (1961).

16. *Selective Draft Law Cases,* 245 U.S. 366, 389-90 (1918).

17. *Sherbert v. Verner,* 374 U.S. 398 (1963).

18. *People v. Woody,* 61 Cal. 2d 716, 394 P. 2d 813, 821-22 (1964).

19. *Sherbert v. Verner,* 374 U.S. 398, 422 (1963).

20. *Pierce v. Society of Sisters,* 268 U.S. 510 (1925).

21. F. Ernest Johnson, "A Problem of Culture," *Religion and the Schools* (Fund for the Republic, 1959), p. 71.

22. Milton Himmelfarb, "Church and State: How High a Wall?" *Commentary,* Vol. 42 (July, 1966), p. 23.

23. *Everson v. Board of Education,* 330 U.S. 1, 16 (1947).

24. *Snyder v. Town of Newton,* 365 U.S. 299 (1961).

25. *Commonwealth* ex rel. *v. School Dist. of Altoona,* 241 Pa. St. 224 (1913).

MILTON HIMMELFARB

Secular Society? A Jewish Perspective

THIS PAPER concerns the place of Jews and Judaism in a society and a culture that are ambiguous mixtures of secularism and Christianity. It is as much about the West ("Christendom") as about the United States, as much about the two hundred years or more since the Enlightenment as about the present.

A convenient point of departure is Ernest van den Haag and others' "Survey of the Political and Religious Attitudes of American College Students" in 1963: "A thorough survey of U. S. colleges leaves the distinct impression of . . . Judaism in decay." *Decay* implies that matters are worse now than they were a generation or so ago. Yet the same survey reports that of Brandeis students measuring their "concern with religious affairs" against that of their parents, about half estimate it to be "about the same"; of the rest, more say their concern is "more intense" than say it is "less intense." Far from showing decay, this shows some improvement, and the improvement would be even more marked if the comparison were made with the attitudes of the parents when they themselves were young.[1] Similarly, young Jewish intellectuals seem somewhat less antipathetic to Judaism and the Jewish community now than their predecessors were in the thirties and forties.[2]

The increasing numbers of Jews who marry non-Jews are sometimes cited as evidence of a decline in Judaism. This would be valid evidence if the lower rate of intermarriages in earlier generations could be taken as an index of fidelity then, but it cannot. Basically, Jewish intermarriage rises with increasing distance from immigrant origins.[3] If anything, the intermarriage of Jews seems less ideological today, less rebellious, than it did in the 1920's.[4] Among the children of immigrants there was a small but *positive* correlation between Jewish education and intermarriage, while among the grandchildren the correlation, though still not high, is negative. About 30 per cent of children born of such intermarriages in America are raised as Jews; this also seems to have been the proportion raised as Jews in Germany a century ago.[5] But this may be misleading. Perhaps proportionately more marriages failed to be designated as intermarriages in Germany because the Jewish partner was no longer a Jew, having become a convert to Christianity before marriage.

The situation of Jews has remained basically unchanged, both in their relation to Judaism and in their relation to the societies and cultures of the West, with its mixture of Christianity and secularism: secularized Christianity and Christian-related secularism. Although the kinds of change that come under the heads of demography, economics, acculturation, and the like are not unimportant, the situation of the Jews today has a continuity that starts from a revolutionary discontinuity at the time of Moses Mendelssohn in the eighteenth century, or even Spinoza in the seventeenth.

Jews, insofar as they have been modern, have wished to be of as well in their societies. They have made progress in this direction, simultaneously or preliminarily moving away from the older Jewish desire and fact of being in but not of their societies[6]; but they have met obstacles. In general, these have been obstacles deposited by the history that secularism was supposed to neutralize or nullify. The various societies, together with their traditions and memories, are still Christian—at least as far as the Jews are concerned. However secular these societies have been from one perspective, they have not been secular in the sense of being neutral between Christianity and Judaism, Christians and Jews.

At the beginning of Jewish modernity, Moses Mendelssohn, its representative figure, was caught up in an experience neatly paradigmatic for all modern Jews since his time. Mendelssohn wished to live in Berlin—the city, the center of Enlightenment and culture. Since Jews needed special permission to live there, he asked a friend to intercede for him with Frederick the Great. The Marquis d'Argens, a French intellectual who was what we would call today a cultural adviser to Frederick, wrote his Francophile (and Judaeophobe) master a letter that is a fine example of eighteenth-century *esprit*:

An intellectual [*philosophe*] who is a bad Catholic begs an intellectual who is a bad Protestant to grant the privilege [of residence in Berlin] to an intellectual who is a bad Jew. There is too much *philosophie* in all this for reason not to be on the side of the request.[7]

Now Mendelssohn was not really so bad a Jew as that, but to be allowed—grudgingly—to live in Berlin, he had to be thought a bad Jew. This, then, was the first lesson that modern Jews learned: If you want to be admitted to the delights and excitements of modern culture, do not be a good Jew. The second lesson was that the only people who were willing to let you live in Berlin were the bad Christians; good Christians would not have you whether you were a good Jew or a bad one. The third lesson, which was learned later than the first two, was that while Jews had to be bad to live in Berlin, Christians could be good or bad as they chose.

But the chief lesson was that reason was the modern Jew's ally; from this lesson it was only a small step to a reverence for Reason. Christians had less reason to revere Reason, since they could live in Berlin without it. Enthusiasm for modernity and secularism was, therefore, unevenly distributed between Jews and Christians.

Especially in Europe, it has been easy, intellectually and emotionally, for Jews to situate themselves in relation to the "good" Christians—the Constantinians, the upholders of the Christian state and the alliance between Throne and Altar. These have been the enemy, from long before the French Revolution to Vatican II, from the Catholic south to the Lutheran north, from Anglican England to Orthodox Russia.[8]

Liberal Christians are harder to place. Some liberal Christian thought has turned out to be harsh toward Jews and Judaism.[9] The society many liberal Christians have seen as secular, either gladly or sadly, is less secular and more Christian from a Jewish perspective. Even those who call themselves secularist rather than Christian tend to have different standards from Jews for judging a culture's secularism and religious neutrality. Two tests of this proposition are the place of Christmas in American life and the question of religious influence in the public schools.

For a Jew, no matter how secular, Christmas must be more problematic than it is for a Christian (or ex-Christian) of equal secularity. Despite all the efforts, frequently by Jews, to show that Christmas is no longer Christian (and never was),[10] even Jews removed from Jewish tradition find themselves obliged to engage in casuistries: a tree in the parlor but no wreath on the door or windows, "Season's Greetings" rather than "Merry Christmas"—the list is long and wryly comical. The great-granddaughter of a Forty-eighter from Germany recalls that when she was a little girl, she asked her mother why their Christmas tree had no star on top and was told that only Christian Christmas trees had a star.

On the more serious matter of religious influence in the public school—prayers, Bible reading, and the like—the Supreme Court has been saying no. To no one's surprise, most of the ensuing expressions of protest and annoyance have come from the Constantinians, but two have come from an unexpected quarter, liberal Harvard. Both the Dean of the Law School and the James Bryant Conant Professor of Education, Emeritus, think that the Court is wrong.

Dean Griswold:

Is it not clear as a matter of historical fact that this was a Christian nation? . . . Are the Mayflower Compact, Anne Hutchinson, Cotton Mather, Jonathan Edwards, William Penn, and many others no part of our history? It is true that we . . . developed a tolerance in matters of religion. . . . But this was not a purely humanistic type of thought. Nor did it deny the importance and significance of religion.

. . . The First Amendment forbade Congress to pass any law "respecting an establishment of religion or prohibiting the free exercise thereof." These are great provisions, of great sweep and basic importance. But to say that they require that all trace of religion be kept out of any sort of public activity is sheer invention. Our history is full of these traces. . . . God is referred to in our national anthem, and in "America," and many others of what may be called our national songs. Must all of these things be rigorously extirpated in order to satisfy a constitutional absolutism? What about Sunday? What about Christmas? Must we deny our whole heritage, our culture, the things of spirit and soul which have sustained us in the past and helped to bind us together in times of good and bad?[11]

Professor Ulich:

The serious opponents [of the Supreme Court's decisions]. . . are aroused by . . . the threat of an unhistorical disruption of national customs and symbols, which today probably have a more patriotic and aesthetic appeal than a deeply felt religious one. But there are even more profound, though sometimes unconscious, reasons for the anxiety of many. . . . The Jewish people would not have survived the long years of persecution without faithful adherence to their rituals, festivals, and prayers. May then the loss of the Christian past not jeopardize the future of *this* nation, just as the desertion from the covenant would have jeopardized the survival of the Jews? Nations, as well as men, though living by bread, do not live by bread alone.[12]

Ulich is right: the decisions and the protests against them have been about symbol, not substance. A Jewish parent can testify that whether or not Christmas is evident in the schools, it is thoroughly evident on television and on Main Street, and these have more effect on children than what formally takes place in school.

Griswold mentions Sunday. As it happens, the Supreme Court has ruled on Sunday in a matter of substance for Jews, or at least for some Jews. The ruling is that a Jew in Massachusetts who does not do business on his Sabbath, Saturday, may not make up for it by doing business on Sunday—though the Massachusetts law refers to Sunday as the Lord's Day, and though a lower court ruled that the state was discriminating against the Jewish merchant on religious grounds.[13]

We may soon have a Sabbath question in the schools. If it is decided that education in the last third of the twentieth century needs six days a week, the sixth day will be Saturday, of course, not Sunday. In the Third French Republic, anticlerical and even irreligious, children attended the state schools on the Jewish Sabbath, not the Christian one. They still do in the Fifth Republic.[14]

While the secular society in the lands that used to be Christendom is neutral in matters of religion, it is more neutral against Judaism than against Christianity. The French distinguish between the legal country and the real country. In the legal country, religious neutrality is imperfect, and in the real country much more imperfect. In every Western nation, Christianity is too inseparable from the national culture for religious neutrality to be truly possible.[15]

Nor does this obtain only in lands where the Revolution paused at the bourgeois stage. It obtains also where the Revolution is or calls itself Marxist. Although all religions are equally bad in Russia, one is worse—Judaism.[16] But 1917's failure to "solve the Jewish problem" is much more recent than 1789's. It was long possible for Jews to believe that only the bourgeois character of the society in which they lived kept them from being truly of it. This belief led many to yearn, with a secularist-messianic fervor, for a socialist transformation of man and society.[17] Now socialist revolutions have come, but for Jews the transformation has not come. Henceforth, faith in socialism as the solution must increasingly be recognized as contrary to experience and reason, if not to Reason.

From this point of view, even a socialist revolution does not go far enough. What is needed is a cultural revolution, or more accurately, a linguistic one. If national languages persist, so will national cultures, and so will the Christianity or the Christian influence—or symbolism, or vocabulary—that is so deeply imbedded in Western culture. How can one understand and appreciate Dante, Shakespeare, Donne, Milton, Racine, Pascal, Hegel, Kierkegaard, Dostoevski, Tolstoi, Hawthorne, or Eliot, if one does not understand and appreciate Christianity?

Since *The Psychopatholgy of Everyday Life,* we have known that it is in trivialities we reveal ourselves. Let us consider some of these trivialities. In English *crusade* is an O. K. word; *Pharisee* or *pharisaic* is a bad word. But *crusade* is O. K. only from the traditional point of view of West European Christianity, not necessarily from the point of view of modern scholarship and certainly not from the point of view of Slavs, Greeks, Armenians, Moslems, and Jews. For the Jews the crusades meant massacres in Europe and Palestine. The First Crusade was more or less the beginning of the Jews' systematic degradation and persecution in England, France, and Germany. Centuries after the Christian Roman Empire had made Jewish proselytism among Christians a capital crime, Jews continued to proselytize. It was the crusades that effectively terrorized the Jews into passivity.[18]

As for *Pharisee* and *pharisaic,* the meaning given to these words is a triumph of Christian (New Testament) propaganda. Yet even secularized Jews, and even secularized Jews who have a somewhat positive attitude toward Jewish tradition and culture, do not hesitate to use these words in preference to *self-righteous* or *hypocritical,* just as they use *crusade* in its honorific sense. Their being unaware of what they are doing would only prove the inherently anti-Jewish force of the culture and its language; their awareness would prove it all the more. They are trying to show—themselves as well as others—that they are not parochial Jews, that they hold truth to be more important than Jewish sensibilities. Actually, they are equating truth with the Christian propaganda that is now ineradicably a part of our secular culture.[19] Western culture prefers Christian to Jewish parochialism—or rather, it takes for granted that Christian parochialism is universalism.

Logically, the best way to solve this problem would be to abolish it. Do the languages of the West transmit old Christian memories and habits? Replace them by a new, universal language, a linguistic (and cultural) *tabula rasa.* Zamenhof, the inventor of Esperanto, was a Jew, and his vision included an element of barely modified Jewish messianism.[20] But in no foreseeable future, whether its emblematic date is 1789 or 1917, are we likely to find Esperanto substituted for English or French or German or Italian or Russian or Spanish; nor, despite the rise of Asia and Africa, are we likely to find the nations and continents that were once Christendom—and Islam, too, for that matter—shorn of all power and influence. Cultures linked to Christianity or Islam cannot be as indifferently neutral in these things as, say, Buddhist cultures.

Even under the sign of Marxism, half a century after the Russian Revolution, some of the noblest and most impressive figures in the lands of the new, socialist cultures are Christian or near-Christian—by deliberate, almost provocative choice: Pasternak, Solzhenitsyn, Sinyavsky, Mihajlo Mihajlov.

From the beginning of Jewish modernity, Jews have had three choices: to be Jews, to be Christians, to be secularists. Many have decided that they cannot conscientiously be Jews because they cannot believe what Judaism requires them to believe: that there is a God, the Creator who revealed himself as Lawgiver to the patriarchs and prophets, that he wishes the children of Israel to preserve themselves in faithful and loving obedience to him, and that all men will yet join them in acknowledging and worshiping him. If a Jew cannot believe this, however freely he interprets it, shall he choose to be a Christian or shall he choose to be a secularist?

If a Jew cannot conscientiously believe in Judaism because he holds it to be unreasonable, then all the more can he not believe in Christianity. If he finds the dogmas of Judaism offensive to Reason, he must find the dogmas of Christianity more so, if only because there are more of them. The dogmas of Judaism are preserved in Christianity, at most with a change of tense (for example, that the Law revealed to the patriarchs and prophets was once binding but no longer is). To these dogmas Christianity adds others, Christological and ecclesiological.

But if not conscientiously, then expedientially, a Jew devoted to Reason can become a Christian. A nineteenth-century biographer tells us that Moses Mendelssohn "despised apostasy as dishonorable, but would gladly have joined his friend Lessing in a society where there were neither Jews nor Christians."[21] Then the years pass. Impatience grows, and with impatience comes a feeling that honor is a costly luxury. So Moses Mendelssohn's son Abraham decides to do the expedient thing, as he later told *his* son Felix:

My father. . . did not want to be a Christian. . . . As long as it was permitted by the [Napoleonic] government under which we lived, I reared you without religion in any form. I wanted you to profess whatever your convictions might favor or, if you prefer, whatever expediency might dictate. But it was not so to be. . . . Naturally, when you consider the scant value I placed on any form in particular, I felt no urge to choose the form known as Judaism. . . . Therefore I reared you as Christians, Christianity . . . being the . . . form . . . most accepted by the majority of civilized people. Eventually I myself adopted Christianity, because I felt it my duty to do for myself that which I recognized as best for you.[22]

Or, as Heinrich Heine said, "the baptismal certificate is the ticket of admission to European culture."[23] A later nineteenth-century oral tradition has it that the Russian scholar Daniel Chwolson said he had been baptized out of conviction—the conviction that it was better to be a professor in St. Petersburg than a wretch teaching the rudiments of Hebrew reading in a mud-sunk village in Lithuania. A similar conviction inspired Bernard Berenson to be (or call himself) an Episcopalian in Boston and a Catholic in Florence.[24] Today, prudential baptisms are apt to be of a somewhat different character. In France, the atheist daughter of Russian Jewish parents has her children baptized as Catholics at birth so that they will not be the prey of a new Nazism.[25]

But, of course, the preferred alternative is secularism, the vision of Lessing and Moses Mendelssohn. Only now, two hundred years later, we ought to see in retrospect what Mendelssohn could not see in prospect—that the secularism of the West is not quite neither Christian nor Jewish equally. Especially does it not have equal effects on the children and grandchildren of the ex-Jew and the ex-Christian.

Suppose that the children or grandchildren, in their turn, rebel against *their* fathers and grandfathers; suppose that they become disillusioned with the religion of Reason and turn to one of the traditional religions. Which will that be? Given the culture they have absorbed not only in the mind but also through the pores, the result is not in doubt. The religion-minded children or grandchildren become Christians.[26] Bergson, a Catholic in spirit, would have been one in fact if it had not been for his honor, which would not allow him formally to abandon the Jews when they were under attack by Hitler.[27] Franz Rosenzweig, perhaps the greatest modern Jewish theologian, was almost baptized; his cousins Hans and Rudolf Ehrenberg were baptized.[28] Edith Stein became a nun.[29] Boris Pasternak became a Tolstoian Russian Orthodox Christian—under the Soviets.[30]

Notably, these conversions were to the particular forms of Christianity dominant in the respective countries: Catholicism in France, Lutheranism and Catholicism in Germany, Eastern Orthodoxy in Russia.[31] Expediential conversions could be to the dominant form of Christianity—Chwolson to Russian Orthodoxy; Disraeli, as a boy and upon his father's initiative, to Anglicanism. But in the Romanoff and Hapsburg empires they tended to be to a minority sect, Protestantism. This was the case in Russia for the family of Vladimir Medem, who was to be an early leader of the Jewish Socialist Bund,[32] and for the banker and economist Ivan Bloch[33]; in Austria, it was almost the case for Freud.[34] A calculation in these conversions to Protestantism in Central and Eastern Europe seems to have been that Protestantism was not "really" so Christian as Catholicism or Eastern Orthodoxy, and that, therefore, one was somehow less of an apostate (to Judaism? to the Jews? to Reason?) if one became a Protestant.[35]

Because Bergson was culturally so French, Pasternak and Frank so Russian, and Rosenzweig's cousins so German, they became sincerely Catholic, Russian Orthodox, and Lutheran.[36] In Western Europe, Jews did not become Eastern Orthodox Christians. In Russia, they did not become Anglicans. This tendency in Jewish conversions does not strengthen the anti-Constantinian argument that Christianity loses by involvement in culture.

These people could become sincere Christians because they had been brought up in the religion of Reason. Few even wished, like Rosenzweig, to "enter Christianity, as did its founders, as a Jew, not as a 'pagan.' "[37] There is no comparable record of sincere conversions to Christianity among those really brought up as Jews.

A Jew who is brought up without religion and who remains without religious feeling may nevertheless marry someone who has such feeling. Statistically, the odds are that that person will be a Christian, not a Jew, and that their children will then be Christians. The religious *potential* of our society is Christian. If a secularist Jew, or his child or grandchild, is to be within reach of a Jewish potential—in the second and especially the third generation—he must actively will it, he must make a decision. To be within reach of the Christian potential needs no decision, no act of will.

In the modern Jewish experience Unitarianism has been perceived as a kind of secularist-Christian hybrid, with the secularist element dominant. But this is a Jewish perception, perhaps even a willful (though unwitting) self-deception. For Jews, at least,

Unitarianism has been a way station on the road toward a more traditional kind of Christianity.[38] Since American Unitarianism has not grown much,[39] we must infer that those who enter are more or less offset by those who leave. Few leave for Judaism. President Taft was a Unitarian; his son the Senator was an Episcopalian.

Ethical Culture was founded in 1876 by Felix Adler, an American. The son of a rabbi, Adler had been studying in Germany to become a rabbi himself when he decided that "right living could stand on its own ground, and was . . . far more important than belief or unbelief about the matters which Judaism and Christianity both deemed essential."[40] From the beginning the movement has attracted many ex-Jews, but it has not realized its ambition of attracting many ex-Christians. For some of the people associated with it, it has served as a kind of passageway from Judaism to Christianity, allowing the passage to extend over two or three generations and obviating the dramatic and traumatic act of formal conversion by baptism. How conscious all this has been we cannot say; but even if not fully conscious, it may still not be unintended. Since Ethical Culture is an alternative to theistic religion, it would be dishonorable for an Ethical Culturist to abandon Jewish for Christian theism; but if it just happened that one's children or grandchildren were raised as Christians by their non-Ethical Culture parent, should one be a religious fanatic and object?

For two hundred years secularist Jews have tried to evade admitting to themselves that they know what this process is. As experience accumulates with the years, the evasion becomes increasingly difficult. The choice for Jews has not really been whether to be a Jew or a Christian or a secularist; it has been whether to be a Jew or a Christian. Other things being equal, secularism has been, for Jews, a propaedeutic to Christianity.

But Jews know that whatever else they may or may not be, they are not Christians. A growing realization that they have only the two choices rather than the three—and the realization may be less than fully conscious or articulate with most—may account in part for the rise in Jewish affiliation, and perhaps sentiment, in the past generation.

This survey makes no claim to completeness. Perhaps nothing need be said here about Zionism and Israel,[41] but two other questions must be touched on, if not answered: America as specifically American, and the autonomy of the future with respect to the past.

Whatever may be the present state of the old cultural and historical controversy over American uniqueness—or, as Marxists used to call it, exceptionalism—America is rather special in the Jewish experience.[42] Unlike Europe, America has had no pre-modern past—no Middle Ages, no feudalism, no union of Throne and Altar. Unlike such multinational states as the Hapsburg empire, ethnically diverse America is a unitary nation; but unlike most unitary nations, it has been religiously pluralist from its earliest days, when the pluralism was Protestant. In America the civic equality of the Jews was never an issue and never had to be legislated, at least nationally. A corollary of the triumph of the American Revolution, so obvious it did not have to be put into words, was that Jews were citizens like all other (white) men. By contrast, the French Revolution is to some degree still, as it once was, the rift that separates France; and the well-being and safety of the French Jews have varied with the fortunes of the French Revolution. As for Germany—

The Jewish folk expression "It's hard to be a Jew" means not only that it is hard to fulfill God's commands as he wishes them to be fulfilled, but also that minority existence is painful. In America today it is less hard to be a Jew, in the second sense, than ever before, anywhere else.

Specifically, therefore, America is different; but the specific difference is enacted within what is generically common to a West that used to be Christendom. The West has become secular—but not all that secular. From the perspective of Jewish experience and of contemporary Jewish reality, the Western secular society is Christian as well as secular—and that includes America.

What of the future? Granted that everything said here has been so and is so, it will not necessarily continue to be so. The future may not be completely independent of the past, but neither is it completely dependent. It has its own realm of autonomy and newness —in a word, of futurity.

Yet, though the openness and newness of the future have been asserted in the past, too, each successive, realized future has been less new than it was expected to be when it was still a future future. All may yet change, and we may be standing at the edge of a newness that will truly be new; but the probabilities are that the past will not give up its old habit of putting its mark on the future.

REFERENCES

1. Educational Reviewer, Inc., "A Survey of the Political and Religious Attitudes of American College Students," *National Review* (October 8, 1963), pp. 287, 291. For the earlier generation, see Nathan Glazer, *American Judaism* (Chicago, 1957), pp. 84-85: "The overwhelming majority of the immigrants' children had deserted Judaism. . . . All during the twenties and thirties it was discovered that the Jewish students had moved much farther from any religious position than Catholic and Protestant students."

2. For instance, compare "Under Forty: A Symposium on American Literature and the Younger Generation of American Jews," *Contemporary Jewish Record* (February, 1944), pp. 3-36, with "Jewishness and the Younger Intellectuals: A Symposium," *Commentary* (April, 1961), pp. 305-59.

3. Erich Rosenthal, "Studies of Jewish Intermarriage in the United States," *American Jewish Year Book,* Vol. 64 (1963), pp. 18-21.

4. Leslie A. Fiedler, *The Jew in the American Novel* (New York, 1959), pp. 14-24; Marshall Sklare, "Intermarriage and the Jewish Future," *Commentary* (April, 1964), pp. 46-52.

5. Rosenthal, "Studies of Jewish Intermarriage," pp. 29-31.

6. Before the last partition of Poland in the eighteenth century, there was official talk of emancipating the Jews, whereupon Jewish communal leadership collected money to send representatives to Warsaw to "forestall the danger so that, God forbid, no new reforms be introduced": cited by Salo W. Baron, *A Social and Religious History of the Jews,* Vol. 2 (3 vols.; New York, 1937), p. 243.

7. Cited by Karl Thieme in "Une Enquête: L'Enseignement chrétien concernant les Juifs," *Evidences,* No. 87 (Paris; January-February, 1961), p. 5.

8. Those who believed that the state was or should be Christian also had to believe that Jews could not or should not be equal citizens with Christians. Cecil Roth, *A History of the Jews in England* (3d ed.; Oxford, 1964), p. 249: "As late as 1818 it was possible to maintain in the courts Lord Coke's doctrine that the Jews were in law perpetual enemies, 'for between them, as with the devils, whose subjects they are, and the Christian there can be no peace.'" Yet for the Jews England was a far more tranquil and tolerant land than most.

In the last quarter of the nineteenth century, in Catholic France and Austria and in Protestant Prussia, "Christian" in the name of a political movement or party usually meant "anti-Semitic." In 1896 the French Dominican Hippolyte Gayraud, for whom "a convinced Christian is by nature a practicing antisemite," urged a convention of the Christian Democrats to have faith that "Christian life itself spreads an effective antisemitism," though "some repressive laws are needed too": Robert F. Byrnes, *Antisemitism in Modern France* (New Brunswick, 1950), pp. 208-09, 215. In our time another French Dominican, a liberal, states the contrary proposition as self-evident; but even in a UNESCO pamphlet he feels he has to justify the record of repressive laws: Yves Congar, *The Catholic Church and the Race Question* (Paris, 1953), pp. 53-54: "As regards religion and respect for the human person and the primary natural rights, the Catholic protest against anti-Semitism is definite, united and absolute; it is equally so in the matter of anti-Jewish discrimination based on racism. As regards the political and sociological aspects of the question, the Catholic attitude is qualified. For example, in pre-1939 Hungary the Catholic bishops, as members of Parliament, accepted the *numerus clausus* laid down for the admission of Jews to certain professions and schools. Here the bishops were acting as national leaders in a country where the Jewish minority (5.3 per cent of the population) had a practical monopoly in a number of spheres (press, theatre, etc.) or at least had a higher proportion of posts than its numbers warranted, even taking its cultural level into account."

The Chief Procurator of the Holy Synod of the Russian Orthodox Church, K. P. Pobedonostsev, was credited with predicting happily that as a result of the policy he was advocating about the Jews, "a third of them would be converted, a third would emigrate, while the rest would die of hunger": Alexander Kornilov, *Modern Russian History* (New York, 1924), p. 284.

In that innocent age before genocide, the Constantinian attitude toward the Jews was generally in consonance with the Eleventh Commandment that Hilaire Belloc, himself a Constantinian and anti-Semite, attributed to the capitalist ethos: "Thou shalt not kill; but neither strive/ Officiously to keep alive."

9. Franklin H. Littell, "The Protestant Churches and Totalitarianism (Germany 1933-45)," *Totalitarianism,* ed. Carl J. Friedrich (Cambridge, Mass., 1954), pp. 108-119; Uriel Tal, "Liberal Protestantism and the Jews in the Second Reich, 1870-1914," *Jewish Social Studies,* Vol. 26 (1964), pp. 23-41; Milton Himmelfarb, "Some Attitudes Toward Jews," *Commentary* (May, 1963), pp. 425-28.

10. For instance, Joseph L. Blau, "On the Celebration of Christmas," *Columbia University Rapport: A Newsletter of the Graduate Faculties* (Christmas 1964-New Year 1965), pp. 3-6.

11. Erwin N. Griswold, "Absolute Is in the Dark. . . ," *Utah Law Review,* Vol. 8 (1963), pp. 173-74.

12. Robert Ulich, "The Educational Issue," in Paul A. Freund and Robert Ulich, *Religion and the Public Schools* (Cambridge, Mass., 1965), p. 40.

13. *Gallagher* v. *Crown Kosher Market,* 366 U. S. 627 (1961): "It would seem that the objectionable language [Lord's Day] is merely a relic." See Milton Himmelfarb, "Festivals and Judges," *Commentary* (January, 1963), pp. 67-70.

14. The Ecole Normale Supérieure, the nursery of the French intellectual elite, trains *lycée* professors. It has traditionally been republican, anticlerical, secularist, anti-anti-Semitic—in short, it affirms the French Revolution:

H. Stuart Hughes, *Consciousness and Society* (Vintage Edition; New York, 1961), pp. 55-57, 347-48. Its student body, which has long included secularist Jews, has in the past generation come to include practicing Catholics as well. Yet Arnold Mandel reports (*American Jewish Year Book*, Vol. 66 [1965], p. 369): "In May [1964] . . . a sensation was produced by the refusal of the Ecole Normale Supérieure to permit the candidacy of a Jewish student who was a Sabbath observer. . . . The examinations [were] on Saturday . . . as French university examinations often were. He asked their postponement on the basis of the freedom of worship guaranteed by the French constitution. The [Ecole Normale Supérieure] replied that Sabbath observance was incompatible with the duties of a civil servant as well as of a student . . . [and that] the young man should give up the idea of attending the Ecole Normale and becoming a teacher. . . . The young man was finally able to take the examinations, which had been postponed to another date, and to enter the Ecole Normale."

15. A presidential address to the American Historical Association, melancholy over the state of history and the historians, notes that "many of the younger practitioners of our craft, and those who are still apprentices, are products of lower middle-class or foreign origins, and their emotions frequently get in the way of historical reconstructions. They find themselves in a very real sense outsiders to our past and feel themselves shut out. This is certainly not their fault, but it is true": Carl Bridenbaugh, "The Great Mutation," *American Historical Review*, Vol. 68 (1963), pp. 322-23.

On America's openness in academic and intellectual life, contrasted to Germany's restrictiveness, see Milton Himmelfarb, "Jewish Sentiment," *Federal Aid and Catholic Schools*, ed. Daniel Callahan (Baltimore, 1964), pp. 90-91; on Durkheim and Marc Bloch in a culture that has Joan of Arc as a central figure, *idem.*, "Two Cheers for Hedonism," *Commentary* (April, 1965), pp. 64-65.

16. Out of many possible references, Walter Kolarz, *Religion in the Soviet Union* (New York, 1961), especially pp. 388-89, and Thurston N. Davis and Eugene K. Culhane, "Religion in the Soviet Union," *America* (February 19, 1966), p. 259. For the testimony of an American philosopher, Lewis S. Feuer, "Jews in the Soviet Union," *New Republic* (November 30, 1963), pp. 11-12; of an American scientist, David W. Weiss, "Plight of the Jews in the Soviet Union," *Dissent* (July-August, 1966), pp. 447-64.

17. Lucy S. Dawidowicz and Leon J. Goldstein, *Politics in a Pluralist Democracy* (New York, 1963), pp. 76-90; R. V. Burks, *Dynamics of Communism in Eastern Europe* (Princeton, 1961), pp. 163-65; Annie Kriegel, "Léon Blum vu par les communistes," *Preuves*, No. 182 (Paris; April, 1966), pp. 44-46; J. L. Talmon, "The Jewish Intellectual in Politics," *Midstream* (January, 1966), p. 10: "Their fatherland was the Revolution which had no frontiers; their country was mankind or the proletariat. . . . What other people had even remotely experienced universalist Messianism with the same intensity? . . . One of Rosa Luxembourg's letters from prison to a Jewish friend [says]: 'Why do you pester me with your Jewish sorrow? There is no room in my heart for the Jewish troubles.' And she goes on to

speak most eloquently of the suffering of the Chinese coolies and of the Bantus in South Africa. Twenty-five years later, after the Germans had occupied it, there was not a single Jew left alive in Rosa's native Zamosc, which was also the home-town of I. L. Peretz [the great Yiddish writer]."

18. Bernhard Blumenkranz, *Juifs et chrétiens dans le monde occidental, 430-1096* (Paris and The Hague, 1960), pp. xivff., 159-212, 382-85.

19. Some Christian scholars have long since written major works about Pharisaism (or classical rabbinic Judaism) that try to penetrate behind the propaganda—for example, H. Travers Herford, *The Pharisees* (New York, 1924), and George Foot Moore, *Judaism in the First Centuries of the Christian Era* (3 vols.; Cambridge, Mass., 1927-30); but only parochial Jews and Christian specialists seem to know about them.

20. For his proposed new religion of humanity, Hillelism, see Marjorie Boulton, *Zamenhof* (London, 1960), pp. 96-105. Zamenhof's father "had abandoned the observance of Judaism and wished to see Jews assimilated into the Gentile community" (p. 1).

21. S. L. Steinheim, *Moses Mendelssohn und seine Schule* (Hamburg, 1840), pp. 27-28, cited by Isaac E. Barzilay, "Moses Mendelssohn. . . ," *Jewish Quarterly Review,* Vol. 52 (1961), p. 92.

22. Cited by Eric Werner, *Mendelssohn: A New Image of the Composer and His Age* (New York, 1963), p. 37.

23. Hugo Bieber (ed.), *Heinrich Heine: Jüdisches Manifest* (New York, 1946), p. 265. Heine also said: "My becoming a Christian is the fault of . . . Napoleon, who really didn't have to go to Russia, or of his teacher . . . of geography, who didn't tell him that in Moscow it's very cold in the winter" (p. 263). Napoleon is the personification of the French Revolution, the friend of secularism and the enemy of religion; if the Revolution had been victorious in Germany, there would have been no need for Heine to be baptized. Cf. Abraham Mendelssohn's statement that as long as the German city he lived in had been under Napoleonic rule, "I reared you without religion in any form," *supra.*

24. Michael Fixler, "Bernard Berenson of Butremanz," *Commentary* (August, 1963), pp. 135-43.

25. Robert Pietri, "L'Antisémitisme: A voix haute, à voix basse," *L'Arche,* No. 109 (Paris; March, 1966), pp. 20-21.

26. Ernest Renan's grandson was Ernest Psichari. Teilhard de Chardin was a collateral descendant of Voltaire.

27. John M. Oesterreicher, *Walls Are Crumbling: Seven Jewish Philosophers Discover Christ* (New York, 1952), p. 43. All seven were born into Mendelssohnian-secularist families. For Simone Weil, see *nn.* 31 and 36.

28. They had in common a great-grandfather whose pride was that, in the approving words of Leopold Zunz, the founder of modern Jewish scholar-

ship (*Wissenschaft des Judentums*), he had taken "a talmudic academy in which a few general disciplines were tolerated" and made it into an "institution in which Talmud was tolerated, and finally a high school without Talmud instruction." At the time of the Revolution of 1848, he urged the Jews to delete from the Passover Haggadah the passage that says, "Though now we are slaves, next year may we be free men": Nahum Glatzer, *Franz Rosenzweig: His Life and Thought* (Philadelphia, 1963), p. xf.

29. Oesterreicher, p. 331, and see *n.* 31.

30. His parents were Mendelssohnian-secularist. For Russian Orthodox influences and symbols in *Dr. Zhivago*, see Edmund Wilson, *The Bit Between My Teeth* (New York, 1965), pp. 427-30, 441-45, 447-72.

31. Another convert to Russian Orthodox Christianity was the philosopher and theologian Simeon L. Frank. When his posthumous *Reality and Man* (London, 1965) was reviewed in the *Times Literary Supplement* (August 5, 1965; p. 683), the reviewer noted that Frank's "mother's father was a practicing . . . Jew"; he went on to associate Simone Weil and Edith Stein with Frank: "And strangely the three . . . are all of Jewish birth. . . ." It would be more exact to say "Mendelssohnian-secularist Jewish birth." See also Nicolas Zernov, *Russian Religious Renaissance of the Twentieth Century* (*London,* 1963) especially pp. 158-59ff. For Simone Weil, see Leslie A. Fiedler, "Simone Weil: A Prophet out of Israel," *Commentary* (January, 1951), p. 43: "Neither she nor her parents nor two of her grandparents had ever seen the inside of a *shul* [synagogue]"; Martin Buber, "The Silent Question: About Henri Bergson and Simone Weil," *Judaism* (April, 1952), pp. 99-109; Hans Meyerhof, "Contra Simone Weil," *Commentary* (September, 1957), pp. 240-49.

32. Vladimir Medem, "Youth of a Bundist," *Commentary* (November, 1950), pp. 477-85: "Oddly enough, all [the members of Medem's family] became Lutherans, as did most [Russian] Jews who joined the Christian church. I believe it was because conversion to Protestantism involved less ceremonial and fewer technical difficulties [?] than Orthodoxy. . . . Only I . . . belonged to the . . . Orthodox church" (p. 479).

33. N[ahum] Sokolow, "The Late M. Jean de Bloch," *Jewish Chronicle* (London; January 24, 1902), p. 11: ". . . his biography? The old story 'that is ever new.' His father was . . . intellectually inclined. . . . He . . . went to St. Petersburg. . . . Having gone over to Calvinism, he developed a capacity for commerce and finance which . . . brought him fortune and influence."

34. Ernest Jones, *Life and Work of Sigmund Freud,* Vol. 1 (3 vols.; New York, 1953-57), p. 167: ". . . Freud thought of joining the Protestant 'Confession' so as to be able to marry without having the complicated Jewish ceremonies [?] he hated so much." Jones was a psychoanalyst. Did he really believe that that was the cause of Freud's thinking of baptism?

35. In the Hapsburg empire in the late-nineteenth and early-twentieth centuries, the philosopher Franz Brentano persuaded a number of Jewish disciples—including Husserl—to be baptized in order to be eligible for pro-

fessorships of philosophy, and, thus, to be able to discharge their moral duty by spreading his philosophical truth in an age when all the positive-historical religions had become outmoded: Samuel Hugo Bergmann, "Emil Utitz: The Tragic Course of a Jewish Scholar" (Hebrew), *Molad*, Nos. 113-114 (Tel Aviv; December, 1957), especially pp. 626-27. Brentano, who had been a Catholic priest, "advised his Jewish disciples to affiliate themselves with Protestantism, which he called, half-jestingly and half-respectfully, 'the religion of the irreligious'" (p. 626). Few could resist the argument that it was their moral duty to do the expedient thing, and that a philosopher had no right to attach more importance to changing his official religious designation than to changing his clothes for an official occasion.

Brentano once wrote Bergmann: "For the more gifted of the members of your people there ought to be no moral prohibition against giving lip service to what they do not believe in their hearts": Hugo Bergmann (ed.), "Briefe Franz Brentanos an Hugo Bergmann," *Philosophy and Phenomenological Research*, Vol. 7 (1946), p. 103. A 1966 addition to the International Library of Philosophy was Brentano's *The True and the Evident*, a translation of *Wahrheit und Evidenz*. Evidently his philosophical truth permitted or rather required creedal falsehood.

36. Simone Weil said that her tradition was "Christian, French, and Greek": Fiedler, "Simone Weil . . ," p. 43.

37. Glatzer, *Franz Rosenzweig*, p. xvii.

38. In 1799 a disciple of Mendelssohn's, David Friedländer, anonymously proposed to a Berlin clergyman that the Jews would become Christians if allowed to subscribe to a unitarian rather than a trinitarian credo: Simon Dubnow, *Weltgeschichte des jüdischen Volkes*, Vol. 8 (10 vols.; Berlin, 1928-29), pp. 202-07.

39. "The first half of the twentieth century for both the Universalists and the Unitarians was from a statistical point of view a time of relative stagnation or decline": Edwin Scott Gaustad, *Historical Atlas of Religion in America* (New York, 1962), p. 128.

40. Henry Neumann, *Spokesmen for Ethical Religion* (Boston, 1951), pp. 3-4. There is a curious lack of objective inquiry into the social history of Ethical Culture.

41. For the "defensive" and the "messianic" elements in Zionist thought, see Arthur Hertzberg (ed.), *The Zionist Idea* (Garden City, N. Y., 1959), especially p. 29f. See also Isaiah Berlin, "Jewish Slavery and Emancipation," *Forum for the Problems of Zionism, World Jewry and the State of Israel*, No. 1 (Jerusalem; December, 1953), pp. 52-68, and Arthur Koestler, *Promise and Fulfilment* (London, 1949), pp. 332-35.

42. The best short statement is Ben Halpern, *The American Jew* (New York, 1956).

JOSEPH L. BLAU

Alternatives Within Contemporary American Judaism

I

Two ACCOUNTS of Judaism misrepresent its history. One, the usual non-Jewish account, sees Judaism, in Arnold Toynbee's term, as a "fossil" faith, a religion that had its normal historical development before 70 A.D., but that has merely remained on earth, without vitality or significance, since the fall of Jerusalem. The other, the account often heard from Jewish traditionalists, maintains that Judaism developed through the rabbinic period to about the tenth century A.D., when its form was fixed and not subject to modification. Neither of these versions can adequately explain the contemporary vitality and the variety of alternatives open to those who regard themselves as living representatives of the oldest religious tradition of the Western world.

This polymorphous Judaism is not easy to define. But, then, none of the major religions of the world is easy to characterize exactly. Those religions to which we refer as "major" have persisted through long periods of time, have spread over large areas of the earth, and have attracted and held the devotion of many adherents. In order to serve the needs of many people under diverse conditions of time and place, a religion must be flexible enough to be an adequate guide to living in multifarious situations, but still maintain its essential stability. The amount of change that may be necessary to preserve the relevance of a religion to any particular situation is not always the same. Indeed, there may be periods in the history of any religion in which only negligible variations occur. Even in eras of major changes, the symbols of the religion may remain unchanged, but the meanings borne by the symbols, the interpretations put upon the symbols, the understandings conveyed by the symbols are ever in flux. Man's religions are constant chiefly in their mutability.

These general remarks are especially valid for Judaism because there have been few periods of relative calm in the history of Judaism. The wandering Jew may be a legend; wandering Judaism is a fact. Wherever in history one starts to use the word "Judaism," the record reveals unstable living conditions and an insecure people, moving about in semi-nomadism or passively shifted by the changing fortunes of empires. With each change of cultural scene, new varieties of Judaism developed, each one incorporating some part of the age-old traditions of the people called Jews and some part of the culture and traditions of their current environment. The history of Judaism, seen from this perspective, is a history of creative cultural synthesis.

In addition to these special crisis-producing shocks sustained more often by Judaism than by other religions, there have been times when the culture of the whole Western world has been in upheaval. The Jews, as one element in this culture, have shared in the general crisis of the times. In periods such as these, all the religions of the Western world, including Judaism, have had to seek an adjustment to novel conditions or to lapse into irrelevance and disappear. Judaism has not disappeared; and thus it has repeatedly demonstrated its adaptability. What it is that has not disappeared—what "Judaism" is—cannot, however, be easily identified or precisely defined.

No one has the right to pronounce authoritatively on what Judaism is today in the United States of America or at any other time or place in its history. There is no criterion within Judaism for orthodoxy or heterodoxy; one recent writer has used the term *polydoxy* to describe Judaism. The only way to answer the question "What is Judaism?" is by enumerating and describing its current varieties. In present-day American Judaism, as in the Judaism of all times and places, there are a number of varieties that differ considerably from one another and from earlier forms of Judaism. The adherents of each of these varieties call their own version "Judaism," and sometimes deny others the right to the name. In addition, both in the general community and among Jews themselves, "Judaism" is used as the name of the class constituted by these various forms.

What, then, is Judaism? It is a name for the many expressions of the spiritual life of those men and women in any place and at any time who regard themselves as Jews. Any one of these expressions may try to move toward a claim to exclusiveness by using its patterns of belief and practice as the criterion of what Judaism is. In our more objective view, however, we are pushed to a more inclusive criterion. Instead of using one form of Judaism as a Procrustean standard for the spiritual life of the Jews, we must use the multi-faceted spiritual life of the Jews as the standard of Judaism.

I *am not* asserting that the many versions of Judaism today do not look back upon a common tradition, both literary and historical; I *am* asserting, however, that the tradition itself is not now, and was not at the times of its expression, a monolith. I *am not* asserting that there is no set of symbols common to all the varieties of Judaism —God, Torah, the people Israel, the Holy Land, Messianism; I *am* asserting that the relative values, the weights assigned to these symbols, differ from age to age and from place to place, and in any one age and place, from group to group. I *am* asserting that the divergent interpretations placed upon these symbols have enabled Judaism to survive the repeated shocks of Jewish history within world history.

The assertion, made all too frequently by Jews as well as non-Jews, that there is one and only one classical form of Judaism is altogether false. There has never been a time in the long history of the spiritual life of the Jewish people when differing varieties of Judaism have not co-existed. There has never been a single universal authority or authoritative body competent to fix the norms of belief or of practice. To use a phrase which has unfortunately become somewhat hackneyed, Jewish life has always manifested "cultural pluralism."

Yet this is not the whole story, for each of the variant interpretations of Judaism, in the time and place of its occurrence, is not merely a random and haphazard emergent, born by chance out of the vagrant thought processes of some charismatic eccentric. It is, rather, the result of an unconscious desire to make the age-old tradition of Judaism sustain a revitalized relevance to the particular conditions of that time and place. The differing interpretations of any one age are, in effect, competing claims on the part of their proponents to be able to serve their adherents most effectively as guides to living. And one does not merely live in the same way in all places at all times without regard to environing conditions; one lives in a context of spatial, temporal, and cultural factors. To serve effectively, an interpretation of Judaism must demonstrate its capacity to focus some aspects of tradition on a current context.

II

The last two hundred years of Jewish history have been especially productive of new interpretations of Judaism, and the Jews of the United States today seem to be receptive to all of them. The reason for the multiplication of varieties, I would suggest, is that the Jews, particularly those of the United States, have been facing simultaneously both the internal crisis of trying to adjust to new conditions of Jewish existence and the general Western crisis of adjusting to the world of modernity. The Jewish situation has been aggravated by a third factor,which might be called a shift in the center of gravity of Jewish existence from a single European focus to a dual one—Israeli and American. Much of the pessimism about Jewish survival is plausible because of the number of challenges that must be met at one time.

The crisis of modernity is shared by the Jews and their non-Jewish neighbors. To the modern mind, religion is peripheral and personal rather than central and social. Judaism in the nineteenth and twentieth centuries has been faced with the need to rethink its own nature in terms of a surrounding environment in which religious affiliation has more and more been regarded as a voluntary individual choice. Total rejection of this environment, while possible, would have involved a rejection of the many individual benefits that have accrued to modern Jews as a consequence of the modern mood; total acceptance of the notion of a completely individualized and open choice of religious affiliation might well have meant the complete disappearance of Judaism. The problem has been one of finding compromise positions suitable to the differing speeds of modernization in the various countries in which Jews live.

Generally, the period starting about 1790 is one in which the political barriers between the Jews and the peoples among whom they lived have tended to be eliminated. The Jews have been emancipated, have become "citizens" rather than "resident aliens." Public careers that were previously closed to Jewish talents have opened up —not everywhere at the same speed, but almost everywhere to some extent. Secular education is far more readily available to Jews than ever before. Even advanced professional training is far more open; the last forty years have seen the virtual disappearance of the *numerus clausus* in European universities and of the equivalent "Jewish quota" at American universities. In many countries, the twentieth century has been marked by a centrality of the Jewish literary figure in the culture of the country. This interesting phenomenon, the subject of a recent study by Irving Malin for the American literary scene, is not by any means unique to America; it has happened in Poland, in Austria, in Czechoslovakia, in pre-Hitler Germany, and to some extent in Russia. Its early stages can even now be detected in England. Jews have come to great prominence in the sciences, and even in engineering, which forty years ago was regarded as a field not open to Jews. These last two hundred years might be described as the time in which the Jews have come out of the ghetto and into the world. They have done so by invitation. In the world into which they have come, men are judged, by and large, on their individual achievements and not on such factors as ethnic origin or religion, which the modern world in theory considers irrelevant—most of the time. Needless to say, there is not the same openness in the social world as there is in the economic, scientific, or political worlds. The new, relatively open society places the burden of proof on the individual; individual Jews no longer compete only against their fellow Jews for the prominent places in the small, enclosed community of Jews; now they are in competition with non-Jews as well.

There is another side to this picture, however; for the discovery of the modern world has meant the need to take a fresh look, re-inforced by the modern physical and social sciences, and grounded in contemporary concepts of intellectual methods and Western notions of aesthetics and morality, at Jewish tradition itself. This is often referred to as a crisis of Jewish identity, but to call it this makes the whole problem one of individual response. It suggests that now, as each American Jew lives the greater part of his life outside of the Jewish tradition, he must inevitably question the remaining fragmentary relation that he has to the Jewish tradition. I would not want to underemphasize this aspect of the problem. Only a few years ago, *Commentary* magazine polled a group of younger Jewish intellectual leaders on the influence their Jewish background, their relation to the Jewish heritage, had had on their development. Overwhelmingly they answered that it had had little or no influence. But this merely points up the social or communal problem of the contemporary crisis in Judaism, for in earlier days the most talented, the most able, the potential and actual leaders among the Jews had perforce to find outlets for their talents within the Jewish community. Their strength re-inforced the Jewish community. As the potential leaders of quality increasingly find the fields for their talent outside the Jewish community in the wider world, internal leadership falls into the hands of the less able, the less original, the less inspiring. At the very time when the most gifted are needed for the reshaping of the Jewish tradition to the modern world, their efforts and their energies are to a very large extent directed elsewhere. In every previous period of Jewish crisis, there were leaders of genius to guide the perplexed. Today's reformulation of tradition must be accomplished more democratically. The democratic experience of the Jewish group in America must become the model of reconstruction for Jews all over the world.

Surely it is obvious that a people that has suffered at least as much as any other people in the world from the conditions of life created by totalitarian governments, especially in Central and in Eastern Europe, should be the first to reject totalitarianism and to receive warmly the notion of a pluralistic, diversified, democratic model for Jewish life. This would certainly be the case if men were as rational in judging their own situation as they are in judging the affairs of others. But, of course, men are most irrational precisely at the point where they themselves are most involved. So during this historical era, when the crying need is for the proposal and experimental practice of as many divergent forms of Jewish life as possible, the pressure for religious uniformity has cropped up within the Jewish world—in the United States as well as in Israel and in England.

In many respects, the Israeli case is the most devastating, because so large a part of the present Israeli population is composed of refugees from the intolerable burden of totalitarianism. Yet, in Israel, since the days of the British mandate, they face the totalitarianism of a state-supported religion that is attempting to impose upon the entire community the views of one fractional fragment, and that a very small one. The situation is comparable to what would exist in the United States if rules for the entire spectrum of Protestant denominations, from the Unitarian-Universalists on the religious left to the most fundamentalist sectarians on the right, were to be officially placed under the control of the Fundamentalists.

III

Whatever has been the case in the rest of the world during these past two centuries of adaptation to modernity, the United States of America and its people have had a special situation to face. First, there were few or no survivals of earlier forms of cultural and social patterning that had to be overcome in order to confront the crisis of modernity. There was no hierarchy. Feudal patterns of tenure barely penetrated the colonies. There were no discriminatory laws handed down from time immemorial. The openness of the situation in the New World allowed a far more rapid adaptation to modern conditions than was the case in any of the old countries. Second, there were, from the beginning of European settlement, many "old countries." The American population, Jewish and non-Jewish alike, came from many different backgrounds and brought along many different types of cultural baggage. Uniformity of any sort was correspondingly more difficult to establish. Third, until relatively recent times, immigration was a continuing process. Each new wave of arrivals brought with it enough differences to prevent the growth of a common pattern.

Consequently, no single "American" version of Judaism has been developed. There have been many attempts, from 1840 to the present day, to introduce some overarching form of communal control in American Jewish life as a first step toward achieving religious uniformity. Some of the outstanding leaders of nineteenth-century American Judaism, like Isaac M. Wise and Isaac Leeser, have tried to work toward centralized control, in the hope of instituting what Wise called a *"minhag* Amerika"—a specifically American constellation of Jewish customs and ceremonies. These efforts, even when led by men of the highest caliber, have failed because in every case there were enough advocates of diversity to frustrate those who sought uniformity. This is not to deny that the Jews of the United States have, from time to time, acted as a virtual unit. Unity and uniformity are different concepts. The occasional unity has, however, come at times when there was a threat to Judaism, to the Jews, or to the State of Israel. It is a "foul weather" unity; when the sun comes out, each group goes its own way again.

The organization of Judaism in the United States is to a considerable extent accidental. In Europe the basic form of organization was the community; within the community, the governing body set up synagogues, hired their functionaries, established schools, and created the necessary philanthropic institutions. In the United States, there were no Jewish communal organizations to undertake these needed functions. Furthermore, the basic pattern of religious organization was Protestant Congregationalism. The Jewish Americans slipped into this Protestant way of organizing themselves, partly because the Protestant way was incorporated into the laws of various states and partly because it was a simpler form of organization for the small Jewish population. The synagogue rather than the community became the focal organization of American Jewish life. This, too, fed the pattern of diversity. Any group of ten or more adult Jews could constitute themselves a synagogue and maintain, both in their directly religious activities and in the religious education of their children, whatever combination of traditional ideas and new or old interpretations they chose.

As a result of these various operative accidents, there are many options available to the Jew in the United States today. It is not merely that there are three major organized movements within contemporary American Judaism. None of these movements has been successful, even within its own affiliates, in fixing a uniform pattern. The three large organizations are federations only; their powers are merely advisory, and their advice is not always taken by their constituent synagogues. In addition, other lesser groups maintain independence from the three large organizations; many of these independent groups claim to be the true "saving remnant," the hope of the future. Individual synagogues, since they are dependent only on the good will and generosity of their members, can also stand aloof and follow their own ways, or, as in the recent case of New York's Temple Emanuel, secede from the corporate body in the wake of some disagreement of principle or policy. Judaism in the United States has been almost completely "Protestantized."

Each of the major organizational groupings represents a range of alternatives rather than a single direction. Among the synagogues affiliated with the Reform movement, there are some whose pattern, set in the late nineteenth century, resembles that of Unitarian churches and whose stated beliefs have more in common with Humanist associations than with rabbinic Judaism. Other synagogues with the same affiliation retain many of the older patterns of traditional behavior and belief and seem closer to historic forms of Judaism than some congregations with Conservative affiliations. Reform Judaism learned early in its history that full Sabbath observance was impossible under the conditions of American life and flirted with the notion of switching the chief service of the week to Sunday morning. This went too far; so an alternative was developed: A non-traditional form of service on Friday evening became the major weekly religious exercise, centering in a sermon or sermon-substitute, such as a forum, a panel, or a review of current affairs from a Jewish point of view. This innovation proved successful and has been adopted by Conservative congregations, and even by some that call themselves Orthodox. Similarly, the Reform group pioneered in translating the liturgy into vernacular modern languages, first German, and later English; Conservative groups followed this pioneering effort, but retained rather more Hebrew in their services. Orthodox congregations have not accepted this innovation. Meantime, with the development in Israel of a modern Hebrew language, Conservative educational institutions began to lay stress on the study of Hebrew as a living tongue. In the last few years, Reform groups have intensified their study of modern Hebrew.

Recently, on the fringes of the Reform movement, an explicitly humanistic Jewish synagogue has been founded in Birmingham, Michigan, by a relatively youthful and well-educated group under the leadership of an able, young ordained rabbi. There has been some grumbling among other Reform groups in the area, especially from older Reform synagogues in Detroit, but the attempt to exclude this humanistic group from the organizational fold is abating. Within the Conservative movement, the Reconstructionist wing has been in existence for forty years and has seemed almost as explicitly humanistic in its conceptions, though considerably less so in its language. The Reform movement, theoretically the more radical, took a generation longer to produce its version of humanistic Judaism than did the Conservative movement.

At the other extreme of Conservatism, there are congregations whose practice conforms to Orthodox standards in every respect except that their rabbis are graduates of the Jewish Theological Seminary of America rather than of one of the Orthodox training schools. The range of practice among Conservative groups is very wide. This is, perhaps, understandable, because it is a middle-of-every-road position. Generally speaking, although even here there are exceptions, the Conservative rabbinical organization is more traditionally oriented than the Conservative lay organization, so that the range is evident even at the level of central organizational statements. It is still true, though less so now than a few years ago, that most of the rabbis associated with the Conservative movement were brought up in Orthodox homes. On the other hand, much of the rapidly growing lay base of the movement consists of people who have come to the movement out of a non-Orthodox and often a non-religious background. This contrast between the rabbis and the laity in the Conservative movement accounts for my having once described Conservative Judaism as "a movement in which rabbis who are a shade to the left of Orthodoxy minister to congregations a shade to the right of Reform."

Orthodox Judaism is perhaps even more fragmented than Reform or Conservative Judaism since there is now a clear and visible split among the Orthodox who reject all participation in ecumenical discussion, those who limit their willingness to enter into such discussions to matters of common social and civic concern, and those who participate with cautious reservations. Moreover, there are differences of practice among Orthodox groups, based ultimately on varying customs in the different countries of Europe from which the members or their parents or grandparents migrated. Finally, we should not forget that the Hassidic (pietistic) movement has recently experienced considerable growth in the United States. Ordinarily one might regard the Hassidim as an Orthodox group, but they would themselves reject this identification. In addition, we should note that Hassidism is not itself a unified movement but rather a loose designation for a variety of often mutually antagonistic groups.

I do not deplore this fragmentation. On the contrary, I welcome it enthusiastically. I find in diversity evidence of the continued creative force in Judaism and of its continued vitality. Diversity is an indication of strength, not of weakness. It is an indication of life, of vitality, of interest, of concern. Uniformity will kill the vital interest of Jews in Judaism—if anything can kill it.

All the current varieties of Judaism are, then, to my mind, legitimate examples of living Judaism. Each is a valiant attempt to produce a synthesis of ancient traditions and present-day knowledge that will hold the allegiance of the mature and attract the devotion of the immature. The Orthodox and modern Orthodox groups may differ in the degree to which they will attend to present-day knowledge, but they agree in making the symbol of Torah, representing the element of continuity, primary to Judaism and central to their definition of a Jew. A Jew is one who manifests his adherence to Judaism by being "Torah-true." Torah itself is not, of course, an absolute fixity or a single, consistent code. Under proper and specified conditions, rabbinic courts can modify Torah by interpretation in our age as they have in past ages. The Conservative and Reconstructionist groups may differ in their readiness to modify traditional liturgies to adapt them to modern situations, but they agree in making the symbol of the people of Israel, *klal yisrael*, "Catholic Israel" as Solomon Schechter called it, primary. Schechter went so far as to say, "The norm as well as the sanction of Judaism is the practice actually in vogue. Its consecration is the consecration of general use, or in other words, of Catholic Israel." In this way, he suggested that what is Torah for any age and any place is what the Jews of that time and place are willing to do and to believe. Instead of making the definition of "Jew" depend on "Torah," Schechter made the definition of "Torah" depend on "Jew." Mordecai M. Kaplan made an even more explicit statement when he said that "Judaism is the folk religion of the Jewish people." Needless to say, the Jewish people, *klal yisrael,* is not an absolute fixity. The opinions of people can and do change as their life experiences change.

Reform Judaism is, in a way, the most difficult of the major movements to characterize, chiefly because in the first state of its development in the nineteenth century it largely denied all the central traditional symbols of Judaism and tried to define itself without reference to nationality or ethnic origin. One might say that for this rationalistic period of Reform, the temple became the central symbol. A Jew, then, might be defined as one who went to temple instead of going to church—but equally a Reform Jew didn't go to *shul.* Torah was de-emphasized by placing stress on the prophetic books of the Bible over against the legal sections and by denying the authority of the rabbinic literature. Customs and ceremonies that had served for centuries to hold the Jewish people together despite their differences of opinion were either totally rejected or made voluntary and optional. More recently, Reform Judaism has entered a new phase of its development in which many of the older symbols and customs have been recalled from oblivion, and some, at least, of the extremes of the early Reform movement have been eliminated. It is still too soon, however, to know what finally will be the direction of twentieth-century Reform Judaism.

The seeming swing toward a more Conservative stance among Reform Jews and the emergence of an Orthodox and even a Hassidic youth movement are perhaps attributable to the holocaust of the Hitler years. The emancipation of the Jews in the nineteenth century held out great hopes for full Jewish participation in an ongoing modern society, and the Jews of the nineteenth century responded warmly to the implied invitation. Especially in the United States, the process of Jewish acculturation was carried on enthusiastically, particularly under the three-faith interpretation of American society. Since Hitler, however, one can see, in addition to the continuing acculturation process, evidence of what Robert Redfield called "contra-acculturation." As Redfield defined this counterprocess, it involves a deliberate attempt to retain the older cultural heritage, partly as a compensation for inferior status, and partly as a badge of distinction to gain prestige in one's own group. We might add that, among Orthodox Jewish youth, contra-acculturation involves a testing of American pretensions. "All right," these young people seem to be saying, "you claim that this is an open, prejudice-free society. Let's just see how far this openness goes when it is confronted with a visible badge of difference."

Howard Brotz, in his excellent study, *The Black Jews of Harlem*, suggests that there is a tension in the Negro community "between the quest for autonomy—moral, cultural, political—of the American Negro as a people or a community *and* the quest for the right to be integrated as individuals into a multiracial, universalistic society." On, I think, a more sophisticated level, a similar tension is apparent among Jews. The emancipation that yielded such rich fruits to individual Jews, who were integrated as individuals into a universalistic society, was harmful, if not disastrous, to the Jewish community. American Judaism today, in its myriad forms, incorporates the desire to restore moral, cultural, and social autonomy to the Jewish community without relinquishing the blessings of integration of individuals into the general society, without the imposition of uniformity, and without giving up any of the advantages to Judaism of its being considered one of America's three great faiths. If this effort is successful, it will be the climax to a most creative age in the history of Judaism.

There is another alternative open to Jews in contemporary America—the alternative of remaining culturally and ethnically Jewish but holding aloof from the organized religious activities of their fellow Jews. In the absence of adequate statistical data, it is impossible to say precisely how large a group of American Jews have availed themselves of this option. To judge their number by the complaints of synagogue officials, the "unsynagogued" constitute a substantial segment of the Jewish population. One cannot talk of this class as having left the Jewish community. They are still very much a part of Jewry in their own minds. Many are leading figures in Jewish communal and charitable associations and are even held in high esteem by their fellow Jews for their services in such causes. We might define the "religion" of the "unsynagogued" by saying that they have substituted Jewishness for Judaism. This definition distinguishes the unsynagogued Jew from the totally assimilated Jew, who rejects Jewishness as well as Judaism.

In expressing their religious zeal and satisfying their spiritual needs through social welfare, ethical activities, cultural creativity, and even political participation in causes of concern to the Jewish community and to the society in general, the unsynagogued pose both a threat and a challenge to the affiliated Jews. In an age such as ours, when the dominant motivations of life are secular and this-worldly, the way of expressing religious dedication through secular service will prove increasingly attractive to the young with consequent loss of membership, income, and prestige to the synagogues. The synagogues must come to do as much for the service of society as the non-synagogal organizations. Certainly from the age of the eighth-century prophets of righteousness, and perhaps even earlier, the theme of social justice has been a major element in the Judaic complex. To many people today the preaching of social justice seems the only *raison d'être* for religious organizations and the striving for social justice the only meaningful form of religiously motivated practice.

Yet it is very hard for the well-established institution, religious or otherwise, to keep such a vision constantly before itself. Pious platitudes are much easier to produce than the self-sacrifice without which there can be no real results. The unsynagogued challenge the synagogues and their members to live their ethical pretensions, under pain of losing touch with Jewish youth if they fail the test. In the hierarchy of traditional Jewish conceptions of philanthropy, there is a level beyond that of charitable giving (*zedakah*)—the level of charitable living (*gemiluth hasadim*). The unsynagogued challenge the members of synagogues of all degrees of traditionalism to aspire to this level. In maintaining this challenge, Jewish moralism presents itself as one among many alternative ways of preserving Judaism in contemporary America.

SISTER MARIE AUGUSTA NEAL

Catholicism in America

RESTLESSNESS CHARACTERIZES Catholicism in America at the present moment, a restlessness experienced as apathy by some, as rebellion by others, and as great expectation by still others. This great expectation is in response to new discoveries: of the goodness of the world, of people, of interpersonal encounters; of the task of making a better world; of the possibility of freedom. It is reflected in the joyous celebration of the new liturgy, joyousness that even borders on the raucous at times and that suggests tremendous release. This release, experienced by some with new wonder and associated with the presence of the Spirit in the sense of a conversion, is concomitantly viewed, if not experienced, by others as the dangerous removal of the cover of Pandora's box, allowing for the uninhibited expression of man's base impulses to affection and aggression uncontrolled by custom or intellectual discipline. This latter kind of response focuses on other realities just as much a part of the present situation as the turn to the world. It is a reaction to the affectively-toned and sweeping criticisms of old, established institutions and organizations through which the Catholic Church has been doing its work in America for the past century, namely, the parochial school system, the parish, the diocesan structure for work and authority among the clergy, the societies of laymen and laywomen, the seminary, the prayer forms, and even the basic meaning of belief. These criticisms, mainly by members of the laity, religious women, and non-administrative clergy, are perceived as dangerous, unfair, and sweeping by some, as valid and useful by others. Many segments of the traditional Church in America, reflected in the local city parish, especially in the ethnic ghetto, are not caught up in the new excitement but, because of its press, must respond to it. The response by those not caught up in the celebration of the new finding of Christ in the world is often severe; it is expressed in a whole range of reactions which may involve anything from restriction of freedom to character attack. These reactions, in turn, elicit expressions of impatience and something close to despair by those who fear that the resisters to change will allow the whole system to become irrelevant through a commitment to signs and customs that no longer speak a meaningful message to the world. These, briefly, are the extremes of a continuum of actions and reactions that characterize the restlessness of the Catholic Church in America at this moment. Their analysis is complex and intricate. A wealth of material exists from which some general lines of explanation may be attempted.[1]

Historical sequence, situational factors, and personality predispositions arising from child-training, and environmental influences such as living apart in ethnic enclaves are a few of the complexities accounting for the different responses to similar or at least related stimuli. They explain the range of response from joyous expectation to anxiety and fear. That the current loosening of old rules may result in the destruction of the entire system of Catholicism or, at least, that segment of it to which one is most deeply committed, is widely believed. The Mass, the Douay version of the Bible, the rosary, devotion to the Blessed Virgin Mary and the Blessed Sacrament, the novena, the retreat, the horarium of a religious community, the religious habit, the Knights of Columbus, the sodality, Sunday school, even Canon Law, the Sacred Congregation in Rome, command-obedience relations in religious orders of men and women, celibacy, institutional ownership, and the long-taught and long-accepted modes of interpersonal relations all suddenly come up simultaneously for re-evaluation. What makes the Catholic situation unique is that its central authority-structure allows that all levels and types of renewal can be stimulated at one time only when an ecumenical council convenes, runs it course, and promulgates to the whole world a new program.[2] The titles of the recent Council documents show a basic and complex range of concerns addressed by the Church in the process of *aggiornamento*. The entire gamut of structural forms is included in the re-appraisal: creed, code, cult; role relations of bishops, priests, religious, and laity; relations with other churches; training, education and mode of expression.[3]

The most striking characteristic of the response to pressures to change is its apparently dichotomous style. The words used to describe the response are familiar to everyone: liberal and conservative. In this context, "liberal" refers to the "great expectations" orientation viewed by the conservative as a naïve unawareness of what man uncontrolled by custom will do when his blind passions are given free expression. "Conservative" is the label applied to those who cherish familiar forms, who plead to go slowly, who seek to introduce changes gradually, and who, in extreme cases, would retain all that is familiar and comfortable in the very recent past because it is good or at least harmless. Both the liberal and the conservative responses are more complex than the distinction implies. Openness to change for interest reasons determines a different set of responses than does openness to change for value reasons. The same is true for resistance to change. At the present moment basic values are frequently involved as determiners of choice but the very pressure of this more self-conscious belief commitment elicits many defensive and unconscious reactions. New theological orientations are more readily available as directives for choice than they were in earlier periods. Their very availability and pressure for social reform explain the current restlessness.[4]

When these two responses—liberal and conservative—selected to some degree because of their congeniality to personality temperament, begin to interact with the exigencies of the current situation, the present patterns characterizing Catholicism merge. Examples are many: the accelerated flow out of the established institutions— seminaries, convents, parochial schools and organizations like the Council of Catholic Men—of persons like Charles Davis and Jacqueline Grennan[5]; the serious re-evaluation of present structures evident in the planning programs for the reconstruction of Canon Law (Fall, 1966); international sociology meetings on the changing role of the clergy (Summer, 1967); a national survey of religious orders for women sponsored by the Conference of Major Religious Superiors of Women's Institutes (Spring, 1967); the widening of lay control in Catholic organizations indicated in periodic news releases of Catholic colleges and universities like Webster College, Notre Dame, Fordham, Marquette, and Catholic University; the assembling of the National Catholic Educational Association to assess the school system (Fall, 1967); and the re-organization of the conference of bishops (Winter, 1967). Other events characterizing the *aggiornamento* include the multiplication of workshops and institutes to review catechetical materials and to plan total rewriting of teaching programs in religious studies not only to mention but to make central the event of encounter with man in his existential situation.

For the third time in eighty years the Catholic Church in America has encountered pressure from its membership to turn from a transcendent to a worldly emphasis. This movement promises to have a more permanent effect than earlier ones. Each of the movements was stimulated by a papal directive, but the earlier two, in the 1890's and the 1930's, had a less articulated value directive as a guide to choice and as legitimation for action. Pope Leo XIII's encyclical on the condition of the working man in 1890 and Pope Pius XI's *On the Reconstruction of the Social Order* in 1930 did not have the theological backing that the Council documents enjoy. At those times, Catholicism was still too other-world-oriented in practice and belief to take these messages as immediate directives for large-scale action. The evidence suggests that the current turn to the world has been so re-inforced by value exploration at several levels of abstraction and by authorization from various echelons of social power that it defines a new course which will result in basic structural changes. Sudden cessation of old styles occurs as structures lose their meaning and usefulness. The building of large training complexes for seminarians and novices is a case in point. Ten years ago, such establishments were the focus of much administrative energy. Today, their usefulness is questioned, and the problem of how to use them effectively is a major issue. The large centralized training centers made sense in the context of an efficient production system to bring Christ to the world, characteristic of Church planning a decade ago. It makes less sense when the Church is defined as "a pilgrim people" finding Christ in the world.

This transition happened so rapidly that personal affections did not have time to de-cathect old forms and move toward new ones except in persons in the vanguard of the toward-the-world movement, persons with a well-developed meaning system giving direction to their psychic energy to move out of the old structures and to adopt new ones. Some analysis of the trends allowing for and encouraging this transition raise the basic question of what determines the direction of history: functional necessity, divine intervention in the form of a prophet, a value system already operating for creative development in society, conflict among interest groups, or a complex combination of these.

The efforts of Catholic priests to organize labor in the 1930's, liturgical experiments by the Benedictines and the Religious of the Sacred Heart in the 1920's, the establishment of the Catholic Interracial Councils in the early 1930's, and the founding of the Catholic Association for International Peace (with its active college segment) in the late 1930's were programs parallel in theme to current pressures to change. But they were too disparate and segmented to make more than a temporary ripple on the surface of an institutionalized system whose value emphasis and normative patterns saw these works as good but of supererogation. The traditional other-worldly orientation of the Church in its religious programs was paralleled by the Church's continuing involvement in the world as another powerful interest group. Criticism and protest were interpreted as deviation from established structure. Efforts toward renewal of the social order, encouraged by Pius XI's encyclical, *On the Reconstruction of the Social Order*, were a response to the social action orientation of Communist programs and, like them, were frequently cast in an authoritarian mode. A theology of social justice was not yet in vogue because the religious message accompanying these new efforts still reflected the dichotomy of the Church and the world. Even so, responses were limited to a few specialists and informal control curtailed large-scale efforts.[6]

Activities of this time included historically-oriented biblical studies, the movement to make the liturgy more community-oriented, civil rights work, peace meetings, and ecumenical dialogue. But these efforts were so segmented and out of line with the more pervasive other-worldly orientation of belief and the ghetto orientation of behavior of the wider Catholic community that even they could be tolerated with little fear of change. The limited action program of the 1930's, however, differed from that of the 1890's. Then explicit condemnation followed the agitation over the Americanist heresy.[7] The kind of activity that is part of the current turn to the world, especially the ecumenical dimension and the involvement in social reform, was seen in the nineteenth century as too secular to be given formal Church support. They were, in fact, in an indirect way formally condemned as heresy. Today, the thrust of social action efforts from the 1890's and the 1930's has reached a point of no return despite the cautious resistance to precipitous involvement in the secular order. The pressure of representatives of the Catholic Church at Selma, in the peace protests, at the population institutes, as well as at the early ecumenical dialogues with Protestants and Jews and at the experimental educational conferences, were external manifestations of ferment in the Church, a breaking away from the image of the Church as a part of the Establishment. As in earlier periods, Catholics initiating social action were treated as deviants, accused of being unholy and worldly, relieved of some of their institutional privileges and, sometimes, of their rights. Though allowed freedom to continue their commitments, they were often forced to accept psychological isolation from their peers, a mechanism of rejection used to effect social control over the deviant by closing him off from the intimate relationships permitted the conformist, thereby subjecting the deviant to character attack or treatment as an oddity. This phenomenon, so well demonstrated by Solomon Asch in the early 1950's, is usually quite effective in repressing a minority effort to reform because the human spirit can endure only a limited amount of isolation unless it has a charisma for antinomianism. It renders the witness powerless for social reform though he remains effective as a model for individual protest with a certain dignity and reverence.[8] The very behaviors that were condemned ten years ago, however, are defined today in many places as legitimate social action, and even as the better way. The Church at the periphery of the city and in small towns is still very much the Church of the ethnic immigrant. It is characterized by a separatist orientation to the world. This situation no longer has the moral approval that it had twenty years ago. New doctrinal emphasis defines the closed community as less holy, as un-Christ-like. This new definition creates some problems of restlessness for the ethnic ghetto-dweller, once rewarded for living apart.

Simply to describe the Catholic Church in America today as an immigrant Church moving into suburbia is to miss several dimensions of the complexity of process. Actually, the current restlessness in the American Church has interlocking roots in at least three historical movements: the evolution of religion in Western history, the development of Catholicism in response to the Protestant reformation, and the growth of American Catholicism within American society. The wider context of religion and Western history requires the consideration of the following propositions. The present restlessness arises out of the dialectic at the heart of Christianity—the great commandment to love God and neighbor. Throughout history one or the other of these great loves has been reflected in style swings. The early Christians prayed and lived as a unit in generous self-giving so that those who knew them exclaimed, "How these Christians love one another." They were responding directly to the gospel injunction: "By this shall all men know you are my disciples if you have a great love for one another." The model of loving membership found in the gospel displayed a unique tension which distinguished its communal form from that of its tribal neighbors: its openness to the neighbor or, better, to the stranger who was to be welcome in his own cultural style. The Gentiles were not forced to accept Jewish customs.[9] By the fourth century, however, the desert-dweller, who withdrew to be holy, reflected a dominant style of Christian life. Later, Benedictine monks returned to the community, in contrast to the desert-dweller who experienced his love of God by removing himself from the organized society. The monastery of the sixteenth century had become a place apart from the town with a special kind of holiness. The Reformation called for a return of the asceticism of the monastery to the market place. It emphasized the spiritual dimension of every man's work as a calling to salvation.[10] Since the Reformation, Catholicism in its spirituality has tended to take on more of an other-worldly aspect and to make private charity its form of social service. Protestantism became the locus of a more this-world-oriented Christianity with stress on public service and self-conscious individualism. This theme will be taken up presently in a discussion of how Catholicism has responded to Protestantism. Before discussing this, however, there is one other point in the dialectic of Western culture to consider: the love and power theme that runs through so much of Western literature, art, and religion.[11]

The love and power dimensions of human interpersonal experience are necessary in the structure of any social relationship possessing permanence; they relate to the maintenance of group life. The first assures the psychic energy that stimulates the membership to want to stay together. The second assures the organization to work to some specific goal. Power is evident as an independent variable if one focuses on the divisions existing in the present restlessness between those with power and those without power, namely, the higher clergy on the one hand, and the laity, religious, and lower clergy on the other. It is among the latter that the expressions of dissent are clearest and that action is most productive. The turn to the world has disturbed the established affection and command style of family roles. The decision-makers in a hierarchical system not only have been defined as fathers and mothers, but also as generals and potentates. The affective bonds defining family-relation terms generate some of the ambivalence, and the whole Jansenistic tradition imposes complexities.[12] This dialectic is at work to change the Church in the areas of command-obedience relations, social responsibility, independence training, respect for the intellectual life, and motivational awareness.[13] The moment is propitious for breaking through institutional forms. By responding to the demands of task and maintenance and the process of cultural lag, conflict of interest and repression of interpersonal affect have created a system too rigid to respond to current exigencies. In broadest terms, the structural differentiation of religion from family and polity, along with the specialization of function characteristic of a modern technologically-based economy, requires that any social system formed before these new divisions of labor became necessary realign its rules of behavior to fit new role expectations. The authority style of the Catholic Church, grounded as it is in the style of the patriarchal family and medieval potentate, is today pressed to re-adjust to technology, to universal education, and to other such modern institutions. The Church in America, therefore, reacts to these pressures, but in the context peculiar to America. The Church, with the charisma of grace, is, as a value-bearing system, re-affirming its basic commitment to love of God and neighbor. It is reforming its rules of procedure to realize more effectively this commitment, free from historically-developed power structures that in the interplay of affection and power became focused on the privileged few to the exclusion of the needy many.

There are, of course, alternate explanations to the power-affection dialectic. A very compelling alternate hypothesis describes the same situation quite differently. It describes religion as an early stage in the process of secularization through which the unknown and frightening was canalized into ancestor-worship by making the gods extensions of the living-together group, the family or tribe. The gods were introduced to reduce anxiety and to make the world more understandable. All this is now giving way, the hypothesis continues, since man's greater knowledge of material realities makes the need for churches established to deal with the unknown, now knowable, not only unnecessary but also anomalous. To proclaim God is dead is necessary so that man will realize what survival demands of him: that he plan his own future in this universe aware that no matter how lonely or frightening his experience and how manifest the acquisitiveness of man, unless he ceases drifting he will destroy himself and all others. The alternate explanation of what is happening includes an intermediate step—the Church's assumption of a State form in the Middle Ages. In Machiavellian terms, a religious belief system which controlled the energies of the peasants during that long period of necessary subjugation was functionally requisite for the survival of man. Shared power in uneasy balance allowed for the relatively effective emergence of modern technological order. But now, with the possibility of an economy of abundance for all, there is no need for formal Church-State relations.

This kind of Darwinian explanation fails to account for several dimensions of current reality: the creative spiritual component of religious doctrine, the reality base of modern man's anxieties in the face of new problems, the precariousness of life in an age dominated by technology, and the relevance of the specific doctrines of existing religious systems. The dialectic of love and power better addresses the human condition of man's historical tendency to use value systems to the advantage of his own specific interest group. Man tries to make his existential condition more predictable and secure by manipulating value systems introduced to direct him away from the status quo.

. Socialization, in this sense, has cycles. In *Religion and Culture*, Christopher Dawson says that all religions at their initial encounter act as agents for social change through the voice and message of the prophet. Christianity, Islam, and Protestantism all set lines for new cultural styles.[14] At other periods in their history, religions become the frame of those cultural styles. Because man, in the face of the unpredictable, tries to handle his anxiety by making his private world secure, the Church becomes a bastion of resistance to change in the styles it has fostered. Functional necessity or utilitarian trend in decision-making which calls for choices among available alternatives and under situational pressure is the context in which religion in the course of its development becomes secularized. To the degree that the institutionalized structure invented for some immediate need itself becomes sacralized, the functional autonomy of its use takes precedence over the realization of the religious values in a new historical setting. The limitations of this pragmatic process diminish the opportunities for man to express or realize his spiritual inspirations. Dissatisfaction with institutionalized forms of religious expression begins to be voiced and responded to by those experiencing the limitations, provided a creative content is available. Creative content is available in the Church at present, and through the Council many of the new theological themes are already legitimated. Current research on the relationship between belief and behavior in American religious orders for women gives substantial weight to this analysis.[15]

Within this description of the dialectic of the Church in Western culture, the response of the Catholic Church to the emergence of Protestantism in the sixteenth century was defensive. It focused on the other-worldly emphasis of faith as opposed to the Protestant this-worldly emphasis on an asceticism of the market place in religious practice. That this turn from the world had become extreme became evident when the Church tried to respond to the moral outrages of recent times. All the Churches failed to fulfill their proper function of passing moral judgment on the public act of the destruction of the Jews in Nazi Germany. They have been unable to stay the tide of racial prejudice since the riots of the late 1930's. The Church in America was immobile when confronted with the use of lethal weapons on the civilian population in World War II. Moral leadership was not forthcoming at the appropriate levels. This neutrality in the face of man's suffering demanded an explicit re-evaluation of the institutionalized patterns of training and behavior within the Church. That churchmen and laity failed to express a moral judgment on those acts of structured evil can be linked to several causes. Specifically, the moral commitment to help one's neighbor, so explicit in the Christian message, was impotent against public policy. Catholic doctrine, it appeared, did not focus on the conditions of the world as its primary point of emphasis. Institutionalized patterns of Catholic behavior allowed a Church founded on moral values which abhor anti-social behavior to tolerate genocide of the Jews, exploitation of the Negroes, violation of world peace, and discrimination in the local community. The Greeley-Rossi study of education of Catholics in America disclosed that there are "very weak" relationships between social consciousness and Catholic education at all levels and that the basic principle of social justice is not operating in the behavior of many Catholics.[16] Until very recently the principle that a man is responsible for the conditions of the world in which he lives was not a part of the value structure of many Catholics. The response of city politicians and businessmen to the conditions in the inner city in 1968 indicates that even now for the rank-and-file Catholic in many areas the principle of responsibility is still not widely known. Yet this principle is central to the belief system of Catholics. When the immediate focus was on the life hereafter, this principle was not explicit. The new theology, however, clearly focuses on the reform of the world.

The Pastoral Constitution on the Church in the Modern World had in its introduction a statement quite commonly accepted by social scientists but not as familiar in religious circles until recently: Man makes his own culture and is responsible for its moral component at any given moment in its history. For many centuries Catholics have acted as if the world and Christianity were two different systems requiring divorce rather than reconciliation. Emmanuel Cardinal Suhard described this orientation in 1946 when he noted for some Christians that it appears that "the duty of believers is not to influence events but to be simply true disciples of Christ in their private lives." [17] Although neither Catholics nor Protestants responded well to the moral exigencies of the 1930's, the causal factors appear to be different. Catholicism was locked in the ghettos of the United States while Protestantism had become a religion legitimizing private enterprise. Their simultaneous failures to respond have encouraged dialogue between the two groups. Although some overlap occurs in the pattern of response in general, Catholics allowed political life in their communities to remain outside the surveillance of religion, while Protestants worked in their milieu to legitimize the existing political structure. Both modes proved inadequate for encountering the moral issues in poverty, minority status, and war.

The emergence of Protestantism in the sixteenth century, its secularization of the monastic model, and its repudiation of the hierarchical structure of the Church, preferring an asceticism of the market place and a communal structure for public worship, were major factors in the continuation not only of the other-world emphasis in the Catholic Church but also of the growing tendency to leave all decisions about policy and social programming to the hierarchy.[18] The extent of this non-involvement and non-concern for the social order is described and explained in *The Act of Social Justice,* an arduous study done in the 1940's by an American priest, William Ferree.[19] He demonstrates that the textbooks for seminary training and catechetical materials were almost completely devoid of emphasis on social justice prior to the time of Pius XI who, in his encyclical, *On the Reconstruction of the Social Order,* and in subsequent Catholic Action directives affirmed the thesis that the man who is aware of social injustice is the man responsible for its repair.[20] Ironically, the more emphasis the Church places on the primacy of the transcendent, the greater the likelihood that Church members will become involved in the secular structure in interest-oriented ways.

This occurs because the Church serves and focuses on non-worldly matters. Not only does it leave the pragmatics of living to those not interested in the spirit, but it leaves the spiritual man without ethical guidelines for the worldly dimension of his own life and work. Thus, even during the period of the development of religious orders to care for the poor, social indifference to the public sector was at its height. This indifference reflected lack of acceptance of the obligation to try to effect change and even of the expectation that change in social structure was possible. Service to the indigent was traditionally a Catholic emphasis. The Catholic way of responding to the needy poor was to bring the suffering person "out of the world" into the safe refuge of a convent or home. The Catholic Church perceived itself as an oasis in a sinful world and expended this care of the indigent only on formal members of the Church. In this way, the very works of charity became modes of separation from the stranger.

Currently two themes in Catholic reform give evidence of reaction to this island-of-safety mentality; the reform of institutions and the respect for persons, two developments gradually more neglected in the centuries-long emphasis on transcendent values and hierarchical control.[21] The Catholic Church shares experiences with different Protestant sects in one or the other emphasis. The Puritans treated the transcendent in a manner similar to that of Catholics but shared no respect for hierarchical control. They needed religious legitimacy for their economic success, for their discovery of human power over the environment, and for the evident joys derived from that environment. Jonathan Edwards' sermons grappled with these issues and made a plea for the re-assertion of God's transcendence and for man to be less involved with the things of the world. Benjamin Franklin secularized this ethic. A century later, Emerson's *Self-Reliance* became a guide to Edwards' descendants in their effort to experience God. According to Emerson, man has to rely on himself to mediate the experience of nature while enjoying the leisure accorded by his work and life style.[22] In the present century, William James and John Dewey have translated this self-disciplining doctrine first into an experiential test of its relevance and then into a genuine concern for the well-being of mankind. Dewey postulated that one should expend this self-sacrificing effort in a mission for all men, that the whole universe is sacred, that social awareness is essential in those devoted to pecuniary gain, that the pursuit of science and the development of political and economic institutions for the enrichment of mankind are good. His themes have become quite familiar to the post-Vatican Catholic. Current American theologians recognize this pragmatism in the Council doctrines, especially as it is expressed in its American forms. Themes characterizing American Catholic thought today include a strong emphasis on service, listening, love, freedom, and encounter in dialogue. The improvement of mankind in this world is continually re-iterated in the context of the Incarnation as an historical event. Historicity is used to explain and to clarify the growing awareness that doctrine and dogma develop as humans develop. Pastoral norms are claimed for judging validity of elements of teaching and life. These norms, in line with American pragmatism, require the tester to legitimate positions taken not, as in the past, by a proclamation of a bishop or even by a direct search of Scripture, but rather from the commonsense Christian judgment of people in whom the Holy Spirit works. Such a focus is related to the new analysis of how God works in history with special concern for the presence of the Trinity where people are gathered and for the expression of the will of God through community members speaking under the inspiration of the Holy Spirit.

Authority as service rather than as the imposition of control is another central theme of American Catholic thought. Its *diakonia,* or service orientation, is rooted in the New Testament, while the structure of authority hitherto used in the Church has been much more the style of the fourteenth-century political command. A personalist philosophy of relation is more congenial to the new emphasis on freedom and personal dignity than is the Aristotelian focus on substance and accident. The view of man as a physical, psychic, social, and historical entity replaces the angelism related to an older asceticism. The hope of creating a better future in an evolving world takes the place of faith as the central theological virtue in this period of transition. Original sin becomes man's apathy in moving toward making a just and loving world.

Moral theology, then, requires a total revamping so that it no longer is dependent solely on natural law but rather on discipleship; that is, on how to become the people Christ invites us to be. The moral theologian's focus on arbitrary rules of conduct is eliminated.[23] Community becomes something to be made, and a limitless ecumenical spirit fits easily into American informal relationships in group encounter.[24] Harvey Cox is the first American theologian to emphasize the spiritual potential of the secular city and to describe God's openness to the world and his evolving work in it through man.[25] The Church becomes a local community of love. Man becomes a listener with whom God communicates through human speech and gesture. Man discovers he needs community in order to become himself; yet, he finds himself constantly threatened by the outer and the inner situation. The "poverty" of the gospel is now defined as sharing all one has, its "obedience" as listening to the Spirit and responding to others through service, while dialogue is the channel to becoming.[26]

There is nothing in this doctrinal sequence that lacks a familiar sound, but in contrast to some of the more recent stresses it is quite new. In the very recent past, the Church recommended, even for the layman, the meditative withdrawing into nature exemplified in the spirituality of the monks who periodically came together for Mass and Latin office. The focus was on salvation of one's own soul and the opportunity to develop a very self-oriented, exclusive type of spirituality where the actors are God and oneself and where the world is alien and sinful though still needing loving succor. This orientation was usually accompanied by secularist behavior which expressed a right to pursue one's own political or economic interests as long as the Church gained in some way. Even today, some Church administrators can still speak of major political or social issues without reference to the Church and its work, rather than as areas of life awaiting the actualization of redemption already realized through the Incarnation. As recently as ten years ago the superiority of the religious life over the lay life as a state of perfection was emphasized and still is in many places. The Church complacently re-iterated that it possessed the whole truth of revelation while other churches had but parts. And in this old style, the quest was made for moral judgments, certain beyond the need for clarification or application through dialogue. Its separation of moral and dogmatic theology was explicit; truths were divided into those of reason and those of faith and were treated as things.

These themes are rapidly disappearing from current Catholic teaching. Many grammar school catechisms and formation programs for religious orders have discarded them. These themes do persist, however, in the thinking of some of the older clergy, families, and monks and nuns who experience a real psychic strain when they are confronted with the new approach.[27] The Council took decisive action in new theological emphases which are developing American themes. Two of the main foci of Vatican Council thought which express the change are its openness to the world and its recognition of the laity as a partner.[28] Stemming from Catholic thought too, and clearly indicated in the documents, is a genuine concern for world poverty. In the spring of 1967, Paul VI's encyclical, *On the Development of Peoples,* further underscored the problem of poverty.[29] For many, this statement re-inforced their thinking. For others in America, it was a revelation of a new orientation, one which stressed the community, ecumenism, and service of the conciliar statements. The encyclical emphasized the dignity of the human person, the responsibility of the actor, freedom. It officially repudiated long-held prejudices. *The Pastoral Constitution on the Church* defines the Church as the "people of God," a servant Church, a pilgrim Church. The definition of the Church as the hierarchical relation among the pope, bishops, clergy, and people is no longer pre-eminent. Awareness of sin and trust in the power of the risen, healing Christ (incarnate in the modern world) to overcome sin is an image of the Council. It is a real turn to embrace the world after a long separation, the joyous turn of a poor, detached, and communal pilgrim people on the move. The Council's rejection of the magic and superstition of an earlier era is explicit. Its assertion, also, of what an openness to the Spirit means is central, as is its limitless extension of the people of God to include all men.

Many of the themes that were incorporated into Vatican II documents were formulated in the decades just prior to the Council by men who, though later the consultants for the Council, were in the late 1940's and 1950's viewed as deviants by the institutionalized Church. Their work was frequently limited in publication and circulation by official Church decree.[30] This phenomenon of rejection which becomes acceptance is understandable when one considers the complexities of the socialization process and the affective relationships and tones involved. A new theology sets different limits on norms and allows for the development of different ranges of behavior. This is threatening to an established structure. A reading public, open to new approaches, becomes the bearer of the new culture. Its reading preferences readily relate to perception and acceptance of change. Reading preference is a major determinant of how the Church in America responds to pressures to change. In one large survey of American Catholic teachers, only 40 per cent feel directly influenced in 1967 by the thinking of Vatican II theologians.[31] This will soon change. The Vatican theology is a response to the European man's developing awareness that institutionalized religion is inadequate to cope with the religious issues raised by the analyses of Feuerbach, Comte, Marx, Nietzsche, Freud, and later writers, who discovered in religious practice and motivation elements stunting growth to maturity. Sermons, catechetical materials, and spiritual direction sometimes allow the national dream—the projection, the myth, the rationalization—to become defined as holy. The unconscious wish to shape the idea of God to one's own image has become so widespread that a thinking man, aware of the processes of his own experience, could not accept the caricature in any serious way.[32] The young American studying sociology and psychology and at the same time examining religious practice becomes aware of these irrational dimensions to religious behavior and responds either by severing his ties or by joining reforms, depending on his experience with the new theologies and on the degree to which his affective ties are bound to local ethnic ghettos.

The American experience of the Catholic Church has a direct confrontation on a large scale with industrialization, urbanization, and bureaucratization. Maurice Stein in the mid-1950's described the effects of these processes on local community life. He concluded that in the relatively secure, established organization of the upper middle-class suburb, many men have already forsaken the trend back to church membership described by Will Herberg as status-seeking. They are substituting psychoanalytic concern for personality development, in addition to an almost neurotic pre-occupation with the development of their children into normal, healthy adults.[33] The current restlessness in the Church describes a possible breakthrough from the total institution complex treated by Erving Goffman in *Asylums* and the pre-occupation with the developing person described by Stein. The restlessness in the Church is as much a response to the de-personalization of modern man by machine and bureaucracy in the wider society as it is to the other-worldly, non-communicating ghetto emphasis. Living in the city outside the ghetto, man retains no resource to turn to when the loneliness of living in the lonely crowd becomes widespread. Catholic Americans experience a similar challenge from the environment as do Protestants, Jews, and agnostics. New themes in American Catholicism focus on creating communities in which strangers are welcome and on developing environments where people have space to become what endowment and grace and social structure allow. A decade ago the ideas of theologians who advocated more adequate response were alien to then current ghetto practices in the churches and were not popularly heard. But they were circulated in the learned journals and in private mailing. America became a place of ready publication for papers expressing the views of the European scholars about making community and developing the person. To some extent the experience of anonymity, of bureaucratization and industrialization was more advanced in this country, and called for alleviation of the psychic stress on the individual as he moved out of the ethnic ghetto and became better educated.

Publishers not previously associated with distinguished spiritual writing brought this sophisticated European thought to the American scene: Sheed and Ward, Newman Press, and later Herder and Company. Four journals presented this material to the lay world: *Jubilee,* a picture magazine for the family, *The Critic, Commonweal,* and *Cross Currents,* each lay-owned and lay-controlled. Three journals for clerics and theologians, *Theology Digest, Theological Studies,* and the *Catholic Biblical Quarterly,* acted equally as media for European thought. The journals published specifically for priests, *The Priest,* the *Homiletic and Pastoral Review,* and the *American Ecclesiastical Review* contained little of the writing of the turn-to-the-world theologians but continued their transcendent emphasis and the world-as-secular focus common to the long tradition.

These different channels of communication are related to the emergence of American Catholics from their separatist experience. A certain sequence in the development of American Catholicism makes its present response unique. Four stages of development have frequently been analyzed in the historical report of Catholicism in America. First was the period after 1688, following the application of the English penal laws to all Catholics in the colonies. They had to perceive themselves as a repudiated group, imprisoned and killed for their beliefs, specifically because the colonists rejected the hierarchical structure of their Church. The second stage encompassed the development of the American Catholic Church in the Protestant style of lay control for lack of an adaptable model in the European hierarchical structure. The next stage involved the reaction of the white, Protestant, Anglo-Saxon communities on the east coast to the wave of migration from Ireland, Germany, and later, southern Europe. This reaction included the establishment of groups like the Know-Nothing Party of the 1850's and the American Protective Association of the 1890's which resented both Catholics and Negroes.[34] The final stage was the Americanization period wherein the Catholic, like the Puritan before him, experiencing his potential for mastering the universe and the delight of the things of this world, participated in the secularization of his own doctrines to permit the legitimation of enjoying the advantages of middle-class status.[35] The first three of these experiences gave an urgency and direction to the development of separatism in the Catholic community in the form of separate schools, newspapers, and welfare service. In time, concern for the local community as a public enterprise was as unformed as in Italy where political participation was specifically forbidden by Church law after 1840 and the rise of socialism. From this time on, neither European communication nor the local American stimulation encouraged joint effort for the common good. This, coupled with an other-world-oriented doctrine, explains the non-involvement of Catholics in the Abolitionist movement and the development in city politics of the local ethnic groups with special interests.[36]

The community studies of the 1940's and 1950's discovered the manner in which the local church becomes the re-inforcer of the values of the community. This can be seen in the comments of local businessmen, lawyers, doctors, commencement speakers at high school graduations, and local news editors. Seldom in any American town or city does the pastor re-iterate a doctrine that violates the complacency of the established business class.[37] A decade of reading these studies seems to confirm the Marxian claim that the Church functions to legitimate the advantage of the established interest groups and acts to resist any effort to threaten its complacency. This thesis, with its claim that religion is epiphenomenal and not the direction-determining impetus the prophet is supposed to be, has led the serious student of sociology to examine very carefully his data, to discern what functions religion exercises in periods of rapid social change.[38]

Durkheim's demonstration that religion is the society and Marx's proof that it is a rationalization for the advantage of interest groups explain well the effects of overinstitutionalization of religious behavior after long periods of uncritical, functional adjustment.[39]

To explain the growing effectiveness of the world-oriented Council doctrines on the American scene, breaking through the institutionalized patterns characterizing the established church, calls for a model that includes the role of the deviant and the prophet. Looking at the response of individuals and groups who experienced strain in the old system and to whom the new themes gave new roles is useful for understanding new directions. Where are the active new voices in the American Church? One may locate them in at least three groups: the articulate laity who, prior to Vatican II, were allowed little decision-making in Church affairs but who are now being defined as "the Church"; women, especially women religious who are treated by the clergy through Canon Law as minors and who in the new theology are, along with everyone else, enjoying a new emphasis on their personal responsibility for choice; and, finally, the non-adminstrative clergy who in Canon Law have no powers or privileges and who in practice have been treated as guests in the pastor's house.[40] There is clear evidence that these groups have in fact produced the people who have persistently and articulately asserted the pressures to change that now affect the Church in America. *The National Catholic Reporter*, the only lay-run national Catholic newspaper, is a prototype for the expressive layman. It is abhorred by many of the hierarchy, but it is defined by many of the laity as the only objective paper. During its three-year existence, it has published extensive articles on the following topics: peace, poverty, birth control, civil rights protest, inter-faith meetings, celibacy of the clergy, renewal in religious life, cities in urban renewal, the role of the laity in the Church, liturgical changes, authority in the Church, pastoral and parish renewal, religious liberty, critiques of parochial education, catechetical renewal, and reports of the flow out of religious orders. It reports in great detail any violation of the rights of individuals in Church structures and any failure of bishops to respond to the needs of groups within their dioceses. *The National Catholic Reporter* has become a symbol of criticism from within the system.[41]

The systematic review of structure undertaken by orders of religious women who staff the health, education, and welfare work of the Church in America is evidence of a genuine response to the invitation to renew and to turn to the world.[42] The development of diocesan and parish councils and clerical senates, as well as the activity of priests in the renewal of cities, reveal a new social concern among the non-administrative clergy. All of these efforts relate to building social structures based on the guidelines of the new theology. The American Church in its restless response to change, now legitimated in Council documents, is more involved in structural renovation and experimentation than any segment of the European Church at the present time with the possible exception of the Dutch Church.[43] The direction the American Church takes in surveying and programming will almost certainly be imitated abroad. In this sense, the American Church will lead in the immediate future in realizing the implications of the work of the Council for the specific efforts to transform the world. The immediate dynamism of this thrust is part of the American experience. It comes from three characteristically American phenomena: the organizational facility which American technological advances have stimulated, the community quest that organizational facility generates in reaction to the anonymity-creating character of bureaucracy, and the emergence of the American Church from its separatist character as old defenses become obsolete through the decline of minority status. Although the themes are mainly European in origin, realization of them is American in form.

Although the stress in this article has been placed on the thrust of new theological orientations and the current activity in the American Church to realize in organizational forms the implications of the new theology, if one wants to understand current restlessness and tension one must also keep in mind that the hold of the traditional structures, developed in the relative isolation of the city ghetto, is still very strong. The local response to world problems of peace, civil unrest, and liturgical changes give evidence of this fact. The prediction that the efforts to reform structure will prevail over the local resistance movements rests on the assumption that new value orientations do have directional force in a social system. This is true especially when the value orientation has been legitimated by official bodies such as the Vatican Council and has been accepted as valid by segments of the membership who, lacking power, have the prestige of trained competence. The professionally-trained laity, clergy, and religious-order members read the journals carrying the new messages and participate in reform efforts. They constitute the body of actual and potential reformers.

REFERENCES

1. See Edward F. Wakin and Joseph F. Scheuer, *The De-Romanization of the American Catholic Church* (New York, 1966), and James Cavanaugh, *A Modern Priest Looks at His Out-Dated Church* (New York, 1967). Also Sr. M. Charles Borromeo Muckenhirn (ed.), *The Changing Sister* (Notre Dame, 1965); Xavier Rynne, *Letters from Vatican City* (New York, 1963), *The Second Session* (New York, 1964), *The Third Session* (1964–65), and *The Fourth Session* (1965–66). Also Mary Perkins Ryan, *Are Parochial Schools the Answer? Catholic Education in the Light of the Council* (New York, 1964), and Leslie Dewart, *The Future of Belief: Theism in a World Come of Age* (New York, 1966).

2. Walter M. Abbott (ed), *Documents,* Vatican Council 2nd, 1960–1965 (New York, 1966).

3. The Council documents include the following titles: *Dogmatic Constitution on the Church; Dogmatic Constitution on Divine Revelation; Constitution on the Sacred Liturgy; Pastoral Constitution on the Church in the Modern World; Decree on the Instruments of Social Communication; Decree on Ecumenicism; Decree on the Eastern Catholic Churches; Decree on the Bishops' Pastoral Office in the Church; Decree on Priestly Formation; Decree on the Appropriate Renewal of the Religious Life; Decree on the Apostolate of the Laity; Decree on the Ministry and Life of Priests; Decree on the Church's Missionary Activity; Declaration on Christian Education; Declaration on the Relationship of the Church to Non-Christian Religions;* and the *Declaration of Religious Freedom.*

4. *The National Catholic Reporter* and the *Brooklyn Tablet* are good examples of newspapers responding differently to change. The *Reporter* represents the whole range of the open-to-change orientation and the *Tablet* responds cautiously. For further analysis of the complex dimensions of the conservative and liberal dichotomies, see Sr. Marie Augusta Neal, *Values and Interests in Social Change* (Englewood Cliffs, N.J., 1965), where the responses to pressure to change of priests in the Boston Archdiocese are analyzed.

5. In the fall of 1966 Father Charles Davis, an outstanding English theologian who had attended the Vatican Council as a consultant, left the Catholic Church, having concluded that the agreed-upon renewal would not be possible within the existing structure. In January of 1967, Sister Jacqueline Grennan, president of Webster College in Missouri, concluding that the definition of the college function as an external work of the apostolate made it quite impossible for her to fulfill her functions in the public sector of American society with the existing control exercised by the diocese, left her religious order to continue her service work as a laywoman.

6. In 1890 Pope Leo XIII proclaimed his encyclical entitled, *Rerum Novarum,* dealing with the conditions of labor in the world of the working-class. In 1930 Pope Pius XI proclaimed *Quadragesimo Anno* dealing with the same topic but changing the content to handle the reconstruction of the social order. In the 1960's Pope John XXIII furthered this social involvement with *Mater et Magistra,* and *Pacem in Terris,* and the Council added the document, *The Church in the Modern World.* In 1967 Pope Paul VI followed with *Progressio Populorum.* It is only in this last document that the implication of the whole series becomes clearly a mandate for reform of political, economic, and social structures.

7. See Thomas T. McAvoy, *The Americanist Heresy in Roman Catholicism, 1895–1900* (South Bend, Indiana, 1963); John Tracy Ellis, *American Catholicism* (Chicago, 1956); and Robert D. Cross, *The Emergence of Liberal Catholicism in America* (Cambridge, 1958).

8. Henry David Thoreau is probably the best American example of the antinomian. For the Asch experiment, see S. E. Asch, "Effects of Group Pressure upon the Modification and Distortion of Judgments," in *Readings in Social Psychology*, eds. Maccoby, Newcomb, and Hartley (New York, 1958), pp. 174–82.

9. St. Paul, *Acts of the Apostles*, Chapter 10.

10. Max Weber, *The Protestant Ethic and the Spirit of Capitalism* (New York, 1958), pp. 89–154.

11. Leo Marx, *The Machine in the Garden: Technology and the Pastoral Ideal in America* (New York, 1964).

12. For a view of this problem within the Church, see Ives Congar, *Lay People in The Church*, translated by D. Attwater (Westminster, Maryland, 1957). For the same problem in the world community, see Norman O. Brown, *Life Against Death* (New York, 1959); Erving Goffman, *Asylums* (New York, 1961); and Erich Fromm, *Escape From Freedom* (New York, 1965).

13. Sister Marie Augusta Neal, *Values and Interests in Social Change*.

14. Christopher Dawson, *Religion and Culture* (New York, 1958).

15. In a survey of the attitudes and perceptions of members of religious orders of women 135,000 have responded to a questionnaire. This research sponsored by the Conference of Major Superiors of Women's Religious Institutes in the United States (C.M.S.W.), is now being analyzed.

16. Andrew M. Greeley and Peter H. Rossi, *The Education of American Catholics* (Chicago, 1966).

17. Emmanuel Cardinal Suhard, *Growth or Decline? The Church Today* (Montreal, 1948), pp. 54–55. For further discussion, see Gustave Thils, *Christian Attitudes* (Chicago, 1959).

18. For a specific example and account of this, see E. E. Y. Hales, *Pio Nono: A Study in European Politics in the Nineteenth Century* (New York, 1964).

19. William Ferree, *The Act of Social Justice* (Dayton, Ohio, 1951).

20. This is the encyclical published in 1930 by Pope Pius XI, forty years after the first statement in encyclical form on the social conditions of the modern world, *Rerum Novarum*, by Leo XIII.

21. Sr. Aloysius Shaldenbrand, *The Primacy of the Person in the Church* (Notre Dame, Indiana, 1967). See also Ives Congar, *Lay People in the Church*.

22. These ideas about Jonathan Edwards and Ralph Waldo Emerson were developed in an American Studies Institute held at Emmanuel College, Boston, Massachusetts, in June, 1967. Leo Marx and Robert J. Roth presented papers on this point for later publication.

23. See F. Simons, "The Catholic Church and the New Morality," *Cross Currents*, Vol. 16 (1966), pp. 429–45; J. Milhaven, "Toward an Epistemology of Ethics," *Theological Studies*, Vol. 28 (1966), pp. 228–41; D. Hurley, "A New Moral Principle—When Right and Duty Clash," *The Furrow*, Vol. 17 (1966), pp. 228–41.

24. See J. Ford and G. Kelly, *Contemporary Moral Theology* (Westminster, Maryland, 1958), pp. 42–153; R. Dailey, "New Approaches to Moral Theology," *Current Trends in Theology*, Chapter IX (New York, 1965), pp. 171–98; J. Doyle, "New Perspectives in Moral Theology," *Homiletic and Pastoral Review*, Vol. 63 (1963), pp. 385–91; P. Murnion, "The Renewal of Moral Theology: Review and Prospect," *Dunwoodie Review*, Vol. 3 (1963), pp. 39–65; S. Pinckaers, "The Revival of Moral Theology," *Cross Currents*, Vol. 7 (1957), pp. 56–66; R. McCormick, "The Primacy of Charity," *Apostolic Perspectives* (August–September, 1959), pp. 18–27.

25. Harvey Cox, *The Secular City* (New York, 1965).

26. John L. McKenzie in *Authority in the Church* (New York, 1966) has developed some of these ideas on authority in the Church. This summary of the American emphasis was compiled mainly from private correspondence with Br. Gabriel Moran, Bernard Cooke, Sr. M. Charles Borromeo Muckenhirn, and Sr. Aloysius Schaldenbrand. The first three speak as theologians, the latter as a philosopher. Ideas were also taken from Gregory Baum, especially those expressed in "Restlessness in the Church," *The Ecumenist: A Journal for Promoting Christian Unity*, Vol. V (1967), pp. 33–36, which he edits and which is published by the Paulist Press.

27. The theologians who have worked out these themes from their scriptural roots are overwhelmingly European. E. Schillebeeck, the Dutch theologian, shows great sensitivity to the new emphasis on the study of man in an anthropological-psychological context to realize the self in a world of experience. His books, *Christ: The Sacrament of Encounter with God* (New York, 1965) and *The Layman in the Church* (Albo House, 1963), develop the person emphasis of American themes. Although McKenzie's *Authority in the Church* is the best American treatment of this new community emphasis on obedience, Alois Muller's *Obedience in the Church*, translated by H. Graef (Westminister, Maryland, 1964), is a German treatment of the theme; Muller also has an article in the fifth volume of *Concilium* entitled "Authority and Obedience in the Church." Hans Kung's *Freedom Today* (New York, 1966) handles well this theme, but Karl Rahner has perhaps the best expression of Christian obedience in "Reflections on Obedience," *Cross Currents*, Vol. 10 (1960) pp. 362–74. Hans Urs von Balthasar in *Christianity and Science* (Westminister, Maryland, 1958) expresses succinctly the focus on man. Piet Schoonenburg handles in a masterly way the question of sin as alienation in *Man and Sin*. The French writer, Piet Fransen, examines authority as *diakonia* and grace as God's love for us, while Jose M. Gonzalez-Ruiz, the Spanish theologian, disengages contemporary spirituality from certainty. See *Information Documentation on the Conciliar Church*, Doss. 66.18, (5.10.66), "Social Prob-

lems and Post-Conciliar Theology," and Doss. 156, "Biblical Foundations for a Theology of the World."

28. See R. P. Theodore Steeman, "Conflict in the Conciliar Church," *Information Documentation on the Conciliar Church*, Doss. 67.14, (5.4.67).

29. *On the Development of Peoples: Encyclical Letter of His Holiness Pope Paul VI* (Boston, 1967).

30. Examples include Ives Congar, Henri de Lubac, M. D. Chenu, and John Courtney Murray. These men did not receive invitations to the first session of Vatican II. Ives Congar's *Lay People in the Church*, Henri de Lubac's *The Drama of Atheistic Humanism*, studies by M. D. Chenu, John Danielou (*Christians Today*), Urs von Balthasar, and others worked out these themes before the Council in forms which had already reached the serious readers in America through such media as *Cross Currents*, "a journal to study the impact of Christianity on our times." Begun in 1953, it carried translations of the themes that later took formal expression as official Church doctrine. Thus the Council codified and promulgated what the serious theologian was already sharing.

31. Results from C.M.S.W. survey of religious women in the United States, research in progress.

32. Albert Dondeyne, *Contemporary European Thought and Christian Faith*, translated by E. McMullin and John Murnheim (Pittsburgh, 1959).

33. Maurice Stein, *The Eclipse of Community* (Princeton, 1960); Will Herberg, *Protestant, Catholic, Jew*. Durkheim, as early as 1912, at the end of *Elementary Forms of the Religious Life* predicted a focus on personality development as a substitute for attachment to institutionalized religions.

34. Ellis, *American Catholicism*.

35. Andrew Greeley, The Church and the Suburbs (New York, 1959); Gibson Winters, *Suburban Captivity of the Churches* (New York, 1961).

36. Oscar Handlin, *Boston Immigrant* (rev. ed., Cambridge, 1959).

37. See Robert Lynd and Helen Merrill Lynd, *Middletown in Transition* (New York, 1937), pp. 303–18.

38. Joseph Fichter, *Southern Parish: Dynamics of a City Church* (Chicago, 1951); Joseph B. Schuyler, *Northern Parish: A Sociological and Pastoral Survey* (Chicago, 1960).

39. Émile Durkheim, *Elementary Forms of the Religious Life* (London, 1915). For Marx, see *Marx and Engels*, ed. Lewis B. Feuer (New York, 1959), pp. 246–61.

40. Canon Law frequently presumes that women are uneducated, inexperienced in business and social affairs, and in need of the prudent vigilance of a wise cleric. The following Canons manifest this presumption: Canons 506, 520–527, 552, 607, and 1109. According to these Canons, bishops must

preside at elections of contemplative orders of women, see that they go to confession weekly, interview young women prior to their taking the vows to be sure they are acting freely, see that women religious do not leave the house without a companion unless it is a case of necessity, and so forth. As for curates, the Canons simply give them no particular rights or authority. The various functions of the parish are the exclusive right of the pastor, including baptisms, weddings, funerals, and so forth. He may order the curate to perform these functions. The curate is subject to the pastor who is supposed to give him paternal instruction and direction (Canon 476); some curates, however, are over fifty years of age.

41. The same themes are treated in a serious and scholarly way by an international documentary service (IDO-C), established by the Dutch during the Council, which now continues to report in seven different languages papers which are given in various parts of the Church that carry out the themes of the Council. A main theme of this service is the examination of new diocesan structures developing to handle the recommendations of the Council for renewal. An American branch of this service began in 1967.

42. Numerous books published within the last few years carry these themes of renewal and reform into all areas of the Church structure. Some of these are: Mary Perkins Ryan's *Are Parochial Schools the Answer?*; Louis J. Luzbetak's edition of *The Church in the Changing City* (Techny, Illinois, 1966); Daniel Callahan's *The New Church* (New York, 1966); *The Changing Sister* and *The New Nuns*, ed. Sr. Charles Borromeo Muckenhirn (New York, 1967); Robert N. Hassenger's edition of *The Shape of Catholic Education* (Chicago, 1967); John D. Donovan's *The Academic Man in the Catholic College* (New York, 1964); and *Vows But No Walls*, ed. Eugene V. Grollmes (St. Louis, 1967).

43. The prophetic themes seem to be in the process of institutionalization in the form Neil J. Smelser describes in *Theory of Collective Behavior* (New York, 1963).

PREDICTIONS AND REORIENTATIONS

DANIEL CALLAHAN

The Quest for Social Relevance

As EVERY politician and social reformer knows, a telling word or a terse slogan can be worth a score of elaborate position papers. The right phrase can point to a goal, elicit a spirit, and provide an emotional peg on which to hang a program. That the slogan, word, or phrase may obscure as much as it reveals is beside the point. What matters is its potency to focus energy and engender vision; the hidden difficulties can be dealt with later, once the forward momentum of commitment has been established. If any single word now current in American Christianity performs this function, it is *relevance*. Typically enough, it is used in the hortatory mode to set a task for the believer and the churches. Christianity must, once again, be made relevant to man and society. It must come to have a fresh function, a new impact, and a contemporary appeal. Used in its negative form, the word is an instrument of condemnation. Christianity is now "irrelevant," having little bite and significance in a world desperately in need of creative departures and radical reform. But the use of *relevance* also reveals, on occasion, a number of anxieties and unanswered questions that exist within the churches today.

1. *Theological relevance.* At the root of the drive for social relevance is a pervasive concern for the intelligibility of the Christian message. If Christianity is to speak to the condition of contemporary man, then it must be able to do so in a language that he can comprehend; thus runs the argument for a reform of traditional theological concepts. In *Honest to God,* a book that has sold well over 500,000 copies in the United States, John A. T. Robinson, the Anglican Bishop of Woolwich, England, wrote that "there is a growing gulf between the traditional orthodox supernaturalism in which our faith has been framed and the categories which the 'lay' world

(for want of a better term) finds meaningful today."[1] Academic theologians can easily point out that the Bishop grossly misunderstands those "traditional" categories he considers "outmoded"—the idea of a God who physically exists "up there" or "out there," to take his most striking example. But they cannot so easily show that popular religion understands matters very differently from the way in which he describes them.[2] Bishop Robinson argues that the idea of the Christian God was formulated at a time when myth still reigned supreme, when men still had an infantile dependence on a problem-solving, gap-filling God, when the categories of Greek philosophy still made sense, when the words *transcendent* and *supernatural* still meant something. Insofar as Christianity persists in stressing these relics of the past, to that extent will it seem unintelligible today.

The same theme finds a sharper expression in the work of William Hamilton and Thomas J. J. Altizer. In *Radical Theology and the Death of God,* they argue "that there was once a God to whom adoration, praise and trust were appropriate, possible and even necessary, but . . . now there is no such God."[3] In Hamilton's formulation, "We are not talking about the absence of the experience of God, but about the experience of the absence of God."[4] For Altizer, the "death of God" means the loss of any possibility of responding "to the classical Christian images of the Creator and the creation."[5] The only possible response to the demise of God, they contend, is a radical embracing of the profane, a complete rejection of "otherworldliness," and a hopeful waiting for the return of God. In a less spectacular vein, Paul Van Buren draws upon linguistic analysis to show that the traditional language used to describe God is empirically meaningless. He contends that the gospel will become significant for contemporary man only when it is understood in a thoroughly secular fashion. Biblical categories must be translated into empirical and ethical terms—the terms of a scientific, technological society.[6] From still another quarter, Paul Cobb asserts that theology must predicate an evolving rather than a static God. Only by adopting the terms of evolution and process philosophy can theology speak meaningfully of creation. Taking up the theme of process philosophy in terms of the Christian understanding of man, a Roman Catholic, E. R. Baltazar, contends that the Aristotelian-Thomistic emphasis on "nature" and "essence" must give way to a recognition of human uniqueness and personality, process and subjectivity.[7] And an Anglical theologian, David Jenkins, believes that the development of a doctrine of God suitable for "post-Copernican man" must be "clearly related to a spiritual discipline and discipleship which is experiential and experimental in relation both to the tradition and to the current situation."[8]

Roman Catholics have, as a rule, been considerably less bold in attempting to find fresh language and concepts for traditional doctrines. Continental existentialism and personalism have influenced reform-minded Roman Catholic theologians far more than the empiricism and pragmatism that have come to dominate Anglo-Saxon theology. Attempts have been made to find a substitute for the word *transsubstantiation* in expressing the metaphysical status of the real presence of Christ in the Eucharist[9]; to express better the nature of the church[10]; and to remove from the theology of the sacraments any suggestion of magic and impersonal mechanisms of grace.[11] Not surprisingly, such expressions as *encounter, intersubjectivity,* and *meeting* loom large in these attempts.

In a somewhat different vein, a major subject of the Catholic "Twenty-Sixth North American Liturgical Week," held in the summer of 1965, was the need for greater moral, liturgical, Scriptural, and theological "relevance."[12] The emphasis there, however, did not fall on translating the old into the new so much as on recapturing those elements of the Christian tradition that have been obscured in the course of ecclesiastical history. Thus, Father Charles E. Curran states that the most telling charge against moral theology is that "it does not appear to be particularly Christian. The reason is obvious: moral theology has not found its basic orientation and inspiration in the word of God itself."[13] A Biblically-oriented moral theology, which would be far more radical than that found in older Catholic theology manuals, would be "relevant in a twofold manner: (1) The absolute character of the New Testament ethics reminds us that we are saved by God and not by ourselves. (2) Man, nevertheless, must continually strive to obtain the goal of complete openness in a union of love with God and neighbor."[14] In another paper, Father Aelred Tegels, O.S.B., felt that the possibility of a relevant liturgy depended upon the implementation of the teaching of Vatican II on the liturgy together with "continuing historical research, sociological and anthropological studies, genuine, controlled experimentation."[15] Finally, a Protestant participant, Jaroslav Pelikan, sounded a cautionary note. He pointed out:

The preoccupation of theology with the need for relevance can be a dangerous thing. It is required of stewards that a man be found faithful, not that he be found successful or relevant; and relevance may very well be one of those things that will be added unto us if we seek first the kingdom of God and his righteousness.[16]

Nonetheless, Dr. Pelikan urged Christian scholars to take a closer look at the "Jewish matrix of early Christian theology" and at the ante-Nicene Fathers. In these sources they would find many keys to two central preoccupations of the ecumenical movement—the problem of unity-in-diversity and the relationship of Scripture and tradition.

2. *Institutional relevance.* Closely related to the drive for theological relevance is a search for a corresponding institutional relevance. The churches' structural life should reflect any new insight into religious virtues. That the churches have failed in this respect is a widespread complaint. Martin Marty's lament is characteristic:

The massive silhouette the churches (Catholic as well as Protestant) create on the American skyline is that of a self-preservative institutionalism. The clergyman exists as a promoter of the organization. . . . Since the institutional self-interest preoccupies the churches and does not directly serve the community, it seems to incarnate irrelevance.[17]

According to Reuel L. Howe, the churches have failed to recognize the complexity of contemporary life and have tended to turn Christianity into an abstraction. Consequently, he maintains, "Much present practice tends to reduce Christianity to the dimensions of a religious cult, and many who are presented for membership drift away from the church partly because it seems irrelevant."[18] Graydon E. McClellan has written of the suburban church's "luxuriant irrelevancy flowing out of its magnificent institutionalism."[19]

Within both Protestantism and Catholicism a common complaint turns on the existence of an impersonal bureaucracy tied to outdated techniques and isolated from the church as a whole. "Theologically speaking," M. Richard Shaull has written, "the church may be a missionary community. In actual fact, however, it has become a major hindrance to the work of mission. The local congregation pulls people out of the world and absorbs their time in a religious program rather than setting them free for their mission in the world."[20] Joseph Cardinal Ritter of St. Louis traces the failure of Roman Catholicism in attracting a sufficient number of candidates to the priesthood to its "failure to present to youth a sufficiently dramatic and meaningful Church to engage their dedication to a life of sacrifice and service."[21] A vigorous attempt is being made within Roman Catholicism to reform the religious orders (ranging from changes in the procedure for electing superiors to the modernization of garb) because "the old structure is no longer relevant to [the] needs."[22] Many Council fathers of Vatican II urged the Catholic Church to address itself to genuine human needs and not just to the exigencies of its own internal life.[23] Although the description of institutionalism is monotonously repetitious, proposed cures are diverse: a change in the structure of parishes; the creation of new lay and clerical organizations within the churches; fresh conceptions of the ministry; less preoccupation with money and buildings.

3. *Social relevance.* Because society places a high premium on social utility, numerous theologians and official agencies of the church have felt compelled to demonstrate (to themselves as much as to others) that Christianity can make a direct contribution to the secular commonweal. As in the institutional and theological relevance already discussed, the initial emphasis has fallen on the churches' abysmal performance. In *The Suburban Captivity of the Churches,* Gibson Winter states flatly that the churches "have suffered dismal failures in the central areas of the metropolis."[24] A similar dirge has been sung by Harvey Cox: "The gods of traditional religion live on as private fetishes or the patrons of congenial groups, but they play no role whatever in the public life of the secular metropolis."[25] In the opinion of Peter L. Berger, "Protestantism has had little to say that would be of relevance to the mighty transformations through which American society has been passing": urbanization, the proliferation of science and technology, affluence, transformations of youth culture.[26] For Gabriel Vahanian, much of the churches' social irrelevance stems from their tendency to dilute the categories of Scripture in a mindless accommodation to society. The idea of the "Kingdom of God is relevant precisely because it is utopian. . . . It becomes turgescent and irrelevant as soon as, transmigrating into Millennarianism and the American Dream, it is domesticated by and conformed to the immanentism of religiosity."[27]

The churches have been indicted for their failure to respond effectively to broad areas of contemporary social concern. Thus Margaret Mead notes that "Christian institutions continue to follow an inappropriate, inadequate, and no longer relevant style of individual Christian charity; in doing so, they surrender to the secular world . . . the wider goals of feeding the hungry, caring for the sick, and protecting the poor."[28] Catholic bishops have been attacked for failing to offer any moral guidance on the Viet-Nam war—on either the ultimate goals of American policy or on the mili-

DANIEL CALLAHAN

tary means used to implement this policy.[29] Despite much improvement in their positions on race relations in the last decade, both Protestantism and Catholicism have been accused of following rather than leading the national consensus and the courts. So it has gone, whatever the issue.

Many Protestants and Catholics within the main stream of theological concern assert that the churches today have an imperative duty to speak to the conditions and problems of society. The literature and rhetoric of "relevance" call for an intense examination of contemporary society and its implications for the work of the churches. The churches must no longer cling to an anachronistic collection of theological concepts, cultural perspectives, and institutional structures. Rather, they must so reform their thinking and interior life that they will be able to speak to the conditions and problems of society. Multiple factors account for the churches' irrelevance. Even when confronted with the phenomenon of secularization, they refuse to recognize that Christianity no longer commands an automatic hearing and homage. In a period of rapid social change, they have been unable to adapt their thought and style to the shifting contexts of social existence. Finally, they have been overassimilated into a society that is being rejected increasingly by youth, intellectuals, and other outsiders.

Unquestionably, the churches have a broad crisis on their hands. In the crisis of leadership, younger, bureaucratically subordinate laity and clergy are pitted against an older, well-entrenched institutionalized leadership; a restless, activist minority against a settled, more melioristic majority. By and large, the cutting thrusts come from those clergy and laity who have committed themselves to the creation of a relevant church. To express this commitment, they have tried to take strong, decisive, and practical steps to meet specific social needs. Progressive young Protestant ministers often come into conflict with reactionary vestrymen in the struggles over church segregation in the South. Inner-city pastors are frequently frustrated in their attempts to interest affluent ministers and laymen from large, established suburban churches in the problems of hard-core poverty areas. Experimental ministries, usually run by isolated individuals and groups, have difficulty gaining the attention and support of city, regional, or national denominational organizations. In Roman Catholicism, younger curates often press older pastors for a re-structuring of parish life. Priests and laymen who want an immediate and total implementation of the spirit and decrees of Vatican II are matched against pastors and bishops who are fearful of rapid shifts in liturgical, organizational, or intellectual patterns. Priests in specialized ministries (racial and poverty work, college chaplaincies) urging radically new approaches frequently clash with a diocesan or religious-order leadership extremely wary of allowing any one group to move in a direction very different from that of the whole establishment.[30]

The institutional ramifications of theology have added another dimension to the crisis confronting the churches today. It is unclear just how much the churches can or should adapt their theology to the exigencies of the moment. A number of different responses to this dilemma have emerged. Among the southern fundamentalist groups, the pentecostal churches, and sects like Jehovah's Witnesses, there has been resolute opposition to any "modernism" in theology; Biblical fundamentalism remains the rule. Within the main-line Protestant churches there has been an uneasy compromise, one result of which has been the appearance of sharply divergent factions within the churches. A comparable division now exists within Roman Catholicism. The ecumenical movement has shown various subgroups within Protestantism and Catholicism that they often have more in common with one another—their supposed "separated brethren"—than with certain members of their own churches.

It remains an acute question whether the churches should undertake the vast task of educating those who will listen so that they may understand the church's traditional language or whether they should forthwith attempt to meet secular man on his own ground. Sharp disagreement exists about whether theology should be made relevant by a fresh return to Scripture and tradition to probe their contemporary significance, or by exploration of primary data well outside traditional limits. In the former instance, the stress will fall on Biblical exegesis, the writings of the church fathers, research into the meaning of the creeds as originally understood and into early forms of liturgy.[31] In the latter, it will fall on sociology, psychology, the arts, and literature.[32] The two approaches are not necessarily incompatible; and, in fact, there are few theologians writing today who do not make at least some use of both. Nonetheless, the conflict in emphasis can be sharp. Opposition to purportedly alien modes of theologizing led the distinguished (and hardly reactionary) Anglican theologian E. L. Mascall to write *The Secularization of Christianity*[33]; and the editor of an important progressive Catholic quarterly, *Continuum,* to complain of theologians who spin "religio-cultural generalities out of Fellini and Camus" and to plead that they instead concentrate on theology's historical task, that of "plumbing the infinite."[34]

On still another level, the crisis is one of action. Most churchmen concede the churches must embody their dedication to the social good, in part, through social action. But there the agreement ends. Many churchmen hesitate to act because of community pressure, bureaucratic or hierarchical immobility, ingrained conservatism, or simply a failure to see that principles require a meaningful concrete expression. James Cardinal McIntyre of Los Angeles refused to oppose passage of the notorious Proposition 14-b for open housing in the California referendum of 1964. The Bishop of Mobile-Birmingham, Thomas J. Toolen, would not permit priests and nuns to take part in the Selma march (they marched anyway); Jesuit superiors silenced Father Daniel Berrigan for picketing and speaking against the Viet-Nam war in 1965; his brother Philip's Josephite superiors censored Philip on the same grounds.

More interesting than specific instances, however, are some of the dilemmas that pressure for social action poses for the churches. First, there is what can be called the "dilemma of specificity." With many avenues of action potentially possible, should the churches choose and commend one option, or should they take only a general position, leaving the choice of means up to individuals and private groups? If, on the one hand, they choose the course of specificity, they run the risk of alienating those members of the church who believe that ecclesiastics are not sufficiently competent to determine the most effective means of social and political action. They lay themselves open to the charge of entering directly into the social and political process and, thus, of blurring the distinction between church and state, the sacral and secular orders. By expending their moral capital on many concrete issues, the churches risk being transformed into just one more pressure group that could, eventually, have no special voice whatever. If, on the other hand, the churches take only general and abstract stands—"do good and avoid evil"—they provide the possibility for people to supply their own moral specifications and, perhaps as often as not, moral rationalizations. Total inaction on race problems, for instance, has been justified on the grounds that the moral good of maintaining peace and order is more important than correcting injustices.

A second dilemma can be termed the "dilemma of authority."

Although the churches vary in the degree of authority they claim over their membership, they all aspire to some degree of moral suasion among those committed to their creed and polity. Yet, conversely, they also desire to grant as much freedom for personal decision to their members as possible. If the ecclesiastical leadership puts all its moral influence behind a specific line of action, it may consequently limit the freedom of those under its sway to come to their own moral conclusions. Authority becomes covertly or overtly coercive, depending upon the status of authority in the church. This dilemma is, of course, most acute in Roman Catholicism where the word of a bishop has traditionally required immediate assent and obedience by the laity. Even under a considerably more permissive and restricted view of episcopal authority, a bishop's recommendation carries heavy weight. Since Vatican II there has been, ironically, an increase both in the demand that the bishops address themselves to concrete problems in a concrete way and in the demand that they cease attempting to prescribe the way Catholics should vote and otherwise implement their social morality.[35]

A third dilemma, the "dilemma of charity," is represented by the conflict between the church's professed aim of speaking to all men and its no less professed aim of bearing prophetic witness to Christian truth. The church must take into account human frailties and yet not temporize in the face of clear moral imperatives. A puritanical ruthlessness can succeed impressively in putting great moral pressure on individuals, but often only at the cost of a total disregard for their psychological preparedness to take a radical moral step. Circumstances of their life might make such a step practically impossible or contextually might entail greater moral loss than gain. Moreover, many people advance morally only if led gently, step by step, from one plateau to the next. This dilemma is strikingly expressed in the implicit conflict between those theologians pressing for a "situation" or "contextual" ethics, especially in the area of personal morality, and those pressing for a sharper, more binding word from the churches in the area of social morality.[36] The former tend in practice toward greater moral permissiveness and variation from case to case; the latter, toward greater firmness and absolutism. The situationist allows the adulterer a flexibility of standards he would not allow the racist.

It is exceedingly difficult for the churches to cope simultaneously with a changing, complex society and with a changing theology. Taken together, these crises and the new conflicts they have introduced into the churches are a source of considerable pathos. On the most human level, almost every church these days has its bewildered, sometimes panic-stricken, members. They neither feel the need for a fresh Christian relevance, nor understand the steps being taken to achieve it. As far as the churches' relationship to society is concerned, they see no need for priests and ministers, bishops and theologians to be issuing statements on social problems. Nor do they approve of sermons, pamphlets, and purportedly religious publications whose content in their opinion is more political than religious. They are distrustful of the new theologies, the new liturgies, and the new forms of Christian social witness.[37] Pathos cuts two ways, however. There is something equally pathetic in the spectacle of ministers, priests, and laymen almost obsessively eager to find a petition to sign, a demonstration to join, a jazz liturgy to perform, or a new cause to promote. At the extreme, they betoken a strand of modern Christianity frantic to find its niche and to prove its cash value in the marketplace of ideas and experience.

Clearly, a good part of the pressure for relevance has been externally induced. A persistent motif of religious writing is that the churches have lost many of their earlier functions. The psychiatrist and the social worker have challenged their place as sources of counsel and guidance; the politician and the technocrat, the artist and the writer, their role as myth-makers and symbol fashioners; the secular ideologues, their status as custodians of ultimacy; and the advertiser and the social planner, their function of shaping values and rendering definitive moral judgments. These popular diagnoses aside, there can be little doubt that the process of secularization and the differentiation of function that mark the movement from a simple to a complex society have radically altered the context of religious belief and the place of religious institutions in society. Differentiation of function in society has meant that no one institution, much less a single individual, can credibly claim competence in more than one or two disciplines or social functions. In a secularized society where "a religious world-view is no longer the basic frame of reference for thought" (to use Thomas O'Dea's expression), religion's function as a synthesizer is greatly diminished. Specialties to which minister and priest could once lay claim (counselor, educator, social arbiter, for instance) have now been taken over by other specialists.

None of these observations, however, provides an answer to two basic questions: In what ways has religion been socially relevant in

America, and in what ways ought religion to be relevant in the future? Yet these questions themselves pose certain preliminary problems. What responsibility, if any, do the churches and individual believers have, as such, toward American society? What can American society reasonably demand of the churches? To what extent ought the requirements of society influence the inner life of the churches?

On the purely secular level, as voluntary institutions participating in the life of society, the churches have a responsibility to promote its welfare, to contribute to its stability, and to be concerned with those persons and institutions that make up the totality of its life. Society may legitimately demand that the churches live up to these minimal obligations. No institution or organization that benefits from society can disclaim social responsibility. At the same time, it would be unreasonable for society to demand the same kind of service from every institution. The churches, the business community, the educational system, the political parties, the academic community, and the philanthropic organizations have different obligations that reflect their diverse capacities and structures. The churches, for instance, are in no position to control the pricing of industrial products, and it would be unreasonable to expect help from them in controlling inflation. Society can demand, however, that the churches put their particular skills and talents, whatever these may be, to the service of the community.

Some immediate general implications leap to mind. Since all of the churches claim a special, overriding interest in moral values and the dignity of man, society can rightfully ask them to make a contribution where moral values and human dignity are pertinent to social problems. The politician, civic leader, or statesman can legitimately call upon the churches for moral support and leadership. To be sure, this poses many dangers for the churches. More than once in American history have they been used by special-interest groups to give moral sanction to immoral political positions. While this possibility complicates the situation—raising, in particular, problems for the conscience of the church—it does not void the general legitimacy of the demand that the churches speak to basic moral and human problems. Nor, from another perspective, would the preference of politicians and civic leaders for churches silent on issues of morality and human dignity be sufficient reason for the churches to be silent. Their obligation to society does not depend upon the wishes of other groups, but upon their existence in and benefit from society. The churches have rights because their members are also citizens. In short, from a purely secular viewpoint, it is equally legitimate for the churches to provide moral support when requested to do so, to withhold support if they cannot in conscience give it, and to find and press moral issues on their own initiative.

Concomitantly, the churches should work to develop the competence, sophistication, and sensitivity necessary to make their contribution to society fruitful. The churches cannot be vaguely opposed to injustice, disorder, and human suffering. Only highly developed technical skills and understanding make any great difference in a society as political and complex as contemporary America. The churches need social, political, and legislative analysts, effective lobbyists, professional staffs, and offices and instrumentalities designed to work at a level commensurate with the complexity of American life. The question is not whether the churches should be institutionalized, but where they should direct their efforts. A self-serving institutionalism is worthy of condemnation, but an institutionalism that is directed toward the service of society need not be at all reprehensible. If the latter were a response to the organizational exigencies of contemporary society rather than an exercise in narcissism, the bad connotations of "ecclesiastical institutionalism" could easily drop away. The churches should be so structured that their aspiration to service is matched by a sophistication and outer-directed organizational apparatus sufficient to realize their desires.

If one takes only the most superficial look at American religion, it becomes easy to see how the churches can establish, by a prima-facie case, that they have been good stewards of their talents and responsible participants in American society. From the Protestant side, serious efforts at social-welfare work and reform began with the Second Awakening. At first, the reform effort was directed toward personal morality, with campaigns against gambling, drunkenness, infidelity, and the like, but was eventually broadened to include a host of larger issues: world peace, human rights, the abolition of slavery, women's rights, the conditions of the working class, prison reform. As early as 1853 one Protestant paper, the *Independent*, was promoting a program of "urban renewal" aimed at lowering rents, cleaning buildings, and developing healthy surroundings.[38] Like efforts were made after the Civil War, culminating, during the first decades of the twentieth century, in the Social Gospel Movement[39] and the Federal Council of Churches. The picture becomes all the brighter if one adds to these developments such efforts as the Woman's Christian Temperance Movement (1874), the Anti-Saloon League (1895),[40] and the widespread Protestant support of the Progressive Party. By the end of World War II, it was generally assumed that the National Council of Churches and major denominational bodies would issue statements on major domestic and international problems, establish task forces and action groups to deal with specific social ills, and institute special funds to give substance to their words. Almost all major denominations established offices in Washington, either as bases for direct lobbying or simply as information bureaus. The Council on Christian Social Progress of the Northern Baptist Convention, the Friends Committee on National Legislation, the Division of Public Relations of the National Lutheran Council, and the Division of Social Education and Action of the Presbyterian Church were some of the more prominent ones. The Catholic record, if less impressive, is still notable. Prior to the Civil War, Catholic bishops directed their concern almost exclusively toward the internal welfare of the church and the preservation of lay loyalty and piety.[41] Even so, they could point to the establishment of numerous orphanages, schools for the indigent, and temperance societies. After the Civil War, efforts were made to care for and educate the newly freed slaves, to promote the welfare of workers, and to provide help to immigrants. The Catholic Lay Congress of 1889 featured a number of papers on the necessity of social justice; a second lay congress in 1893 was primarily devoted to demonstrating the church's concern for human welfare.[42] The formation of the National Catholic Welfare Conference shortly after World War I gave even greater impetus to these concerns.[43]

Yet this kind of evidence is misleading. It tells nothing about the cumulative impact of the churches on society, only what the visible leadership was writing, doing, and discussing. In failing to mention currents within the churches hostile to social concerns, it gives an overly optimistic view of the inherent sense of social responsibility felt by believers and the churches. Still, the special crusades of the churches and small Christian groups were often highly influential. One has only to recall the effectiveness of Protestant prohibition efforts in bringing about dry laws, the powerful leverage Protestant churches brought to bear against relaxation of gambling laws, the long success of Catholics in keeping old divorce and birth-control laws on the books, and, more recently, the powerful support given by the churches to civil rights legislation.

These crusades often engendered bitter discord within and among the churches. Yet they demonstrate that when any large and powerful church or group within the church sets its mind to influencing mores and legislation, it has usually been able to do so, at least temporarily. No less important, failure of the churches to lend support to social reform has significant negative consequences. The foot-dragging of both Protestantism and Catholicism in the South on Negro rights was for decades important in preserving the *status quo*.

The easily documented efforts at relevance lead many churchmen to reject indignantly any charge that the churches are unconcerned about their civic responsibilities. But the presence of so much ambiguity concerning the nature, motives, and effectiveness of the churches' efforts leads reformers (outside the churches and within) to question the unfairness of this charge. These very different perspectives provide an important reason why debates within the churches on social issues can be so furious. Yet it should be evident that the internecine arguments are significant. The history of religion in America shows that concerted and systematic campaigns of public persuasion can make an immense difference in public opinion and legislation, mores and civic attitudes. It matters greatly, therefore, what tactics the churches decide to adopt and how far they are prepared to go in influencing public opinion; which issues they believe part of their responsibility and choose to press; which call for direct, specific action and which for indirect comment. When the Cardinal Archbishop of Los Angeles decided that fair-housing legislation was a "political" and not a "religious" matter, it made a difference. When the Cardinal Archbishop of Boston decided that urban renewal was a "religious" as well as a "political" matter, it also made a difference. In each case, attitudes were affected and legislation influenced.

Whatever might be said about the broad influence of religion,[44] there can be little doubt about the continuing potential of the churches to influence public opinion on certain issues. Political leaders and legislators still fear organized religious opposition, as was clear from debates on changing abortion laws in California and New York in 1965. Catholics still fear the power of Protestant groups to deflect federal legislation that might provide some benefits for parochial schools. Planned Parenthood still fears the power of the Catholic hierarchy to influence legislation on birth-control aid and information. The frequency with which religious leaders are sought to lend their sanction to some social reform, international cause, or moral crusade further substantiates the belief that the churches and their constituents can provide some helpful social and political leverage.

The phrase *social and political leverage,* loosely used in the preceding sentence, is crucial. It has often been argued that the churches' function should be restricted to influencing the moral tone of their members. Churchgoers should have the Word preached to them, be given some broad, general moral guidance, and then be left free to apply their Christianity as they see fit in their daily personal and civic lives. If the churches do more than this, they step beyond their competence. The churches should help form good men. The combined force of such men can then make an indirect, but nonetheless real contribution to society. Although this has been a common enough argument, it has never stopped the churches from applying specific pressures when they believed some vital interest of their own to be at stake. The same Protestant churches in the South that did not hesitate to conduct openly political campaigns to retain dry laws disclaimed "political" competence when it came to racial laws.

There is a fundamental objection to this general stance of political neutrality. It would be exceedingly difficult to prove that broad, vague moral guidance—exhortations about love, responsibility, and justice—makes any real difference in the way people make decisions. Without some specification of what a genuinely moral decision might be in concrete situations, many people are likely to endow their *de facto* choices with *de jure* moral justifications. This is borne out by the way in which almost every political and social stance in American history has been able to gain some religious support and justification. Moreover, in a highly political and organized society—a society that achieves social progress through pressure groups and social leverage—moral generalities rarely have any substantive meaning until they are translated into specific programs of legislation and action. Hence, the course of realism, honesty, and consistency would seem to require that the churches take concrete positions on concrete matters. Since few political issues are totally devoid of moral implications, the churches should not hesitate to speak on a wide range of practical issues. They should use their social and political leverage to the fullest extent. To be specific is to be relevant; to be general is to be irrelevant. Thus should the "dilemma of specificity" be resolved today.

Protestantism and Catholicism in America have each exhibited different strengths and weaknesses in this respect. The strength of Protestantism has been its persistent concern for the welfare not just of Protestants but of the nation as a whole. Coupled with a moralistic attitude toward religion, this has produced a heavy emphasis on the churches' duties toward American life. But there has also been an attendant weakness, well expressed by William Lee Miller:

The characteristic contribution of American religion to American politics . . . has been—not perspective, wisdom, depth of insight—but the rousing of sentiments and energies of charity, generosity and social reform; the characteristic vices have been those of a tremendous over-simplification and sentimentalization of politics.[45]

To these vices might well be added the frequent presumption that only Protestant values are genuinely American values; the considerable amount of Protestant political activity that has been directed at thwarting the demands of other religions; and, as Reinhold Niebuhr has argued, the ambivalence in American Protestantism about the idea and use of power. To cite Miller again, "The remarkable image one gets of the American Protestant enterprise is that of an intention to embrace the world, yet without compromise; to be a sect and yet to mold the whole culture; to reject power and yet to be powerful."[46]

The strength of American Catholicism is that it has rarely presumed any special moral mandate in America. With the exception of a few areas of sexual morality, it has accepted its lot as a minority religion, content simply to live its own life as it sees fit. Yet this attitude has also engendered certain weaknesses: notably its failure to show much concern for the rights and needs of other minority groups. Catholics were notoriously anti-abolitionist prior to the Civil War, late in taking seriously Negro rights after the war, indifferent to women's rights until the last decade, and generally disinterested until the present in questions of civil liberties. Catholicism was prone to take seriously only those causes that bore directly on its own institutional needs and those of its people. It promoted pluralism in education primarily because of its own system of parochial schools; the rights of the working man because so many Catholics were workers; religious freedom because (though not exclusively) this freedom was its only hope in an overwhelmingly Protestant nation. Much of this has changed of late, but the words of Father Joseph H. Fichter, S.J., are still pertinent:

Catholics share in the anti-Semitism of the Northeast, in the isolationism of the Midwest, in the prejudices against the Mexican in the Southwest. . . . On this level we are dealing with the moral and social problems on which the American people are confused, and on which Catholics demonstrate their achieved Americanization by sharing in that confusion.[47]

The churches' greatest success in exercising social leverage has been in domestic politics, especially when some clear, easily understandable value has been at stake—racial equality, urban renewal, labor relations, and public welfare. Their greatest failure has been in those areas marked by a complexity of interests, the need for technical sophistication, and the necessity of ecumenical cooperation. The churches' provincialism partly explains this difference in their effectiveness. Though their concerns are proclaimedly universal, their organizations and techniques have been geared primarily to the local level. Protestant churches in America belong to the World Council of Churches and, in some denominations, to world executive bodies and federations, but these relationships are tenuous and do not offset the provincialism in American religion. Roman Catholicism fares little better; although joined to Rome, the different national hierarchies throughout the world are almost totally independent when it comes to finances, positions on international politics, and internal social policy. Even within the different dioceses of one nation there is a tradition of independence.

The explanation of provincialism also rests partly in the relatively great distance between the churches and the academic, scientific, and diplomatic communities. The presence of the churches in the universities is, at best, peripheral. Nor are the churches present in scientific laboratories, in technically advanced industries, or at international political conferences. Individual churchmen may, on occasion, be in all of these places. Still, by the time they have been able to relay information or suggestions to the churches (assuming they are even in a position to do so; and many are not), events may have moved on to the next stage. Evidence of this gap is to be found in the churches' failure to say anything of note at the time about saturation bombing during World War II or about the atomic bombing of Hiroshima and Nagasaki. They had, in the first place, no information about the facts, and secondly, no well-developed moral theology that could have been quickly and tellingly brought to bear even if they had known the facts. The minimal response of the churches today to cybernation, automation, the emergence of anti-colonialist African and Asian nationalism, international agreements on control of nuclear weapons, and aid to underdeveloped nations shows the persistence of this pattern. Lacking close contacts with decision-makers in these areas and the technical competence to deal with the complex issues, the churches have trouble being heard or being taken seriously when they try to speak.

The very diversity of the churches and their memberships provides another obstacle. As a result of widespread social mobility, fewer and fewer of the major churches can be identified with any one social class, economic interest, region, or party affiliation. Just as Roman Catholicism can no longer be thought of as an exclusively urban, lower-class religion with fixed leanings toward the Democratic Party, American Protestantism is losing to a considerable degree its earlier identification as a middle-class, predominantly rural religion. A movement to the suburbs among white Protestants and to the inner-city ghetto among Negro Protestants accounts for much of this change.

This greater political and ideological diversity within the churches has made it increasingly difficult for a church to attain a consensus within its membership. Although the churches are still capable of bringing social pressure to bear, the frequent lack of internal agreement on issues, strategy, and tactics nullifies much of their political power. Where there is a "religious witness" on both sides of any given fence, church pronouncements will be tempered, as positions on the Viet-Nam war clearly testify. By contrast, the churches have now achieved something of a consensus on race, signaled by the formation of the ecumenical National Conference on Religion and Race in 1964. But even this consensus often disintegrates at the local level because of disputes over tactics.

Social relevance requires the gaining of technical competence and the achieving of a working consensus. There is no easy route to either of these goals. On the question of competence two basic steps would be helpful. First, the two major institutional bodies, the National Council of Churches and the National Catholic Welfare Conference, need to enlarge considerably their professional staffs. Each now has divisions responsible for various areas of social concern, but they are small in comparison with the magnitude of the tasks they face. The same can be said for the various denominational offices and, at a still more local level, the denominational and diocesan offices in cities and states. Where it is a matter of scientific and technological problems—especially some of the moral dilemmas posed by advances in medicine, methods of warfare, psychological conditioning, psychiatry, automation, and cybernation—it is doubtful that there now exists even *one* professional staff in any of the churches charged with the duty of attempting to master the problems and disseminating guidance to the local churches. By and large, the best-endowed and most heavily staffed offices remain those answering the strictly institutional needs of the churches—fund-raising, missionary activities, and public relations. Yet even if the churches were determined to establish staffs in the areas suggested, they would immediately encounter difficulty finding qualified personnel. Neither seminary training nor life in the ordinary local church is geared to turning out specialists in advanced contemporary problems. The numerous graduate schools and seminaries of religion are considerably stronger in this respect, but their strength lies in well-established areas of church concern —race, urban life, the impact of industrialization rather than in the newer areas created by advances in physics, the biological sciences, and psychiatry.[48] The practice of many Roman Catholic religious orders in sending priests and nuns on for graduate work in secular disciplines is a notable exception to the general rule. The churches must clearly make a more systematic attempt to develop specialists. This could be done in two ways: by the establishment of funds devoted to the training of technical staff personnel and by a fellowship system designed to attract theological students and others into specialized church work after providing them with money for advanced work in secular disciplines.[49]

The achievement of a working consensus on social issues within the churches poses far more complicated problems. Professional staffs, assuming they could skillfully communicate their findings to the local churches, would obviously help to provide some consistency and order in the kinds of data channeled into the churches. But more realistically, at least for the near future, only broadened ecumenical relations among the churches are likely to provide real leverage. No single church today is able to exert a major *positive* influence solely on its own. Working alliances will have to be formed by like-minded groups from different churches. Already evident in the area of race and urban renewal, this practice will have to be extended to many other areas. Similarly, the churches will have to learn how to work with non-religious groups much more effectively than has been customary. One of the notable features of the "March on Selma" in March, 1965, was the way in which ministers, priests, nuns, and laymen from different churches all placed themselves under the command of Martin Luther King and his staff.

None of these comments, however, touches on the main problem: the will of the churches to enter the social arena in full force. The churches have consistently given a comparatively low priority to social issues. Now that they are beginning to make efforts to change their parochial priorities, they are discovering how ingrained the old pattern is. As R. Morton Darrow has pointed out in a masterly essay, the Protestant churches for decades avoided any massive social commitment:

In church after church, movements for social and economic reform led by individual clergymen or laymen were squelched by vestrymen or the equivalents, who, viewing society from a lofty perch of affluence and high status, could see no need for drastic changes. Nor can it be said that there was any loud clamor for active participation of the churches—largely middle class in the white, Protestant churches outside the South.[50]

Practically, this resulted in ecclesiastical bureaucracies structured to deal mainly with internal matters. These structures remain dominant today. Moreover, the very success of the churches in creating a large empire of inner-directed buildings, facilities, and staffs has meant that they are now saddled with their maintenance. Should the Catholic Church, for instance, make the (unlikely) decision to reduce or close the parochial-school system and divert the funds saved into social projects, it would face the extraordinarily difficult task of disposing of school buildings and property. It would also have to find work for the thousands of nuns, brothers, and priests in the school system. Thus, it is hardly surprising that the past continues to dominate the present and to curtail the future. Only the most drastic kind of revolution could make a difference. There is no evidence that the established leadership is prepared for such a large-scale reversal of traditional priorities.

Although these complications suggest how unrealistic it would be to expect the churches suddenly to become powerful levers in effecting social reform and progress, there still remain many immediate ways by which they can increase their contribution. A relatively quick competency could be achieved in four areas within the existing structures or where an incipient competency already lies.

1. *The collection of facts.* In *The Idea of a Secular Society*, D. L. Munby has pertinently observed that "in the field of overall social

policy . . . we need to know . . . the actual aims, intentions, impulses and motivations of the various groups in society."[51] To this may be added the need for facts about how people live, what their needs are, and where they are not being served by governmental bodies. If only because of their number and widespread distribution, the local churches in America are strategically placed to assist in gathering this information. Moreover, because the churches are voluntary organizations, they could on occasion be in a better position than governmental agencies to gather and publicize facts. Although official agencies can and do collect information, too often crucial groups are missed or the information, once gathered, is not properly and effectively disseminated, either within or outside the government. The signal effectiveness of Michael Harrington's book *The Other America* in calling public attention to some critical data on poverty (most of it from official sources) shows the value of private efforts in this respect. To some extent, naturally, the churches already serve as information-gathering bodies, particularly in conjunction with denominational offices, the National Council of Churches, and the National Catholic Welfare Conference. But by and large these efforts remain sporadic and relatively unscientific, usually limited to personal impressions and random surveys. Even so, the data on dope addiction collected in Harlem by small groups of Protestant ministers, on urban housing by priests and ministers in Boston, and on the living conditions of migrant workers in California and the Southwest has been a valuable supplement to that collected by other groups. The addition of trained sociologists to the staffs of regional or municipal church bodies would help to systematize these efforts.[52]

2. *The utilization of experience and facilities.* Again, one of the churches' great advantages is the number and local distribution of congregations. The ministers, priests, and perceptive members of these parishes have a good vantage point from which to see the problems of American society firsthand. More than that, these churches have buildings and facilities, some experience in reaching and organizing people, and some access to the local secular officialdom. Many parishes and churches have taken advantage of these assets; it is not difficult to find in every American city of any size interparish committees specializing in counseling the indigent and helping them find jobs, in caring for the elderly, in working with youth, drug addicts, alcoholics, broken families, and the mentally ill. An important new development has been the availability of Of-

fice of Economic Opportunity funds to churches sponsoring job and educational programs for youth. Yet such activities are by no means common. On the contrary, they remain scattered and relatively unorganized ventures dependent upon the initiative of individual clergymen and churches rather than an integral part of the ecclesiastical organizations. The primary concern of the local churches remains Sunday worship, the maintenance of facilities, and the preservation of a genial social life. Roman Catholicism varies from this pattern only by adding the upkeep of the parochial schools to the main concerns of the parish.

3. *Acculturation of immigrant groups.* Though it is commonly assumed that the massive immigrations characteristic of the late-nineteenth and early-twentieth centuries came long ago to an end, this is only relatively the case. While the number of immigrants coming to America from abroad does not amount to a large figure today, large numbers of people can still be called immigrants if one broadens the concept of "immigration" to include those groups that move from one part of the country to another, from one environment to another (rural to urban, South to North, East to West). The movement of southern Negroes from the rural South to the urban North, of poor whites from the Appalachian and Ozark regions to large cities, of Mexican-Americans from rural Texas and Southern California to cities like San Antonio, Forth Worth, Oakland, and Los Angeles, of elderly people from the North to Florida and Arizona often involves as great a cultural shock as that experienced by Old-World immigrants coming to America. The needs of these new immigrants are many: the learning of a different style of life and a new language or a new dialect in some cases; the gaining of jobs, housing, and education for the kinds of work available to them; the finding of a community in which they will feel comfortable. The potentialities for church assistance in all of these areas are clear. The churches can provide neighborhood social centers, organize information desks, undertake the work of leading newcomers through the usually bewildering channels of civic bureaucracy, run child-care centers, establish counseling services. The possibilities are almost as limitless as the needs. Above all, few highly specialized skills would be needed to provide service. Again, to be sure, it is possible to find local churches and in some cases city-wide church groups doing just this kind of work. The East Harlem Protestant Parish in New York has for many years worked with Puerto Ricans, and the Archdioceses of New York and Chicago,

as well as some Texas and California dioceses, have special training programs for priests who will be working with Spanish-speaking groups. But, again, these efforts are not nearly so widespread and imaginative as they could be. This is particularly unfortunate because a sizable number of the major American churches have at least some historical experience in integrating newcomers into a new milieu. German Protestantism in the Midwest and Irish Catholicism on the East Coast for decades found ways to introduce their immigrant brethren to American life, and they did so with extraordinary success. Once the great influx slowed down in the 1920's, however, most of these talents were put aside. There was, in particular, no transfer of the kind of concern felt for the churches' own unacculturated members to those new members of the community who had no religious affiliation with the established churches.

4. *International relations.* While it is now common for church groups and leaders to issue statements on issues of world peace,[53] to sponsor inter-church and ecumenical discussions on modern warfare and international relations, few attempts are made to bring church leaders from disputing nations together to carry on discussions independent of their governments. During the years preceding World War II, for instance, one would have thought that American and German bishops and church leaders might have attempted to convene a conference to discuss their mutual roles and responsibilities in the growing crisis. No such attempts were ever made. Although an important segment of South Viet-Nam's populace is Catholic, no attempt has been made—or even proposed—to bring American and South Vietnamese Catholic leaders together to discuss the war. Though some of the churches in South Africa, notably the Anglican and Roman Catholic, are in the forefront of opposition to *apartheid*, there are no known attempts being made to bring spokesmen from these churches together with church leaders in other countries to discuss the problem. The power of nationalism, on the one hand, and an abiding fear of seeming to interfere in national politics, on the other, have effectively kept church leaders isolated from one another in moments of crisis. Such contacts seem imperative. When serious crises involving the relations between nations arise, would it not be appropriate for the Roman Catholic Pope to invite to Rome immediately representative church leaders, clerical and lay, from the nations involved in order that they might sit down together and attempt to form a consensus on the moral issues at stake? Similarly, could not the World Council of

Churches invite to its headquarters in Geneva similar Protestant leaders? Even better, Rome and Geneva might jointly convene a conference. Such a move—a religious "summit conference"—could well add a new dimension to the churches' scattered attempts to speak to political and military crises. At the very least, it would help focus the attention of the churches on the moral dilemmas posed by international conflict.

There is no magical key to the achievement of relevance; only a great variety of moves at the highest and at the grass-roots levels is likely to have a cumulative significance.[54] A revolution in the thought and action of the churches is necessary, but the signs favoring a radical overthrow of the long, deeply ingrained tradition of hesitancy, complacency, and social conservatism remain comparatively few. That the Second Vatican Council saw fit to devote only two documents out of sixteen, one on communications and one on the "Church in the Modern World," to a direct confrontation with contemporary social problems is a good indication of prevailing priorities in world Christianity, including the United States: first the internal affairs of the church, then society. There is rarely much energy left to deal with the latter.

Ideally, the churches could perform two very broad, but essential tasks in society. They could, in the first place, think much more consciously of themselves as potent communities of reconciliation. One of the great, almost unparalleled assets of the churches is their very diversity of membership. This may make unanimity on particular issues difficult to achieve, but it also means that the churches can provide a place where very different kinds of people can come together in a context they all share—their commitment to Christianity and their church. Such contexts are rare in our society, where most voluntary secular institutions are organized for special-interest groups pursuing narrow ends. The churches, by contrast, are in principle so structured that they are open to a great variety of people. Confrontations of social problems within the churches should, then, be able to cut across class, ethnic, racial, educational, and economic lines far more easily than they can in other institutions. (It should be unnecessary to point out that where the churches are *de facto* enclaves of exclusivism, they will have to work for the kind of universality they claim.) People may not agree with one another in the churches, but at least it ought to be possible for them to communicate there.

A second task the churches could perform would be to recognize that they are almost the only remaining institutions in American society that have an interest in the whole man, in ultimate values, and in the deepest ground of the common good. In the past, the churches were apt to think that the Christian heritage of the West, the antiquity of the churches, and the claimed origin of their wisdom in revelation gave them an exclusive mandate to shape values in society. The non-Christian was never prone to accept pretensions of this kind, and even the Christian has come to relinquish most of his claims to preferred status. Without in any sense suggesting that the churches attempt to regain their privileged status, there is no reason why they should not continue to see one of their major tasks as that of placing before the public the broader issues of human life, society, and culture. If they do this in a non-coercive way, using the techniques of reason and moral suasion, there need be no threat to the maintenance of pluralism or the separation of church and state. When the churches attempt to illuminate the human situation, when they point to the existence of human needs in society, when they try to take steps to alleviate these needs (especially in conjunction with other groups), when they work to preserve the idea of human dignity and justice, they are being socially "relevant." More than that, they are also being faithful to the best in their own traditions.

REFERENCES

1. John A. T. Robinson, *Honest to God* (Philadelphia, 1963), p. 8.

2. Cf. *The Honest to God Debate,* ed. David L. Edwards (Philadelphia, 1964), *passim.*

3. Thomas J. J. Altizer and William Hamilton, *Radical Theology and the Death of God* (New York, 1966), p. x.

4. *Ibid.,* William Hamilton, "The Death of God Theologies Today," p. 28.

5. *Ibid.,* Thomas J. J. Altizer, "Theology and the Death of God," p. 95.

6. Paul Van Buren, *The Secular Meaning of the Gospel* (New York, 1963).

7. E. R. Baltazar, "Teilhard de Chardin: A Philosophy of Procession," *Continuum,* Vol. 2 (Spring, 1964), pp. 87-97.

8. David Jenkins, "Whither the Doctrine of God Now?" *New Theology No. 2,* eds. Martin E. Marty and Dean G. Peerman (New York, 1965), p. 73.

9. Pope Paul VI's encyclical *Mysterium Fidei,* issued in 1965, complained

about the expression *transsignification* as an adequate expression of the doctrine propounded by the Council of Trent.

10. *The Constitution on the Church,* promulgated in 1964, placed its emphasis on the church as a "community" and as the "people of God." At the same time it gave a minimal amount of attention to such older concepts of the church as a "perfect society" or the "Mystical Body of Christ."

11. The most notable effort in this respect is E. Schillebeeckx, *Christ the Sacrament of the Encounter with God* (New York, 1963).

12. "Jesus Christ Reforms His Church," *Proceedings of the Twenty-Sixth North American Liturgical Week* (Washington, D.C., 1966).

13. *Ibid.,* "Relevance: Contemporary Moral Concerns," p. 3.

14. *Ibid.,* p. 6.

15. *Ibid.,* "Relevance: The Present Liturgical Reform," p. 21.

16. *Ibid.,* "Relevance: The Preoccupations of Theology," p. 30.

17. Martin E. Marty, *Second Chance for American Protestants* (New York, 1963), p. 65.

18. Reuel L. Howe, "The Psychological Sciences," *New Frontiers of Christianity,* ed. Ralph C. Raughley, Jr. (New York, 1962), p. 43.

19. *Ibid.,* Graydon E. McClellan, "The Ministry," p. 130.

20. M. Richard Shaull, "The Form of the Church in the Modern Diaspora," *Princeton Seminary Bulletin* (March, 1964), p. 43.

21. National Catholic Welfare Conference News Service (June 29, 1966). In *Priest and People* (New York, 1965), Father Joseph H. Fichter, S.J., presents the results of a survey of priests that showed that in the larger American dioceses half of the priests have no significant personal contact with their bishop.

22. Sister Marie August Neal, S.N.D., "Sociology and Community Change," *The Changing Sister,* ed. Sister M. Charles Borremeo Muckenhirn, C.S.C. (Notre Dame, Ind., 1965), p. 47.

23. *Council Speeches of Vatican II,* eds. Hans Küng, Yves Congar, Daniel J. O'Hanlon (Glen Rock, N. J., 1964), *passim.*

24. Gibson Winter, *The Suburban Captivity of the Churches* (New York, 1962), p. 15.

25. Harvey Cox, *The Secular City* (New York, 1965), p. 2.

26. Peter L. Berger, *The Noise of Solemn Assemblies: Christian Commitment and the Religious Establishment in America* (Garden City, N. Y., 1961), p. 35.

27. Gabriel Vahanian, *The Death of God* (New York, 1966), p. 15.

28. Margaret Mead, "Introduction," *Christians in a Technological Era*, ed. Hugh C. White, Jr. (New York, 1964), p. 17.

29. These attacks have appeared most prominently in *Continuum, Commonweal,* and *The National Catholic Reporter.* By the summer of 1966 only one Catholic prelate, Lawrence Cardinal Sheehan of Baltimore, had issued any kind of formal statement on the morality of the Viet-Nam war; and his was a very broad statement that took no specific stands.

30. Two books, one by a layman and one by a priest, succeed well in dramatizing (and sometimes overdramatizing) these various tensions: Edward Keating, *The Scandal of Silence* (New York, 1965) and Father William DuBay, *The Human Church* (New York, 1966).

31. The discussion of "relevance" at the Twenty-Sixth North American Liturgical Week, cited *supra* in footnote 13, provides a good example of this style of theologizing.

32. The work of Harvey Cox and, even more, that of William Hamilton, provides salient examples of this style.

33. E. L. Mascall, *The Secularization of Christianity* (New York, 1966).

34. "Theology and the Uses of History," an editorial in *Continuum,* Vol. 4 (Spring, 1966), pp. 95-96.

35. In this context it is worth recording the remarks of John Cogley, William Clancy, and John Leo during a *Commonweal* symposium in 1964: "*Cogley:* It is interesting that in California just recently some Catholics were demanding that the bishops tell other Catholics how to vote. This may seem a welcome assist on the particular issue of fair-housing legislation at stake, but I am not happy that we have a group in the Church, and liberals at that, criticizing bishops for not instructing the faithful how to vote. *Clancy:* This was the strange situation in the 1950's. Our secular liberal friends are usually scared to death of the bishops saying anything; but in 1952 they were demanding that the bishops speak out on McCarthy. They were morally outraged that the American hierarchy didn't condemn him. . . . *Leo:* I wonder if Catholic liberals haven't consistently been playing the game both ways. If it is a measure they like, they ask the bishops to intervene. Otherwise they are quick to point out that the political order belongs to the layman." "Fortieth Anniversary Symposium," *Commonweal,* Vol. 81 (Nov. 20, 1964), pp. 266-67.

36. Cf. Joseph Fletcher, *Situation Ethics* (Philadelphia, 1966); John A. T. Robinson, *Christian Morals Today* (Philadelphia, 1964); and Paul Lehmann, *Ethics in a Christian Context* (New York, 1963).

37. On the Protestant side, the editorial pages of *Christianity Today* and *The Christian Herald* provide good examples of the forms this reaction can take. On the Catholic side, the pages of the *Brooklyn Tablet* and *The Wanderer,* as well as the statements and publications of the "Catholic Traditionalist Society," perform a like function.

38. A succinct account of these efforts can be found in Winthrop S. Hudson, *Religion in America* (New York, 1965), p. 197ff.

39. C. H. Hopkins, *The Rise of the Social Gospel in American Protestantism, 1865-1915* (New Haven, 1940) and James Dombrowski, *The Early Days of Christian Socialism in America* (New York, 1936) are basic for an understanding of the movement.

40. Peter H. Odegard, *Pressure Politics: The Story of the Anti-Saloon League* (New York, 1928).

41. *The National Pastorals of the American Hierarchy, 1792-1919* (ed. Peter Guilday [Westminster, Md., 1954]) shows an almost unrelieved omission of reference to American social problems except where they bear on the welfare of Catholics.

42. *Souvenir Volume of the Centennial Celebration and Catholic Congress* (Chicago, 1893).

43. The most exhaustive treatment of these matters can be found in Aaron L. Abell, *American Catholicism and Social Action* (Garden City, N. Y., 1960).

44. A poll conducted by George Gallup for the *Catholic Digest* early in 1966 found that belief in God has declined slightly in the past fourteen years and that the certainty of that belief has declined even further. The greatest decline was found among Jews: in 1952, 70 per cent of the Jews interviewed said they were certain of God's existence, but in 1966 only 39 per cent of the Jews interviewed were certain. Such polls, however, obviously do not measure the intensity of social commitment of believers and, for this reason, they are unilluminating concerning the social impact of belief. For a strong argument that religious beliefs continue to make a considerable social difference, see Andrew Greeley, "The Secular City," *Commonweal*, Vol. 83 (Nov. 12, 1965), pp. 181-84; and Gerhard Lenski, *The Religious Factor* (Garden City, N. Y., 1961).

45. William Lee Miller, "American Religion and American Political Attitudes," *Religious Perspectives in American Culture*, eds. James Ward Smith and A. Leland Jamison (Princeton, 1961), p. 103.

46. *Ibid.*, p. 91.

47. Father Joseph H. Fichter, S.J., "The Americanization of Catholicism," *Catholicism and the American Way of Life*, ed. Thomas T. McAvoy, C.S.C. (Notre Dame, Ind., 1960), p. 124.

48. It should be noted that there is considerable interest in psychiatry so far as it bears directly on pastoral counseling. The existence of the Society for Religion and Mental Health is a sign of this concern.

49. It is at present notoriously difficult for scholars working in the field of religion to find fellowship money to support post-graduate work. Only the Danforth Foundation, in conjunction with the National Council on Religion in Higher Education, offers any substantial help. Nor have the large

denominational organizations made any serious attempt to support scholarship.

50. R. Morton Darrow, "The Church and Techniques of Political Action," *Religious Perspectives in American Culture*, p. 184.

51. D. L. Munby, *The Idea of a Secular Society* (New York, 1964), p. 27.

52. Roman Catholicism already has a number of sociologists specializing in such matters as the parochial schools, vocations to the priesthood and religious orders, and Catholic family life. There is no reason why some of them could not be recruited by diocesan bodies to do research on less parochial matters.

53. During the summer of 1966, for instance, there was a heavy flurry of statements on Viet-Nam: The National Council of Churches urged President Johnson not to pursue a policy of military escalation; delegates to the eighteenth biennial congress of the Greek Orthodox Church of North and South America voted "wholehearted" support of the United States' stand against "all aggression, particularly in Vietnam"; Pope Paul VI urged negotiations; delegates to the World Council of Churches' conference in Geneva, "Christians in the Technical and Social Revolutions of Our Time," condemned American foreign policy in Viet-Nam.

54. Stephen C. Rose has sketched some basic goals for local churches in "The Grass Roots Church," *Christianity and Crisis*, Vol. 26 (July 25, 1966), pp. 168-71. Among the noteworthy initiatives being taken by larger groups are the following: Urban America, Inc., an urban-planning group that will work cooperatively with several major Protestant church bodies to stimulate and help finance construction of low-cost housing; strict anti-discrimination clauses being written into Catholic diocesan building contracts; the Metropolitan Urban Service Training Facility, an ecumenical venture sponsored by the Methodist Church to train community leaders in methods of influencing civic power structures toward social change; the sponsorship by the Protestant Episcopal Church of an agency designed to facilitate church participation in community organization programs; the transformation of the United Church Board for Homeland Ministries from a primarily educational to a primarily action-oriented emphasis; the multifaceted work being freshly undertaken by the various agencies of the older national organizations, especially the National Council of Churches and the National Catholic Welfare Conference—agencies specializing in race, poverty, old age, family life, rural life and housing—and the Catholic Interracial Council, the Episcopal Society for Cultural and Racial Unity, the Baptist Action for Racial Brotherhood.

HARVEY G. COX

The "New Breed" in American Churches: Sources of Social Activism in American Religion

FIVE YEARS AGO the colorless Hudson River city of Newburgh, New York, flashed briefly into national attention when its city manager proclaimed a "get-tough" policy with what he called "welfare chiselers." State and national welfare officials took a dim view of his program, however, and it was quickly terminated. The town dropped once again into obscurity. But this year, Newburgh was back in the news. On May 2, 1966, *The New York Times* carried a story with the headline: "CLERICS UNITE IN ATTACK ON NEW-BURGH'S COLOR LINE." There followed an account of a rent strike in the city's Negro ghetto, a protest organized and supported by a group of the town's white and Negro clergy. Despite the opposition of most of the white population, the clergy said they would continue the strike until repairs were made to the dilapidated tenements in question. If their stated reason for being involved in this action ("The church must witness to the poor, and this includes the Negro") persuaded only a minority of white churchmen to support the action, this minority was still a conscious and articulate one.

Newburgh is not an unusual city. It has simply been fated, twice in five years, to become a stage for a larger drama. Five years ago its welfare crisis disclosed a national uneasiness with welfare policies. Today the battle raging there between socially militant churchmen and such custodians of the *status quo* as banks and real-estate institutions is part of a nationwide phenomenon: the emergence of a "New Breed" of socially activist clergy.

Churches today are facing an unprecedented institutional and theological crisis in their mission to the city. Most of their social services have been taken over by the municipal, state, and federal governments, or by secular agencies. This partial loss of function has precipitated a wrenching reappraisal of urban church strategy in America. It has also provided the occasion for the New Breed of church leaders to seize the initiative and to move the churches away from a social-service view of urban problems toward a political one.

The New Breed has brought to the fore a style of theology and a political vision that have lain dormant for some years although they have deep sources in the Christian tradition and in the American religious experience. In Buffalo, Philadelphia, Kansas City, Chicago, Oakland, and dozens of other cities, the New Breed can be found organizing welfare unions, tenants' councils, rent strikes, and school boycotts. Wherever they are at work, they have evoked opposition, both inside and outside the churches. The resulting tensions have made church politics livelier and more interesting today than they have been for decades.

In this paper I wish to examine certain of these tensions in church politics, describe the New Breed of activist churchmen, and indicate some of the theological and sociological factors operative in the situation.

I

Although the present battle within the churches has profound theological significance, it is not debated in overtly theological terms. Rather, the debate turns on questions of church strategy and policy. The best example of this is the discussion now going on inside the churches over what they should do about poverty. The poverty question comes up in many ways: Should the church remain largely as one of the "helping agencies" and thereby continue its traditional social-service view of poverty? Should it cast its lot with non-governmental organizers, such as Saul Alinsky, investing money, staff, and prestige in building political power for the poor? These, not the Virgin Birth or the inerrancy of Scripture, are the issues church leaders discuss most ferociously today.

Protestant church historian Martin Marty describes the two sides this way: One side says that the Christian church should be involved in the struggle of today's poor in the city and on the farm—at the side of the delinquent, the racially oppressed, the politically exploited. The other side says the church should love these people, but should not become involved in the politics of their problems. As the new strategic-theological altercation unfolds, it becomes clear that the dispute involves three principle parties. Each has a strategy, and a theology to back it. One group simply wants the church to "stay out of politics." It includes people who hold that religion should focus on a world beyond this one, on an inner or "spiritual" life separated from political conflict—the traditional pietists. It includes others who, though they believe the church should concern itself with justice, feel that it should not squander its efforts in the shifting sand of city politics, but should concentrate on larger, more universal quests.

Another group consists of the churchgoing Bourbons. They want the church to act as the custodian of property rights and the traditions of the *ancien régime*. These people regard religion as the sacred cement that binds a society to its past. They are not against the church becoming involved in controversial issues, so long as it always upholds the conservative side. This group is small but wealthy and disproportionately influential. It is linked with conservative business interests and with such reactionary religious publications as *Christian Economics*. Though it usually maintains an aura of respectability, on its right wing it shades into fanatical Birchite groups and Billy Joe Hargis' "Christian Anti-Communist Crusade."

The third group, also small but growing quickly in size and influence, is the New Breed, those laymen and clergy who are bent on moving the church toward a more direct role in supporting and inducing social change.

No one knows just how large the New Breed is. Certainly it includes a sizable minority of the ministers graduated from the main interdenominational seminaries and some of the denominational ones in the past ten years; it also includes some educated laymen who have been influenced in the years since World War II by college pastors and professors of religion.

Still, the main symbol of the New Breed is the socially activist clergyman. An indication of the weight of the New Breed's impact can be seen in the radical metamorphosis the public image of the American clergyman has undergone in the past few years. A decade ago, he was often depicted in cartoons and stories as a pompous bore, a disagreeable zealot, or a genial incompetent. Although these images still persist in certain areas, the average man is now just as likely to think of nuns, priests, and ministers leading protest marches, standing in picket lines, or organizing debates on Viet-Nam. This change in the stereotype of the churchman has affected the minister's self-image. It separates the New Breed from the Old. Among the clergy, the clear demarcation is between those who participate directly in the political or social struggle and those who do not.

The New Breed fights its battles mainly in the city. Although there are examples of church social activism in rural areas, the major theater of operations for the New Breed remains the American city. True, ministers and priests played a major role in the dramatic strike of the Delano, California, grape workers this year. Also, the Mississippi Delta Ministry sponsored by the National Council of Churches is perhaps the most controversial program operating under church auspices anywhere in the country. Yet the priests and ministers involved in these activities often come from urban backgrounds and hold many of the values and beliefs of the much larger group of New Breed churchmen now at work in the cities.[1]

Spokesmen for the New Breed have in the past decade moved into key positions in churches, seminaries, and city-mission structures. This group has accepted the "political" rather than the social-service definition of the crisis of urban poverty. Its leaders sharply criticize the traditional programs of churches and mission societies. They advocate the utilization of church resources to help mobilize the poor in various types of community organizations. They speak unapologetically of the struggle for power in the city and the churches' responsibility to enter into the struggle on the side of the exploited and powerless.[2] In Rochester, Buffalo, Chicago, and other cities they have used church funds to support Saul Alinsky or other organizers in setting up energetic programs for organizing the poor. Negro ministers who hold positions of leadership in the civil rights movement are a crucial component in the New Breed. They have helped churches form coalitions with civil rights groups, neighborhood action organizations, and political reform movements.

Some people believe that this surprising new role the churches are playing in the cities has already begun to have an important effect. Saul Alinsky said in a recent interview that the churches in the 1960's have assumed the role played by the labor unions in the 1930's. "The unions are now the haves—they're part of the *status quo*," says Alinsky. "The Christian churches are now taking the leadership in social change." Alinsky has worked with priests and ministers to organize the poor in the ghettos and grey areas of a dozen American cities. He has had years of experience, but he recently conceded that he has never seen the equal of the "pure flame of passion for justice you find in these young ministers today." Although he admits that large sections of the church remain inert or reactionary, he still contends that the church is often less compromised than most other large urban institutions and that, in any case, it has a gospel that "constantly forces it to think about siding with the poor," even when such a posture militates against its own institutional interests.

Since Alinsky's work exposes him mainly to the militant minority within the churches, his evaluation is undoubtedly biased. He may underestimate the strength of those elements in the church today that are more sclerotic than any fossilized labor union and far removed from the hope and hates of the urban poor. But he has spotted an important trend. There is a new mood in the churches, and it is gaining ground quickly.[3]

The debate unleashed by the New Breed is far-reaching. It simmers just below the surface at the national meetings of denominations, church agencies, and church organizations. It often breaks out into open opposition as it often did against Eugene Carson Blake. Blake is now Secretary-General of the World Council of Churches; until May, 1966, he was Stated Clerk of the United Presbyterian Church. One of the first top church officials to be arrested in a civil rights demonstration, Blake is a hero of the New Breed. In an article on the task the church currently has before it, Blake said:

The Church must identify itself much more radically with the interests of the poor, the "losers," the outcasts and the alienated. . . . The mark of the presence of the awaited Messiah is still related to the poor having the Gospel preached to them and the captives being released.[4]

The debate also erupts frequently in city councils of churches. In Rochester, New York, the Council of Churches voted in 1964 to raise $100,000 to support a militant community organization among poor Negroes. The local radio station WHAM threatened to cancel the Council's weekly religious program. When the churches persisted in their plans for the community organization, they were shut off the air; the case is now before the F.C.C. The Council's executive insists that even though the church's radio voice has been silenced, the church is preaching the gospel by its identification with Rochester's dispossessed.

This argument rages in city after city and church after church.

Although the fight seems at first to be about tactical considerations, it actually has profound theological overtones. It raises the most basic questions about the mission of the church, the nature of its faith, and the central problem of where men encounter God in an urban secular world.

II

Why has a movement of militant, politically conscious churchmen emerged in American cities in the past decade? There are both sociological and theological reasons; the phenomenon cannot be understood without exploring both dimensions.

Sociologically, the emergence of the New Breed can be accounted for by the change in the distribution of power among ethnic and religious groups that has taken place, especially in the older cities of America, in recent years. A Catholic mayor and city council, who usually have close ties with the Irish, Polish, and Italian poor, have in some measure replaced the Protestant oligarchies in the city power structure. Of course, there are still many poor Catholics, but the noisy "new poor" in American cities are often Negroes and Appalachian whites, and mostly Protestants.

The sociological and political basis for the new role churches are playing in urban politics may be the common antagonism for City Hall shared by displaced middle-class white Protestants and by disinherited white and Negro poor. The coalition these groups form is sometimes strengthened by other partners: reform-minded Jews of the type who swallowed ethnic sentiment and voted against Beame and for Lindsay in New York, and "new" Catholics who are heartened by Vatican II and whose Catholicism is a matter of conviction rather than a badge of ethnic identification.

Admittedly this alliance of disparate groups is a recent one; and the connections between the parties, tenuous. Middle-class Protestants and Jews tend to have a League-of-Women-Voters mentality. On the whole, they are devoted to civic improvement, interested in constitutional reform, but suspicious of noisy, conflict-inducing community organization and of sharply partisan politics. Poor whites cooperate uneasily with the Negroes. Catholics are upset when they are accused of "betraying their kind." But however flimsy this coalition may sometimes appear, it is the expression of important social and political realities. If the coalition combines the vigor of the New Breed in the church and the energy of today's Negroes, we may be witnessing the appearance of a formidable new ingredient in the mixed stew of American urban politics. If so, it is a force that politicians will ignore to their peril.

The bureaucratization of religious organizations is the second factor contributing to the entrance of church groups into the political arena as forces to be considered. Although this may sound unlikely to some church members and even to some religious activists, there can be little real doubt that it is true. As Max Weber said, the rationalization of religions produces a group of religious specialists; these specialists then refine, restate, and clarify the beliefs and practices of the religion, often in ways that laymen disapprove. At the upper levels of governmental and private bureaucracies one sees today the development of a group of people who are in command of information and technical competence and can exert influence and leadership that goes considerably beyond the views of the people they are supposed to represent. Such professional initiators of policy populate the research staffs of many elected officials and of numerous public and quasi-public agencies. They often staff the foundations and the command posts of large voluntary associations. They can also be found on the staffs of church organizations, and this raises an important question about the relations between lay and professional members in religious groups. It is especially important for many Protestant groups where all authority ostensibly flows from laity to designated officials. Despite explicit doctrines of congregational autonomy and grass-roots authority, something like a "managerial revolution" has taken place in the church. Many church leaders form and lead rather than merely reflect and represent the opinions of their constituencies.[5]

The coming of the managerial revolution to Protestantism means that the wrangle between the New Breed and its opponents is in no sense a battle for the freedom of laymen against a dominating clergy. It is often the reverse. Activist ministers must frequently contend with the socially conservative laymen who sit on the boards and committees that rule the churches. This is particularly important to point out in view of the vocal demands among Catholic laymen today for a wider responsibility in the governance of their church. Protestantism in America, at least in its main-line denominations, is far from being completely lay controlled, but it is often where lay control is most powerful that the social-service mentality and opposition to social action has been most vociferous. Correspondingly, where the managerial revolution has freed ministers and church executives from subservience to laymen, there is *more* of a tendency toward social involvement. Studies have shown that ministers who do not serve a local parish, and hence are somewhat more insulated from direct lay control, are much more likely to demonstrate and become involved in direct action than are pastors of local churches.[6] Of the hundreds of clergymen who flew to Selma, a disproportionate number were denominational and interdenominational staff people, college and university chaplains, and ministers of mission churches not directly dependent on a congregation for their financial support. The same could be said for involvement in urban political issues. Ministers not directly answerable to lay constituencies are joined in New Breed activities by pastors, including Negroes, whose congregations approve their involvement. Ministers of conservative congregations in suburbs or downtown are less likely to lean toward New Breed activism. Likewise priests who belong to religious orders are more likely to take unpopular stands than are the secular priests who serve parish congregations.

Thus, the emergence of the New Breed can be understood in part from a strictly sociological perspective. It expresses a new constellation of political groupings in the American city. It springs from the bureaucratically secured freedom of church executives who have been liberated by tenure and specialization from immediate answerability to lay sentiment. But such explanations always leave much unsaid. One study shows that ministers who belong to denominations that have taken stronger stands on civil rights tend to become more deeply involved in this struggle than ministers whose national church bodies have issued weaker statements. In other words, there are religious and theological variables at work. Unless we specifically examine what Gerhard Lenski calls "the religious factor,"[7] our picture remains incomplete. Without a "religious factor," for example, it would be hard to explain why the behavior of certain Catholics conflicts markedly with ethnic and class expectations, or why church leaders urge courses of action that may threaten their class and institutional interests.

III

Two elements in the belief systems of the churches have a direct bearing on the emergence of the New Breed. One is the "holiness of the poor," the special status assigned to the poor in

Christian theology. The other is the idea of the "blessed community," the high value put on equality and personal participation in the congregation and in the society as well, especially in religious groups deriving from the English Reformation. The Negro freedom movement, particularly as it is embodied in such charismatic leaders as Martin Luther King, has often served as the vehicle through which churchmen have moved toward activism on a wider range of issues. But King's persuasiveness lies in part in his ability to appeal to values that are deeply enmeshed in the American religious tradition. The Negro becomes the present embodiment of "the poor," while "integration" points to the vision of a holy community. All this is made explicit on such ritualistic occasions as the 1963 March on Washington where the ritual culminated in King's "I Have a Dream" sermon.

It is also essential to notice that the two elements, the holy outcast *and* the blessed community, must go together. Without the vision of restored community, the holiness ascribed to the poor would fall far short of politics and result in a mere perpetuation of charity and service activities. But the two together, mediated to American theology from the classical theological tradition by the emphasis on the Kingdom of God and the Social Gospel, produce a powerful ideological stimulus without which the New Breed remains incomprehensible.

Let us look first at the place of the poor in Christian theology. Saul Alinsky is correct in saying that whatever their degree of institutional compromise, the churches have an inconvenient gospel that constantly reminds them that they should be the protagonists of the poor. This tradition has deep roots. Although the ancient Jews saw prosperity as a sign of divine favor, they also believed that God would severely judge those in power who abused the poor. This is evident, for example, in Nathan's parable to King David (II Samuel 12:1-6) and in the preaching of such eighth-century prophets as Amos, Isaiah, and Micah. The Mosaic legislation and particularly the Priestly Code make the poor—especially widows, orphans, and sojourners—objects of special solicitude (see Leviticus 5 and 19). Among the Israelites, the poor had the privilege of gleaning and the right to the produce of the land during the sabbatical year.

From the outset, the outcast has occupied a special place in Christian theology. In Jesus' teaching it is the poor who inherit the Kingdom; his recorded utterances fairly seethe with invective against the rich. Whether these sayings are really his or whether they reflect the ethos of the early church is not important for our purpose. In either case, the poor, the disenfranchised, and the underprivileged were believed to be holy; they were thought to be in some way especially favored of God.

Most early Christian congregations were made up of poor people, as Paul discloses in the opening section of his first letter to the Christians at Corinth. Passages critical of the rich may reveal, therefore, an element of *ressentiment*. Still, these ideas were fixed in canon and liturgy and have periodically exerted an important influence on the church. This is obvious when one thinks of the continuous impact that one single text, "Sell all you have and give to the poor," has had throughout church history. It was a crucial determinant in the birth of the monastic movement and the Franciscan order among others. This case and countless others demonstrate the importance of value and belief to social change.[8]

With the rise, after Constantine, of the Medieval Catholic Church and the resulting alteration in the class composition of Christianity, there was a corresponding retreat from the mystique of the poor. Although the monastic movement tried to emphasize its religious importance, poverty was eventually defined, along with celibacy and obedience, as one of the "counsels of perfection" required of the dedicated religious elite within the church but not of the vast majority of believers. The poor, both clerical and lay, were viewed as those whose presence in the society provided the needed occasion to give alms and exercise the virtue of charity. In a subtle way, the virtue seen by early Christians in the poor themselves was now transferred to those who gave to the poor.

With the coming of the Protestant Reformation and the rise of capitalism, the idea that the poor were especially dear to God temporarily lost favor. Moral strictures on the poor became common. Their failure to flourish was interpreted as evidence of the displeasure and wrath of God. Still, the value of compassion for poor people was never wholly lost, and England passed its first real poor-relief act in 1601, emphasizing work relief for able-bodied men and apprenticeships for children. But the suspicion that pauperism came mainly from sloth rather than from the inability to find a job caused relief payments to be kept lower than the wages paid to the poorest workers. In many European countries, the churches retained control of poor relief until the nineteenth century.

Throughout Western history, contempt for the poor as morally inferior people was constantly challenged by the belief in their holiness. The idea that the indigent were bearers of special virtue and religious significance was always kept alive. Roman Catholic orders stressed the value of poverty. Heretical groups such as the Waldensians, founded in 1179 by Peter Waldo as "The Poor Men of Lyons," tried to call the whole church back to apostolic poverty. Moravians and Methodists spread their doctrines at first mainly among the poor. Among modern Roman Catholics, writers such as Dorothy Day and her followers of *The Catholic Worker* kept the idea of God's presence among the poor alive in a church that was often debased and cheapened by American success standards. It is noteworthy that Michael Harrington, whose eloquent book on poverty *The Other America*[9] made such a mark on the American conscience, began his writing career with *The Catholic Worker*.

But this traditional emphasis on the holiness of the poor in Christian theology could not by itself have produced the New Breed. A tradition of *concern* for the poor could just as easily lead the churches today into the social-service rather than the political attitude toward poverty. The other operative theological and ethical tradition is the equalitarian vision of the blessed community in which everyone participates without distinction. Although this image recurs many times in the Bible, it is perhaps best seen in Jesus' parable of workers in the vineyard, each of whom receives the same pay although they have worked different lengths of time. This parable illustrates the radically equalitarian eschatology of Christianity, in contrast, for example, to the ancient Egyptian belief that royalty would still reign and slaves still serve in the next life. When the principle of radical equality before God and equal participation in the community is applied to the present society, and not just to the church or to the world to come, it has explosive consequences for secular polity. This belief in "participatory democracy," along with a devotion to the poor and dispossessed, supplies in one way or another the theological fuel for today's New Breed.

Where did this conviction originate? The rankless equality of participants was a central feature of the earliest Christian congregations. The Apostle Paul speaks of equality between slave and free, Greek and barbarian, and men and women. With the development of a hierarchically ordered church and the assumption by Christian priests of the *privilegien* once accorded the priests of the imperial cultus, the principle of radical equality was, however, eclipsed. Again, as in the case of poverty, it was emphasized if not always practiced by the religious orders. Some historians contend that the practice of full electoral democracy began in the West in the Benedictine monasteries.

With the Reformation, the religious equality of all was again strongly emphasized. Although the left-wing Reformers wanted to extend the idea to the entire society, Luther insisted that to confuse equality before God and equality among men was a serious error. It was in seventeenth-century England that the value of "participatory democracy" was most successfully lifted from the religious congregation alone and applied to society as a whole. In Cromwell's army "even cobblers and tinkers" were exhorted to reflect upon political problems. Thus the ideal of a society where everyone participates in politics, where no one is excluded in principle from decision-making in the commonwealth, entered the Anglo-Saxon tradition. It is still operative today and is unquestionably one of the beliefs motivating the New Breed of churchmen.

Not only were all men called by God to political participation, according to the Puritans, but it was possible to establish certain elements of God's Kingdom here on earth. The Calvinism of the English Puritans, as Michael Walzer has shown in *The Revolution of the Saints,* "appropriated worldly means and usages: magistracy, legislation, warfare. The struggle for a new human community, replacing the lost Eden, was made a matter of concrete political activity."[10]

This impulse toward the reconstruction of the political community along lines that would insure a greater realization of ethical and religious values continues to operate in our society today. When combined with a theologically grounded compassion for the poor, it produces a potent motivational factor. But it required a view of the possibilities of the outcast and his potential for political participation that had not been present during the medieval period. Puritanism supplied this missing link. As Walzer goes on to say, the Puritan program required "a recognition that all subjects were knowledgeable and active citizens, rather than naïve political children, that government was not a household, the state not an extended family, and the king not a loving father."[11]

This same set of beliefs about man, when applied to the American scene today, results in a rejection of the social-service definition of poverty and an endorsement of the political definition. It provides the often unspoken assumption by means of which the young turks can argue that "poverty" is not merely the lack of money and of services by some people, but the failure of the political community as a whole.

IV

With the coming of the New Breed, the American churches have begun to reclaim a central element of their past. H. Richard Niebuhr has argued that the ideal of establishing the Kingdom of God on earth is the most persistent and pervasive theme in the history of American theology.[12] It brought many of the first settlers to a foreboding new continent. It helped inspire the founding fathers of the republic. It came to fervent expression in the nineteenth century in the Social Gospel Movement under Washington Gladden and Walter Rauschenbusch. In turn, the Social Gospel greatly influenced the social thinking of the Federal Council of Churches in its famous "social creed of the churches" of 1908. With the coming of World War I, the Social Gospel Movement, for which pacifism was a central tenet, began to lose momentum. Later it was displaced theologically by the so-called neo-orthodox movement. Reinhold Niebuhr, with whom neo-orthodoxy is usually associated in this country, perpetuated many of the elements of the Social Gospel, though he was often critical of what he took to be its naïveté about power.[13]

The present renewed interest in political action for the poor among New Breed churchmen is not just a "return to the Social Gospel." It is more than that. It is a reclamation of the main stream of theology in America, a stream that was only temporarily diverted by the European existentialist theologies after World War I. Those who see in the New Breed a mere outburst of secular activism reveal a lack of familiarity with the history of religion in America. The Kingdom of God, which in the neo-orthodox period had become an "impossible possibility," has become once again something for which to work.

Still, there are differences between the current crop of socially militant churchmen and their spiritual forebears. The views of the New Breed tend to be more provisional. They do not believe that one push will bring in the Kingdom. They tend less to identify particular utopian schemes, such as socialism or pacifism, with the gospel. They are more appreciative of secular allies and see the church more as a supporter and strengthener of movements already under way than as a vanguard. They rely less on preaching and are more willing to lead the institutional church directly into the struggle for power for the poor. The New Breed has learned its lessons from Reinhold Niebuhr and combined them with the spirit of the Social Gospel. It has renewed the quest for the Kingdom of God on earth, but it has done so with a deeper realization of the intransigence of evil and a more realistic idea of power and how it functions.

This, then, is the theological perspective of the New Breed. It underlies its claim that the social-service agencies, including those operated by the church, do little to remove poverty. According to the New Breed, these agencies merely reduce the guilt of the nonpoor by fostering the illusion that "something is being done." And this illusion leaves little strength or inclination to make the structural changes necessary to close the gap between the culture of poverty and the majority. So strong is the New Breed's contempt for the Lady-Bountiful attitude toward the poor that certain church agencies have advised their local congregations *against* any cooperation with the government's War on Poverty unless the programs guarantee power and participation for the poor. The April 1966 *Newsletter* of the Division of Church Strategy and Development of The United Presbyterian Church in the U.S.A. warns its readers about the War on Poverty:

There are serious dangers in the way current community action programs are being structured. Lines of control are being drawn tightly to a central bureaucracy. Vital dynamic elements in the city are in danger of being smothered by the kinds of control of the local citizens which are built into the operations of the city poverty operation. Full endorsement seems inappropriate.[14]

Here the traditional Christian interest in the poor and their welfare has been informed by a social eschatology, a dedication to the restoration of full participation in the commonwealth. This hope for the realization of the blessed community, though expressing itself in secular political form, is, as we have seen, authentically religious in origin.

The New Breed of activist churchmen stands in the succession of Roger Williams and William Penn, both of whom sought to establish a colony of heaven on earthly soil. They witness to their faith in a style that would have been familiar to their forefathers among the Free-Soilers, Abolitionists, Feminists, and Social Gospelers.

This tradition, which was partially eclipsed by a generation of church theologians heavily influenced by Europe, represents the reappearance of an authentically American religious stream. The New Breed may appear "secularized" to some, but they have an honorable religious history behind them.

What will happen to the New Breed? They will probably not succeed completely, either in their efforts to win control of the church from the Old Guard or in their attempt to abolish poverty, war, and injustice in our society. They may even grow old and complacent. But at the moment, these young activists are trying with some real success to lead the American churches away from their nostalgic dream of the rural past and into the peril and promise of an urban future. In doing so they may restore to visibility a religious tradition at least as old as the American experience itself. Even if they do not fully succeed, they are writing a fascinating chapter in the history of not only the American church, but of the republic as well.

REFERENCES

1. See Leon Howell, "The Delta Ministry," *Christianity and Crisis*, Vol. 26, No. 14 (Aug. 8, 1966), pp. 189-92.

2. For example, see the February 1965 issue of *Social Action*, published by the Council for Christian Social Action of the United Church of Christ. The entire issue is devoted to "Strategy for Community Change."

3. For a good account of the debate in the churches over Alinsky, see Stephen C. Rose, "Saul Alinsky and His Critics," *Christianity and Crisis*, Vol. 24, No. 13 (July 20, 1964).

4. Eugene Carson Blake, "The Church in the Next Decade," *Christianity and Crisis*, Vol. 26, No. 2 (Feb. 21, 1966), p. 17.

5. Paul Harrison, *Authority and Power in the Free Church Tradition* (Princeton, 1959).

6. See some of the recent work of sociologist Jeffrey K. Hadden, especially "A Study of the Protestant Ministry of America," *Journal for the Scientific Study of Religion*, Vol. 5, No. 1 (1965), pp. 10-23.

7. Gerhard Lenski, *The Religious Factor* (Garden City, N. Y., 1961).

8. See J. A. Sanders, "The Banquet of the Dispossessed," *The Union Seminary Quarterly*, Vol. 10, No. 4 (May, 1965), p. 335.

9. Michael Harrington, *The Other America* (New York, 1962).

10. Michael Walzer, *The Revolution of the Saints* (Cambridge, Mass., 1965), p. 28.

11. *Ibid.*, p. 33.

12. H. Richard Niebuhr, *The Kingdom of God in America* (New York, 1959).

13. See Robert T. Handy (ed.), *The Social Gospel in America 1870-1920* (New York, 1966).

14. See "Strategy for the Response of Religious Institutions to the War on Poverty," page 6.

MICHAEL NOVAK

Christianity: Renewed or Slowly Abandoned?

PROFOUND CHANGES have begun to become apparent in the field of
religion in the latter half of the twentieth century. This paper
attempts to analyze these changes, as they are occurring among
younger Americans. As one who is involved in these changes, the
author has, in part, been assigned the task of recording the sense
and momentum of these changes "from within." The title of a sober
pastoral letter of Emmanuel Cardinal Suhard of Paris, issued at the
conclusion of World War II, states rather well the fundamental
question: "The Church Today: Growth or Decline?"[1]

The transformation that Christianity, in particular, is now experiencing is unique in its rapidity, profundity, and intensity, although it is not without partial historical analogues. Our task will
be to sort out the ambiguities that arise from these changes: Is
Christianity slowly exercising its perennial powers of assimilation
over yet another culture, or is it dying the death of a thousand
qualifications? Our procedure will be to report other statements
and interpretations of the present religious situation, and then to
offer an analysis of our own.

I. Something Is Dead

The evidence that a profound ambiguity has stolen into contemporary Christian consciousness is so overwhelming that one
hardly knows where to point. Perhaps the testimony of a conservative Anglican divine will be most telling. Professor E. L. Mascall
takes as a leitmotif for his book, *The Secularization of Christianity*,
the following quotation:

There is no longer a Christian mind. It is a commonplace that the mind of modern man has been secularized. For instance, it has been deprived of any orientation towards the supernatural. Tragic as this fact is, it would not be so desperately tragic had the Christian mind held out against the secular drift. But unfortunately the Christian mind has succumbed to the secular drift with a degree of weakness and nervelessness unmatched in Christian history. It is difficult to do justice in words to the complete loss of intellectual morale in the twentieth-century Church.[2]

Ever since the appearance in England and the United States of Bishop John A. T. Robinson's *Honest to God*,[3] the literate public has become aware of the themes of "a religionless Christianity," a "secular Christianity," and, finally, a "death-of-God theology." The young German minister, Dietrich Bonhoeffer, who was executed by the Nazis at the age of thirty-nine and whose enigmatic reflections in *Letters and Papers from Prison*[4] largely inspired the present interpretations of what is happening to Christianity, has been featured in *Life* and *Time*. Bonhoeffer, writing within an orthodox, world-despising Lutheran context, discovered in prison that the world had "come of age," that it was in its "adulthood." In order to drive men to their knees, the traditional Christian apologetic sometimes attempted to humiliate them or to point to something "beyond" that they lacked. It must now give way to a "worldly Christianity," an optimistic fullhearted engagement of Christians in secular tasks. Christ, "the man for others," is found in worldly service. Christians should appeal not to a transcendent but to an immanent God, "the Divine in the midst of things." They should live "as if God does not exist," since God as *deus ex machina* is no longer needed by men.[5]

The excitement that such reflections generated among those Protestants who had been trying to live with the Barthian, neo-orthodox, transcendent God, the "wholly Other," is not difficult to imagine. The long years of "crisis theology" had begun to weigh too heavily.[6] Bonhoeffer's optimism regarding the world came as a great release, especially for younger men[7] too long dominated by the unchallenged views of Barth, Tillich, Reinhold Niebuhr, and Bultmann. Concomitantly, the entrance of many Christians into the civil rights movement and into the struggles of the "inner city" seemed to corroborate Bonhoeffer's vision. Christians who were involved in "religion" often had little sympathy for the necessary social and political reforms. Christians involved in living "for others" dreamed dreams of a new kind of society in the United States.

They felt all too keenly the "irrelevance" not only of the religious establishment but also of the religion of the past. The project of working out a new "radical theology," without reference to the traditional transcendent God of Christianity, seemed quite plausible precisely to some who were most motivated by Christian impulses to "love their neighbor."

A classic story in the literature of our culture, told over and over again in the works of such writers as Dreiser, Farrell, Anderson, Roth, and Updike, concerns an odyssey from a religious upbringing to "enlightenment." Observers who do not believe in God scarcely share the excitement of Christians regarding the new age of religionless Christianity. Miss Marghanita Laski wrote: "Religionless Christianity, though often profoundly exciting to those who have hitherto taken an organized church for granted, seems to the unbeliever a natural response to the often noted fact that the vitality of impulses atrophy as they become institutionalized." She was not impressed by the attempt, as she saw it, to invent "a mishmash of apparently less controversial religion."[8] Alasdair MacIntyre opened his review of *Honest to God* with one memorable sentence, "What is striking about Dr. Robinson's book is first and foremost that he is an atheist," and closed it with another, "The creed of the English is that there is no God and that it is wise to pray to him from time to time."[9] W. W. Bartley III, himself a former Protestant become enlightened, reviewed some of the Bonhoeffer literature and wondered whether, had he not been executed, Bonhoeffer might not later have quite simply "forsaken Protestant theology." Bartley registered a characteristic Anglo-American philosophical complaint about the "shallow and woolly eclectic thinking, as well as the occasional downright incompetence and self-deception" of the earlier giants of American Protestant theology, Paul Tillich and Reinhold Niebuhr. Then he concentrated on Bonhoeffer:

It becomes rather urgent for a person holding a view like Bonhoeffer's— that there is literally no need for Christianity or for God in an adult world—to explain what if anything does distinguish a Christian from others and why, indeed, anyone should in such circumstances remain a Christian. It is precisely at this point that Bonhoeffer, who is rarely profound but usually clear, becomes as vague as any conventional German theologian. The role of the Christian is conceived now as a fundamentally ethical one of total engagement in social and personal life in full collaboration with like-minded liberal secularists.[10]

There is in these comments by nonbelievers a little of the *a priori* confidence enunciated some years ago by Sigmund Freud. "I think," Freud calmly addressed an imaginary believer, "you are defending a lost cause." He continued:

Our God *Logos* will fulfill whichever of these wishes nature outside us allows, but he will do it very gradually, only in the unforeseeable future, and for a new generation of men. . . . On the way to this distant goal your religious doctrines will have to be discarded. . . . You know why: in the long run nothing can withstand reason and experience, and the contradiction which religion offers to both is all too palpable. Even purified religious ideas cannot escape this fate, so long as they try to preserve anything of the consolation of religion. No doubt if they confine themselves to a belief in a higher spiritual being, whose qualities are indefinable and whose purposes cannot be discerned, they will be proof against the challenge of science; but then they will also lose their hold on human interest.[11]

Religious thinkers, thus, seem to be impaled on the horns of a dilemma. If they do not come to a more sophisticated understanding of their faith, tutored by reason and experience, they will be bypassed by the religion of *Logos;* if they do come to a more sophisticated understanding, they will lose all interest in religion, or at least their less educated constituency will. In fact, Freud interprets religious interests as the expression of a need for consolation felt among the less educated and the less mature. If this interpretation is correct, religious people cannot learn from reason and experience, religious thought cannot progress beyond infantile or adolescent defenses, and religion as a cultural force is essentially fixed and static. "My illusions," Freud writes, "are not, like religious ones, incapable of correction."[12] It seems to be a necessary tactic for the nonbeliever to think that religion is closed to further development, incorrigible under the pressures of inquiry and experience. A story is current about a distinguished American positivist who, on hearing Paul Tillich deliver a highly intelligent funeral sermon for a mutual colleague, sputtered angrily: "Why Tillich isn't a Christian at all!"

A second factor, besides their own opposite commitments, makes it difficult for nonbelievers to understand developments in religious life and thought. The inhibitions of the Victorian era, as Gordon Allport relates,[13] have been reversed. In polite public conversation it is no longer embarrassing to speak openly of sex, but it is embarrassing to speak of religion. Academic writers about religion commonly begin with apologies. "Among modern intellectuals—especially in the universities—the subject of religion seems to have gone into hiding. . . . The persistence of religion in the modern world appears as an embarrassment to the scholars of today."[14] Surveying possibilities for inquiry in his own field, a political scientist writes:

Religions appear to be virtually untouched. Certainly no American political scientist has provided a noteworthy analysis of the idea-system (or idea-systems) that characterizes religions in general. Neither has an American political scientist carefully explored the significance for legal government of the belief-system, organizations, and rituals we call Christianity.[15]

It is difficult to see how political scientists can understand political events in Viet-Nam, or even the different political styles of such American politicians as Goldwater, Johnson, Stevenson, and Kennedy, without a knowledge of the alternative experiences of religion.

The cautious observer, consequently, will not wish to assent too quickly to the proposition that the transformations being undergone by Christianity in our time are all in the direction of capitulation to atheistic or agnostic secularism. Contemporary atheistic secularism, particularly in America, carries so great a weight of Christian conviction that it does not confront a sophisticated Christianity so much with an antithesis as with a sympathetic stimulus. In our society there are real differences between the world view of the agnostic and that of the Christian. These differences must be located with care; conclusions about their practical consequences ought not to be rashly and ideologically assumed.

In the first place, American atheists or agnostics are not often tempted by nihilism. Dostoevski once wrote that if there is no God, everything is permitted. But nontheistic humanists in the United States do not appear to be less moral, less critical, less concerned with values than theistic Americans. On the contrary, nontheists in America appear to retain a profound conviction concerning the possibilities of intelligence in history, a fundamental and hopeful orientation toward a better future for men, a marked capacity to accept responsibility and to act, and a profound respect for the human person and his freedom. These are startling values, on the face of it; but we take them so for granted that we do not wonder about them.

Moreover, because the Christian churches, as institutions, have often set their faces against the advance of science, philosophy, and social reconstruction, the extent to which theist and nontheist alike share many basic values has been masked. Men are commonly blind to the presuppositions that motivate them. Their conscious arguments pivot upon too superficial a plane. No doubt the nontheist wishes to carry his reconstruction of the beliefs and motives of our civilization through to the end. "Atheism is a long-range affair," Jean-Paul Sartre writes.[16] But the point to be doubted is that this reconstruction has yet been completed. "The Middle Ages," wrote Alfred North Whitehead, "formed one long training of the intellect of Western Europe in the sense of order. . . . The habit of definite exact thought was implanted in the European mind by the long dominance of scholastic logic and scholastic divinity."[17] Whitehead spoke then of the "instinctive conviction" of our culture, "the instinctive tone of thought and not a mere creed of words . . . the inexpugnable belief that every detailed occurrence can be correlated with its antecedents . . . —that there is a secret, a secret which can be unveiled." He added:

When we compare this tone of thought in Europe with the attitude of other civilizations when left to themselves, there seems but one source for its origin. It must come from the medieval insistence on the rationality of God, conceived as with the personal energy of Jehovah and with the rationality of a Greek philosopher. Every detail was supervised and ordered: the search into nature could only result in the vindication of the faith in rationality. Remember that I am not talking of the explicit beliefs of a few individuals. What I mean is the impress on the European mind arising from the unquestioned faith of centuries.[18]

Because he is a Catholic, Christopher Dawson's view is often taken with less than neutral credence, but his remark on this point seems sound: "Nowhere is the dynamism of Western religion more strikingly manifested than in the indirect and unconscious influence it has exercised on social and intellectual movements which are avowedly secular."[19] After wryly confessing his belief in "our God *Logos*" and the primacy of intellect, Sigmund Freud observed: "The primacy of the intellect . . . will presumably set itself the same aims as those whose realization you expect from your God . . . namely the love of man and the decrease of suffering."[20] "Take our moral philosophers, for instance," Albert Camus wrote, "so serious, loving their neighbor and all the rest—nothing distinguishes them from Christians, except that they don't preach in churches."[21] Bertrand Russell points out that his own views on individual and secular ethics are "in close harmony with Christian ethics." The impulsion toward creativity and moral exaltation is "the basis of what the Gospels call duty to God." But this impulsion is, of course, "separable from theological belief."[22] One may agree with Russell that human values are, in principle, separable from theological belief. But one may wonder whether the theoretical separation, however estimable, has been carried out in our society even among practicing nontheists. To step outside Christian institutions is not *ipso facto* to step outside Christian values. The virtues that Walter Kaufmann commends in *Faith of a Heretic* are perfectly compatible with various orthodox understandings of Christian faith. From a Christian point of view, they are superior to many poor but popular statements of that faith.[23] The mien does not make the atheist any more than it does the monk.

Nevertheless, it must be granted that the world view of Judaism and Christianity by which the Enlightenment and secular optimism lived even while nontheists renounced specific religious beliefs and eschewed religious organizations, has altered swiftly during the past generations. The twin shocks of the Nazi barbarism in Europe and of the new technology in the United States have constituted a turning point in the spiritual history of the West. "The central fact of modern history in the West—by which we mean the long period from the end of the Middle Ages to the present," William Barrett writes, "is unquestionably the decline of religion." This decline means:

. . . Religion is no longer the uncontested center and ruler of man's life, and . . . the Church is no longer the final and unquestioned home and asylum of his being. . . . The waning of religion is a much more concrete and complex fact than a mere change in conscious outlook; it penetrates the deepest strata of man's total psychic life. . . . The loss of the Church was the loss of a whole system of symbols, images, dogmas, and rites which had the psychological validity of immediate experience, and within which hitherto the whole psychic life of Western man had been safely contained. . . . Western man has spent more than five hundred years—half a millennium—in stripping nature of these projections and turning it into a realm of neutral objects which his science may control.[24]

Thrown into the horrors of Nazi occupation, during which torture was a commonplace and death no mere unpleasant accident to be avoided but a daily instructor, many European thinkers came to reject the cosmic world view of the Enlightenment—to reject the intermingling of religious and secular assurances by which Europe had long lived. "We were never more free," Jean-Paul Sartre has written, than during the German occupation. We had lost all our rights, beginning with the right to talk. Every day we were insulted to our faces and had to take it in silence. Under one pretext or another, as workers, Jews, or political prisoners, we were deported *en masse*. Everywhere, on billboards, in the newspapers, on the screen, we encountered the revolting and insipid picture of ourselves that our suppressors wanted us to accept. And because of all this we were free. Because the Nazi venom seeped into our thoughts, every accurate thought was a conquest . . . exile, captivity, and especially death (which we usually shrink from facing at all in happier days) became for us the habitual objects of our concern. We learned that they were neither inevitable accidents, nor even constant and inevitable dangers, but they must be considered as our lot itself, our destiny, the profound source of our reality as men.[25]

Yet even existentialism seems to be derivative from Christian faith. Sartre's own language is full of re-interpreted Christian symbols, and Christian theologians have speedily absorbed existentialism.

In the United States, as in England, religion appears to be struggling not so much with doubt or unbelief as with irrelevance. Technology, rather than *blitzkrieg* and brutality, seems to call for a new view of human experience. Alasdair MacIntyre writes:

Christianity provided pre-industrial England with a common frame of reference, with a sense of over-all meaning and with a pattern which gave form to life. . . . But industrial society has never been able to accommodate a religious interpretation of its own activities. The founders of atheist humanism hoped for and predicted secularization not merely in the sense of abandonment of religious belief and practice, but in the sense of a transformation of human goals and hopes from other-worldly into this-worldly. The present was to be judged and transcended, not by looking to the justice of heaven but by looking to that of the future. The hope of glory was to be, and in some . . . measure was, replaced by the hope of Utopia.

But we have neither glory nor Utopia to hope for. The hope that a secular Utopian tradition, whether Liberal or Marxist, sought to provide was never realized. The routine of working-class life, the competitive ladders of the middle classes absorb us into immediacy. We are dominated by a present to which the idea of a radically different future is alien. What conventional politics promises us is always a brighter version of what we have now. . . . In this situation the substance of religious belief is no longer with us, but in our ordinary secular vocabulary we have no language to express common needs, hopes, and fears that go beyond the immediacies of technique and social structure.[26]

Professor MacIntyre does not agree that the secularization of the modern world is "an accomplished and recognized fact." He detects no "sense of triumph in secular writers." Instead he finds among them "the same uneasiness" that he discovers in theologians.

Between the ten per cent or so of clear and convinced Christians at one end of the scale and the ten per cent or so of convinced sceptics at the other, there is the vast mass of the population, most superstitious to some degree, using the churches and especially the Church of England to celebrate birth, marriage and death, and to a lesser degree Christmas. This use or misuse of the churches is rooted in a set of vague, half-formulated and inconsistent beliefs.[27]

The relationship between Christianity and Western culture is, it appears, ambiguous. In order to understand what is transpiring within American Christianity today, we will need a few more specifics and, more than that, a new set of interpretive tools.

II. *The Inadequacy of American Christianity*

"Jesus, I love that car," an American father exclaims on his deathbed, in a story by John Updike. Does any symbol touch contemporary Americans so closely as their own cars? The dying man's son reflects later in the closing lines of the story:

Any day now we will trade it in; we are just waiting for the phone to ring. I know how it will be. My father traded in many cars. It happens so cleanly, before you expect it. He would drive off in the old car up the dirt road exactly as usual and when he returned the car would be new, and the old was gone, gone, utterly dissolved back into the mineral world from which it was conjured, dismissed without a blessing, a kiss, a testament, or any ceremony of farewell. We in America need ceremonies, [this] is I suppose. . . the point of what I have written.[28]

The American imagination sometimes seems impoverished, governed by machines, the human subject driven out. "We in America have from the beginning been cleaving and baring the earth, attacking, reforming the enormity of nature we were given, which we took to be hostile. We have explored, on behalf of all mankind, this paradox; the more matter is outwardly mastered, the more it overwhelms us in our hearts."[29] The basic experiences of human life in which religious life is renewed—finitude, suffering, evil, compassion, wonder, freedom, joy—are not widely celebrated in our culture. Homogeneity is our mark. We do not so much live as undergo processing. John Updike describes a young hitchhiking sailor:

He had the full body, the frank and fresh blue-eyed face of the docile Titans—guileless, competent, mildly earnest—that we have fattened, an ocean removed from the slimming Latin passions and Nordic anxieties of Europe, on our unprecedented abundance of milk and honey, vitamins and proteins. He had that instinctive optimism of the young animal that in America is the only generatrix of hope we have allowed ourselves; until recently, it seemed enough.[30]

The analytical, technical, verbal mind, moreover, is pre-eminent in the academies and the journals. Everywhere the living sources of religion are rendered arid. Of a rural Pennsylvania church Updike writes: "The nave was dimly lit, the congregation small, the sermon short, and the wind howled a nihilistic counterpoint beyond the black windows blotted with garbled apostles. . . . There was a strong sepia flavor of early Christianity: a minority flock furtively gathered within the hostile enormity of a dying, sobbing empire."[31] All the more is this true in Manhattan: "The churches of the Village had [a] Second Century quality. In Manhattan, Christianity is so feeble its future seems before it. . . . One hastens homeward afterward, head down, hurrying to assume the disguise—sweaters and suntans—of a non-churchgoer."[32] Even in private conversation, the atheist is a threat to the believer:

I feared [the astronomer's] visit. I was twenty-four, and the religious revival within myself was at its height. Earlier that summer, I had discovered Kierkegaard. . . .

He had an air of seeing beyond me, of seeing into the interstellar structure of things, of having transcended, except perhaps in the niggling matter of lust, the clouds of human subjectivity—vaporous hopes supported by immaterial rationalizations. It was his vigorous, clear vision that I feared. . . .

"My Lord, Walter," Bela said, "why are you reading [Plato]? Is this the one where he proves two and two equals four?" And thus quickly, at a mere wink from this atheist, Platonism and all its attendant cathedrals came tumbling down.[33]

The educated believer, aware of the decline of the Judaeo-Christian world view in his own psychic life and in that of the educated public, cannot escape facing the possibility that Christianity has reached the end of the line. He may meet this question by distinguishing between the Judaeo-Christian world view and the actual Christian faith. Is the ancient Judaeo-Christian world view, constituted by confidence in the final rationality of history and in the ultimate importance of individual personality, required for the life of faith? Supposing that the bases of a technical, secular, international culture are significantly different from the bases of the Hebraic-Greek-Roman world in which Christianity took root, can Christianity survive?

The evidence that the end of the line has been reached is impressive. In the United States, the theological content of Christian belief appears to be minimal. The vast majority of American Christians do not seem to be concerned about the problems involved in attempting to straddle two so widely different world views as those of the traditional Judaeo-Christian world and the recent technical world. "An observer of the American church scene of today," writes Wilhelm Pauck, "can hardly fail to note that theology is not in the center of concern among Protestants. In the main the laity of the churches is unconcerned about theological questions, and few ministers appear compelled to orient their work to clear theological principles." Ministers, he goes on, "cannot but be aware of the fact that today Christian truth goes nowhere unchallenged, indeed, that Christianity is actively being opposed by rival 'secular faiths' of scientism, humanism, nationalism, socialism, and even the democratic faith." Moreover, ministers do not appear to be "guided by a theological awareness of the specific nature of Christianity."[34]

Yet precisely here emerges the nub of the question. The rapid strides made in science, communications, and technology since World War II have suddenly made the "specific nature of Christianity" problematic even for theologians. The transplantation of primitive Christianity into the Greek categories of the third and fourth centuries, or the transformation of Platonic Christianity into Aristotelian categories by Aquinas in the thirteenth century, or the upheaval that separated post-Reformation from pre-Reformation Christianity might possibly offer historical parallels for the profound adaptations required of Christianity today. But each of these preceding stages had more in common with one another than any one of them has with the situation today. The elements to be emphasized, moreover, are not only the vast complexity but also the suddenness of the transformation Christianity faces today.

III. *The Required Transformation and Its Risks*

To what extent can Christianity be separated from the world view that once so thoroughly dominated Western culture, the world view implicit for example in the Declaration of Independence and even in the Preamble and Bill of Rights of the Constitution? Let us suppose that there is no pattern of rationality to human history, no Creator who granted "inalienable rights" to individual human beings, no intervening Providence watching over the affairs of men and ultimately making Liberty and Justice prosper. Let us suppose that there is no integrated, interrelated cosmos, in which the individual has a "place," "a station," or even a "steward-ship." Let us suppose that the ideal of the "whole man," of the "integrated personality" who is "reconciled to his lot" and "realizes his talents," of the man who receives "a vocation" from God is not sufficiently open-ended. Let us suppose that human life in a tech-nical world is bound to be fragmented, a little frantic, often im-personal, and scarcely dependent upon "God" for control of storms and rain, famine, illness, and poverty. Let us suppose that, since the strategy of concentrating upon soluble problems proves much more immediately productive, man's sense of mystery should atrophy. Let us further suppose that most human beings define as the meas-ure of their personal value the contribution they can make toward the worldly welfare of this and future generations. Do such sup-positions establish a context in which "the specific nature of Chris-tianity" has evaporated? Is a Christianity that accepts such pre-suppositions unfaithful to itself? Can there be a "secular" Christianity, just as valid as a "Platonic" Christianity, an "Aristotel-ian" Christianity, or a "deistic" Christianity?

Such questions have come to exercise Christian theologians in this decade; but they have arisen during a moment of embarrass-ment. On the one hand, there are countless Christians living quite obliviously and contentedly (and often productively, in their fash-ion) according to half-understood and contradictory symbols in-herited from the past: symbols of a manipulating Providence, a Creator immanent within Evolution, a cosmic Policeman[35] who guarantees the importance of the individual in "the scheme of things." Competitive life in a pragmatic, technical, pluralistic so-ciety has, of course, blunted the edge of many Sunday-morning symbols. During weekdays the force of such symbols may not be much in evidence. But, on the other hand, even the educated Christian elite has recently borrowed most of its cherished language from Kierkegaard, from Buber, from Heidegger; from European, and largely Germanic, existentialism and personalism. In the United States, Paul Tillich and Reinhold Niebuhr have been, for an elite, the prime molders of religious language. Tillich has attempted to stand "on the boundary" between classical ontology and con-tinental existentialism, and to mediate these to the more pragmatic, concrete American temper.[36] Reinhold Niebuhr has attempted to return to the mythical language of the ancient Hebrews, the language of "the self and the dramas of history." Neither Tillich nor Niebuhr speaks the spare, technical, secular language of the non-religious intellectual elite in this country. Their tone of voice, their key concepts, and their symbols derive largely from the European context of Schleiermacher, Schelling, Barth, and Bultmann.

So long as America remained a Protestant country, the insularity of Protestant theological life (it goes without saying that American Catholic theological life has been far more insular) could exist without being noticed. But recently American Protestants have been discovering that the American university is dominated philosophically by Anglo-American language analysis and more generally by the pragmatic methods and categories of physical science, the social sciences, and technology. In today's workaday world, moreover, American culture is not rural and Protestant but urban, utilitarian, and secular. In the world of politics, questions of power and pragmatism—often weak points in Protestant thought—loom large, and the captivating style is that of John F. Kennedy. In the field of social reform, the Negro is the moral hero. In the world of letters, music, and painting, and only somewhat less so in the worlds of psychology and sociology, where the *lingua franca* of American intellectual life is now forged, the Jewish community provides far more than its share of leaders. The cultural hegemony of the white Anglo-Saxon Protestant has been shattered; he must now take seriously interpretations of human life other than his own. Thus only now, a century later, is he experiencing Nietzsche's perception that God is dead, only now is he facing the accumulated secularization of daily life in America.

Many of the younger Christian theologians wish to break more decisively than Niebuhr and Tillich have with the thought patterns of the past. Some of them are attempting to speak the language of contemporary secular fiction and drama[37]; others the language of sociology[38]; still others the austere language of Anglo-American linguistic analysis.[39] It is not yet clear whether "the specific nature of Christianity" can be articulated in these special languages. But one reason for this uncertainty is the prior uncertainty concerning what constitutes the "specific nature of Christianity." To what propositions, to what style of life, to what symbols, to what method of resolving issues is a Christian specifically committed? How *in fact* does a Christian differ from an atheist? The cultural transition forced upon Christians by the shape of the emerging technical civilization has posed radical, fundamental questions.

Moreover, the new technological, secular society that is rapidly sweeping the world has its center of maximum intensity in the United States. It is America that one half of the world, at least, now imitates. It is a serious question whether American theologians, renouncing the only theological languages they presently have, German ontology and German existentialism, have the resources to carry through an intellectual transformation of Christianity. The bias of American theology, left to itself, is toward ethics and activism. Whether, for example, American theologians of the past accepted the immanent God of European liberal theology, or the transcendent God of European neo-orthodoxy, the result tended to be the same: social action. Can there be an intellectual transformation of Christianity if Christianity is reduced to an effort at social relevance? Christians would then have nothing to say to one another that nonbelievers could not say to them.

Critics both inside and outside the churches warn about the dangers of attempting to relate Judaism or Christianity too easily to the patterns of thought and predilections of any cultural epoch. Judaism and Christianity are for the ages, not for this epoch merely. No bias is more seductive than the bias of the present, the bias of identification with an avant-garde to whom the future belongs. A young Jewish rabbi recently warned me, as I prepared this article, not to ignore the potential overt conflict between religious and secular values. He wrote: "I think that liberal Catholics are mistaken when they believe that their recent absorption into the intellectual, social, and political establishment removes all sources of tension. Indeed it may, but only at the expense of their religious integrity. This has already been evidenced among the Jews."

H. Stuart Hughes doubts whether the great changes prompted by the Johannine revolution within Catholicism

can take place within the framework of the Church as it has been traditionally understood. I find the conservatives in the Italian and Spanish hierarchies not wholly in the wrong when they warn of the perils ahead. I do not believe that Catholicism will cease to exist. But I think it quite possible that the post-Johannine Church—at least the Church of the educated—will become so private, so personal, so enmeshed in the vocabulary and concepts of the secular world as to be almost unrecognizable as the Catholicism of the past. Whether this will be a loss or a gain is for the members of the faith alone to decide.[40]

The stakes, then, are high. Few are unaware of the risk involved. Certain astute observers, in fact, think that some of those engaged in the *aggiornamento* of Christianity, whether Protestant or Catholic, are undergoing a fundamental crisis, not of renewal but of belief: They have lost heart, but disguise this fact from themselves by frenetic efforts to reform the institutions in which they no longer feel at home.[41] Again, Christianity is a historical community whose pilgrimage across the centuries is made through the medium of a clumsy, inefficient, steadily evolving but indispensable set of institutions. Yet many Christians seem to think of the church as a collection of individuals who must forever be recalled to a non-institutional, interior, spiritual renewal. Such critics are apt to be ready to abandon the traditional symbols and institutions of Christianity in order to establish new institutions that might preserve their own fervor into the future. Others seem to accept, without a sense of historical ambiguity, the slogans of "secular" Christianity and the program of social and political "relevance." They seem to forget that what to one generation appears to be "relevant" to secular culture may to a later generation of prophets appear to have been a betrayal of the faith. They forget that the scars left by the relevance of some past forms of Christianity have not yet healed.

IV. *Beginning the Task*

The Christian community is, and ought to be, pluralistic. It is not likely that all Christians will accept any one theory of how the needed transformation is to be accomplished. The age cries for experimentation and for diverse initiatives even in contrary directions. The advantage of belonging to such a community is that each member helps to correct the mistakes of the other. Out of the finite insights of many individuals and many churches comes a rounder wisdom than could be achieved by one man or one church alone. The Christian community extends temporally as well as spatially. In the testimony of the past there is leverage against the biases of the present, which are, especially in a culture boasting of rapid change and swift obsolescence, the most compelling of all. The danger of belonging to such a historical community is to fail to meet the new on its own terms when the hour is ripe. The advantage is to learn to demand evidence concerning an identification of the new with the true, particularly where human values are at stake. In recent Western history, the church seems to have erred most frequently, often grievously, on the side of conservatism.

My quiet conviction is that Christianity is now entering upon one of the most creative periods of its history. Dissatisfaction with the present and a longing for renewal have been generated in the almost universal anguish of two world wars. I believe that Christianity is true; it offers in the round, and in connection with other beliefs from other sources, the most adequate interpretation of human nature and destiny that we have. Certainly many of the themes that it prominently asserts seem as if they are true. Russell, Freud, Camus, and many others borrow from them to some depth. In any case, no argument for Christianity is of serious interest unless such claims to truth are made. Every human group in our time faces the radical transformation of beliefs and values that Christianity faces. As Alasdair MacIntyre has pointed out, few secular men today speak triumphantly. No one holds the keys to human destiny in his hands. We live with large areas of gray and with still larger areas of black. Our brightest light illuminates best only immediate things. Some human beings will prefer the security of clarity, but others are bound to venture into the area of mystery.

At this point Christianity and Judaism become "relevant." Because the world view that supported Christianity for so long has fallen away, the inner life of many Christians is bound to be shaken. We may expect to see larger and larger defections from the churches in the next two or three decades. Sociologists may tell us that more people are going to church than ever before, and even that this churchgoing is part of a more general and authentic search for values in American society.[42] But if some of these churchgoers are seeking a tidy cosmic picture in which they will find their place and learn what is expected of them, Christianity—if it is faithful to itself—will increasingly disappoint them, for Christian theologians are increasingly detaching themselves from the Judaeo-Christian world view of the past. They are prepared to be much more modest in the clarity and sense of structure they claim to attain. They are trying to devise a Christian style for living in the gray and blackness, for employing the pragmatic techniques of the small area of brightness. In the latter task, they are often at one with secular social reformers. In the former task, they keep alive the human sense of mystery, of wonder, of awe, of finitude, of longing, of courage and adventure that is proper to those who explore the reaches of the human spirit in solitude and in community.

To be sure, there are many persons in our culture whose sense of mystery has atrophied. They are busy men, technical, humane, but practical. The freedom and diversity of a technical civilization offer them many avenues of preoccupation apart from reflection upon the mysteries of human destiny. But to others such a life seems less than human. Christianity becomes relevant for these people precisely when it draws them into reflection upon who they are and how they relate to one another. Freed from the Judaeo-Christian world view, Christianity does not try to escape the real obscurity of human destiny. Evil men prosper; rain falls on just and unjust alike; God does not coddle those who accept his covenant. The world seems as if the atheist could be right. Hence the psalmist's plea: "Let not my enemies rejoice, O Lord; let me not blush and be confounded." Dachau and Belsen symbolize vividly the power of evil and the silent patience of God, who does not intervene. Life is not a morality play.

But is not appeal to a hidden God only a play on words? How does a completely hidden God differ from no God at all? The Christian believes himself always in the presence of One who understands and wills all the contingencies, even the crippling ones, of human life. For the Christian, events are not flat, mechanical, literal; other persons, events, and things are what they are, but they are also "alive" and symbolic. They are part of a conversation with God. The Christian does not visualize human life as part of a great, stable cosmic picture. He affirms that life, though often as unpredictable and contingent and erratic as a tale told by an idiot, signifies something. But what it signifies is not entirely clear; the mystery is not dispelled. The Christianity of the present has, of necessity, shed the securities promised by the Judaeo-Christian world view of the past. The Christian today knows how profound is the darkness in which he has been left. A greater modesty, a greater sense of contingency and darkness, a greater sense of comradeship with non-Christians do not ill become Christians. What is being abandoned is not Christianity but the cultural world view that was its first matrix, its cocoon, for the first two millennia of its existence.

V. *The Relationship of Christian Faith to Atheism*

The task of re-interpreting basic Christian symbols in the open-ended scientific context of the new era will not be accomplished swiftly. But if the Judaeo-Christian world view is now adjudged inadequate, it was always inadequate. Only our ignorance prevented us from seeing its inadequacies earlier. Assuming that Christian faith is true, not only must its disengagement from the Judaeo-

Christian world view be possible, but there must already have been signs of strain in the past. Were not medieval Christians too smug in their Ptolemaic world, thinking themselves the center of the universe? Were not Reformation Christians too dogmatic and too pessimistic? Were not liberal Christians too sanguine, thinking that knowledge is powerful and power innocent? When one looks back at "ages of faith," or "golden eras," one is not always certain that there were then better Christians, only a different style of Christian. It has always been a struggle to be a good Christian; no age mass-produces them. When the Son of Man returns, Jesus asked, will he find one in ten thousand faithful to his word? Now that the illusions of Judaeo-Christian culture are passing away, Christians will again become accustomed to being a few, a tiny remnant, among the multitudes of men.

In this new context, one pressing inquiry is how the Christian differs from the atheist. No one way of working out this question has found universal acceptance,[43] but public discussion seems, at least, to be identifying the area in which the answer lies. Two basic propositions underlie my own proposal. The first conviction is that man is a question-asking animal; the second is that he is a symbol-making animal. Appeal is not made to a special "religious experience," nor to a personal "encounter with the Transcendent." Rather, each man is asked to reflect upon the experience of human life that he already has. Each man decides for himself who he is, and so works out his own destiny. From this point of view, Christianity is not conceived as "filling a need," in the sense in which food and water fill human needs. Men are obviously able to live, and to live well, apart from Christianity.

Under the tutelage of other world religions, men have been taught in other, but often similar, ways about the mysteries of human life.[44] Among Western atheists and agnostics, important convictions nourished by Christianity have been widely diffused. The historical dynamism of liberalism, confidence in the preciousness of human life, trust in the intelligibility of the contingent and the empirical, compassion, a thirst for justice and equality, an assumption that progress in history, though ambiguous, is possible—such beliefs, even if they are now separable from Christian institutions and symbols, do not contradict, but rather express the basic imperatives of Christian life.

Two historical tragedies of vast dimensions prevent some observers from reading the relationship of Christianity to contemporary culture in this way. First, Christian institutions and symbols have often been used in opposition to those efforts at philosophical, scientific, and social reconstruction that have built the modern age. Many Christians now wish to say that, far from being normative for the Christianity of the future, the Christianity of the preceding era was defective in its openness and wisdom; it should have joined more thoroughly than it did in the social and intellectual revolutions of the last four centuries. As a Jewish rabbi and philosopher has asked:

Why has the modern Church on the whole been lukewarm, indifferent or downright hostile to liberal drives when it might well have wholeheartedly embraced or spearheaded them? . . . Why has the liberalism of the modern age been allowed to be shot through with a thoroughgoing secularist bias, when it might conceivably have been given a religious and Christian impetus? . . . How could [Christian and Jew] ever have been indifferent, lukewarm, or hostile to the liberal ideal—and this in the name of their faith! . . . when that ideal is the most authentic modern secular expression of their faith? How could they have ever feared the free scientific exploration of the world when, long freed of idolatrous worship of the world, they should have been the first of all scientific explorers? Why afraid of technology, when they were the first to believe that the earth is handed over to human rule? Above all else, how could any Jew or Christian who ever believed in one Father of all men have failed to rally to the modern struggle on behalf of man's common humanity, or have sabotaged secularists who led this struggle?[45]

Secondly, missionaries, exporting to other cultures not only Christianity but the Judaeo-Christian culture as well, stifled a native response and an original testimony. We have thus been deprived of learning what an indigenous Asian or African Christianity would have been like. If Christianity is for all men, we are impoverished by its limitation to Western forms. Why could not other cultures have been as free as the Greeks and the Romans, the Goths and the Huns, to develop their own style of Christian life?[46] We suffer now for the historic power and the arrogance of Western Judaeo-Christian culture.

Nevertheless, it seems sensible to envisage an anthropology, a sociology, a psychology of man that will be flexible enough to relate in one view all the types of human culture, all the varieties of men. One strand of such a hope is the prosaic fact that men ask questions. Men have the capacity to raise ever further questions, to question their own presuppositions, to alter their lines of inquiry and routines of behavior, and to turn in ever new directions. In this capacity is rooted the possibility of human development in history, the variety of human life, and the sense of self-transcendence that arises in human consciousness. This drive to ask questions is of itself unrestricted and unstructured; it is prior to and more fertile than the presuppositions and concrete determinations of any particular line of inquiry. It is open-ended, capable of coping with new and unexpected experiences, and able to revise its methods and its conclusions. Some men detect in man's restless, unrestricted drive to question a sign of the presence of God. Hardly a writer concerned with the search for God does not point to this capacity as the basic evidence for, and guide to the meaning of, a transcendent principle in human experience.

To be sure, this evidence is ambiguous. Some men interpret the evidence in a materialistic sense; others see no signs of God in the relentless drive to question. Those who believe in God, however, seem both to become aware of his presence and to govern their language about him through the kind of self-transcendence experienced in exercising their drive to understand, their capacity to wonder, and their inability to regard any finite system as adequate to human aspiration. The atheist seems to take the drive to understand as a matter of plain fact; the believer reflects upon it, is led to wonder, and then silently to adore.

A generation ago it was, perhaps, somewhat easier to take the basic drive to inquire as a matter of plain fact. Many thinkers seemed to assume that there was an obvious and "objective" method of inquiry, which spared them the perils of subjectivity and mystery; there was, for example, scientific method, Freud's "reason and experience" whose symbol was *Logos*. To assume, with Sidney Hook and Bertrand Russell, that "All knowledge that we have is scientific knowledge"[47] was to take a short cut to a sense of security and self-esteem. Those who took such a short cut were *tout court* rational and objective. This was due to no merit of their own, but merely a consequence of adopting the scientific method. But in our generation it is not so obvious why one should adopt the scientific method. If the world in which we live is absurd—and by *world* I do not mean some vast metaphysical cosmos, but the immediate crises and issues facing human society, like domestic social reform, environmental control, and political conflict—then it is not obvious that fidelity to scientific method will assuage our ills. On the contrary, if human existence is, in fact, impervious to intelligence, then the attempt to be intelligent may only heighten our peril. Perhaps the examined life is not worth living. Moreover, there is no necessary connection between science and liberalism.

I am not arguing against fidelity to scientific method or against a commitment to the employment of intelligence in human affairs. I am only trying to expose the presuppositions that are prior to such fidelity and such commitment. Even if one does not reflect upon these presuppositions, they are operative in the decision to commit oneself to science and intelligence, for other options—nihilism, irrationality, escape—are available. Thus, a commitment to science and to intelligence requires a justification. It does not merely "happen." The swiftest justification, of course, is that to raise the issue of justification is already to appeal to intelligence. Moreover, in practice, men cannot help justifying their choices. One may choose to live as a sheep; what one cannot do, once that choice is made, is to justify one's choice. Still, men can, astonishingly enough, successfully employ science and intelligence in understanding and taking responsibility for their environment. What kind of world is this, in which such a situation is true? There is no short cut to an interpretation of human life, by way of an incantation of phrases like "science," "scientific method," and "our God *Logos*." Even less so is there a short cut by way of the argument that "contemporary philosophers say. . . ." Why should anyone accept, without inquiry into basic presuppositions, what contemporary philosophers happen to think?

In short, it seems apparent to many younger thinkers that atheists and agnostics, particularly those who are committed to scientific method and intelligent analysis, are—from a formal point of view—as much involved in fundamental interpretations, decisions, and commitments as is a man of religious faith. Insofar as science is a method, it is as available to theists as to nontheists. Insofar as it is a way of life, it must justify itself by meeting the tests of human living, just as a religious faith must justify itself.

At this point, the second proposition, that man is a symbol-making animal, enters the discussion. Human actions have not only a pragmatic, literal, immediate meaning. They also reveal the character, self-image, intentions, and purposes of their agents. Men do not act only according to verbal, analytical statements of abstract principle; they also act according to imaginative models, symbols, or styles of human behavior. For some men, it appears, a human being is to be understood as an especially complicated machine; for others, as an instrument in the betterment of the lot of future generations; for still others, as an end in himself. There are those for whom the style of human action is best symbolized by Sisyphus, or Prometheus, or a rhinoceros, or outcasts waiting for perhaps nothing at all, or an expert in a white coat, or a careful and detached observer, or a calculator who thinks of life as an instance of game theory, or a crisp but affable executive. Men who perform the same actions, which achieve roughly the same pragmatic effects, operate under different core symbols. A rebel may rebel out of Promethean defiance or out of a humble passion for justice. Democracy succeeds because it recognizes the freedom available to individuals and communities on the level of basic symbols, even when common pragmatic purposes are to be achieved.

But it would be a mistake to believe that symbols are unimportant. The relationship between motivating symbol and concrete action is not so clear and direct as the relationship between a verbal premise and its implications. What one surrenders in changing basic symbols may not become apparent immediately in one's actions. But it would be very surprising to anthropologists, sociologists, and psychologists alike if, after a change in social or personal symbols, changes in action did not follow. Christian faith, it must be apparent, has traditionally employed cultural symbols of various sorts—one time, one set of symbols; another time, another set— as vivid interpretations of human existence and as motives of action. The strain put upon the symbols used in the preceding cultural epoch has reached a point of maximum intensity; this strain is also apparent among human beings generally.

But there are several reasons why there is hope that Christian symbols will regain their vigor, in a fresh style and an authentic interpretation. Already some Christians have lived according to a new style even though a theory of what they were doing was not yet available; such diverse Christians, for example, as John F. Kennedy and Pope John XXIII. Kennedy articulated a realism, a pragmatism, a modest hopefulness that once again makes political action in the name of freedom and compassion possible. He transplanted the ideals of Christian life in the world from the Judaeo-Christian context into the technical, fluid, secular context of a new era. Pope John XXIII began a renewal so thorough in one of the most ancient of Western institutions that the shape of world politics and world cultural forces has been radically altered, for any change in Roman Catholicism powerfully affects the self-definition of many other institutions, religious or secular.

Secondly, one of the first fruits of Pope John's revolution is a renewed ecumenical movement—a movement of cooperation, mutual criticism, and mutual support that is beginning to touch not only Protestants and Catholics but Christians and Jews. Ultimately, it will reach all men of all religious faiths and of none. Religious people are beginning to think of themselves less as separate sects than as brothers, whose differences, however important and mutually enriching, do not outweigh their common sense of mystery and humanity. In particular, the ecumenical movement has brought enormous mutual stimulation to the various Christian bodies that lived for so long in intellectual isolation from one another. During the period of isolation, differences of social status, temperament, and personality were often institutionalized. Belonging to a sect, a man was content to be in some ways less than fully human; he adhered to a limited style or pattern of life. There was a "Protestant principle," a "Catholic principle," and many subtypes of complacent differentiation. Now each of the Christian communities is putting pressure on the others. Admiration is leading to emulation. Certain Catholics are closer in spirit to some Presbyterians than either are to many members in their own religious communities. Moreover, in each communion, traits usually associated with other communions are beginning to emerge—Protestants learn Catholic attitudes toward worldly things like food and drink; Catholics learn prophetic criticism of institutional idolatry. Christianity is ceasing to be sectarian; it is becoming more roundly human.

A third factor for hope is that a profound spiritual change is occurring in the academy. The serious study of religion is moving outside the seminaries and into the universities. Fred M. Hechinger has reported in *The New York Times*[48] that at universities around the country, "students have been enrolling in courses on religion in record numbers. Some institutions," he continues, "find it difficult to recruit enough faculty members to fill the demand." According to Mr. Hechinger's survey, the interest in courses in religion is largely intellectual. He concludes: "Many students who are volunteering for the Peace Corps were identified as those most interested in courses in religion." Now that philosophy has become analytical, and literature courses are often technical, courses in religion offer a privileged neutral opportunity for studies in the comparative interpretation of basic human values like freedom, love, justice, and openness. It should be added that theology is becoming the province of laymen; applications to the few university graduate schools in theology in the country are extremely high. Moreover, since the Second Vatican Council, newspapers and journals like *Commentary, Harper's,* and *The New Republic* have given an increasing proportion of space both to reporting and to analyzing events and trends in contemporary theology. *The New York Times* made a major addition to its staff in 1965 in assigning John Cogley as religion editor. The most pertinent and complete account of theological developments is now often to be found in the "secular" press. Frequent international consultation among theologians assures the continued flow of ideas. In these ways, religion is ceasing to be sectarian and parochial.

More important, there are signs of a new type of inquiry within the academy. "The trend seems to be," Mr. Hechinger reports from comments of one academic spokesman, "that the faculty is not afraid of religion any more and does not feel a threat to it—does not feel that it's a form of superstition left over from the middle ages."[49] It seems plain to many students, if not to members of an older generation, that in a pluralistic society there are many interpretations of human life, only one of which is represented by the pragmatist who is confident that mankind can make progress, can find some degree of happiness, can be assured that the success of science is no illusion. If I read some members of the younger generation correctly, their marked commitments in ethics are leading them to reopen metaphysical questions. They have not started with an ontology, on which they then "base" their ethics. They are driven to metaphysics not by crisis and despair, but by reflection upon their own hope. Their metaphysics is not one of sickly reflection apart from action, but of action illumined by reflection and of reflection prompted by, required by, and terminating in action. The young are healing the Kantian breach between thought and action.

It would, of course, be a mistake to estimate that there is a widespread religious revival among the young. Those who identify Christianity with the obsolete Judaeo-Christian world view continue to leave the churches in great numbers. For many God is irrelevant. He figures in nothing that they do, or understand, or hope. But many thoughtful students, particularly those, believers or not, who are concerned about questions of values, recognize that people who are serious about their Christian faith or their atheism have much in common. Neither group has seen God, and both are passionately concerned about the fate of human beings. Our ecumenical age has perhaps discovered that the debates of even a generation ago be-

MICHAEL NOVAK

tween theists and anti-theists were, on both sides, insufficiently modest. Many Christians are discovering that the Judaeo-Christian world view was an illusory support of their faith, while many atheists are discovering that their own convictions have the structure of a faith.

Thus, in particular, some serious atheists discover that, from a purely formal point of view, they live by three basic principles. With or without intellectual justification, they believe that to pursue intelligence, to try to make our social order (in Mississippi, for example) more intelligent, is to live fruitfully and well. They have a principle of vision: to create out of chaos a more intelligent, if fitful, center of light. Secondly, they do not expect to be totally successful in history. Their hopes are modest. We cannot eliminate suffering from the world, Camus tells us, but we can diminish by a little the amount of suffering; and this suffices for a human life. Many live by such a principle of resignation. Thirdly, many find that they experience deep compassion regarding any human being who is suffering, and they think that such compassion is good. They care about human beings as they care about no other phenomenon in the universe. And they are glad to care.

How, then, speaking formally, do these principles of vision, of resignation, and of compassion differ from the faith, hope, and charity of the believer? The believer does not see God. The only proof he has that he loves God, whom he does not see, is that he loves those human beings whom he does see (I Jn: 4). If they are serious, believer and unbeliever live by love for men. Yet those who love human beings are not many but few. Those few who are serious about their atheism or their belief require one another, for the battle against the hucksters, who daily increase and multiply, striving to possess the earth, is desperate. In the churches as in the buildings of our cities, there are countless petty men for whom persons are not ends but means: fodder for organizations, functions of society, useful citizens, faithful followers.

God did not "so love the church"; he loved the world. The church is for the world, not world for church. In the darkness, believer and unbeliever, by loving human beings, do what best becomes human beings and are brothers.

VI. A Renewed Creativity

Religion, then, appears to some young people as a function of

408

the question-asking and the symbol-making man. Who am I? What may I hope? What should I do? These questions put them in the midst of the mysteries of human destiny. Such young people are not pleased with what they have seen in the churches. They do not often find satisfaction there for the question-asking or the symbol-making impulse. Nevertheless, even the most unrelieved and oppressive of the institutional churches convey (sometimes despite themselves) a sense of history, a sense of community, a sense of mystery. But, ironically, while the symbol-making impulse is encountering new sympathy and serious inquiry in the universities, the symbols and sentiments prominent in the institutional churches repel by their dishonesty and irrelevance many who would be prepared to respond to what the churches are supposed to be. Although some of the young, motivated perhaps by their work among the poor, are prepared to accept the style and limitations of the religion of the uneducated, the religion of the middle classes shocks them by its pettiness.

The key religious symbols of Judaism and Christianity speak of freedom, love, justice, openness to events, to others, and to the world; they speak of the mystery and tragedy of human life, of the kind of hope that leads to action without sentimental illusions. Emil L. Fackenheim writes:

Here it is at long last time to bear direct witness to Him who has been the God of Israel for more than three millennia, and the God of the Christian Church since its inception. *He is the One who is infinite, yet relates Himself to finite men; who in His power does not need man, yet in His love chooses to need him; who in His self-sufficiency does not require the world yet wishes to require it—and bids man do His will in it.*

Such a God does not require demythologizing. He already *is* demythologized, and has been so ever since He first revealed Himself in an infinity destructive of all finite idols. (Only the images man forms of Him require demythologizing, but even these are *recognized* as being mere images.) . . .

The infinite value of the human person, always part of both Jewish and Christian faith, must now by faith be accepted as . . . a goal demanding secular realization—by and on behalf of all men. And in accepting this demand, modern Jew and Christian must descend into this secular world, from what has often been, and still is, a remote Heaven.[50]

Such a testimony is necessary, because it is a temptation for the believer today to state publicly only what a secular thinker might affirm; there is a seductive absolutism in the widespread ignorance and indifference regarding religion. On the other hand, the believer is becoming increasingly aware of the nontheistic alternative. Religion is becoming self-critical; the first condition of renewed creativity is therefore present. Because of the advance of secular intelligence, human capacities, and alternative viewpoints, it has become increasingly difficult for the man of religious faith to take for granted the world view that he receives from his parents. No one can be born a Christian. Being born into a Christian family usually involves inheriting patterns of thought, images, and sentiments that must be replaced by other more authentic patterns. But the nontheist must also grope for a set of imaginative symbols, a moral style, and appropriate attitudes by which to live humanly in the technical world we are building. There is no *a priori* argument for deciding whether theism or nontheism is a more adequate interpretation of human life. Although proportionally the numbers of Christians continue to grow less, those who remain Christian are working toward a clearer view of what their interpretation of human life entails. In living this interpretation they will test its empirical and pragmatic justification.

Perhaps a statement of the character of Christianity, however fragmentary and incomplete, is called for at this point. Christianity offers a community of inquiry in which to pursue one's concern for human values and the mystery of human life. Its eucharistic liturgy has an intimate, audacious power. Christianity is not merely an instrument of social relevance nor does it honor mere meditation apart from responsibility for the survival and the welfare of the human race. Christianity is not a form of activism. In a culture of increasing leisure, it can teach men how to contemplate and how to explore important depths of the human spirit. It recognizes that social action comes to fruition in the free personal development of each man.

Moreover, human actions have, like liturgy, a social context. In the world in which we are coming to live, this context embraces all men: One's neighbor is the Viet-Cong, the Russian, the Harlemite, or the Nob Hill matron. Christianity offers no escape from the complexities and ambiguities of the new world culture; nor does it offer (as Judaeo-Christian culture often did) a complacent satisfaction that one has all, or even any, complete answers. Rather, it offers a historical community of inadequate human beings, who are trying to be faithful to the good news that God, despite appearances, loves the world and asks men to take responsibility for building a human community of freedom and truth, justice and compassion.

It offers a rich history of reflection upon the crushing difficulties involved in such a task. But it does not allow us to think ourselves innocent, as mere victims of a pathetic fate. It does not rescue us, as President Kennedy said one spring and then experienced one autumn before our eyes, from the inequalities of fate. It demands that we take ourselves as we are, assuming responsibility for those evils of ours that increase the common suffering. It teaches that God is present everywhere. It does not offer security, but reconciliation: a wellspring of creative, painfully growing brotherhood.

REFERENCES

1. Emmanuel Célestin Suhard, *The Church Today* (Notre Dame, 1948).

2. E. L. Mascall, *The Secularization of Christianity* (New York, 1966) quoting from Harry Blamires, *The Christian Mind* (New York, 1963), p. 3.

3. John A. T. Robinson, *Honest to God* (Philadelphia, 1963).

4. Dietrich Bonhoeffer, *Letters and Papers from Prison* (New York, 1953).

5. The passages most commented upon are *ibid.*, pp. 208-15; 217-20; 222-27; 236-44.

6. In a passage popular with the new theologians, Saul Bellow deplores talk of human suffering "in the mouths of safe, comfortable people playing at crisis, alienation, apocalypse and desperation. . . . We must get it out of our heads that this is a doomed time, that we are waiting for the end, and the rest of it, mere junk from fashionable magazines. Things are grim enough without these shivery games. People frightening one another—a poor sort of moral exercise." *Herzog* (New York, 1965), pp. 385-86.

7. The most widely discussed theological book of 1965 was Harvey Cox's *The Secular City* (New York), with the jacket inscription: "The Secular City: A celebration of its liberties and an invitation to its discipline." William Hamilton and Thomas J. J. Altizer, in *Radical Theology and the Death of God* (New York, 1966), also announce a new optimism. See, e.g., p. 113, for the way in which Hamilton chooses Bonhoeffer over against Niebuhr and Tillich.

8. *Punch*, June 23, 1965, quoted in *New Theology*, No. 3, eds. Martin E. Marty and Dean G. Peerman (New York, 1966), p. 17.

9. Alasdair MacIntyre, "God and the Theologians," *Encounter*, Vol. 21, No. 3, reprinted in part in *The Honest to God Debate*, ed. David L. Edwards (Philadelphia, 1963), pp. 215-28.

10. W. W. Bartley III, "The Bonhoeffer Revival," *The New York Review of Books*, Vol. 2 (August 26, 1965), p. 16.

11. Sigmund Freud, *The Future of an Illusion* (New York, 1964), pp. 87-89.

12. *Ibid.*, p. 86.

13. Gordon Allport, *The Individual and His Religion* (New York, 1950), p. 1.

14. *Ibid.*

15. Charles S. Hyneman, *The Study of Politics* (Urbana, Illinois, 1959), pp. 62-63.

16. Jean-Paul Sartre, *The Words* (New York, 1964), p. 253.

17. Alfred North Whitehead, *Science and the Modern World* (New York, 1948), pp. 12-13.

18. *Ibid.*, p. 13.

19. Christopher Dawson, *Religion and the Rise of Western Culture* (London, 1950), p. 22.

20. Freud, *op. cit.*, p. 88.

21. Albert Camus, *The Fall* (New York, 1961), p. 133.

22. Bertrand Russell, *Authority and the Individual* (Boston, 1960), pp. 70-71.

23. Walter Kaufmann, *Faith of a Heretic* (New York, 1961), see especially pp. 291-342.

24. William Barrett, *Irrational Man* (New York, 1962), pp. 24-25.

25. *Ibid.*, pp. 239-40, quoting from Jean-Paul Sartre, *The Republic of Silence.*

26. *Op. cit.*, pp. 225-26.

27. *Ibid.*, p. 223.

28. John Updike, *Pigeon Feathers and Other Stories* (New York, 1962), p. 279.

29. *Ibid.*, p. 248.

30. *Ibid.*, p. 263.

31. *Ibid.*, p. 250.

32. *Ibid.*, pp. 251-52.

33. *Ibid.*, pp. 179, 181-82.

34. Wilhelm Pauck, "Theology in the Life of Contemporary American Protestantism," *Religion and Culture: Essays in Honor of Paul Tillich,* ed. Walter Leibrecht (New York, 1959), p. 270.

35. See J. B. Phillips, *Your God Is Too Small* (New York, 1961), p. 8, for a brief popular exposition of some dozen or more "inadequate conceptions of God which still linger unconsciously in many minds."

36. See Paul Tillich, "The Conquest of Intellectual Provincialism: Europe and

America," *Theology and Culture,* ed. Robert C. Kimball (New York, 1959), pp. 159-76; a remarkable essay in which Tillich reflects on what it meant for him, as a German, to rethink his theology in an American context.

37. Gabriel Vahanian, *The Death of God: The Culture of Our Post Christian Era* (New York, 1961); Thomas J. J. Altizer and William Hamilton, *op. cit.*

38. Harvey Cox, *op. cit.*

39. Paul M. Van Buren, *The Secular Meaning of the Gospel* (New York, 1963).

40. H. Stuart Hughes, "Pope John's Revolution: Secular or Religious?" *Commonweal,* Vol. 83, No. 10 (December 10, 1965), p. 303.

41. Daniel Callahan, *Honesty in the Church* (New York, 1965).

42. Talcott Parsons, "The Pattern of Religious Organization in the United States," *Symbolism in Religion and Literature,* ed. Rollo May (New York, 1960), pp. 152-77, esp. pp. 173-76.

43. I have attempted to deal with this problem in *Belief and Unbelief* (New York, 1965), and in "The Christian and the Atheist," *Christianity and Crisis* (March 21, 1966). The reader might also consult Daniel Callahan, "Freud Saw It Coming," *Commonweal* (June 3, 1966), pp. 312-313, and the exchange of letters in *ibid.* (July 1, 1966), pp. 405, 423-25. See also, Justus George Lawler, "Theology and Its Uses of History," *Continuum* (Spring, 1966), pp. 92-101; and Eugene Fontinell, "Reflections on Faith and Metaphysics," *Cross Currents* (Winter, 1966), pp. 15-40.

44. The young Roman Catholic theologian Hans Küng contends that, from a Christian point of view, other world religions are the ordinary sufficient human means of salvation; Christianity is an extraordinary means. See Hans Küng, *Freedom Today* (New York, 1966).

45. Emil L. Fackenheim, "A Jew Looks at Christianity and Secularist Liberalism," *The Restless Church,* ed. William Kilbourn (Philadelphia, 1966), pp. 87, 98 (italics his). Professor Fackenheim urges Jews and Christians to address the secular liberal "so as to embrace his liberalism and repudiate his secularism." *Ibid.,* p. 97.

46. Paul Tillich, *Christianity and the Encounter with World Religions* (New York, 1963) and *The Future of Religions* (Chicago, 1966).

47. Sidney Hook, citing Russell, in *The Quest for Being* (New York, 1961), p. 214.

48. *The New York Times,* May 8, 1966.

49. *Ibid.*

50. Fackenheim, *op. cit.,* p. 97.

NOTES ON CONTRIBUTORS

NOTES ON CONTRIBUTORS

ROBERT N. BELLAH, born in 1927 in Altus, Oklahoma, is Ford Professor of Sociology and Comparative Studies at the University of California, Berkeley. He is the author of *Tokugawa Religion* (Glencoe, Illinois, 1957) and editor of *Religion and Progress in Modern Asia* (New York, 1965).

JOSEPH L. BLAU, born in 1909 in Brooklyn, New York, is Professor of Religion and chairman of that department at Columbia University. He is the author of *Modern Varieties of Judaism* (New York, 1966); *The Story of Jewish Philosophy* (New York, 1962); *Men and Movements in American Philosophy* (New York, 1952); and *The Christian Interpretation of the Cabala in the Renaissance* (New York; rev. ed. 1966).

DANIEL CALLAHAN, born in 1930 in Washington, D.C., is Associate Editor of *Commonweal* and Visiting Professor of Theology at Marymount College. He is the author of *The New Church* (New York, 1966); *Honesty in the Church* (New York, 1965); and *The Mind of the Catholic Layman* (New York, 1963). He has also edited *The Secular City Debate* (New York, 1966) and co-edited *Christianity Divided: Protestant and Roman Catholic Theological Issues*.

WILLIAM A. CLEBSCH, born in 1923 in Clarksville, Tennessee, is Professor of Religion and Humanities and executive head of Special Programs in Humanities at Stanford University. Mr. Clebsch has written *A New Historiography of American Religion* (Indianapolis, 1967); *Pastoral Care in Historical Perspective*, with Charles R. Jaekle (Englewood Cliffs, New Jersey, 1964); and *England's Earliest Protestants, 1520–1535* (New Haven, 1964).

HARVEY G. COX, born in 1929 in Chester County, Pennsylvania, is Associate Professor of Church and Society at the Divinity School of Harvard University. He is the author of *The Secular City* (New York, 1965). Mr. Cox is an editor of *Christianity and Crisis* and writes a regular column on the city for *Commonweal*.

EMIL L. FACKENHEIM, born in 1916 in Halle, Germany, is Professor of Philosophy at the University of Toronto. Mr. Fackenheim is the author of *Metaphysics and Historicity* (Milwaukee, 1961) and *Paths to Jewish Belief* (New York, 1960). He has contributed numerous articles on philosophy and Judaism to *The Review of Metaphysics, Commentary, Judaism,* and many other journals.

EDWIN S. GAUSTAD, born in 1923 in Rowley, Iowa, is Professor of History at the University of California, Riverside. He is the author of *A Religious History of America* (New York, 1966); *Historical Atlas of Religion in America* (New York, 1962); and *The Great Awakening in New England* (New York, 1957).

LANDON GILKEY, born in 1919 in Chicago, is Professor of Theology at the Divinity School of the University of Chicago. Mr. Gilkey is the author of *Shantung Compound* (New York, 1966); *How the Church Can Minister to the World Without Losing Itself* (New York, 1964); and *Maker of Heaven and Earth* (New York, 1959).

MILTON HIMMELFARB, born in 1918 in New York, is editor of the *American Jewish Year Book*. Mr. Himmelfarb is also a contributing editor of *Commentary* and the Director of the Information Service of the American Jewish Committee. At present he is writing a book in which he will treat the theme he discusses in this issue.

WILBER G. KATZ, born in 1902 in Milwaukee, Wisconsin, is Professor of Law at the University of Wisconsin Law School. Former Dean of the University of Chicago Law School, Mr. Katz has written *Religion and American Constitutions* (Chicago, 1963); *Introduction to Accounting* (Chicago, 1954); and, with Felix Frankfurter, *Cases on Federal Jurisdiction* (Chicago, 1931).

FRANKLIN H. LITTELL, born in 1917 in Syracuse, New York, is President of Iowa Wesleyan College. President Littell, consultant in Religion and Higher Education for the National Conference of Christians and Jews, is the author of *The Anabaptist View of the Church* (paperback edition, 1964) and *From State Church to Pluralism* (New York, 1962). He was the co-editor of *Welt Kirchenlexikon* (Stuttgart, 1960).

MARTIN E. MARTY, born in 1928 in West Point, Nebraska, is Chairman of the Church History Field at the University of Chicago Divinity School and Associate Editor of *The Christian Century*. Mr. Marty has published, among other titles, *Varieties of Unbelief* (New York, 1964); *Religion and Social Conflict* (Oxford, 1964); *The Infidel: Freethought and American Religion* (1961); and *The New Shape of American Religion* (New York, 1959). Mr. Marty co-edits *Church History,* the professional journal of the American Society of Church History, and the annual *New Theology*.

WILLIAM G. McLOUGHLIN, born in 1922 in Maplewood, New Jersey, is Professor of History at Brown University. The author of *Billy Graham* (New York, 1960); *Modern Revivalism* (New York, 1959); and *Billy Sunday* (Chicago, 1955), Mr. McLoughlin has recently written *Isaac Backus and the American Pietistic Tradition*, published in 1967, and is editing the diaries and travel journals of Isaac Backus for the Brown University Press. He has also completed a history of the separation of Church and State in colonial New England to be published by Harvard University Press.

DONALD MEYER, born in 1923 in Lincoln, Nebraska, is Professor of History at Wesleyan University. Mr. Meyer has written *The Protestant Search for Political Realism* (1960) and *The Positive Thinkers* (1965).

SISTER MARIE AUGUSTA NEAL, S.N.D., born in 1921 in Brighton, Massachusetts, is Associate Professor of Sociology and chairman of the Sociology Department at Emmanuel College. She is the author of *Values and Interests in Social Change* (Englewood Cliffs, New Jersey, 1965) and has contributed essays and articles to numerous books and periodicals. Sister Marie Augusta is the Director of Research for the Conference of Major Superiors of Women's Religious Institutes in the United States, Associate Editor of *Sociological Analysis*, and a member of the Commission on Human Rights, Archdiocese of Boston, and the Governor's Commission on the Status of Women.

MICHAEL NOVAK, born in 1933 in Johnstown, Pennsylvania, is Assistant Professor in the Special Program in Humanities at Stanford University. The author of *Belief and Unbelief* (New York, 1965); *The Open Church* (New York, 1964); and *A New Generation: American and Catholic* (New York, 1964), Mr. Novak is an editor of *The Journal of Ecumenical Studies* and a contributing editor to several other journals.

THOMAS F. O'DEA, born in 1915 in Amesbury, Massachusetts, is Professor of Sociology and Chairman of the Department of Religion at Columbia University. The author of *The Sociology of Religion* (Englewood Cliffs, New Jersey, 1966); *American Catholic Dilemma* (New York, 1958); and *The Mormons* (Chicago, 1957), Mr. O'Dea has contributed numerous articles to scholarly journals.

HAROLD P. SOUTHERLAND, born in 1934 in High Point, North Carolina, is an associate in the law firm of Quarles, Heriott & Clemons in Milwaukee, Wisconsin. Mr. Southerland was co-author with Abner Brodie of "Conscience, the Constitution, and the Supreme Court: The Riddle of *United States v. Seeger*" in the 1966 *Wisconsin Law Review*.

BRYAN R. WILSON, born in 1926 in Leeds, England, is the reader in sociology in the University of Oxford and a fellow of All Souls College. Mr. Wilson has written *Sects and Society* (Berkeley, 1961) and *Religion in Secular Society*. He edited and contributed to the volume *Patterns of Sectarianism* (London, 1967).

INDEX

INDEX

Abernathy, Ralph, 64
Abortion laws, and Catholic church, 352
Acculturation of immigrant groups, 360
Adler, Felix, 291
Adventist groups, 53, 55, 56
Aggiornamento, 109, 398; in Roman Catholic journalism, 233, 313
Alinsky, Saul, 89, 369, 371–372, 376
Alliance for Progress, 48
Allport, Gordon, 387
Altizer, Thomas J. J., 161, 340; and "death of God," 340; *The Gospel of Christian Atheism*, 216–220
Amalgamation of culture and religion, 164
America, discovery linked with religion, 26
America as a world city, 42
American Association of Pastoral Counselors, 251, 262
American Catholic thought today, 324; central theme of, 324, 326
American Catholicism, four stages of development of, 328; number of followers, 112–113; since 1850, 112–113. *See also* Catholicism in America
American Civil Liberties Union, 279
American clergymen, metamorphosis in public image of, 370ff. *See also* Clergy
American Council of Christian Churches, 59, 61, 129
American *Geist*, acceptance of secular context of life, 148; characteristics of its relation to religion, 144ff; harmony between secular and religious, 144; religion as personal, inward phenomenon, 145

American Humanist Association, 271
American Jewish communities, 30
American Jews, and attitude toward death camps, 179; and civic equality, 292; cultural and charitable enterprises, 38; opposition to aid to religious schools, 278. *See also* Jews, American
American pastoral profession, laicism in, 89–91, 260–261; specialization in, 91, 98, 99, 262–264. *See also* Specialization in American pastoral profession
American pietism today, 53
American Protestants, "neither fear of hell nor hope of heaven," 171; policy of recruitment of, 38
American religious life, influence on European religious life, 146; inherent secularity of, 149; secular influences on, 159–164; and social welfare, 350
American religious patterns, 121
American sense of mission, 66
American theology, 137ff; and America as "promised land," 149; concern with economic justice, 159; and concern for love of neighbor, 141ff; emphasis on service to fellow man, 143; impact of secular concepts on, 156, 159–164; indigenous character of, 152; influence of history on, 139; influence of modern culture on, 141; influence of psychoanalytic theory on, 160; influence of science on, 138, 159; literature's influence on, 161; pragmatic character of, 147; and pragmatism, 324; recent radical, 163; relevance in American life, 164; roots of, 148; separation between

Index

Index

Hiltner, Seward, 254
Himmelfarb, Milton, vi, 278, 282
Hippies, the, 84
Hocking, Ernest, 179
Hook, Sidney, ix, 403
Horton, William M., 60
Howe, Irving, ix
Howe, Mark deWolfe, 272–274
Howe, Reuel L., 342
Hughes, H. Stuart, 397
Hume, David, 195

Ideological cleavage in American Protestantism, 75, 76
Image of America as a Christian nation, 35
Industrial Areas Foundation, 89
Industrialization, effect of, on religion, 175ff
Institutionalism, ecclesiastical, 350

James, William, 50, 154, 253, 323
Jeffers, Robinson, 19
Jefferson, Thomas, 8, 174; second inaugural address, 9
Jehovah's Witnesses, 45, 46, 50; foundation of, 57; membership in, 128; opposition to "modernism," 345
Jenkins, David, 340
Jewish communities, American, 30, 306, 307; synagogue as center of, 306
Jewish identity, crisis of, 303
Jewish matrix of early Christian theology, 342
Jewish population in the U.S., 118; geographical, 119
Jew's right to his Jewishness, 209–210
Jews, American, 38, 59, 299–311; and celebration of Christmas, 284; competition among branches of faith, xi; Conservative, 307; and conversion to Christian faith, 288–290; Hassidic (pietistic) movement, 308; intermarriage with non-Jews, 282; membership in religious family, 118; and observance of Sunday, 285–286; Orthodox, 307–310; philanthropy of, 124; place of, in American society, 282ff; Reform, 307–309; reform-minded, 373; secular education of, 302; and secularism of the West, 289; "unsynagogued," 310. See also American Jews
John XXIII, Pope, 178, 179, 180, 232,

405; *Journal of a Soul,* 168; *Pacem in Terris,* 40
John Birch Society, the, 16, 370
Johnson, Dr. F. Ernest, 278
Johnson, Lyndon B., 10
Jones, Samuel Porter, 54
Judaeo-Christian norms, as basis of value judgments, 41; tension between secular values and, 203; world view, 393, 399–402, 407
Judaism, adjustment to modern world, 302–306; Conservative, 306–307; definition of, 300–301; history of, 299–300; Orthodox, 307–308; Protestantization of, 306; Reform, 261, 300, 307; and reversal of traditional fronts, 204; and secular liberalism, 205
Judaism, American Reform, 261, 300, 307

Kant, Emmanuel, 143, 152, 195, 207
Kaplan, Mordecai M., 309
Katz, Wilber, v, 269
Kaufmann, Walter, 390
Kennedy, John F., 3, 65, 396, 405; ceremony following death of, 178; inaugural address, 4
Kierkegaard, Søren, 152, 155, 196, 395
King, Martin Luther, x, 63, 64, 114, 178; "March on Selma," 358; 1963 March on Washington, 376
Koinonia, 79
Küng, Hans, 234

Labor unions, and the urban poor, 371
Laicism in American pastoral profession, 89, 90, 91, 101, 260–261
Laity, age of, 37
Language analysis, influence on theological formulations, 157, 396
Language philosophy, 157, 166
Laski, Marghanita, 386
Lawrence, T. E., 201
League of Women Voters, 373
Leakey, L. S. B., 192
Leeser, Isaac, 305
Lehmann, Paul, 152
Lenski, Gerhard, 171, 375
Leo XIII, Pope, 315. *See also* Catholicism in America
Levelers, the, 51
"Liberal Protestant" consensus, 52
Liberal Protestant theology, breakdown of, 59

Index

Index